AIN'T GONNA LET NOBODY TURN ME AROUND

To: Karen

In Black Sisterhood and Struggle

Barbara Smith

3-31-15

To Karen

For your unwavering commitment through the decades. 3-31-15

SUNY series in New Political Science
Bradley J. Macdonald, editor

AIN'T GONNA LET NOBODY TURN ME AROUND

Forty Years of Movement Building with

BARBARA SMITH

Edited by
Alethia Jones
and
Virginia Eubanks
with
Barbara Smith

Cover photo of Barbara Smith by Vicki Smith.

Published by State University of New York Press, Albany

For information, contact State University of New York Press, Albany, NY
www.sunypress.edu

Production by Ryan Morris
Marketing by Fran Keneston

Library of Congress Cataloging-in-Publication Data

Ain't Gonna Let Nobody Turn Me Around: Forty Years of Movement Building
    with Barbara Smith / Alethia Jones and Virginia Eubanks, eds., with Barbara Smith
ISBN 978-1-4384-5115-2 (hc : alk. paper)
ISBN 978-1-4384-5114-5 (pbk. : alk. paper)
ISBN 978-1-4384-5116-9 (ebook)

2014947017

0 9 8 7 6 5 4 3 2 1

From Alethia
For my mother, grandmother, and Angela and the sacrifices they made.
For my sister, Tamara, if only . . .

From Virginia
For my second family, the feminist activist community of the Capital Region
of New York, for their integrity, fearlessness, and compassion.

From Barbara
For my sister, Beverly, and everyone who takes a stand for justice.

Contents

Illustrations

Figures

Foreword

I'm a part of the women's movement that doesn't really get that much play, even to this day, because it's the part of the women's movement that ... pushes for looking at how capital and imperialism ruined the lives of virtually everyone on the planet except for the members of the ruling class and a few people who benefit from the crumbs.

—Barbara Smith, interview by Loretta J. Ross, May 7–8, 2003, Voices of Feminism Oral History Project, Sophia Smith Collection, Smith College

Barbara Smith is a revolutionary. There is no other way to put it. Yes, she is recognized as a singular voice in the women's movement and one of the most important Black feminists on the planet. Yes, she is a pioneer of independent progressive publishing and a founder of Black women's studies. Yes, she is a long-time lesbian activist committed to social transformation, not just marriage equality and mainstream acceptance of the LGBT community. And yet, anyone who knows Barbara Smith and has followed her work over the past four decades understands that these categories—*as they are commonly understood*—do not fully capture the range of her thought and activism. To suggest that she is "more" is not to diminish Black feminism but rather to insist that Smith's own definition of Black feminism goes to the root of oppression and power and seeks ways to end all forms of exploitation, redistribute power, and transform society. Her description of the Combahee River Collective's objective perfectly articulates her vision of Black feminism: an "antiracist, feminist *practice* with a radical, anticapitalist analysis." So it should not surprise us that Barbara Smith has played an active role in the most important movements and intellectual developments of our time: she fought for Civil Rights, human rights, peace, environmental justice, stood on the front lines against apartheid and all forms of racism, against U.S.-backed death squads in Central America and all forms of imperialism, against police brutality and all forms of state violence, against poverty and all efforts to deny people a living wage, welfare, and housing. And she played a central role in the formation of ethnic studies, women's studies, sexuality and gender studies, and queer theory. Despite these monumental accomplishments and an unparalleled record of struggle, she has only recently begun to receive the critical attention she deserves. This extraordinary collection of interviews and conversations will send a new generation scouring the internet in search of Smith's oeuvre.

I first discovered Barbara Smith around 1982 in my university library, before there was an internet. As a student at Cal State Long Beach, I practically lived between two call numbers: E 185, where all the African American studies books resided, and HX—home to books on Marxism. It was on those shelves, some place around E 185.86, that I came across a book titled *All the Women Are White, All the Blacks Are Men, But Some of Us Are Brave: Black Women's Studies*, edited by Gloria T. Hull, Patricia Bell-Scott, and Barbara Smith. The cover photo, dating back to the early twentieth century, depicted two fierce Black women in matching plaid outfits and elaborate hats, looking straight into the camera. One of the women sported what appeared to be a man's necktie and belt. I discovered the book just about the time I declared Black studies my minor and history my major.

Finding that book was both unsettling and exhilarating. In those days, Black studies at Long Beach State was run by hardcore Black nationalists and was considered a masculine endeavor. Most of my professors used "the Black man" and "the White man" as shorthand for describing America's racial terrain. Many of us were also concerned about the epidemic of racist police violence. The same year Smith and her coeditors released *But Some of Us Were Brave*, Long Beach State was at the center of controversy when a fellow student and star football player named Ron Settles was found dead in a holding cell in Signal Hill, California, a tiny township encircled by the city of Long Beach. Settles had been arrested the night before while driving through Signal Hill and charged with cocaine possession—a strange charge in light of the fact that he had no prior history of drug use. According to the police department's official narrative, a distraught Settles mysteriously obtained a blunt object, beat himself, and then hanged himself in his cell. Of course, the police assaulted and killed Black women, too, but to my peers at the time, Black men were the targets, the endangered species.

It is not as if Black women were invisible. As nationalists, we had posters of Namibian and Angolan women with babies on their backs and AK-47s strapped to their shoulders, though we lacked the theoretical sophistication to recognize how these posters ultimately reinforced patriarchy by depicting women militants as primarily responsible for motherhood and the domestic sphere. Black women writers also achieved unusual prominence around this time: Alice Walker's *The Color Purple* appeared in 1982, along with Gloria Naylor's *The Women of Brewster Place* and Audre Lorde's *Zami: A New Spelling of My Name*. Toni Morrison had been publishing novels for a decade, Michele Wallace's controversial *Black Macho and the Myth of the Superwoman* appeared three years earlier, and in 1981 Angela Davis released *Women, Race, and Class.*

But the brand-new clothbound book I held in my hand that day in 1982 was unlike any of these other texts because it announced the formation of a new field: Black women's studies. Reading the very first sentence in Smith and Hull's introduction to the book stopped me in my tracks: "Merely to use the term 'Black women's studies' is an act charged with political significance." That is to say, merely to assert the positive existence of Black women is a political statement, and to act not only to make Black women visible but to acknowledge and battle the multiple forms of oppression they endure, is an "act of political courage" (xvii). More than anything I had read before about Black studies, Smith and Hull's statement made the strongest case for critical analysis as a mode of praxis, insisting that there has to be a deep, organic, dialectical link between Black women's studies and the Black feminist movement, and that Black women's studies must necessarily be "feminist, radical, and analytical" (xvii). Looking back, it is pretty clear now that *But Some of Us Were Brave* contributed so much more than making Black women visible. By calling for a critical analysis of race, gender, and sexuality, Smith anticipates so much of the scholarship that now falls under the rubric of queer studies and critical race theory.

What struck me most out of everything packed into those 385 pages was the short but incisive Combahee River Collective Statement. Today it is regarded as one of the most important political documents of the late twentieth century, but in 1982 it had only been circulating a few years, primarily among socialist feminists and radical Black women. For me, reading the statement was a revelation—one of the critical turning points in my political life. The context is important here. I was nineteen-going-on-twenty, in the throes of a transition from cultural nationalist to "revolutionary nationalist" to Marxist-Leninist, and in all of these movements the *manifesto* represented the essential principles around which activists build a strategy for change. It is an assertion of what is wrong with the world, how to fix it, and what the world might look like if we won (or for that matter, what the world would look like if we didn't win). The Combahee River Collective Statement was the closest thing to a "perfect" manifesto I'd ever read. Smith and her two coauthors (her sister Beverly Smith and Demita Frazier) argued that a nonracist, nonsexist society could not be created under capitalism, nor could socialism alone dismantle the structures of racial, gender, and sexual domination. Smith could see this because, as an activist, theorist, literary critic, poet, she considered the whole of life. To her the struggle wasn't just the public fight in the streets or the public fight for representation, nor was it just socialism defined as providing resources in a very public way—decent jobs, collective labor. Rather, she made connections between production, reproduction, household labor, the exploitation of children, sexual violence, and physical abuse—issues that rarely find a place on the agenda of a lot of Black nationalist organizations, let alone socialist ones.

Suffice it to say, I looked for anything that had Barbara Smith's name on it. I read everything from "Toward a Black Feminist Criticism" and "Racism and Women's Studies" to "Soul on Hold" and "Where's the Revolution?," collected her many political essays, picked up *Home Girls* as soon as it came out, and later devoured *The Truth That Never Hurts*. Reading Barbara Smith not only hastened my migration from Black nationalism to Marxism, but she convinced me that it is impossible to be a revolutionary without becoming a feminist. What I did not realize at the time is that she paid an enormous price for her radical politics—which included choosing to live as an out Black lesbian. One of the heart-wrenching truths revealed in these interviews and conversations is the degree to which Smith's writing and political work was ignored, ridiculed, and buried for so many years. Black intellectuals viciously attacked (and egregiously misread) her pioneering "Toward a Black Feminist Criticism" when she first presented the work in 1977. White feminists sometimes shut her out when she exposed racism in their ranks. The "mainstream" LGBT movement often found her to be too radical and kept her at arm's length. She was not invited to major conferences, including Black Women in the Academy: Defending Our Name in 1994, I believe the largest gathering of Black women intellectuals in the twentieth century.

By the late 1990s, things began to change. She was part of the opening plenary session at the historic Black Radical Congress in 1998, proving to be one of the most influential and politically lucid voices at that event. And then a growing number of scholars have begun to revisit the movements of which she was a part and to examine her ideas with greater care and urgency. Thanks to the tireless work of Beverly Guy-Sheftall, Patricia Hill Collins, Duchess Harris, Kimberly Springer, Wini Breines, Alexis Pauline Gumbs, Roderick Ferguson, and, of course, Alethia Jones and Virginia Eubanks, among others, anyone with even a cursory understanding of intersectionality, queer of color critique, or the new histories of Black feminism will know Barbara Smith. And right now, as the extreme Right wages a relentless war against women's reproductive rights, sexual freedom, labor, immigrants, the poor, public education, on democracy itself, and continues to promote neoliberal policies that redistribute wealth upward and destroy what's left of public institutions and the social safety net, we *need* to know Barbara Smith. And as progressives try to roll back the draconian laws passed by Republican governors, state legislatures, and Congress, we desperately need to know Barbara Smith.

Her work speaks to all of the critical struggles we are confronting—war and empire, poverty and wealth redistribution, racism and democracy, and sexual politics. Consider, for example, our national turn toward homonormativity. On the one hand, "don't ask, don't tell" has been repealed and gay marriage is winning support in many states and is now championed by President Obama. And yet, as liberals—straight and gay—shout victory and express their pride in being an American, as more and more celebrities come out of the closet and in doing so increase their Twitter following, women's reproductive rights are being destroyed; Planned Parenthood is being dismantled; and access to various forms of birth control under insurance coverage is under attack. All of these issues disproportionately affect poor and working-class women. Violence against queer people has not abated, but much of it has been wreaked upon transgender people, whose stories of dislocation, alienation, and oppression sound alarmingly like the experiences Smith writes so eloquently about when she came out in the 1970s.

Finally, it is precisely because Smith sees and analyzes the whole of life that her ideas are fundamental for developing a vision for building a sustainable, radical movement capable of winning key local struggles and moving the nation in a new direction. How do we understand the current conditions and build local, national, even international movements that can effect change, challenge the oppressive institutions that seem to grow more powerful and more draconian over time, and build solidarity across divisions of race, ethnicity, gender, and generation? Even amid some of the most powerful mass insurgencies in generations (Occupy Wall Street, the Wisconsin revolt, etc.) an often-divided and confused Left has tended to elide institutional racism and sexism in favor of a class rhetoric that corrals everyone into the big tent of the 99 percent. Smith knows it is not that simple. She understands that a "politics of identity" is not interest-group or single-issue politics but a politics that considers the whole human being— the full range of her oppressions, needs, desires, and experiences. She has been telling us all along that paying attention to inequalities of race, sex, and gender in addition to class does not hinder strong solidarities but strengthens them. She has always recognized the transformative nature of social movements and the space of empathy required to build a movement. The point is to stand up against injustice everywhere, and in doing so we expand our horizons, change our perspectives, deepen our solidarity. Barbara Smith always walked the talk, standing up for all those in struggle, no matter their race or nationality, gender or sexuality, consistently fighting from a standpoint of "antiracist, feminist *practice* with a radical, anticapitalist analysis." This is the definition of a revolutionary. And if we are serious about achieving real justice and a lasting peace, we need more revolutionaries like Barbara Smith.

Robin D. G. Kelley
August 19, 2012
Los Angeles, California

Preface

My politics are indelibly shaped by the era in which I came of age. Movement leaders and scholars who stood out like Ella Baker, Kathleen Cleaver, Angela Davis, Dave Dellinger, Barbara Deming, and Howard Zinn fundamentally questioned the status quo and worked tirelessly to change it. As Michael Eric Dyson asserts in his book, *I May Not Get There With You: The True Martin Luther King Jr.*, King's views were much more radical than the mainstream acknowledges. By speaking out against the war in Vietnam and explicitly focusing upon economic injustice, the perspectives King held later in life dovetailed more and more with positions held by members of the Left.

One consequence of *Ain't Gonna Let Nobody Turn Me Around*'s publication with which I have had to grapple is coming out again, not as a lesbian but as a radical. In my current work as a member of the Albany Common Council, I do not generally discuss the core of my political beliefs, although it is well known that I am a progressive. Now, at a time when our moderate first African American president is regularly accused of being a socialist, I actually declare that I am one.

Radical politics or politics considered to be radical at the time have in fact brought about some of society's most needed changes. The abolition of slavery, the enfranchisement of Black people and women, the dismantling of Jim Crow, the institution of the eight-hour workday, the implementation of workplace safety rules, the toppling of colonial empires, the ongoing struggles against oppression based upon gender, sexuality, and gender expression were all considered too radical or downright impossible before they succeeded. One of the questions this book may lead readers to explore is whether working for reform has any relationship to challenging systematic oppression.

Ain't Gonna Let Nobody Turn Me Around was conceived of as a collection of interviews, but I experience it as a series of many layered conversations. The central conversation has been with the exceptional editors, Alethia Jones and Virginia Eubanks. In 2007 when Larin McLaughlin, an editor at State University of New York Press, approached me about doing a book that would include new interviews, she asked if I had suggestions for an editor. Although Alethia and I had not known each other long, I decided to ask her if she would consider taking on this task. I am so grateful that she said yes. Neither of us had any idea of how gargantuan and complex this project would turn out to be, but Alethia did not hesitate, and she also had the presence of mind to enlist another comrade for the journey, her friend and colleague Virginia Eubanks. Mishel Filisha, a doctoral student in sociology at the University at Albany, was also a key member of the team. She did meticulous and innovative research to uncover materials for us to consider for inclusion in the finished work. Mishel also documented some of my current activities on film. As the manuscript neared completion, I suggested that we ask my longtime friend and political comrade Naomi Jaffe to read and comment on it. Naomi's years of movement experience and her stellar editorial skills made a tremendous contribution to the book. Together, these women's vision, intelligence, and generosity have shaped what you hold in your hands.

After Alethia, Virginia, and I arrived at the topics we wanted the book to cover, we discussed who might conduct each interview. In every single instance each of the potential interviewers we invited said yes. Their willingness to take time out of their schedules and in many cases to travel in order for us to meet and talk was wonderful. Sitting down with old friends and valued colleagues was one of the most fulfilling aspects of the conversations that make this book. Because of Virginia and Alethia's decision to combine sections from different interviews that address the same topic, I feel as if these distinguished scholars and activists are also in conversation with each other, are literally on the same page as we tease out the often invisible stories of Black women's struggles and lives.

I am excited at the possibility that *Ain't Gonna Let Nobody Turn Me Around* may enable me to engage in conversations with new communities of readers, especially conversations across generations. I am humbled that the work I have been driven to do and have (mostly) loved is being recognized in these pages.

Barbara Smith
August 20, 2012
Albany, New York

Acknowledgments

FROM THE EDITORS

We thank Barbara Smith for inviting us to do this project and the incredible journey that commenced. She has been warm, generous, responsive, and forthcoming. She helped to make a detailed and circuitous project a joy to work on over an extended period of time. Any and all income derived from this book will go to Barbara, whose sacrifices and dedication have meant a fulfilling life but one without jobs with pensions, healthcare, and the like.

Without Mishel Filisha this project would not have had the auspicious start that it did. We knew there would be enough material to work with but none of us (Barbara included) had any idea of the overwhelming volume until Mishel assembled all the documents (over 200) in one place. And Mishel has remained with the project for the duration. She attended and recorded as many interviews as possible and shot video at community and other public events. We are forever grateful for her dedication, thoughtfulness, thoroughness, and efficiency. She has our unending support as she completes her PhD in sociology, and we know that generations of students have and will benefit from her wisdom and sharp insights.

We thank all the interviewers. Each and every one said *Yes!* immediately. Their perspectives and follow-through were vital to the final shape that the book took. They were flexible with scheduling and generous with their time before, during, and after the interview itself.

Early in the process, Alethia and Virginia spent a week in the Myles Horton House at Highlander Research and Education Center in New Market, TN, pondering what this book could be. We are deeply indebted to all the staff at Highlander, but especially benefitted from conversations with Pam McMichael, Susan Williams and Elandria Williams. The organizations that hosted each of the interviews also deserve special mention. Our first interview occurred in Albany's Women's Building, home to Holding Our Own: The Women's Foundation and one of only two such buildings in the country. The Women's Building has been wholly owned and independently operated by feminists for over four decades. We could not think of a better place for starting this project. The second interview occurred at the Women's Research and Resource Center at Spelman College, which remains the only such space that we know of at an HBCU (historically Black college and university).

The Lesbian Herstory Archives in Brooklyn, New York, is a very special place run by very special women. So many hard-to-find pieces that would otherwise be lost to history have a home here on one of four floors of this Brooklyn brownstone. The archives is run 100 percent by volunteers. They opened just for our interview. We thank archivists Shawn(ta) Smith (aka "Your Lesbian Librarian") and Paula Grant (who commuted an extended distance and stayed quite late to help us adjust to some extenuating circumstances). They were also a wonderful and generous resource for Mishel's research. In addition, the Sophia Smith Collection at Smith College also made some of the wonderful riches within its archives available to this project.

The Murphy Institute of the City University of New York (CUNY) also deserves special mention. It hosted us for three interviews on two days. We extend our thanks to Gregory Mantsios and Paula Finn for doing so much to create a space in the heart of the city that is devoted to the cause of worker, economic, and social justice and making access and use feel effortless. We also thank our home academic institution during this project, the University at Albany, State University of New York. Specifically, the Center for Policy Research at Rockefeller College of Public Affairs and Policy, the School of Social Welfare, and the Department of Women's, Gender, and Sexuality Studies provided institutional support.

Special angels appeared along the way who gave critical insight, advice, and service at crucial moments. Victoria Kereszi readily agreed to film Barbara to ensure we had documentary footage of her on the campaign trail in 2009. She generously donated her documentary filmmaking skills, her time, and delightful energy. Kayo Denda, from the Rutgers University Libraries, provided much-needed support and advice for dealing with the immense raft of permissions requests this volume required. Naomi Jaffe and two anonymous reviewers provided insightful and thorough comments on the manuscript. For transcription, we thank Mishel as well as Alethia's mother, Jeanette Jones, who unexpectedly and quickly worked on two interviews at a crucial moment in the project.

We must thank the State University of New York Press who made this project possible. The concept for the book came from Larin McLaughlin, who first approached Barbara with the idea of producing a volume of interviews and conversations that would document her life and legacy. Under the new editorial leadership of Beth Bouloukos, the enthusiasm and support of the press has continued.

Neither one of us is a Black women's studies scholar. We want to acknowledge those scholars who are and the incredible work, built over decades, that they have created. Their intellectual contributions remain, too often, unacknowledged by theorists, scholars, and academics in related fields. This book aims to share Barbara's work and legacy with a broad general audience. However, we wish to especially mention Alexis Pauline Gumbs's dissertation, "We Can Learn to Mother Ourselves: The Queer Survival of Black Feminism 1968–1996." Completed in 2010 at Duke University, this amazing collection of interviews, archived material, and social theory enlightened us to many of the cutting-edge questions of the field. It also reveals the deep sacrifices and hidden histories of the many, many women who have courageously and creatively stood for the authentic audacity of their lives and the lives of those they love.

We certainly hope we have not overlooked anyone. If so, the responsibility is ours.

Finally, we would like to thank each other. Alethia appreciates Virginia's love of lists and her insistence that if we print each page and put it in a binder, it will eventually become a book. Virginia appreciates Alethia's flexibility around deadlines—most of the time—and her passionate commitment to inspiring dialogue, loving critique, and creating movements and institutions that heal us all. We started as friends and colleagues and are leaving this project lifelong comrades and collaborators.

CREDITS

Chapter 2

Barbara Smith. "Interview by Loretta Ross." Voices of Feminism Oral History Project, Copyright © Sophia Smith Collection, Smith College, 2003. Reprinted with permission of the Sophia Smith Collection.

Jewelle Gomez and Barbara Smith. "Taking the Home Out of Homophobia: Black Lesbian Health, A Conversation between Jewelle Gomez and Barbara Smith." In *The Black Woman's Health Book: Speaking for Ourselves*, ed. Evelyn C. White. Copyright © Perseus Book Group, The Seal Press, 1994. Reprinted with permission of Perseus Book Group.

Photo by Dudley Brumbach. "The body of the Rev. Bruce W. Klunder." *Cleveland Plain Dealer*. Reprinted with permission of The Plain Dealer/Landov.

No author. "Klunder, Bruce W." *The Encyclopedia of Cleveland History*. Copyright © Case Western Reserve University, Cleveland: Case Western Reserve University, 1997. Reprinted with permission of Case Western Reserve University.

Chapter 3

Combahee River Collective. "The Combahee River Collective Statement." In *Capitalist Patriarchy and the Case for Socialist Feminism*, ed. Zillah Eisenstein. Copyright © Monthly Review Press, 1979.

Barbara Smith. Excerpt from "Black Feminism: A Movement of Our Own" (originally titled "Barbara Smith on Black Feminism"), reprinted in *Frontline Feminism 1975–1995: Essays from Sojourner's First 20 Years*, ed. Karen Kahn and Robin Morgan. Copyright © Aunt Lute Books, 1997. Reprinted with the permission of Aunt Lute Books.

Chapter 4

with permission of Alumnae Association of Mount Holyoke College and Barbara Smith.

Barbara Smith. "Racism and Women's Studies." In *Frontiers: A Journal of Women's Studies*. Copyright © University of Nebraska Press, University of Nebraska Press, 1980. Reprinted with permission of University of Nebraska Press.

Chapter 5

Modern Language Association Commission on the Status of Women in the Profession. "Black Women and Publishing: Statement by the Modern Language Association Commission on the Status of Women in the Profession." Copyright © the authors, 1976. Reprinted with permission of Gloria De Sole, Joan Hartman, Ellen Messer-Davidow, Deborah Rosenfelt, Cynthia Secor, and Barbara Smith.

Barbara Smith. "Our Stories: Women of Color." Copyright © *The New Statesman*, The New Statesman, 1984.

Barbara Smith. "A Press of Our Own: Kitchen Table: Women of Color Press." In *Communication at the Crossroads: The Gender Gap Connection*. Copyright © *ABC-CLIO*, ABC-CLIO Inc., 1989.

Sojourner Editorial Collective. "Packing Boxes and Editing Manuscripts: Women of Color in Feminist Publishing." Copyright © the authors, Sojourner, 1993. Reprinted with the permission of Martha Ayim, Deborah Barretto, Matt Richardson, Barbara Smith.

Chapter 6

Barbara Smith. "Soul on Hold." Copyright © *Village Voice*, LLC, Village Voice, 1985. Reprinted with permission. First published in *Village Voice*, a Village Voice Media publication.

Amy Gluckman and Betsy Reed. "Where Has Gay Liberation Gone? An Interview with Barbara Smith." In *Homo Economics: Capitalism, Community, and Lesbian and Gay Life*. Copyright © Taylor & Francis Group, Routledge, 1997.

Ted (Tito Ben-Ysrael) Beck, Mandy Carter, Chandra L. Ford, Kara Keeling, and Barbara Smith. "Will People of Color Pay the Price? A Statement by People of Color in Support of the Ad Hoc Committee for an Open Process." Copyright © 1999 by the authors. Reprinted with permission of Ted Beck, Mandy Carter (cofounder Southerners On New Ground [SONG] and National Black Justice Coalition [NBJC]), Chandra L. Ford, Kara Keeling, and Barbara Smith. Reprinted with permission of the authors.

Barbara Smith. "Organizing in Albany: Justice for Diallo." Copyright © *News & Letters*, News & Letters, 2000. Reprinted with permission of News & Letters.

In Our Own Voices. "I Am Gay and This Is Where I Pray." Copyright © In Our Own Voices, 2010.

Barbara Smith. "Please Don't Fan Flames of Bigotry." Copyright © *Albany Times Union*, Albany Times Union, Inc., 2011. Reprinted with permission of Michael Spain, Associate Editor.

Chapter 7

Chapter 8

1
Chronicling an Activist Life

Virginia Eubanks and Alethia Jones

We started *Ain't Gonna Let Nobody Turn Me Around: Forty Years of Movement Building with Barbara Smith* in 2008, at the height of the sub-prime mortgage crisis and in the midst of the ongoing economic collapse. The devastation to communities and families in the United States called into question free-market capitalism and representative democracy. By 2013, a flowering of social justice organizing and an upswell of courageous and principled action appeared around the world: the Arab Spring and other anti-totalitarian struggles in the Middle East and North Africa; the Puerta del Sol Square occupation of "Los Indignados" in Madrid, Spain; protests by tens of thousands of people in Britain and Greece against draconian austerity measures; and Occupy Wall Street, which inspired hundreds of occupations in cities across the United States and the globe.

Occupy Wall Street, one of the most hopeful recent efforts in the United States, was nevertheless beset with issues of classism, sexism, racism, and homophobia. It is not the first movement to earnestly struggle with these issues, and it won't be the last. But how do the organizations, coalitions, and movements we are building attend to issues of hierarchy, leadership, and transparency? How do we build new ways of being with each other that incorporate fairness, respect, and accountability across our differences? How can we pursue strategies and construct organizations that embody the futures we wish to create? Attention to these matters is at the heart of Martin Luther King Jr.'s call to create "beloved community" and of Barbara Smith's efforts to work with political movements to create a more just world.

This book is not a memoir, a biography, or a reader. It is a reflection and a conversation. *Ain't Gonna Let Nobody Turn Me Around* samples a lifetime of political work and commitment to liberation struggles, providing a mixed-media collage of voices and experiences from a variety of movements that, we hope, conveys useful lessons about the gritty work of pursuing social justice. The book uses Barbara Smith's life and work to dissect, analyze, and derive lessons from the freedom struggles she experienced, shaped, and supported. Often, we critique the hierarchies "out there" while ignoring how we internalize them and reproduce them "in here," in our movements and institutions. This has real consequences for organizing. One result is that the most privileged among us—those closest to the white, middle-class, heterosexual, male, able-bodied ideal—often reap most of the social status, political rights, and economic benefits fought for by people's movements. Barbara Smith's membership in multiple oppressed groups—Black, female, lesbian, working class—combined with her anti-racist and anti-imperialist stance led her to operate from an approach that refused to see any group as disposable and to insist that all of her identities be respected. Then and now, she challenges movement organizers to pursue innovative strategies that promote inclusion and accountability, forging patterns different from the hierarchical and exploitative models that we have inherited. We have drawn from her movement-building work and her participation as a scholar, organizer, writer, publisher, elected official, and activist. The documents and interviews juxtaposed in this book illustrate direct resonances between the current historical moment and the fervent movements for Civil Rights, Black feminism, women's liberation, peace/anti-war, and gay and lesbian liberation that shaped the 1960s and 1970s.

Activist Grace Lee Boggs argues that the next revolution is not only about massive, visible protest in the streets—though some of the largest demonstrations the world has ever seen have taken place in the last decade—but about cultural change that allows us to combine spiritual growth, healing, and practical actions to reinvent the material and political reality of our daily lives. In *The Next American Revolution: Sustainable Activism for the Twenty-First Century*, she writes,

> All over the world, local groups are struggling, as we are in Detroit, to keep our communities, our environment, and our humanity from being destroyed by corporate globalization. . . . Most of them are small and barely visible, but together they are creating the largest movement the world has ever known. . . . This movement has no central leadership and is not bound together by any *ism*. . . . But they are joined at the heart by their commitment to achieving social justice, establishing new forms of more democratic governance, and creating new ways of living at the local level that will reconnect us with the Earth and with one another. (Boggs and Kurashige, 2011: 42)

In her four decades of activism, teaching, and publishing, Barbara has grappled with some of the most difficult dilemmas faced by broad-based diverse movements for social change. Her faith in sweeping political change—the belief that massive shifts in consciousness, institutions, and power can occur at any moment—is founded in her own experience where again and again, so-called ordinary people make history. This book offers lessons from that experience intended to help us all work more deeply to secure liberation for everyone in the next American revolution.

In some ways, this book is "typical" Barbara. You will learn about her, but the book is really about the freedom struggles to which she has devoted her life. So many sisters, mothers, aunts, godmothers, grandmothers, sista friends, girlfriends, and others have inspired us because they stood up for our dignity and gave voice to our humanity and dreams. When they weren't allowed in the front door, they used back doors, side doors, windows, alleys, and every which way to make change for our communities. Like other dedicated grassroots activists, Barbara attends too many meetings, forges ties across many players, strategizes and analyzes to identify points of leverage, creates new initiatives and programs, and when needed, puts herself on the front line to bring about meaningful social and political change. She traces her activist lineage to Black women—like Harriet Tubman, Sojourner Truth, Fannie Lou Hamer, Ella Baker, and countless others—who spoke truth to power in order to free their people and to bring all humanity closer to creating a just world. She roots herself in the legacy of Black female movement activism and its distinctive mode of action, which is tenaciously committed, constantly present, and fundamentally humane. The Black feminist movement that Barbara helped to build in the 1970s grew from a tradition that existed for centuries and will continue into the future as long as injustice exists.

So many of these glorious women are unnamed in our history books and their stories are not told. Barbara sees this grassroots movement-building work as historically significant. As a scholar, writer, and publisher, she sought to preserve movement history whenever and wherever she could, and her devotion to leaving a historical record makes this book possible. Over the past four decades, Barbara's work on the front lines of a diverse array of movements has produced over two hundred books and articles. We selected the best and hardest to find pieces and combined them with a dozen new interviews commissioned exclusively for this project. In bringing together these otherwise scattered remnants of struggles and strategies into one place, we seek to facilitate a new generation of learning and leadership.

The decades Barbara spent insisting on full inclusion hold lessons others will find useful. The resulting truths may be uncomfortable, but, as Barbara says elsewhere, they are ultimately "truths that never hurt" (Smith 1998). The anxiety and discomfort these truths may provoke are simply growing pains that come from a deepened understanding and awareness of the world around us. We hope the book inspires your quest to fight for social justice in a world that is both riven with inequalities yet filled with endless possibilities for freedom.

Lessons in Movement Building

After mining the archives, talking to Barbara's contemporaries, and listening in on the interviews conducted for this project, we identified core themes that operate as key touchstones for the entire book. We share them explicitly here. We offer them not as a "how to" primer that lays out a blueprint for growing social movements but as a "what to ask" guidebook to fundamental questions and ideas that social justice practitioners should grapple with to pursue their work with heightened integrity, accountability, courage, and humor.

We do not claim originality. The eight points we identify are grounded in the principles and practices of Black feminism that Barbara and her colleagues spent decades articulating. Black feminism originates with Black women's experiences. The commitment to eradicate the injustices committed against Black female bodies and psyches creates a unique political analysis and practice. But this approach is not essentialist; it does not assume that membership in a biological or demographic category automatically confers an oppositional consciousness. Instead, Black feminist analytical methods pay close attention to the particularity of lived experiences. Consequently, we learn by analyzing our relationship to, or membership in, oppressed and degraded social groups. We also learn through our collective efforts and struggles to transform our experiences with injustice into sources of liberation, freedom, respect, dignity, joy and love. By highlighting them here, they serve as guideposts to help readers navigate through the rich array of perspectives and experiences shared in this book.

The eight points consist of four conceptual pillars—*identity politics*, *coalition building*, *intersectionality*, and *multi-issue politics*—and four core practices—*awareness*, *integrity*, *courage*, and *redefining your own success*. We see the pillars and practices as matched pairs where a key political principle is joined with an individual behavior that strengthens one's ability to operate effectively in constructing each pillar. These eight points allow us to deepen movement building and enrich political consciousness.

Identity politics insists that the most insightful analysis of power often arises from a deep knowledge of the material circumstances of oppressed people's lives. That means understanding where we come from, our identities, and the forces that shape us. To do so requires cultivating *awareness* by deepening our capacity to examine our own identities. Awareness helps us gain consciousness of the structures of privilege and oppression that permeate our lives. We experience our humanity through our distinct embodiment—the time, place, gender, race, nation, class, sexuality, physical body, age, languages, and political and social culture that we inhabit. It is imperative to know, understand, and respect that all people have unique social locations from which they experience the world. With awareness we become more responsible in our actions.

The dominant culture holds that to name our specific social location is to be exclusionary, to be narrow, to limit what is possible. Black feminists demonstrate the opposite, that naming can be liberatory. Instead of colorblindness, Black feminists pursue universal human rights grounded in the distinct histories of actual people. As argued by members of the Combahee River Collective, for example, a society that respects Black women is a society with institutions and people who have the capacity to be just, inclusive, and fair to everyone without compelling conformity to a single standard. Creating such a society requires a most thorough revolution of the institutions and cultural practices that assign worth and privilege.

The second pillar, *coalition building*, connects the hard work of knowing ourselves to the even more difficult task of working with others across difference. Coalition building asks us to reach outward from our individual and local experiences to create connections and shared agendas with others nationally and globally. As Barbara says in "Where Has Gay Liberation Gone?": "How limited would my politics be if I was only concerned about people like me!" (p. 186). Battles for social justice are long hauls that require the combined efforts of a variety of movements to succeed. Because reaching out is complicated, dangerous work, it requires *integrity*. It entails the genuine pursuit of something other than self-interest and personal advantage, and acting in ways that are consistent with your internal values. Coalition work calls upon us to be honorable, sincere, and principled in our dealings, even when others are not. It requires us to approach others with a spirit of revolutionary optimism, despite past disappointments, because diverse connections are the only way to win in light of our enormous, shared, global challenges.

Intersectionality demands that we each account for our specific social location within interlocking webs of power and privilege and understand that different strands of injustice—racism, sexism, heterosexism, classism, xenophobia, trans-hatred, ageism, and others—are complexly interwoven. The concept of intersectionality*—which finds one of its origins in the Combahee River Collective Statement of 1977 (p. 45) as the phrase "interlocking oppressions"—holds that those who inhabit multiple categories of disadvantage cannot be served by single-issue politics or analysis. Because oppressions are experienced simultaneously, our political analyses and strategies must also be multidimensional. Intersectionality also suggests that each of us embodies a complex mix of disadvantage as well as advantage. Each of us must recognize and contend with the oppressor within, as well as value and nurture the aspects of ourselves that yearn for liberation. The recognition of this complexity can yield more nuanced organizing strategies than simplistic formulations that are rhetorically appealing but furnish little guidance to the complex inner dynamics of movement building. All of us have

---

*The concept of intersectionality has been elaborated by many scholars, most notably Kimberlé Crenshaw (1991) and Patricia Hill Collins (1998a and 1998b).

the capacity to reinforce oppression or to further liberation. Our choices and our analysis deeply matter.

Choosing to speak about identity can unmask many taken-for-granted social, economic and political conventions that affix categories of worth. Thus, this pillar takes enormous *courage*, a determination to look at difficult subjects and to speak the truths that you see. Truth telling means identifying root causes of problems; speaking the reality of our experiences in the service of justice and freedom, even when it's inconvenient; and not being afraid to be challenging when necessary. Barbara has repeatedly chosen to speak uncomfortable truths. These truths are the foundation on which institutions and attitudes that respect those who are too often disrespected, neglected, and exploited can be built. The costs of telling the truth in the face of a status quo based on falsehood are real, and the intellectual and political work necessary to create broadly representative, multi-issue coalitions for social justice should not be underestimated. But earnest engagement is fundamental. These truths are often unwelcome and can inspire backlash and social recrimination. We chronicle some of the costs that Barbara has borne as a result of her courage in the chapters that follow.

"Each of us must develop the capacity to recognize and contend with the oppressor within, as well as to value and nurture the aspects of ourselves that yearn for liberation."

Finally, *multi-issue politics* insist that we not prioritize the liberation of one group of people over any other and that we deliberately work together to dismantle overarching systems of oppression, not just to seek rights and benefits for a single group or victories on a single issue. All justice-seeking interventions must simultaneously attempt to eliminate economic exploitation, racism, sexism, homophobia, and violence in society at large. If our aim is to bring transformative changes in society, then we must be *willing to redefine success* away from narrow, temporary, or qualified gains. We must move beyond a focus on winning a law, election, or court case here and there and pursue instead the genuinely inclusive, democratic politics that we seek to build. In fighting for social justice, we pursue liberation for everyone. To do so, we need to see conditions for what they really are and also to forge different ways of being and acting. As the Black Radical Congress Principles of Unity state, "Our discussions should be informed not only by a critique of what now exists, but by serious efforts to forge a creative vision of a new society" (p. 205).

Black feminism challenges us all to forge effective alliances for social justice across difference because our futures are bound up in each other. Black feminism is grounded in an identity and operates as a political practice. It is an active commitment to fighting an exploitative and dehumanizing power structure. In order to achieve full humanity for all people, dominant cultural messages of inferiority imposed upon those marginalized from the mainstream for being the "wrong" race, gender, ethnicity, sexuality, or class must be combatted; for those who derive power from conforming to the status quo, dominant cultural messages of superiority must be excised. Liberation for everyone or liberation for no one is a statement of strategic and moral fact.

Why We Did It and What We Learned

Alethia

When Barbara invited me to edit this book, I welcomed the opportunity to trace her journey from activist to elected official. I met Barbara when she was a member of Albany's Common Council, the legislative body of New York State's capital city. She soon guest-lectured in my graduate class, Inequality and Public Policy. "How," I wondered, "did a member of the legendary Combahee River Collective and a pioneer of identity politics find her way to public office?" As an urban politics scholar and practitioner, I am always delighted when grassroots activists deploy the principles, practices, and skills forged in a life of movement building toward the conventional political arena. Major progressive shifts in politics and policy can result. I invited colleague and friend Virginia Eubanks to join this project because her background in women's studies and her work on welfare rights and economic justice organizing complemented my strengths in race, ethnicity, and urban politics.

I was raised by my mother and grandmother in post-independence Jamaica in an atmosphere that regarded my Blackness and femaleness as positives and as sources of strength. Our newly independent nation designated Nanny, an escaped slave who successfully led insurrections to defeat the British, as a national shero. Once in the United States, the notion that I was less than anyone else because I was Black or female was ludicrous. This stance led me to detect the hypocrisy of elite education in the United States as I won scholarships to various Ivy League institutions. Educational scholarships were not a favor of benevolent whites for unprepared minorities but belated recompense for killing (literally and spiritually) so many talented and gifted people of color. I quickly realized that my opportunities at Columbia University were directly tied to the sacrifices of illiterate sharecroppers during the Civil Rights movement. I soon learned that many Caribbean activists fought for Civil Rights and dignity alongside African Americans, and that many African Americans dedicated themselves to international struggles to end colonialism and imperialism. I gradually came to understand that my presence in the United States is a product of globalized capitalism that originated with the Atlantic slave trade but now operates through new systems of coerced migration. Immigrants may migrate to seek a better life, but they often do so in a context of colonial domination, U.S. cold war geopolitics, and of lopsided international loans that cripple the economic prospects of many Global South nations.

Reading dozens of Barbara's essays and interviews for this book provoked me to reexamine my educational experiences in the United States. Although I studied racism and colonialism in urban politics, and engaged in on-campus battles for dignity and respect as a student leader, it took reading Smith's "Racism and Women's Studies" and "Toward a Black Feminist Criticism" to understand the source of deep ennui that permeated graduate school at Yale University and my academic career. Barbara's analysis helped me realize that racism and sexism invisibly shaped the hidden curriculum that defined *how* I studied race and public policy. Educational institutions socialize us into the dominant individualistic career achievement model that renders the study of everything, even freedom movements, as individual intellectual pursuits.

Barbara's articles and interviews filled in much of what was missing in my formal education and shifted inchoate feelings to crisp analysis. Her work validates the discomfort and dis-ease borne from the daily lived experience of elite liberalism, where few overt racist references emerge but unstated presumptions of white superiority—wrapped in language of individuality, rationality, and qualifications—are pervasive. Barbara's work names what is missing—an explicit discussion of the ways in which research bolsters or challenges structures of power and disadvantage. Too often we are encouraged to use our education to secure individual career kudos and financial security as our primary, if not our only, goal. In that framework, education becomes a means to fit in and get ahead rather than a tool of broader social change that helps to unravel the biases and assumptions that justify an oppressive status quo. I was drawn to work that would make the world a better place and relied on intuition to find allies and collaborators. But I wonder how a more self-conscious awareness of the link between scholarly projects and liberation movements would have altered my own academic work.

Barbara's writing stirs up questions about one's daily practices and strategic choices. I suspect that if I had the benefit of Black feminism's "close examination of the conditions of Black women's lives in a racist, capitalist, sexist, and heterosexist hierarchical society" earlier in my life, I would have navigated the obstacles to building a life devoted to social change differently. I learned that Black feminism did profoundly shape my life, but not through intellectual encounters, like reading and teaching the Combahee River Collective Statement or encountering Audre Lorde's *Sister Outsider*. Instead, extended relationships with grassroots institutions with Black feminist roots helped me to reshape and reroute my life path. (Those roots were unknown to me at the time and came to light during this book project.) During and after college, I participated in a local Black Women's Health Project support group (later Be Present, Inc.). In 2004 I started working closely with the Women's Theological Center (now Women Transforming Communities) in Boston.

Though the political roots of these organizations were not explicit, their politics were evident in their work—deep, deliberate, and abiding attention to creating spaces to heal the scars of oppression and support women in creating a more healing, whole, and transformed world. Through these and other experiences, I gradually learned the art of crafting healing dialogues that advance social justice. Increasingly, designing and facilitating customized educational experiences for community and social justice groups grew in importance as crucial sites of political action. In these spaces, activists sharpen their tools to create a more democratic and just world. I locate my work in the tradition of Civil Rights activist Septima Clark, an educator who worked directly with ordinary people engaged in the social, political, and economic struggle to transform the conditions of their lives. I started this book as an assistant professor, but it ends with me in the labor movement directing education programs for 1199SEIU UHWE, a social justice healthcare union. It seems appropriate that this realignment of the personal and the political occurred while working closely with Barbara.

Virginia

Barbara and I first came into contact through the welfare rights and economic justice organization I cofounded—Our Knowledge, Our Power: Surviving Welfare (OKOP). Many OKOP members live in the Common Council district of Albany, New York, where Barbara serves as a local elected official, and she reached out to express her support for our work. Our first real connection, thus, was through shared political commitments, though I had also assigned the Combahee River Collective Statement and *The Truth That Never Hurts* to my women's studies students. I am glad that Barbara and I had already developed a "solidarity through practice" before Alethia invited me to contribute to the book. To be honest, I was deeply intimidated by the prospect of trying to capture her legacy in this collection, which required doing crazily nerve-wracking things like editing "Toward a Black Feminist Criticism," an utterly groundbreaking document, down to a handful of pages. Without prior knowledge of Barbara's remarkable kindness, generosity, and humor, I never would have had the guts.

I came of age as an activist in the 1990s at the height of what the Left called "identity politics" and the Right called "political correctness." UC Santa Cruz, the progressive state school where I received my undergraduate education, boasted a plethora of racially, ethnically, and sexuality-specific clubs, organizations, centers, curricula, and events. As a straight, middle-class, white student, I had a mixed reaction to these experiences. On one hand, they helped me recognize my racial privilege, name my own experiences with gender oppression, and understand others' experiences. On the other hand, I was often wracked with guilt—for example, for not being "marginal" enough to have a legitimate political analysis—and struggled to find a way to connect to activism.

Working on this book, I came to understand that during my college years, I misunderstood the nature and the contribution of identity politics and intersectionality to activism. First, I assumed that intersectionality only applies to those who inhabit multiply marginalized positions, not to those of us who inhabit relatively privileged subject positions. Second, I naively assumed that identity politics referred only to the demographic position you inhabit, not to principled struggle to understand and transform the unjust realities you encounter, whatever your subject position. These misunderstandings left me feeling that I should "give up" my privilege rather than using it for social change and led me to take a backseat in work for social change. In the end, I developed what I hope is a realistic awareness of the impact of unquestioned privilege on organizing, but for a time, my confusion kept me from bringing my whole self to movement building. A long period of paralysis might have been avoided if I found Barbara's work earlier.

When I talk to friends about the process of researching, writing, and editing this book, I call it my "master class in feminism." As expressed in "Racism and Women's Studies," Barbara's is still, I think, the best articulation of a broad, inclusive, expansive feminism:

> Feminism is the political theory and practice that struggles to free all women: women of color, working-class women, poor women, disabled women, lesbians, old women, as well as white, economically privileged heterosexual women. Anything less than this vision of total freedom is not feminism, but merely female self-aggrandizement. (p. 134 in this volume)

Exploring Barbara's legacy has helped me reinforce, reaffirm, and strengthen lessons I have learned in the last decade while working in multiracial, multi-issue, cross-class feminist organizations: feminism must be based in practice; must respond to the real, lived material conditions of women who are most oppressed and exploited; and must focus on liberating *all* women.

For example, OKOP has developed an analysis of the welfare system that recognizes the multilayered nature of oppression and privilege. In light of the recession, anti-immigrant fervor, and an increasingly conservative political culture, many working-class families are accessing public assistance programs for the first time. Desperate to see their need for financial support as the result of extraordinary factors out of their control, they often define existing recipients as socially and culturally "Other"—more poor, more female, and more Black or Brown—in order to separate "good" welfare recipients (new ones like themselves) from "bad" ones (those who needed help before the recession). This leads to a situation of enormous horizontal violence, where recipients blame each other for what are widespread structural and economic problems. In welfare rights work, not having an intersectional analysis can be deadly. It makes us blame those closest to us—our natural allies—for problems that are created by systems of domination.

Based partly on insights from Barbara's work, OKOP has chosen a different path, developing strategies that rely on an economic human rights framework and public "truth telling" to help poor, working-class, and middle-class people see shared issues and concerns across race, gender, and sexuality. Framing our work in this way has opened up vast and exciting new alliances, leading us to build coalitions with remarkable national and international organizations such as the Poor People's Economic Human Rights Campaign and the World Courts of Women, and to develop a multi-issue agenda that recognizes that a society that respects and supports mothers on public assistance is a society that encourages a fuller humanity for all people.

Barbara's work has also inspired in me the courage to tell the truth about race, something that I, as a white woman, have been carefully conditioned not to discuss, or even acknowledge. In these times of "post-racialism" and "colorblindness," Smith's insights provide an important corrective. She demands that we tell the truth about our own lives. Better yet, she provides tools to build organizations, public forums, and social movements where we can be honest about the nature of our social experience and live to tell about it. As *Ain't Gonna Let Nobody Turn Me Around* developed, I found myself thinking, "I wish I had this book twenty years ago!" With it beside me, I would have felt less crazy, less alone, more resilient, more courageous. It would have made a vast difference in my practice, my thinking, my relationships, my life. I hope that the fundamental principles that Barbara and so many of her colleagues fought for and shared, and our small contribution in putting these resources into a single volume, do the same for you.

Roadmap to the Book

In traversing four decades and two hundred publications by and about Barbara, we selected items to create a book that sparks conversation and provokes reflection. We created a "remixed" format that, we hope, allows readers to experience Barbara's key intellectual and political contributions in ways that inspire innovation in scholarship, activism, and organizing today. Each chapter has a clear theme that captures major segments of Barbara's life and activism in more or less chronological order. However, we carefully blended a selected mix of key writings by Barbara, pictures and movement ephemera, and previously unpublished contemporary interviews. Each chapter features a primary interview, but we interweave excerpts from different interviews throughout every chapter to create "virtual conversations" about key events.

The interviews, which were commissioned specifically for this volume, allow the reader to "listen in" to an honest conversation with knowledgeable colleagues who are motivated and inspired by Barbara's life and legacy. In some cases, interviewers are contemporaries with whom Barbara had organized and strategized, such as Beverly Guy-Sheftall, Joo-Hyun Kang, Vera "Mike" Michelson, Barbara Ransby, and Matt Richardson. In other cases, they are activist-academics who have closely studied the legacy and meaning of Black feminism, such as Alexis Pauline Gumbs and Kimberly Springer. Loretta Ross, while not contributing an interview specifically for this volume, conducted an extensive (unpublished) oral history with Barbara in 2003 and kindly allowed us to include sections of it in this book. We each conducted interviews with Barbara to explore areas of our own interest and to fill in holes in the narrative as the book developed. You will find sections of our interviews threaded throughout the book, weaving together and highlighting what we think are important themes.

We concentrated on finding materials—writings by or about Barbara, key historical documents, and archival photographs—that are not easily available elsewhere. For example, you will not find what is perhaps Barbara's most well-known essay, "Toward a Black Feminist Criticism," here, but you will be able to read a speech she gave at the Howard University Black Writer's Conference in 1978—which included parts of that essay—and also experience the audience's rejection of Barbara's unprecedented effort to perform a lesbian reading of Black literature. We also chose to illuminate some aspects of Barbara's work that we think deserve more attention, such as her trenchant analysis of class and capitalism. Nearly all of the documents in the book were extensively edited for length. We encourage you to search out the pieces that most interest you and read them in the original. Despite including many fascinating, important, and hard-to-find documents, we do not claim to have put together the definitive account of Barbara's life and legacy. Rather, we hope to offer one interpretation of how her work can be used to inform and inspire principled action today.

2

Home Grown

Early Roots of Activism

> There is nothing more important to me than home . . . and all the women
> there that raised me. It was undoubtedly at home that I learned the rudi-
> ments of Black feminism. . . . Critics of feminism pretend that just because
> some of us speak out about sexual politics at home, within the Black
> community, we must have sprung miraculously from somewhere else. But
> we are not strangers and never have been. I am convinced that Black
> feminism is, on every level, organic to Black experience.
>
> —Barbara Smith, *Home Girls* (1983)

Much of Barbara's writing and activism honors the beauty and sacrifice of the lives of ordinary Black women. The interviews, writings, and historical documents in this chapter illuminate how one family contended with institutional oppression and the lessons these struggles conveyed. Barbara recounts and reflects on her growing-up years—from the circumstances of her birth to becoming an activist to coming out as a lesbian.

Barbara's family took part in the historic Great Migration, serially relocating from the small town of Dublin, Georgia, to a vibrant, cosmopolitan African American neighborhood in Cleveland, Ohio. Away from the most direct impacts of Southern racial terrorism, aunts, uncles, great-aunts, and grandparents joined their labors and their money to create a multigenerational, extended family home with loving commitment to, and high expectations for, Barbara and her twin sister Beverly.

Sadly, Barbara and Beverly lost their mother, Hilda, at age nine. This tragic loss is both personal and political, and provided Barbara with an early and unforgettable lesson about how the United States undervalues the lives of Black women. In the circumstances of Barbara's growing-up years, we can see the incredible need for a politics specific to the material realities of being Black, female, working class, and lesbian in the 1950s and 1960s. In Barbara's response to those conditions, we can also discern the beginnings of an astute analysis of collective experience that the Combahee River Collective would famously call "identity politics." We see that Barbara's activism is deeply personal, rooted in the lessons her grandmother taught her. We learn why home is something worth fighting for.

But the story in this chapter is not only Barbara's personal history; it is the history of the growth of our movements. It is an anatomy lesson that traces the lifeblood of progressive work over the last four decades. The beating heart at the center of this account is the insight that grounding ourselves in the particularity of our lives is the key to fighting injustice. Paying attention to our histories, our legacies, and the politics we learn at home—and telling the truth about these experiences—can provide a source of understanding powerful enough to save all of our lives.

The primary interview anchoring this chapter comes from friend and activist Loretta Ross, who cofounded SisterSong Women of Color Reproductive Health Collective. In addition, Ross is one of the first African American women to direct a rape crisis center in the 1970s and is a coauthor of *Undivided Rights: Women of Color Organize for Reproductive Justice* (Silliman et al. 2004). We extracted excerpts from a previously unpublished oral history that was conducted in 2003 for the Voices of Feminism Oral History Project, a unique and comprehensive resource that is part of the Sophia Smith Collection at the Women's History Archives at Smith College.

Roots of Beloved Community

In this section, Barbara shares how her family's move North during the Great Migration shaped her experience of growing up in Cleveland, Ohio. As a teenager in Cleveland's Civil Rights movement, Barbara participated in the fight to end school segregation and experienced firsthand the struggle to end U.S. apartheid and to build a "beloved community" that recognized everyone's full humanity. We illuminate Smith's early political consciousness with photographs that convey the indelible marks of her first forays into activism. Interviews conducted for this volume with Alethia Jones and Barbara Ransby demonstrate how early experiences provided the wellspring from which later political analysis arose.

Barbara Smith, "Interview by Loretta Ross," Voices of Feminism Oral History Project
(Smith and Ross 2003)

Barbara Smith (to Loretta Ross): I was born on November 16, 1946, in Cleveland, Ohio. I was the first of a set of twins, the only children that our mother had. I came from a family of Black southern women. Even though I grew up in the

North, the kind of rearing that my sister and I had was very southern and very traditional because everyone in our family had come from a little town in Georgia called Dublin, which is between Macon and Savannah. They had done a serial migration, starting probably in the late 1920s up to the 1940s. I think all of my grandmother's sisters were in the North by the time I was conscious.

Because of their roots in the South, I got the best of both worlds. They had moved North to get away from Jim Crow white supremacy and white racist terrorism, besides also wanting the economic possibilities that living in the industrial North might bring to them. But as far as values, point of view, all those things, I feel very rooted in core Black culture, which is traditionally the culture of the South.

My mother was a college graduate. She graduated from Fort Valley State College in the mid-forties, a small Black college at that time—segregated Black college—in Georgia. My father had been in World War II, or at least he was in the armed services. Given our birth date, it was as the war was ending that they were together. According to this first cousin of my mother who I always called Aunt Isabel, he came to Cleveland with a ring. And he stayed at the YMCA. Apparently he did not pass muster with my grandmother and with the great-aunts. From what I understand they disapproved of the marriage and so my mother ran away with him, which is highly romantic. And that may be why I'm such a romantic, or failed romantic.

So they ran away together—I don't know where they went—and then she returns. She was looking extremely sad. Aunt Isabel was somewhat younger than my mother, she was still a teenager, and she also was a real party girl and just having a lot of fun. So she said, "I'm bobbing around and I'm having so much fun and I didn't know what was wrong with Hilda. So one day I ask Hilda, 'What's wrong? You're just so down.' And my mother said to her, 'Don't you know?'" What Isabel did not know is that my mother was pregnant with my sister and myself.

As twins we were born quite prematurely. We were told that we weighed less than five pounds together. Today, that's a high-risk baby, but back in 1946, an incubator in those days was nothing but an egg carton with some lights. [laughs] And we were in the incubators. My sister, who is seven minutes younger than I, she had pneumonia, so she stayed in the incubator longer, and stayed in the hospital longer. We were really hanging by a thread. I always felt, because of these stories that I'm telling you, that I had a destiny. Obviously I was supposed to make it and be sitting here today.

Our mother died when we were nine years old, and we were raised by extended family. Our grandmother was always our primary caretaker because our mother had to work, like most Black women, and particularly a Black woman who did not have a husband. So our mother, with her college degree, a Bachelor's of Science in Education, the two jobs that she had during my young life were as a nurse's aide and as a supermarket clerk. She was a supermarket clerk when she died, with her Bachelor's of Science in Education. That's a typical Black woman's story, in relationship to racism and employment, during that era, and for most of the years that we've been in this country. She tried to get certified [as a public school teacher] in the state of Ohio as we were beginning kindergarten. But they sent her to schools that had some of the worst problems in the city. She was so disheartened by what she found there, that she decided to go back to the supermarket where she was the head clerk.

I will never forget telling a white woman therapist about my mother being a college graduate and the kinds of jobs she had and having this therapist tell me that my mother obviously had a self-image problem. The diagnosis was that I had a similar problem—no self-confidence. What this white woman did not understand was that there had been generations of Black college-educated people, men and women, who were denied jobs that their education had prepared them for. And maybe my mother did have a self-image problem—after all, she was a Black single mother in the 1940s with two little children and she had to take any damn job she could find! In her day, there were Black folks with PhDs working in the U.S. postal service because they couldn't get jobs elsewhere. That's just the way that was.

Our mother was born in 1922, and she had had rheumatic fever as a child. This is when they're living way down in Dublin, Georgia; who knows what the medical facilities for Black people were like then. In the spring of 1956—although these two incidents are unrelated, they were related in our minds, my sister's and mine—she was on a public city bus that had an accident, and she was injured. I think she was treated. That was kind of the beginning of the period of our mother being ill. This accident was very upsetting. Then, not long after that, she went into the hospital, never to return, because the rheumatic fever had weakened her heart.

Education was the bottom line in my family. Most people in this country, whether they were Black, white, male, or female, did not have college degrees in the 1940s. The high school diploma was the thing that most people sought, and many did not even get that. So our mother was highly educated for a Black woman of her time, even though she was not able to use that professionally. She brought that to us. We got started on the absolute right track.

Although many people in my family did not go to college, all of them were really educationally motivated. My grandmother and her sisters taught school in the segregated schools of the South in the early twentieth century, even without having completed any college. My Aunt Rosa did take normal courses at Spelman, summer courses.*

---

* Normal courses prepared students to be teachers, conveying the "norms" of teaching, what today is known as pedagogy that teaches teachers how to teach. Many historically Black higher educational institutions, such as Hampton, Claflin, Spelman, Tougaloo, Bishop, and others, sought to "prepare young men and women to be leaders in educational efforts among their people" by offering these courses (Trustees of the John F. Slater Fund for the Education of Freedmen, 1882: 13).

My Aunt Rosa, all my great-aunts, were very important to me. At least one of them lived with us through my entire growing up years. Aunt Rosa treated us like we were two of her little pupils. So I mean I know how to do every little craft there is. [laughs] I know how to make a May basket to this day, valentines, shamrocks, Easter eggs, you name it. Cut out and decorated!

One of the things I love about my family's attitude toward education is that it was always about the thing itself and not what it was going to get for you. So that's probably why I don't have a pot to piss in to this day [laughs], because we were never motivated around things. There were so many things that were so much more important than material objects. They were purely committed to using your gifts, whatever they were, to the best and most challenging level of your ability, and they were big readers. The people in my family read all the time. My grandmother read primarily the Bible and other religious books and pamphlets. Our family subscribed to two daily newspapers; there were three in Cleveland at the time. We got the Black newspaper that was published once a week. We had magazines.

As you can tell, we were not dirt poor. Of course, my grandmother, who was born in 1887, whenever we would ask for something, either money or some object, she said, we're poor people. [laughs] The family was obviously doing better than they had been in Georgia. My dear uncle—who died in 2001, outliving his sisters by many decades—said that the house they had down in Dublin, you could look down and see the earth through the floorboards and you could look up at the ceiling and see the sky.

Alethia Jones: Where did your class analysis come from?

Barbara Smith: Our grandmother told us on a daily basis that we were poor people. By the time my sister and I had arrived, things had gotten better. But my family didn't stop identifying with the lives that had shaped them. I think there was a basic sense of what's *fair*. It was not right that some people have all the clothes and all the food and all the beautiful places to live and all of whatever it is they think is valuable, and then there are kids on the street. The people who raised me, they were pretty fair. We saw people operating around us who had real ethical compasses.

My sense of justice is also shaped by the fact that my sister and I experienced something miserably unfair when we were nine years old. Our mother died. We had, right up in our face, an experience of what isn't fair. It's not fair for your mother to die when you're nine years old. I have never gotten over it. I never will.

Because my family had education, because they had drive, and because they pooled their resources, we did not grow up in poverty. We were by no means upper-class and we were by no means "sadiddy" [i.e., uppity, stuck up]. We were a working-class, lower-middle-class family. When we were six years old, in first grade, our family made a decision to become homeowners. We moved from a house that we rented to a house that they bought and owned. It was a two-family house, by no means luxurious. We lived on the first floor—our grandmother, our mother, our great-aunt, sometimes another great-aunt, and Beverly and myself. That's quite a few people in a five-room suite. Our Aunt LaRue and her husband lived on the second floor. It really was all about an extended family working together: our aunt, our mother's sister, her husband at the time, and our mother, all their incomes were flowing into this one household. The family wanted to move to this house because it was near some of the best public schools in the city.

We had lived in what was called the "Central Area," which was closer to downtown and quite prosperous. There were many Black-owned businesses and there were people who owned their homes. People who lived in our new neighborhood [Mount Pleasant], who were also Black, had similar goals and similar desires for their children. There were also very poor Black communities, like Hough. There were some schools that were notorious for how poor they were and how violent they were. But in those days, violence was fights and maybe a knife, it wasn't about guns.

Cleveland was one of the ten largest cities in the country at the time. We did not know at the time that we were growing up in a very cosmopolitan setting. We had a vast public school system: hundreds of elementary schools, dozens of high schools. We were very, very fortunate. But I was born about eighty years after slavery ended. Slavery hadn't been over for one hundred years at the time my sister and I arrived on earth. That had impact. My growing up years were affected by that experience; people still had a collective memory of how slavery had shaped our goals and our desires. Black people were not thought of as human beings. At the very most, we were considered inferior human beings. The people who I grew up with, they were bound and determined to prove that wrong. They were bound and determined to say, "We're not going to fall into the stereotypes. Whatever you think we are, we're going to show you something else."

Our aunt used to take us to the Cleveland Museum of Art, our public schools went to concerts performed by the Cleveland Orchestra on a regular basis, we got introduced to live theater as children because Karamu House was a launching pad for Black actors and performers. So we got to see live theater, including Shakespeare, done by Black actors. I just thought that was the way life was. I thought that was normal. It didn't occur to me that not every little girl was seeing a Black cast perform *Little Red Riding Hood*. Talk about being lucky. So lucky. That's the kind of life I would like everybody to have.

The value system in my home was to identify with Black people as a group. We were never told to look down on anyone. We were not in the Black elite, that upper stratum of doctors and attorneys. Our aunt regretted so much that she had not had the opportunity to go to college because she was so bright. She would have thrived there. But she had a really good white-collar job working at the main branch of the Cleveland Public Library.

The injustice of poverty. Class oppression is the bottom line. It's a basis and a way of understanding other kinds of oppression. Race and class in this country are completely intertwined.

Barbara Smith (to Loretta): We went to Robert Fulton Elementary School. One of the things about [Mount Pleasant] is that it had a lot more white people in it. At our old school there were virtually no white people except for the teachers. I will never forget the first day of school at the new school. Our mother told my sister and myself, she said, "There are going to be more white children in your class from now on." And she said not another word about it. [laughs] It wasn't like, "They're going to act like this and this is how you're supposed to feel." No attitude. Just facts. There are going to be a lot more white people there.

"Class oppression is ... a basis and a way of understanding other kinds of oppression."

There was definitely racism. The first racism we experienced was in an educational context. The summer that we were eight, we were picked from kids all over the city and the suburbs to take French at Western Reserve University. There were perhaps three or four Black students in an average-size class, and my sister and I were very shy, which doesn't mix very well with learning to speak a language. You had to really put yourself out there in a way that a shy child might be reluctant to do. We weren't causing any other kind of problem for our teacher, but she was incredibly mean to us. She treated us horribly.

The teacher, that was one thing. But because it was a long class, about three hours every morning, there would be a break and kids would bring snacks. It was the fifties, so most people's mothers were not working then, and they would bring snacks that their mothers had made for them. Although our mother worked, she was a great baker, and we loved making cookies with her and cakes, too. So we asked her, begged her, "Could you please make cookies for us so we can take them to class and we can share them with the other children?" Well, out of her full-time work schedule, she of course complied and made chocolate chip cookies, and we took them to class. And do you think any of those white children would touch them? I will never forget it as long as I live.

People don't know about U.S. apartheid. I grew up under apartheid, under segregation, even though it was the North. People forget the level of demonization and vilification and dehumanization that was part and parcel of being a person of African heritage living in this country before the Civil Rights movement. I lived under that. One of the worst examples that I can think of is when these yahoos, these creatures, rejected my dear mother's cookies . . .

Figure 2.1: Barbara Smith and Beverly Smith, circa 1956, Cleveland, Ohio. Barbara and Beverly were featured in the *Cleveland Plain Dealer* in the 1950s after Barbara's question "What is a petrified forest?" was selected for publication in a children's column. They received the prize of a set of encyclopedias, which the family always wanted but could not afford.

We went to Alexander Hamilton Junior High School and John Adams High School, which was one of the best academic high schools in the city of Cleveland. We had a wonderful guidance counselor, Miss White, who was, of course, white. She was an incredibly important person in my life because she challenged all of us to apply to the most competitive schools she thought we were qualified to apply to. Because of the Civil Rights struggle, and *Brown v. Board of Education* in 1954, schools were under pressure.* In order to get or keep federal funding, they had to desegregate. That really opened the dam for what public institutions, including educational ones, had to do in order to be compliant. It wasn't about benevolence—if they wanted to keep getting those federal dollars they had to demonstrate that they were not segregated institutions.

---

* *Brown v. Board of Education of Topeka, Kansas* (1954) is the landmark unanimous Supreme Court decision that ordered the end of "separate but equal" public education, finding state-funded Black-white segregation inherently unequal.

My sister and I aced every test we took, standardized or otherwise. Our guidance counselor was in touch with Charles McCarthy [an official at Yale's Cooperative Program for Educational Opportunity]. When he saw our PSAT* scores, he called Miss White up and he said, "Have them apply to every single school they want to," and they paid our application fees.

Interview with Barbara Ransby

Barbara Ransby: Can you tell me a bit about your experience in the Civil Rights movement?

Barbara Smith: I always describe it as my first movement and the one that has been most formative of my perspective about organizing, politics, and justice. It was not just the first that I was involved in chronologically, but it actually changed my social status within my lifetime.

When I was born, in 1946, segregation was the law of the land. So even though I was growing up in the North, I lived in a country where segregation was absolutely the rule, condoned, supported, institutionalized. Civil Rights is the movement that made the most difference in my life as far as what I am able to do versus what I would have been able to do had it never occurred. I grew up under segregation, and I lived in a time of domestic terrorism, the threat of lynching and vigilantism, and an even more unequal justice system [than we have now].

I came of age during the height of the Civil Rights era. I was in elementary school in 1954, when the Supreme Court ruled on *Brown v. Board of Education*. The Montgomery bus boycott happened in '55. Emmett Till was murdered. All these things happened during the time I was coming of age. It was such a terrible time to be Black. I lived in a world where Black people were assumed to be inferior, to be less, to be incompetent, incapable, criminal, immoral.

I was sheltered in some ways because of being a child in the North, where we had de facto segregation, instead of the South's harsher de jure version. I was a teenager, in the early 1960s, and in Cleveland, the Civil Rights movement had a focus on school desegregation. They did a really good job of getting youth involved. So the first demonstration I ever went to, I will never forget it, it was the spring of 1964, on a Saturday, and it was all these kids from all over the East Side of Cleveland. It was just exciting.

It was a mobilization on the Saturday before the citywide boycott of the public schools had been called. I had never felt like that before, I had never been to anything that was like that. I was so amazed. I was really shy and socially

---

*Pre-Standard Admissions Test, the precursor to the full standard admissions test for college in the United States.

"Klunder, Bruce W.,"
The Encyclopedia of Cleveland History (1997)

KLUNDER, BRUCE W. (12 July 1937–7 April 1964) was a martyr in the campaign to desegregate the Cleveland public schools. Born in Greeley, Colorado, son of Everett and Beatrice Klunder, he moved with his family to Oregon where he was educated. Klunder earned his bachelor's degree from Oregon State University (1958) and there met his future wife, Joanne Lehman. The couple wed 22 Dec. 1956, and had two children, Janice and Douglas.

Klunder and his wife moved to New Haven, Connecticut, where he enrolled in the Yale Divinity School. He was graduated with his B.D. in 1961. In Sept. 1961 Klunder came to Cleveland as executive director of the Student Christian Union of the YMCA. He was ordained to the Presbyterian presbyterate in Cleveland at the Church of the Covenant on 4 March 1962. In April, 1962, Klunder was a founding member of the Cleveland area CORE (Congress of Racial Equality). Klunder believed his calling demanded social activism and was soon a leader in the Civil Rights movement. He frequently did picket duty, demonstrating for fair housing, and against segregated public facilities and discrimination in hiring.

When the Cleveland City School District decided to build new schools which would have reinforced the pattern of segregated neighborhood enroll-ment, Klunder took the lead in attempting to stop construction. On 7 April 1964, he and four other protesters gathered at the construction site for Stephen E. Howe Elementary School on Lakeview Road. He lay down behind a bulldozer while four other pickets blocked its forward path. The operator, seeking to avoid the protesters in front of him, unknowingly backed over Klunder, instantly killing him. His death was ruled an accident.

The next day 150 people marched in silent memorial in front of the Board of Education Building downtown. Funeral services were held at the Church of the Covenant with Eugene Carson Blake, head of the United Presbyterian Church delivering the eulogy, and 1,500 attending. Klunder's ashes were interred in the columbarium of the Church of the Covenant.

From *The Encyclopedia of Cleveland History*, 1997. Reprinted with permission of Case Western Reserve University.

Figure 2.2: The body of the Reverend Bruce W. Klunder, 1964. From the photograph's original caption: "The body of the Rev. Bruce W. Klunder lies in front of the bulldozer that has just crushed him to death. At upper left stands a mother holding her child." (*Cleveland Plain Dealer*, photo by Dudley Brumbach. Reprinted with permission of The Plain Dealer/Landov)

uncomfortable, but I felt like I belonged there. They wanted all of us to be there, we were seen as an important part of this [struggle].

When my sister and I graduated from high school—we were mid-year graduates because of the overcrowding in the Cleveland public schools, so we graduated in January of 1965—we got jobs, but we also made a real effort to work with CORE. We had a Congress of Racial Equality chapter in Cleveland, and one of the reasons we were able to do very interesting work with CORE is because the executive director was a Black woman who was an Oberlin College graduate, and she was very open to having two young Black women at the office.

We canvassed on housing and other issues of concern to poor Black communities. She had us go with an adult volunteer, a wonderful man whose first name was Chuck, who was blind. We could help each other: he was an adult who could make sure we were safe going up to strangers' doors; we could help him by saying, "There are some steps here. Or, there's the railing." We would ride the bus together and go door-to-door. It was a wonderful relationship; he was a very nice person. So we got involved in canvassing, one of the basic building blocks of organizing, at a very, very early age.

BOARD TO BUILD MORE SEGREGATED SCHOOLS

"Keep informed on the problems and issues that continue to affect the education of our children." That was the message David Cohen, CORE's Education Chairman, emphasized at the last general membership meeting.

Here, briefly, are the general facts Cohen outlined:

The Cleveland School Board is spending taxpayer's money to support segregation. They are now moving at breakneck speed to build three schools in Glenville. Board members insist their only purpose is to alleviate overcrowding in Hazeldell. Yet if this is their aim, why don't they transport some of the students to the 12,500 empty elementary pupil places in Cleveland?

This would be cheaper, it would integrate some classes, and it would not perpetuate the segregated neighborhood school.

The answer is that the board will pay any price to end the present transportation program because it now requires integration. The new schools are not being built for the Negro students in Glenville, but to appease Whites in Collinwood and Murray Hill who oppose integration.

The neighborhood school must be replaced with consolidated educational centers. They would be integrated; and they would offer efficient, economical and high quality education.

The School Board must drop its committment to the neighborhood school.

CLEVELAND
CORE
CHAPTER
POST OFFICE BOX 5614
CLEVELAND, OHIO 44101

U.S. POSTAGE
PAID
CLEVELAND, OHIO
Permit No. 2065

Figure 2.3: "Board to Build More Segregated Schools," selection from CORE Newsletter, spring 1964. The Cleveland chapter of the Congress of Racial Equality (CORE) organized against the construction of segregated schools throughout the early 1960s.

Barbara R.: Were your parents supportive of your activism?

Barbara S.: By that time, I didn't have parents. My mother died when I was nine years old, and we never had contact with our father. So I had my wonderful maternal aunt, my grandmother, my great-aunts, and a maternal uncle in the same neighborhood.

One of the things I so value and love, when I think about that early part of my life, is that my aunt, who really became my parent, when we would talk to her about wanting to go to a demonstration, she would ask a few basic questions about our safety, give us a little bit of advice, and then she'd let us get on the bus and go. It's amazing to me that she had such faith in our judgment, and didn't want to hold us back. I think that's one of the most wonderful things that could ever happen to me, to any young person. That is, to have someone who is responsible for you, but who gives you enough leeway, and who treats you with enough respect, that they think you can actually make a good decision. Obviously these were building blocks to some of the things that I do now.

Of course, the people in my family obviously wanted to see racism addressed! They'd come from the Jim Crow South, and Georgia was no joke. But we didn't have to hide, fight, or debate. What I was being exposed to was the transformative struggle of my people. The people who seemed to me the most heroic, and the most interesting, at the time were the people who were involved in that struggle: Martin Luther King Jr., of course, and James Baldwin, who was my hero. We were excited about people who were noble and absolutely courageous.

Barbara R.: The focus of my research is on Ella Baker and SNCC [Student Nonviolent Coordinating Committee], which has been a great source of inspiration for a lot of the political work that I've done. I know SNCC was very influential in a number of ways in shaping your political consciousness. I'm wondering if you can say something about that.

Barbara S.: I never met Ella Baker, but I did have the privilege of meeting Fannie Lou Hamer briefly. I also remember watching her speak at the 1964 Democratic Convention [on television] and being transfixed because it was like, "Black people never get to talk on TV about anything. Particularly Black women." This is the era when the first TV show with a Black main character was just rolling out, *Julia*. It was about a Black single mother, widowed. She was a nurse and she was perfect. She was absolutely perfect. Not a wrinkle. The contrast between that first attempt to show Black family life on TV and Fannie Lou Hamer just giving a reading of the entire U.S. democracy! That's what she was doing. She was doing a reading of the failures of the entire U.S. democracy. I believe she said, "Is this America? Is this America?" She could talk with such authority about how it was not functioning. But when I met her she certainly did strike me as being very kind, and [reminded me of] the people in my family who were from the same part of the country.

Barbara R.: That was certainly what I took away from my work on Ella Baker, this tough, sharp, smart strategist with enormous human compassion and caring. She was there for people when the smoke of battle cleared. She was worried about human beings and their lives.

Barbara S.: I idolized SNCC. I was fortunate to see Howard Zinn do a presentation when I was in college. I was just so struck [by him]. He was a professor, he was clearly so committed to the things I thought were most important, and he had written this wonderful book, *SNCC: The New Abolitionists*. I went out and got it the very next day, read it, and I was just like, "This is it!" Just so exciting. SNCC was the most remarkable organization because it was people who were young. It was also people who were willing to push the envelope. It was not religious-based organizing. To me, that was *the* organization.

Barbara R.: What was your direct connection to the Civil Rights movement? The experience of seeing Fannie Lou Hamer and watching this unfold? Hearing Howard Zinn? What were some other points of connection?

Barbara S.: I've been a part of many movements for political, economic, and social change and justice. I was reading Fanon before I even thought about Black feminism. I was admiring the Panthers before I ever thought about Black feminism. I was protesting the war in Vietnam before I could understand feminism.

College Life and Activism

In excerpts from interviews with Loretta Ross, Barbara Ransby, Matt Richardson, and Alethia Jones, Smith describes her activism during her undergraduate years at Mount Holyoke College, a highly competitive women's school in New England, and explores the relationship between her activism, her upbringing, and her education as a young adult.

Barbara Smith, "Interview by Loretta Ross," Voices of Feminism Oral History Project

(Smith and Ross 2003)

Barbara Smith (to Loretta Ross): The Ivy League was completely closed to women at that time, so Wesleyan, Williams, Dartmouth, Yale, Harvard—none of that was even on the agenda. We couldn't apply because we were females. So ironic, given the fact that we were also Black.

But once I found Mount Holyoke College I knew that was the one. It is the oldest of the Seven Sisters,* and it has a very different tradition than the rest. It was founded in 1837 by a visionary woman, Mary Lyon, who had a dream of starting an educational institution for women when girls and women were not being educated. She literally collected pennies from New England farm wives to start the school. I'm not saying it wasn't elitist. I'm not saying it wasn't racist. I'm not saying [laughs] it wasn't white supremacist. And I'm also not saying I did not suffer the trials of the damned.

> **"I went to a women's college because they were some of the best and most elite colleges in the country for female students at the time. I'm not saying it wasn't elitist. I'm not saying it wasn't racist. I'm not saying it wasn't white supremacist. And I'm also not saying that I did not suffer the trials of the damned."**

I went to a women's college because they were some of the best and most elite colleges in the country for female students at the time. There was also the comfort of a women's environment. One of the things I thought to myself at the time was, I know that I'm going to be dealing with racism if I go to any predominantly white institution. So if I go to a women's college at least I will not be dealing with negative assumptions about me because I am a girl. Now, the women's movement was definitely in a quiescent stage in the fifties and early 1960s, so when people think that I chose to go to a women's college because I was such a staunch and righteous feminist, I say, "Please, read your history books!" [laughs] I didn't even know the word feminist in those days, but there was greater comfort being with women.

It was rough going my first two years. I knew I was going to finish college, because I wanted to have a better life than not going would provide for me. But after my first two years, I transferred out of Mount Holyoke and spent my junior year at the New School for Social Research in New York City, because I was done, really done. I lived in the East Village in 1968. I'd always wanted to get to New York City. That time was extremely important. It was a nontraditional program, and I concentrated on the social sciences. That's where I first read Marx, Freud, Weber, Hegel—all them bad boys, and had wonderful discussions with teachers and the disaffected youth who were my classmates.

My dreams, they were not about materialism, they were about going to Paris

---

*Seven private liberal arts women's colleges on the East Coast founded in the nineteenth century. Radcliffe merged with Harvard and Vassar became coed.

and being an expatriate Black writer. I thought the only way you could really be a Black writer was to get your behind over to Paris [laughs] because the great ones did that! You know: Wright, Baldwin, Chester Himes. Hey, good enough for them, good enough for me! But in the end, I decided to go back to Mount Holyoke for my senior year and I finished there. I was going to finish college. That had to happen.

Interviews with Barbara Ransby, Matt Richardson, and Alethia Jones

Barbara Smith (to Barbara Ransby): By the time I left for school in the fall of 1965, the Civil Rights movement was shifting from a Civil Rights perspective to a Black Power perspective. Some might say it was winding down. But there was an organization at Mount Holyoke called the Civil Actions Group, and a lot of the students whom I most admired were a part of it.

In 1965 and 1966, we organized fasts against the war in Vietnam. They caused controversy. Mount Holyoke is a women's college, which means it was outside of the box in the sense that it thought women were intelligent and could lead. But, it was certainly conservative as far as its social expectations. We had to wear skirts to dinner! [laughs] There were people who did not think we should be fasting. I will never forget, going to the music history class that I was taking and the instructor made some really cutting remarks about those of us who were fasting. And I was so upset, so angry.

Barbara R.: This speaks to the issue of how we assume certain institutions, either women's colleges or historically Black colleges, by the nature of how they define their constituency, are going to be progressive. That is so not the case!

Barbara S.: In the fall of 1968 Mark Rudd spoke about the Columbia [University] struggle* nearby, and we went over to see him. We thought it would be good for him to come over to Mount Holyoke, which rumpled quite a few feathers . . .

Barbara R.: All the administrators were locking their doors?

Barbara S.: They were fit to be tied, because we didn't ask! You know that phrase, "I'd rather ask forgiveness than permission?" We were operating on that basis. That was the first time I ever met anybody who described themselves as a part of women's liberation. He was traveling with a woman who was part of the women's liberation movement, and I was like, "What is *that*?"

Barbara R.: And how old were you?

Barbara S.: I think I was twenty-one at the time. I just couldn't get it. The historical relationship between Black women and white women is extremely

---

*Mark Rudd, a junior at Columbia University, led the campus's Students for a Democratic Society (SDS) chapter, which organized sit-ins where students occupied key administration buildings to protest the war in Vietnam, U.S. imperialism, and the proposed construction of a Columbia gymnasium in Harlem that activists called "Gym Crow." The occupation gained national media attention and became known as "Columbia '68." Rudd was promptly expelled.

fraught, defined in many ways by the experience of slavery, and, of course, post-slavery, peonage and share cropping, et cetera . . .

Barbara R.: . . . and then the domestic relationship . . .

Barbara S.: Black women working in white women's homes and taking care of white women's children, and being completely marginalized as far as any kind of social access or equality is concerned. So when your past relationship with white women is that they were your boss, and often your very, very abusive and disrespectful boss, it's like, "What does Miss Ann need with a liberation movement?" She already has everything anybody could possibly want . . .

Barbara R.: . . . and is she really asking me to join her?

Barbara S.: Right, indeed. But as time went on, and I got out of college and into the world, I began to understand what women's issues were. I got a gift certificate as a Christmas present, and you know what I went and bought with it? Kate Millet's *Sexual Politics*. I read it cover to cover. I was fascinated by it because her examples were primarily drawn from literature. That was the beginning of a click. It would have been hard to escape the movement during those years when I was coming of age. But it didn't make much sense to me at that point.

Matt Richardson: Were you involved in activism at Mount Holyoke, and what kind?

Barbara S.: Yes, I was. We were in the generation of students that were desegregating these elite private colleges and universities for the first time. There were fewer than thirty Black students in the entire school, and the enrollment at that time was about 1,600 students.

The Civil Actions Group focused on Civil Rights, but it was also getting very involved with anti–Vietnam War organizing. In the spring of 1967, which was my sophomore year, there was this major demonstration in New York City against the war in Vietnam, a march to the United Nations. That was the first time I ever saw hippies, and there was also a contingent that had come from Harlem. One of the speakers was Martin Luther King Jr., who gave one of his first major speeches [against the war]. In fact, the speech he gave at Riverside Church during that period was just a few days before that demonstration.[*]

[The year that I went to the] New School for Social Research, my junior year, was the year that Columbia University went out on strike, and we closed in solidarity. The New School had its own chapter of Students for a Democratic Society (SDS).[†] Even though I shared political perspectives with people in SDS,

---

[*] Smith is referring to King's landmark speech, "Beyond Vietnam," given on April 4, 1967. The protest at the United Nations was on April 15, 1967. Over one hundred thousand people marched and listened to speeches by Martin Luther King Jr., Floyd McKissick, Stokely Carmichael, and Dr. Benjamin Spock. Prior to the march, nearly two hundred draft cards ordering males to fight in the Vietnam War were burned by youths (mostly young men) in Central Park.

[†] SDS (1962–1969) became virtually synonymous with the New Left movement and college student political organizing and was a major vehicle for anti-Vietnam War organizing and for young men to resist the draft. Its Port Huron Statement is a classic call for participatory democracy. For more, see Miller (1994).

I just didn't see any way to be involved. It was obviously about white guys, or at least white people. Everything was so white and male and compartmentalized.

I went back to Mount Holyoke College my senior year, and got involved in a huge amount of organizing that directly addressed issues on campus. [For example,] we demanded that there be some kind of a building for an Afro-American Center. I learned a lot about basic organizing during those years. We were negotiating with administrators, and, at a certain point, those discussions were not leading anywhere. We just said, "Okay, now we have to go to the next step," and we had a sit-in in the administration building. It was very lady-like. [laughs] We let people get to where they needed to go, we didn't bar anybody from doing their work, but we sat on this staircase in the administration building for most of the day. And do you want to know what I was reading that day? James Weldon Johnson's *Autobiography of an Ex-Colored Man*.

[The campus administration] said that the Board of Trustees would have to decide if we could have this Afro-American Center. We demanded that we meet with them ourselves. One faculty member, a wonderful professor of political science, was very supportive and agreed to go with us to meet with the Board of Trustees in New York City, at the top of the Time-Life Building. I think we were the first students who ever met with the Board of Trustees of Mount Holyoke.

We were the "turning-the-tide" generation at these schools. I entered in '65 and I graduated in '69, and a lot changed in the society as a whole between those dates. In the summer of 1967, I was a resident tutor in the A Better Chance Program at Mount Holyoke College, and studying and discussing James Baldwin's *The Fire Next Time*. It was incredible because the title so resonated with the urban insurrections that were happening during that period. I remember walking to the one drugstore in South Hadley, Massachusetts, and buying either a *Time* or *Newsweek* that had the Newark riots on the cover. Imagine being in this incredibly beautiful, bucolic setting and going to get these magazines showing what was happening in cities like the city that I grew up in. Cleveland went off in the summer of '66. In '68, I was working at Western Reserve University as a counselor in the Upward Bound Program in the summer, and that was the year of the Glenville shootout.* We literally were on lockdown in our dormitories with lights turned off for safety, because of all the shooting.

---

* The Glenville shootout was a series of violent episodes that took place between the Cleveland Police Department and armed Black militant groups in July of 1968. Carl Stokes was the first Black mayor of a major U.S. city. He was elected in 1967 and sworn in January 1, 1968. *The Encyclopedia of Cleveland History* records that

> Before the [first] night [July 23, 1968] was over, 7 people were dead: 3 policemen, 3 suspects, and 1 civilian; and 15 were wounded. When it became clear that the police were neither trained nor equipped to handle the disorders, Mayor Carl Stokes requested and received the assistance of the National Guard that following day. Stokes believed that putting African Americans in control of their own community would prevent further bloodshed, and the afternoon of 24 July he decided only Black policemen and Black community leaders would be allowed in Glenville with the rest of the police and the guard stationed on the perimeter of the cordoned-off area. ("Glenville Shootout," 1998).

Alethia Jones: How did you decide to go to Chicago in 1968, which became so violent?

Barbara S.: By the time I went to Chicago for the Democratic National Convention demonstrations in the summer of '68, I was starting my senior year. I thought I was grown. I really went through quite a process of deciding whether I was going to go or not. I knew it was going to be dangerous. I was talking to someone this weekend about times where there has been a lot of violent activity in the United States, and they mentioned Chicago. They said, "Then there were the riots in Chicago in 1968." I said, "Yeah. The *police* rioted." I wasn't rioting. I was there for a demonstration. My sister and my aunt were at home watching it on TV. They must have been so worried.

I lived in revolutionary times. That's where people's heads were at. There were people who were willing to stand up to injustice, speak truth to power, risk arrest, risk all kinds of things in order to stand up. After being in Chicago, we went out to California. You'd see Panther posters on street corners in Oakland, Berkeley, all over the Bay Area. One of the things being raised by Black militants, who were very committed to the struggle, was a concern that people who were getting really fabulous educations would forget all about our communities and turn our backs on them. I will never forget Stokely Carmichael coming to Mount Holyoke College my senior year and basically accusing us of that. The question of: Are you down with the folk? Are you doing this to serve yourself, to line your pockets, or do you have a commitment to the greater good of your community? It was an event that was coordinated by our new Afro-American Society, and he felt like he needed to put down the Black student leaders, who were all female because it was a women's college, from the stage. I will never forget it as long as I live. There was a gender dynamic going on there.

Barbara S. (to Matt Richardson): The reason I went to graduate school, and the reason I chose English, is because I was committed to teaching Black literature, African American literature, which, virtually, was not being taught at that time.

Matt: How was University of Pittsburgh? You were in the English department?

Barbara S.: Yes, I was. I was just there for two years. I'm such a nerd! I have always had positive relationships with teachers, not across the board, but any place that I've studied, there's always a teacher that I remember with great fondness and great admiration. I met a professor at the University of Pittsburgh whose name was Thomas Philbrick, and he was a Melville scholar. I took his Melville course the first semester I was there and just *loved* Melville.

Because I had dealt with an exclusive Eastern college, I knew I did not want to go to an Ivy League school to work on my PhD, so Mr. Philbrick recommended that I go to the University of Connecticut, because there were some great Melville scholars there. That's why I went to the University of Connecticut. Because of *Melville*! [laughs] There was also a wonderful Black professor there named Donald Gibson, and he was one of the few Black professors on a graduate faculty in literature at a predominantly white university at the time.

Matt: So you got a master's degree at . . .

Barbara S.: University of Pittsburgh . . .

Matt: And then went to the PhD program . . . in English [at University of Connecticut, Storrs]. So what was going on at this point in terms of your activism while you were in graduate school?

Barbara S.: I felt like I would never be involved in political organizing again. There was a really strong Black studies program in development at the University of Pittsburgh, and Black nationalism was just the rule of the day. There was not much space for Black women in those movements.

I was still involved in peace organizing to end the war in Vietnam, and I took a lot of criticism for going to a major mobilization in Washington the first fall that I was at the University of Pittsburgh. There were people who were very critical, and who said that that was a white issue, despite the fact that the vast majority of U.S. military people who were dying in Vietnam were young men of color. And why were they there? Because of poverty and racism.

I was constantly writing and keeping journals. I wrote something that was never published, called "The Last Demonstration," that was about going to the major mobilization against the war in Vietnam in November of 1969 in Washington, D.C., and thinking that I would never be involved in anything like that again. I met some women when I was at the University at Pittsburgh who were interested in beginning to do work in women's studies. I met with them, but there was such a disconnect for me, because it was like, "What do white women have to complain about?" It was just hard to imagine people who had had such a domineering, exploitative, and oppressive relationship to Black women saying they now wanted to be liberated. [Nevertheless,] I had experienced sexism myself—it was sometimes hard to separate sexism out from racism—but I had definitely experienced it, particularly after leaving Mount Holyoke. So I [became] interested in the women's movement.

My sister, Beverly, had gotten married in 1970, and her husband was a television director or producer of the first Black news show in New York City, which was called, I believe, *Black News*. They moved [to New York], and then, eventually, she got a job working at this little magazine called *Ms.* [laughs] By that time, we were really getting interested in women's issues and trying to see how it would apply to us. And would it ever! Because of her working at *Ms.*, I found out that the National Black Feminist Organization was going to have its first Eastern regional conference in November of 1973. And then, the rest is history.

Barbara R.: You mentioned Martin Luther King Jr. I've recently been speaking in different places about the King holiday. Every year, I think of his term "the fierce urgency of now" and how much he evolved in the course of his career. But you heard him speak in 1967. How did you see King? What do you think about King's role in the movement? His legacy? He is characterized as a kind of patriarch of the movement; that image belied some of the grassroots work that was going on. Here you were, this budding feminist. How did you see King as a force in the movement?

Barbara S.: There was such great admiration for him in my family because he was from the South, from Atlanta. They were from Georgia. So he was from home, and just on that basis alone, there was that fellow-feeling and identification. Then the fact that he was a minister, and that he was helping to blow the top off of the system that had motivated them to escape from the South and come somewhere else to try to do something different and have better opportunities. They admired him.

By the time I was in college, I certainly was absolutely impressed by the fact that he was speaking out against the war, which I knew was a courageous stance to take when many Black people were not doing the same. Later, as his very short life evolved, he became more and more radical. At the time of his death, he was talking about capitalism and poverty, and how you can't have justice under an unjust economic system. And that *will* get you killed, besides everything else.

Barbara R.: So funny how people only remember the "I Have a Dream" speech. As Vincent Harding says, that's a very deliberate amnesia about King. There were such radical speeches—the "Beyond Vietnam" speech; even the "I've Been to the Mountaintop" speech the night before he died; the Riverside Church speech, exactly a year before he was assassinated—were anti-imperialist, critical of capitalism, supportive of workers, and so forth.

Barbara S.: He gave the Riverside Church speech within days of the speech that I witnessed. We were talking coming down on the train [for this interview] about this notion of volunteerism, of taking the King holiday and turning it into an opportunity to volunteer. That is absolutely not what he was about. I say, yeah, volunteer to be put in jail, volunteer to be beaten, volunteer to be knocked over by fire hoses and bitten by police dogs. That's what you're volunteering for. We're not talking about going to a homeless shelter and serving some meals. People want to water that down. The right wing in this country, the conservatives in this country have cherry-picked from his written record and from his speeches . . .

Barbara R.: . . . Hijacked! Stolen! Absconded!

Barbara S.: For those of us who lived through it, it's like, "How can you get that out of this?" It makes no sense whatsoever. We were living in a situation of racial warfare. We were living under U.S. apartheid.

Barbara R.: And the obscenity of the folks who have carried out a crusade against affirmative action, doing so under this rubric of Civil Rights. One of the organizations that fought against affirmative action programs on college campuses calls itself the Civil Rights Institute. This idea of being colorblind, and that affirmative action is reverse racism, is such a crude betrayal of that legacy.

Barbara S.: Indeed. A colorblind society? If you came into this room and you said, "I don't see any tables in this room; there's just furniture!" Huh? You know? It's just . . .

Barbara R.: . . . denial of reality.

Barbara S.: Colorblindness, from [the Civil Rights] period, would have meant that we understand that people come from a variety of ethnic and racial backgrounds, and nationalities. We understand that and we do not see anyone as less in the incredible diversity of human populations. That's what colorblindness would mean. It's not this idiotic, simple-minded, "I don't see color, I just see a person." Shut up. Just shut up! The other one that gets me is when people say, "I don't care if you're green or purple." It's like, no. Because we don't have green people, and we don't have purple ones. So let's just talk about reality.

"One of the things about the Civil Rights movement is that it had a value system that was very loving and valued us as human beings. . . . We really were trying to get a transformation, not just of the laws and of the institutions, but of the human spirit."

Barbara R.: It's a kind of escapism. I started high school in 1971, and I felt like the people who were facing the world and changing the world in the most courageous way, and probably in my teenage vision, the most romantic way, were radicals and revolutionaries and activists. There was a sense in the Civil Rights era that something was being won in the fight against the most visible forms of repression. When I came of age the repression was much more covert; it was COINTELPRO and the FBI doing a lot of behind-the-scenes things.* It wasn't dogs attacking people in Birmingham . . .

Barbara S.: . . . and bombing churches and little girls dying. One of the things about the Civil Rights movement is that it had a value system that was very loving and valued us as human beings. As opposed to, "You're just a cog. You represent this. You embody this. You are a part of the proletariat, but I don't really want to know you. I'm not very interested in you." There was that attempt for a beloved community. There was a real valuing of the human beings who were the community in struggle. One of the examples of that was when students from the North, who were predominantly white but not entirely, went South. They were always so touched by how poor Black people in the rural South treated them, and how embraced they were. That's the humanity of the Black community in which I was raised.

I'm always struck by the humanity of people who have nothing, people who are in some ways the most oppressed, [whose example disproves] the notion

---

*COINTELPRO was a clandestine, unauthorized domestic spying program created by FBI director J. Edgar Hoover to disrupt, discredit, and destroy those deemed "domestic threats." Undercover agents infiltrated Civil Rights (and other political) organizations creating internal dissension, imprisonment, and sometimes assassinations. For more, see O'Reilly (1991) and Rosenfeld (2012).

of oppression being so dehumanizing that it takes people's [humanity] away. Sometimes, the generosity of people who have very, very little, their sense of commitment to other human beings, is what they have. It is their wealth. I write about that in the introduction to *Home Girls*, when I talk about how Black women formed a community of support and caring. I see that as part of a value system of the Civil Rights movement, too. We really were trying to get a transformation, not just of the laws and of the institutions but of the human spirit.

It's hard for those of us who come out of the mid-twentieth century, when movements were vibrant, when social relations were altered in a major way, changed, transformed by movement organizing, to remember that those transformations grew out of a historical time. So much that we take for granted now resulted from the movements of that period. But you can't remake a historical time. You can take advantage of opportunities for organizing, for activism, and for change in the historical period in which you live. But we can't recreate all of the factors that made the mid-twentieth century phenomenal.

It was a time when all the apple carts were getting upset. You had the anti–Vietnam War movement, the peace movement, you had Third World countries' liberation from colonialism, globally. You had the Civil Rights movement, the women's movement, and the gay liberation movement. You had all of that happening, all at one time. And it was my generation; it was the baby boom. But the majority of the baby boomers were never involved in the movements that I'm talking about. They were affected by, and helped to create, the youth culture of that period, but the majority of people of my generation were not involved in movements . . .

Barbara R.: I think that's an important historical lesson, too. Because the further we get from that decade, I think it's easier for young people today to kind of romanticize—"It was a time when *everybody* was in motion!" Everybody wasn't.

So Barbara, thank you for all the good work that you did, and do. I think the fact that you've had the perseverance and the commitment to struggle in so many different terrains, around so many different issues . . .

Barbara S.: . . . in so many improbable circumstances!

Barbara R.: And you still look twenty-nine.

Barbara S.: Oh, stop it!

Barbara R.: Struggle keeps you young, that's the moral of the story.

What Would It Mean to Be a Lesbian?

These excerpts from the Loretta Ross oral history provide a frank and personal account of Barbara's responses to her early attractions to other women. With poet and writer Jewelle Gomez, Barbara shares the costs and contradictions of publicly sharing (or not) one's true sexual identity and the impact that homophobia has on mental health.

Barbara Smith, "Interview by Loretta Ross," Voices of Feminism Oral History Project

(Smith and Ross 2003)

Barbara Smith (to Loretta Ross): I was terrified of the possibility that I might not be "normal" and that I might indeed be something, a word I probably couldn't even think of, a lesbian. It was a really, really difficult time to have those feelings, because there was no movement. Stonewall happened a few days after I graduated from college.* I personally know women [from other women's colleges] who were expelled for being lesbian, having lesbian feelings, lesbian lives, who were a part of my generation.

Now, as it happened, going to Mount Holyoke, I was surrounded by lesbians! [laughs] But of course the word wasn't used. There were lesbian students, there were lesbian professors, there were lesbian administrators. I'm not saying they were the majority, but women's colleges have always been a safe space for women-identified women. Some of these women had never been sexual, were never sexual with each other. But these all-women's environments were safe spaces at a time when there was no other such place in the society.

Some of my friends from college turned out to be lesbians, but we never discussed it. Those who were actually having sexual relationships during our college years were terrified. One friend of mine told me, "I was just terrified all the time." I also want to say, and be very clear, that I had crushes on other students while I was there. They were not acted upon, but they were deeply felt.

I was involved with a man for a few years in the early seventies. We were together for a few years and I remember that once, after we had made love, I got up to go to the bathroom and you know what I was thinking? I was thinking, "Hmmm, now all I need is a good woman!" Whoa! Where did that come from? Did I say that? [laughs] Did I think that? I certainly didn't say it. But the thoughts were there. So, what was little Barbara going to do with these very unconventional feelings, particularly given how I was raised?

Like most people, particularly Black people, I thought being queer, being lesbian, being gay, being a bull dagger was tantamount to being a criminal. Prostitute, thief, murderer, sinner, crazy—all kinds of bad things. I just thought, "Oh my goodness. My family did not sacrifice the way they sacrificed for my sister and I to have the kind of lives they could only wish to have—they didn't

---

* The Stonewall Inn in Greenwich Village of New York City was the site of a series of uprisings where gay and lesbian patrons resisted and fought back during a routine police raid of the bar. The uprisings were undertaken primarily by the most marginalized gays and lesbian of the time—youth, transgender people, gays and lesbians of color, poor and working-class queers, street hustlers, and drag queens. Today, Gay Pride marches are held annually to commemorate the event, which is generally seen as the origin moment of the movement for gay and lesbian liberation. For more on Stonewall, see Carter (2010), Duberman (1994), and Faderman (1992).

do all that so I could suddenly become a low-life." [laughs] That's really how I felt about it.

That was really the dilemma, in addition to not knowing how to negotiate the transition known as coming out. How could I become a person like *that* after my people have poured so much energy into me being a contributing member of the race? These are the contradictions that African American and Black lesbian, gay, bisexual, and transgendered people are still dealing with.

"Taking the Home Out of Homophobia: Black Lesbian Health"
Jewelle Gomez and Barbara Smith (1990)

There've been lesbian and gay men, Black ones, as long as there've been African people. You know how they say that the human race was supposed to have been started by a Black woman? Well, since she had so many children, some of them were undoubtedly queer.

Writer Ann Allen Shockley has a wonderful line that I use often, "Play it, but don't say it." That's the sentiment that capsulizes the general stance of the Black community on sexual identity and orientation. If you're a lesbian, you can have as many women as you want. If you're a gay man, you can have all the men you want. But just don't say anything about it or make it political. The difference today is that the lesbian and gay movement prides itself on being out, verbalizing one's identity and organizing around our oppression. With the advent of this movement, the African American community has really been confronted with some stuff that they've never had to deal with before. . . . The issue is not whether gay people have been here since forever. It's that we are telling our community that it has to deal with us differently than before. That's what contemporary Black gay and lesbian activists are doing. . . .

Women become lesbians because they are deeply attracted—sexually—to other women. To me, that's the bottom line. There was a notion during the early Women's Movement, in which I was involved, that you could choose to be a lesbian. But I think the important point is whether you choose to be out, to act on your lesbian feelings. . . .

Those of us who were coming out just before Stonewall knew that we had feelings, passion and lust for other women. We didn't necessarily have a place for our feelings that felt safe. But we knew intuitively—not because we read it in a book somewhere—that gay was good. Today people have women's studies courses, out lesbian teachers, all kinds of stuff that we didn't have. . . .

Homophobia affects one's mental health—I lived my adolescence and young adulthood in terror. Some people think that coming out during the Women's Movement was an easy thing. But I'd just like to say right here for the record that from puberty on, I had screaming nightmares, because I was having dreams of being sexual with women. I would wake up and my grandmother would be standing looking over me and I thought she knew what I was dreaming. . . .

I think that conscious lesbianism lived in the context of community is a positive thing. It can be a really affirming choice for women. The connection of homophobia and sexism is deep, though. Homophobia is a logical extension of sexual oppression because sexual oppression is about roles—one gender does this, the other does that. One's on top, the other is on the bottom. . . .

"We pay a heavy toll for being who we are and living with integrity. Being out means you are doing what your grandmother told you to do, which is not to lie. Black lesbians and gays who are out are not lying."

[W]e pay a heavy toll for being who we are and living with integrity. Being out means you are doing what your grandmother told you to do, which is not to lie. Black lesbians and gays who are out are not lying. But people really need to understand that there is entrenched violence against lesbians and gay men, much like, and parallel to, the racial violence that has characterized Black people's lives since we've been in this country. . . . [A]s out Black lesbians we have to live—we do live—with an incredible amount of courage.

Barbara Smith, "Interview by Loretta Ross," Voices of Feminism Oral History Project

(Smith and Ross 2003)

Barbara Smith (to Loretta Ross): You know that thing I said about surviving as a really premature infant? I think one of the reasons that the universe permitted me to survive was so I could be outspoken around issues of sexuality as an out Black lesbian. I've been out as a Black lesbian since the mid-1970s, not long after Stonewall. Finding Black feminism allowed me to come out, because I needed to meet Black women like myself who were out and proud lesbians. That made me think, "Well, gosh, if they can do that maybe I can do that, too." That was really the key. But I was a Black feminist before I was a Black lesbian, at least before I was a self-declared Black lesbian. I like people to know that because again, within our Black communities, so often lesbianism and feminism are seen as absolutely identical and the same thing. Lesbian identity is an expression of sexual orientation; feminism is a politic. And anybody can be a feminist.

I came out at the height of lesbian feminism in the twentieth century. Going through my papers recently, I got little glimmers of like, weren't we some kick-asses back then? Wasn't it something when you thought you had found the way, the truth, and the light? There was so much collective and communal excitement about finally coming out from the shadows and out of the closet. Not just in the context of lesbian and gay liberation, but in the context of feminism. There was an extreme amount of exhilaration, an extreme amount of energy, all this wonderful synergy going on at that time.

The hardest thing to me about being a lesbian is being rejected by my Black brothers and sisters. That's the hardest thing, without any doubt. White people were never down with me, so I never expected acceptance, caring, love, or support from them as a group. I absolutely expect those things from other people of color, particularly from African Americans, because that's the group that I come from. The hardest thing to me is to feel like I don't belong, that I don't deserve to be respected, that I'm ostracized. . . .

I never felt that in order to deal with these two disparate identities, I had to run away from the Black community. Oh, no. That's not going to happen. You've got to be kidding. [laughs] So, because I have maintained, in a deep way, my connections—personally and also politically—to other Black people, whatever their sexual orientation, I have survived.

Building Black Feminism

Feminism is something I claim because I claim it in the name
of Black women.

—Barbara Smith, "Black Feminism:
A Movement of Our Own" (1984)

Black feminism begins with the simple idea that Black women's lives have
worth and value. Because society habitually denigrates and oppresses Black women,
this assertion of basic humanity is deeply political, even revolutionary. The pursuit
of a vision of global human transformation—while simultaneously naming the
distinct experiences of Black women—is at the heart of Black feminism.

This chapter covers the period of defining and living Black feminism. Black
feminists craft arguments, organizations, strategic actions, and interventions
designed to change how individuals and institutions treat society's most neglected
and abused. To this end, Black feminism is a political movement formed to
assert and obtain dignity, autonomy, and self-determination. When the story
of mainstream U.S. feminism is amended to reflect the formative roles of Black
women, other women of color, lesbians, and working-class women, it will show
how many feminists audaciously tackled racism, classism, and heterosexism
within the women's movement, as well as sexism in their own communities, in
their quest to build a more just world.

> **"The pursuit of a vision of global human transformation—
> while simultaneously naming the distinct experiences of
> Black women—is at the heart of Black feminism."**

In this chapter, we follow the development of two major conceptual contributions
of Black feminism: identity politics and interconnected oppressions. As Barbara
suggests in her interview with coeditor Virginia Eubanks, insisting that Black
women, working-class lesbians, and others with multiple identities "had a *right* to
create a political agenda that was relevant to addressing the oppressions that they
faced . . . was groundbreaking" (p. 43, in this volume). Barbara and her collaborators
insisted that understanding the ways that different facets of one's identity—and

different kinds of institutional oppression—intersect and mutually reinforce each other is crucial to building inclusive, ethical, and effective politics. Identity politics is, then, the political analysis and practice that arises out of careful attention to the lived realities of experiencing interlocking oppressions.

In the seventies, Black feminism was responsible for an incredibly important expansion of the familiar feminist saying, "the personal is political." When a dozen Black women were murdered in Boston in 1979, the Combahee River Collective—most well-known for their statement on Black feminism, reproduced in this chapter—was able to quickly marshal an analysis of the wave of murders that explained its origins not just rooted in racial injustice and violence but in widespread hatred and victimization of women. From this analysis, the collective was able to suggest a political practice that went beyond "Don't walk alone at night" and forged coalitions that were able to effectively challenge racist/sexist violence. This chapter also focuses on the tools and strategies Black feminists developed to save women's lives. Black feminists build solidarity through practice on a variety of issues, from sterilization abuse to taxi drivers' strikes, through collaborative political organizing, consciousness-raising, and dialogue.

While we concentrate on the early years of 1970s Black feminism in this chapter, Black feminism is not—and should not be—relegated to the past. The conditions that required the development of Black feminism still exist; so does Black feminist resistance, organization, and mobilization. The case of "African American Women in Defense of Ourselves," a response to the Anita Hill–Clarence Thomas hearings in the early 1990s, shows how a Black feminist politics and lens made the hearings' erasure of Black female subjectivity visible. The legacy of the work of the Combahee River Collective, and so many other Black feminist organizations of the era, held the seeds of a critique that grew into a vocal movement for gender and racial justice. It still does; so this chapter also highlights terrific ongoing work being done by Black feminists.

The primary interview anchoring this chapter comes from Kimberly Springer, who has written extensively on Black feminism, race, sexuality, and social movements. She is author of *Living for the Revolution: Black Feminist Organizations, 1968–1980* (2005), editor of *Still Lifting, Still Climbing: African American Women's Contemporary Activism* (1999), and coeditor of *Stories of Oprah: The Oprahfication of American Culture* (2009).

A New Era of Black Feminism

The Black feminist movement blended insights from the African American Civil Rights movement, the second wave of the U.S. women's movement, Black nationalism, a socialist analysis of the economy, and other political interventions to form a distinct point of view on the nature of oppression and the necessity of opposing it. This section includes two of its classic founding documents: the National Black Feminist Organization (NBFO) Statement of Purpose and the Combahee River Collective Statement. The NBFO (1974–1977) was a short-lived but historic organization that provided a national forum for articulating a Black feminist political agenda. The Combahee River Collective began as a chapter of NBFO in 1974. Its widely circulated statement of principles was written in 1977 but published in 1979 in Zillah Eisenstein's book, Capitalist Patriarchy and the Case for Socialist Feminism. *This now classic statement is believed to be the first published use and definition of the term "identity politics." In it, Barbara, her sister Beverly, and their comrade Demita Frazier articulate one of the defining contributions of Black feminism—interlocking oppressions—an idea that finds currency today as intersectionality. The statement succinctly addresses the liberatory insights borne from close attention to the interconnections of racism, sexism, classism, and homophobia.*

Interview with Virginia Eubanks

Virginia Eubanks: How important do you think it is to locate your political and intellectual work in your own experience?

Barbara Smith: I think it was crucial. It may not be as important now, but certainly at the time we were building Black feminism, it was critical. People now see women of color in popular culture, having positions that we never would have dreamed they would have. We see interracial relationships and families in TV commercials. It's a whole different world, what's acceptable and what is not. So there are lots of things that people take for granted.

Many don't understand what it felt like to be Black and female growing up in the fifties, sixties, and coming of age in the 1970s, and being absolutely devalued. Everywhere you looked, you felt that you did not count, that your voice was not heeded, that you needed to just get back and let the real people make all the decisions. When we asserted the things we did in our Combahee River Collective Statement, and in other places, we were really stepping out there! To say that Black women, many of whom were lesbians, and were either working class or identified with their working-class roots, to say that people who had those multiple identities actually had a *right* to create a political agenda that was relevant to addressing the oppressions that they faced, that was *groundbreaking*!

We took a lot of heat for saying that we thought that our combined, multiple identities, which also were linked to oppressions, had meaning. By saying that we needed to address the injustices, bigotry, oppression, and violent terrorism we suffered as a result of these connecting identities, we were asserting something very, very big and very, very new.

The work that we did has opened the way for people to be a lot more sane, respectful, and open to differences. In the most radical parts of the women's movement, that's what we were all concerned about: How do we organize across differences? How do we not erase each others' identities? How do we not be defensive when people raise issues that are not necessarily directly our own? How do we create a real women's movement that is inclusive and for everybody? That's what we were trying to do. A lot of different voices, and a lot of individuals, made major contributions to that dialogue and that struggle.

From our position in Combahee, building identity politics gave us a platform, an analysis, and a certain sense of confidence that we deserved to be part of the dialogue. If we had not done that, where would women of color be, as far as being able to assert the legitimacy of our concerns and the particularity of our point of view? We empowered ourselves by looking at our situation, making observations about it, drawing conclusions, and saying, "We're here, we deserve to be here, and understand that when we talk, we're talking from all these different experiences." Our experience is complex; it should be intriguing to you. That made it possible for us to be much more effective political actors than if we had stayed silent and invisible.

What people did not necessarily understand about identity politics was that it was not to say that "Your problems are not worthy of consideration" or that they are beneath ours. That's not what we were saying at all. What we were saying was that we have a constellation of multiple oppressions, when they combine, it's not just arithmetic, it's *geometric*. When you get up in the morning, you don't get to decide which of your identities you are going to lay aside. You are the full package. In any event, it was not exclusionary, and in practice, it really had the possibility of liberating everyone, because we were dealing with all of the isms.

"National Black Feminist Organization Statement of Purpose"
National Black Feminist Organization (1973)

The distorted male-dominated media image of the Women's Liberation Movement has clouded the vital and revolutionary importance of this movement to Third World women, especially Black women. The Movement has been characterized as the exclusive property of so-called white middle-class women and any Black women seen involved in this Movement have been seen as "selling out," "dividing the race," and an assortment of nonsensical epithets. Black feminists resent these charges and have therefore established the National Black Feminist Organization, in order to address ourselves to the particular and specific needs of the larger, but almost cast-aside half of the Black race in Amerikkka, the Black woman.

Black women have suffered cruelly in this society from living the phenomenon of being Black and female, in a country that is *both* racist and sexist. There has been very little real examination of the damage it has caused on the lives and on the minds of Black women. Because we live in a patriarchy, we have allowed a premium to be put on Black male suffering. No one of us would minimize the pain or hardship or the cruel and inhumane treatment experienced by the Black man. But history, past or present, rarely deals with the malicious abuse put upon the Black woman. We were seen as breeders by the master; despised and historically polarized from/by the master's wife; and looked upon as castraters [*sic*] by our lovers and husbands. The Black woman has had to be strong, yet we are persecuted for having survived. We have been called "matriarchs" by white racists and Black nationalists; we have virtually no positive self-images to validate our existence. Black women want to be proud, dignified, and free from all those false definitions of beauty and womanhood that are unrealistic and unnatural. *We*, not white men or Black men, must define our own self-image as Black women and not fall into the mistake of being placed upon the pedestal which is even being rejected by white women. It has been hard for Black women to emerge from the myriad of distorted images that have portrayed us as grinning Beulahs, castrating Sapphires, and pancake-box Jemimas. As Black feminists we realized the need to establish ourselves as an independent Black feminist organization. Our aboveground presence will lend enormous credibility to the current Women's Liberation Movement, which unfortunately is not seen as the serious political and economic revolutionary force that it is. We will strengthen the current efforts of the Black Liberation struggle in this country by encouraging *all* of the talents and creativities of Black women to emerge, strong and beautiful, not to feel guilty or divisive, and assume positions of leadership and honor in the Black community. We will encourage the Black community to stop falling into the trap of the white male Left, utilizing women only in terms of domestic or servile needs. We will continue to remind the Black Liberation Movement that there can't be liberation for half the race. We must together, as a people, work to eliminate racism, from without the Black community, which is trying to destroy us as an entire people; but we must remember that sexism is destroying and crippling us from within.

"The Combahee River Collective Statement"
Combahee River Collective ([1977], 1979)

We are a collective of Black feminists who have been meeting together since 1974. During that time we have been involved in the process of defining and clarifying our politics, while at the same time doing political work within our own group and in coalition with other progressive organizations and movements. The most general statement of our politics at the present time would be that we are actively committed to struggling against racial, sexual, heterosexual, and class oppression, and see as our particular task the development of an integrated analysis and practice based upon the fact that the major systems of oppression are interlocking.

The synthesis of these oppressions creates the conditions of our lives. As Black women we see Black feminism as the logical political movement to combat the manifold and simultaneous oppressions that all women of color face.

1. The Genesis of Contemporary Black Feminism

Before looking at the recent development of Black feminism we would like to affirm that we find our origins in the historical reality of Afro-American women's continuous life-and-death struggle for survival and liberation. Black women's extremely negative relationship to the American political system (a system of white male rule) has always been determined by our membership in two oppressed racial and sexual castes. As Angela Davis points out in "Reflections on the Black Woman's Role in the Community of Slaves," Black women have always embodied, if only in their physical manifestation, an adversary stance to white male rule and have actively resisted its inroads upon them and their communities in both dramatic and subtle ways. There have always been Black women activists—some known, like Sojourner Truth, Harriet Tubman, Frances E. W. Harper, Ida B. Wells Barnett, and Mary Church Terrell, and thousands upon thousands unknown—who have had a shared awareness of how their sexual identity combined with their racial identity to make their whole life situation and the focus of their political struggles unique. Contemporary Black feminism is the outgrowth of countless generations of personal sacrifice, militancy, and work by our mothers and sisters.

"We are actively committed to struggling against racial, sexual, heterosexual, and class oppression, and see as our particular task the development of integrated analysis and practice based upon the fact that the major systems of oppression are interlocking."

A Black feminist presence has evolved most obviously in connection with the second wave of the American Women's Movement beginning in the late 1960s. Black, other Third World, and working women have been involved in the feminist movement from its start, but both outside reactionary forces and racism and elitism within the movement itself have served to obscure our participation. In 1973, Black feminists, primarily located in New York, felt the necessity of forming a separate Black feminist group. This became the National Black Feminist Organization (NBFO).

Black feminist politics also have an obvious connection to movements for Black liberation, particularly those of the 1960s and 1970s. Many of us were active in those movements (Civil Rights, Black nationalism, the Black Panthers), and all of our lives were greatly affected and changed by their ideologies, their goals, and the tactics used to achieve their goals. It was our experience and disillusionment within these liberation movements, as well as experience on the periphery of the white male Left, that led to the need to develop a politics that was anti-racist, unlike those of white women, and anti-sexist, unlike those of Black and white men.

There is also undeniably a personal genesis for Black Feminism, that is, the political realization that comes from the seemingly personal experiences of individual Black women's lives. Black feminists and many more Black women who do not define themselves as feminists have all experienced sexual oppression as a constant factor in our day-to-day existence. As children we realized that we were different from boys and that we were treated differently. For example, we were told in the same breath to be quiet both for the sake of being "ladylike" and to make us less objectionable in the eyes of white people. As we grew older we became aware of the threat of physical and sexual abuse by men. However, we had no way of conceptualizing what was so apparent to us, what we knew was really happening.

Black feminists often talk about their feelings of craziness before becoming conscious of the concepts of sexual politics, patriarchal rule, and most importantly, feminism, the political analysis and practice that we women use to struggle against our oppression. The fact that racial politics and indeed racism are pervasive factors in our lives did not allow us, and still does not allow most Black women, to look more deeply into our own experiences and, from that sharing and growing consciousness, to build a politics that will change our lives and inevitably end our oppression. Our development must also be tied to the contemporary economic and political position of Black people. The post–World War II generation of Black youth was the first to be able to minimally partake of certain educational and employment options, previously closed completely to Black people. Although our economic position is still at the very bottom of the American capitalistic economy, a handful of us have been able to gain certain tools as a result of tokenism in education and employment which potentially enable us to more effectively fight our oppression.

A combined anti-racist and anti-sexist position drew us together initially, and as we developed politically we addressed ourselves to heterosexism and economic oppression under capitalism.

2. What We Believe

Above all else, our politics initially sprang from the shared belief that Black women are inherently valuable, that our liberation is a necessity not as an adjunct to somebody else's but because of our need as human persons for autonomy. This may seem so obvious as to sound simplistic, but it is apparent that no other ostensibly progressive movement has ever considered our specific oppression as a priority or worked seriously for the ending of that oppression. Merely naming the pejorative stereotypes attributed to Black women (e.g., mammy, matriarch, Sapphire, whore, bulldagger), let alone cataloguing the cruel, often murderous, treatment we receive, indicates how little value has been placed upon our lives during four centuries of bondage in the Western hemisphere. We realize that the only people who care enough about us to work consistently for our liberation are us. Our politics evolve from a healthy love for ourselves, our sisters and our community which allows us to continue our struggle and work.

This focusing upon our own oppression is embodied in the concept of identity politics. We believe that the most profound and potentially most radical politics come directly out of our own identity, as opposed to working to end somebody else's oppression. In the case of Black women this is a particularly repugnant, dangerous, threatening, and therefore revolutionary concept because it is obvious from looking at all the political movements that have preceded us that anyone is more worthy of liberation than ourselves. We reject pedestals, queenhood, and walking ten paces behind. To be recognized as human, levelly human, is enough.

We believe that sexual politics under patriarchy is as pervasive in Black women's lives as are the politics of class and race. We also often find it difficult to separate race from class from sex oppression because in our lives they are most often experienced simultaneously. We know that there is such a thing as racial-sexual oppression which is neither solely racial nor solely sexual, e.g., the history of rape of Black women by white men as a weapon of political repression.

Although we are feminists and Lesbians, we feel solidarity with progressive Black men and do not advocate the fractionalization that white women who are separatists demand. Our situation as Black people necessitates that we have solidarity around the fact of race, which white women of course do not need to have with white men, unless it is their negative solidarity as racial oppressors. We struggle together with Black men against racism, while we also struggle with Black men about sexism.

We realize that the liberation of all oppressed peoples necessitates the destruction of the political-economic systems of capitalism and imperialism as well as patriarchy. We are socialists because we believe that work must be organized for the collective benefit of those who do the work and create the products, and not for the profit of the bosses. Material resources must be equally distributed among those who create these resources. We are not convinced, however, that a socialist revolution that is not also a feminist and anti-racist revolution will guarantee our liberation. We have arrived at the necessity for developing an understanding of class relationships that takes into account the specific class position of Black women who are generally marginal in the labor force, while at this particular time some of us are temporarily viewed as doubly desirable tokens at white-collar and professional levels. We need to articulate the real class situation of persons who are not merely raceless, sexless workers, but for whom racial and sexual oppression are significant determinants in their working/economic lives. . . .

A political contribution which we feel we have already made is the expansion of the feminist principle that the personal is political. In our consciousness-raising sessions, for example, we have in many ways gone beyond white women's revelations because we are dealing with the implications of race and class as well as sex. Even our Black women's style of talking/testifying in Black language about what we have experienced has a resonance that is both cultural and political. We have spent a great deal of energy delving into the cultural and experiential nature of our oppression out of necessity because none of these matters has ever been looked at before. No one before has ever examined the multilayered texture of Black women's lives. An example of this kind of revelation/conceptualization occurred at a meeting as we discussed the ways in which our early intellectual interests had been attacked by our peers, particularly Black males. We discovered that all of us, because we were "smart" had also been considered "ugly," i.e., "smart-ugly." "Smart-ugly" crystallized the way in which most of us had been forced to develop our intellects at great cost to our "social" lives. The sanctions in the Black and white communities against Black women thinkers [are] comparatively much higher than for white women, particularly ones from the educated middle and upper classes. . . .

We have a great deal of criticism and loathing for what men have been socialized to be in this society: what they support, how they act, and how they oppress. But we do not have the misguided notion that it is their maleness, per se—i.e., their biological maleness—that makes them what they are. As Black women we find any type of biological determinism a particularly dangerous and reactionary basis upon which to build a politic. . . .

3. Problems in Organizing Black Feminists

During our years together as a Black feminist collective we have experienced success and defeat, joy and pain, victory and failure. We have found that it is very difficult to organize around Black feminist issues, difficult even to announce in certain contexts that we are Black feminists. . . .

The major source of difficulty in our political work is that we are not just trying to fight oppression on one front or even two, but instead to address a whole range of oppressions. We do not have racial, sexual, heterosexual, or class privilege to rely upon, nor do we have even the minimal access to resources and power that groups who possess any one of these types of privilege have.

The psychological toll of being a Black woman and the difficulties this presents in reaching political consciousness and doing political work can never be underestimated. There is a very low value placed upon Black women's psyches in this society, which is both racist and sexist. As an early group member once said, "We are all damaged people merely by virtue of being Black women." We are dispossessed psychologically and on every other level, and yet we feel the necessity to struggle to change the condition of all Black women. In "A Black Feminist's Search for Sisterhood," Michele Wallace arrives at this conclusion:

We exist as women who are Black who are feminists, each stranded for the moment, working independently because there is not yet an environment in this society remotely congenial to our struggle—because, being on the bottom, we would have to do what no one else has done: we would have to fight the world.[1]

Wallace is pessimistic but realistic in her assessment of Black feminists' position, particularly in her allusion to the nearly classic isolation most of us face. We might use our position at the bottom, however, to make a clear leap into revolutionary action. If Black women were free, it would mean that everyone else would have to be free since our freedom would necessitate the destruction of all the systems of oppression.

"If Black women were free, it would mean that everyone else would have to be free since our freedom would necessitate the destruction of all the systems of oppression."

Feminism is, nevertheless, very threatening to the majority of Black people because it calls into question some of the most basic assumptions about our existence, i.e., that sex should be a determinant of power relationships. Here is the way male and female roles were defined in a Black nationalist pamphlet from the early 1970s:

We understand that it is and has been traditional that the man is the head of the house. He is the leader of the house/nation because his knowledge of the world is broader, his awareness is greater, his understanding is fuller and his application of this information is wiser. . . . After all, it is only reasonable that the man be the head of the house because he is able to defend and protect the development of his home. . . . Women cannot do the same things as men—they are made by nature to function differently. Equality of men and women is something that cannot happen even in the abstract world. . . . The value of men and women can be seen as in the value of gold and silver—they are not equal but both have great value.[2]

The material conditions of most Black women would hardly lead them to upset both economic and sexual arrangements that seem to represent some stability

---

[1]Wallace, Michele. "A Black Feminist's Search for Sisterhood," *The Village Voice*, 28 July 1975, pp. 6–7.

[2]Mumininas of Committee for Unified Newark, Mwanamke Mwananchi (The Nationalist Woman), Newark, N.J., ©1971, pp. 4–5.

in their lives. Many Black women have a good understanding of both sexism and racism, but because of the everyday constrictions of their lives, cannot risk struggling against them both.

The reaction of Black men to feminism has been notoriously negative. They are, of course, even more threatened than Black women by the possibility that Black feminists might organize around our own needs. They realize that they might not only lose valuable and hardworking allies in their struggles but that they might also be forced to change their habitually sexist ways of interacting with and oppressing Black women. Accusations that Black feminism divides the Black struggle are powerful deterrents to the growth of an autonomous Black Women's Movement.

Still, hundreds of women have been active at different times during the three-year existence of our group. And every Black woman who came, came out of a strongly-felt need for some level of possibility that did not previously exist in her life. . . .

4. Black Feminist Issues and Projects

During our time together we have identified and worked on many issues of particular relevance to Black women. The inclusiveness of our politics makes us concerned with any situation that impinges upon the lives of women, Third World and working people. We are of course particularly committed to working on those struggles in which race, sex, and class are simultaneous factors in oppression. We might, for example, become involved in workplace organizing at a factory that employs Third World women or picket a hospital that is cutting back on already inadequate health care to a Third World community, or set up a rape crisis center in a Black neighborhood. Organizing around welfare and daycare concerns might also be a focus. The work to be done and the countless issues that this work represents merely reflect the pervasiveness of our oppression.

Issues and projects that collective members have actually worked on are sterilization abuse, abortion rights, battered women, rape and health care. We have also done many workshops and educationals on Black feminism on college campuses, at women's conferences, and most recently for high school women.

One issue that is of major concern to us and that we have begun to publicly address is racism in the white Women's Movement. As Black feminists we are made constantly and painfully aware of how little effort white women have made to understand and combat their racism, which requires among other things that they have a more than superficial comprehension of race, color, and Black history and culture. Eliminating racism in the white Women's Movement is by definition work for white women to do, but we will continue to speak to and demand accountability on this issue.

In the practice of our politics we do not believe that the end always justifies the means. Many reactionary and destructive acts have been done in the name of achieving "correct" political goals. . . . We believe in collective process and a nonhierarchical distribution of power within our own group and in our vision of a revolutionary society. We are committed to a continual examination of our politics as they develop through criticism and self-criticism as an essential aspect of our practice. In her introduction to *Sisterhood Is Powerful* Robin Morgan writes:

> I haven't the faintest notion what possible revolutionary role white heterosexual men could fulfill, since they are the very embodiment of reactionary-vested-interest-power.

As Black feminists and Lesbians we know that we have a very definite revolutionary task to perform and we are ready for the lifetime of work and struggle before us.

Interviews with Kimberly Springer, Barbara Ransby, Alethia Jones, and Virginia Eubanks

Kimberly Springer: When you were in Combahee, did you think about that work as building a movement?

Barbara Smith: Absolutely. We were very clear that we were building something really, really important. The Combahee River Collective was originally a chapter of the National Black Feminist Organization, so we knew we were part of something bigger than just what we were doing in Boston. We were networked with Black feminists in different parts of the country: up and down the East Coast, and also in Chicago and California. Wherever we could find each other by phone or by letter.

I always knew we were changing history with the work that we were involved in. Most of us had been involved in other Leftist movements, so we had a sense of historical meaning and how organizing develops and moves forward. We knew we were not operating in a vacuum.

If you knew about SNCC [Student Nonviolent Coordinating Committee], for example, you at least had in the back of your mind that we're doing similar kinds of interventions around racial and gender politics and sexual politics, sexual identity politics. We were part of politically significant traditions.

There was a person in the Combahee River Collective named Sharon Bourke who was older than most of us—we were mostly in our twenties, she was in her forties. She had a long history with the Black cultural and Black power movements. She was involved with the Institute of the Black World in Atlanta, and also was a very, very well-informed and well-educated Marxist. Demita Frazier was from Chicago, but I believe had had some involvement with the Black Panthers. When we were having our Black feminist discussions and building our analysis and practice, people would say, "When I was in the Panthers . . ." or "When I was at the Institute of the Black World . . ." or "When I was protesting the war in

Vietnam . . ." We didn't just spring up whole from nowhere. We knew we had roots, and at the same time, we did work that connected us to other movements, other progressive organizing, and other radical organizing that was going on in Boston and around the country and the world at that time.

Kimberly: What do you think the role of a writer is in a movement for social change?

Barbara S.: All of our movements for justice and for liberation have writers' names associated with them: Frantz Fanon, James Baldwin, Frederick Douglass. The word has always been connected to action. The feminist movement, and the lesbian feminist movement particularly, was a movement of the word in many ways. Literary pursuits and literary initiatives really characterized the second wave of feminism: the periodicals, bookstores, presses, publishing. The fact that there were these incredibly talented writers like Audre Lorde and Toni Cade Bambara and Adrienne Rich, June Jordan, Ntozake Shange, so many people whom we could name who are really tearing the lid off things that people had experienced but had never spoken about and had never written about. Seeing the film *For Colored Girls* recently reminded me of the power of that particular artistic piece to change social and power relations. Just by articulating the fact that we exist, we're here, we have a different experience that's just as valid as those of you who are considered the mainstream or a part of what's important.

Kimberly: So the writers that you mentioned are really key in what, in academia, we call intersectionality. You invented intersectionality! Do you think your contributions, and those of the authors you mentioned, are adequately recognized for providing the basis for intersectionality?

Barbara S.: I don't think it is sufficiently recognized, actually. I think that the term "identity politics" was used for the first time in the Combahee River Collective Statement. About a decade ago the phrase "identity politics" was being bandied about generally by the right wing, but they didn't understand what we meant.

Kimberly: Can you talk about what you meant and what they meant, and how they are different?

Barbara S.: We meant to assert that it is legitimate to look at the elements of a combined identity that included affiliation or connection to several marginalized groups in this society. There is meaning in being not solely a person of color, not solely Black, not solely female, not solely lesbian, not solely working class or poor. There is a new constellation of meanings when those identities were combined. *That's* what we were trying to say. One of the reasons we were saying it so strongly is that Black politics as they were defined at the time were not sufficient to address our objective material conditions and the realities of our political status and our oppression. Black politics at that time, as defined by males, did not completely or sufficiently address the actual circumstances of real, live Black women. They just didn't.

For example, domestic violence and economic situations might keep women in physically abusive situations, and that's of course going to be more prevalent in communities that are economically oppressed. We need to have an analysis for that reality. That's what we were talking about. We were asserting that we exist, our concerns and our experiences matter. We named that "identity politics," because we said that it is legitimate to look at the elements of one's own identity and to form a political analysis and practice out of it.

"We were asserting that we exist, our concerns and our experiences matter. We named that 'identity politics,' because we said that it is legitimate to look at the elements of one's own identity and to form a political analysis and practice out of it."

What the right wing meant by identity politics was that those people who are not white, not male, not straight, and not rich, it was not legitimate for them to assert anything, because they just wanted special privileges and special rights in a context of: "Enough rights already." White males who are heterosexual and have class privilege—the system does work pretty well for them. There was a great resentment that these other people, these people they considered to be marginal and undeserving of the same kind of privileges and access, they were irritated that those people were asserting that, again, it made a difference whether you were an immigrant of Muslim heritage or religious beliefs, living in the United States, and maybe even queer at the same time. They didn't want to hear about that. They used it as a way of beating people over the head and saying, "You don't count, you don't matter, we're going to keep on doing things the way we're doing them."

Kimberly: But it seems like there are some on the Left who might let the Right co-opt the term "identity politics" by talking about the differences that they think identity politics creates. It seems like the disparagement of identity politics is something that works against having unity within a movement. So, if people are recognizing that there's value in their own situation and their own identity, how does that work with the goal of solidarity?

Barbara S.: That was another aspect of it. Because the watered-down version of identity politics was just what you described. Which was, "I'm an African American, working-class lesbian with a physical disability and those are the only things I'm concerned about. I'm not really interested in finding out about the struggles of Chicano farm workers to organize labor unions, because that doesn't have anything to do with me." The narrow, watered-down dilution of the most expansive meaning of the term "identity politics" was used by people as a way of isolating themselves, and not working in coalition, and not being concerned about overarching systems of institutionalized oppression. That *was* narrow.

Lesbian separatism was a kind of identity politics that frequently did not take into account that there were many, many people in this country and around the globe who were terribly and horribly oppressed and didn't happen to be white lesbians. They weren't really interested in that, because they saw one major contradiction, which was patriarchy. But we never meant that. I put Bernice Johnson Reagon's article "Coalition Politics: Turning the Century" at the end of *Home Girls* very purposefully. I wanted the thought, the frame of reference with which people left the book, to be that coalition politics are really, really vital. Reagon talks about people being in their little barred rooms. That's not what we were talking about.

"The way you come together is to recognize everyone fully for who they are, respect and understand who they are, as we work toward common goals of justice and liberation and freedom."

We were asserting our validity and our right to exist, to examine our political situation, and to organize to change that situation. We never were asserting that no one else's political status, social status, economic status, or oppression was important. We never thought that. We actually believed that the way you come together is to recognize everyone fully for who they are, respect and understand who they are, as we work toward common goals of justice and liberation and freedom.

It was not a narrow view. But it's hard to be invisible, and before we began to assert identity politics and the importance of a Black feminist stance we were, by and large, invisible.

Barbara Ransby: Before intersectionality became a shorthand label to capture a certain kind of race and class analysis, that was your work. People like you and Ella Baker have embodied a whole tradition of Black feminist and feminists of color tradition of identity politics that is grassroots, radical, and connects different issues. You write about it, but more importantly, you live it. When we commodify these terms, we don't think of what work gave rise to us even conceiving of a particular model of social justice organizing. The Combahee River Collective Statement comprehensively articulated this important tradition so cogently—it's amazing to me the longevity of the document!

Barbara S.: We sat down and wrote it for Zillah Eisenstein because she wanted us to contribute something to her anthology *Capitalist Patriarchy and the Case for Socialist Feminism*—just the title of the book shows the radical way we understood the system of power and systems of oppression we were living under. We were attuned enough and in sync enough that we could actually write something that belonged in that book.

Barbara R.: Hearing you talk about that refutes the notion that [second wave feminism was] a bourgeois movement that didn't deal with class. There was always a grappling with class inequality, economic injustice, the realities of capitalism as a part of figuring out a radical feminist vision.

Barbara S.: Women [in the second wave] started all kinds of institutions, including women's schools, where women who had expertise or a skill shared their knowledge with other women. At one of the women's schools in the Boston area, they held a course on Marxism. We had so much fun. I had been introduced to these thinkers, philosophers, and political analysts before [as an undergraduate student at the New School for Social Research in New York City]. But when I took the course at the women's school, we talked about how the work that we were reading applied to our lives. So we were reading Lenin and Trotsky and, of course, Marx, and we would talk about their perspective on the woman question and how it was for us in the 1970s, actually forming movements.

That commitment to class analysis was also reflected in our practice. For example, some of the work we did with the socialist feminists in the Boston Women's Union was in the area of reproductive rights and freedom. Just as the Combahee River Collective was starting, they were starting to organize the Committee to End Sterilization Abuse (CESA). Dr. Helen Rodriguez-Trias visited Boston to attend a women's health conference and inspired our organizing around sterilization abuse. Some of the people in Combahee got involved in CESA's Third World Women's Committee. A couple of years later, when the Hyde Amendment was passed,[*] we also formed the Abortion Action Coalition, which had its own Third World Women's Committee. These organizations became the platform for organizing women of color health presentations and discussions, a strategy that was right out of the *Our Bodies, Ourselves* playbook.

We would have discussions, events, programs at a community school in the South End, a historically multiracial working-class neighborhood. These were just discussions with women who lived in the community about what concerns us, what do we do to keep ourselves healthy, and what are the systematic barriers that we face to that being the case? We never did things that solely focused upon the issue of abortion. It was always the whole context of how can you be healthy in a system that doesn't have a great health care delivery system and where there are so many factors that you're dealing with that mitigate against your being healthy? We talked about their children, not just them. It was very different from a narrow focus.

---

[*]The Hyde Amendment, passed by Congress in 1976, bars the use of certain federal funds, primarily Medicaid, for abortions. Political resistance to the Hyde Amendment focused on the fact that the provisions of the amendment would unduly impact poor and working-class women who lacked access to health insurance through their employers. The amendment also impacts federal employees, such as military personnel and their families, federal prisoners, and Indian Health Service clients, all of whom must pay for abortions out of pocket.

Barbara R.: Both linking sterilization abuse to reproductive choice and abortion and the terms "Third World women" and "Third World feminism" are historically specific. Young activists aren't always familiar with where they come from, but they are very anti-imperialist terms. The campaign against sterilization abuse recognized what was happening beyond the continental United States, in Puerto Rico, explicitly, and other places. So this idea that a woman of color feminism or Third World feminism was one that was inherently global and anti-imperialist even in choosing the terms and issues, it broke out of a very narrow, exceptionalist view of things.

Barbara S.: Absolutely! Absolutely! People of color in the Left during that period did use the term Third World to describe ourselves. We saw ourselves as being subjected to internal colonization. We had external colonies that were put in place by super powers and other primarily European nations. Then we had internal colonies that were put in place by the same people that affected people whose origins were in that Third World. As time went on, we looked at Nicaragua, we looked at Grenada, Cuba, where a different kind of economic system—certainly influenced by Communism, socialism, Marxism, et cetera—was a reality and where we saw a lot of hope and inspiration.

Barbara R.: When you look for hopeful places on the planet where revolutionary governments are doing it differently, sometimes when you get to issues of gender and sexuality, they come up short. Have you felt that need to reconcile a feminist politics and criteria for progress, success, radical transformation with the socialist sensibilities?

Barbara S.: There are real contradictions there, particularly because some of us who were doing some of the most groundbreaking work and asking some of the most cheeky, unsettling questions—we were lesbians. So of course we had a different perspective on the world. We knew that we were not necessarily welcome in any context. We weren't welcome under U.S. capitalism, necessarily. We weren't welcome in revolutionary societies, either.

I went to Cuba in 1995 in a lesbian and gay delegation. So that was really quite historic. It was during a period when there was a lot of opening up of discussions about these issues in Cuba, pretty much driven by that movie, *Strawberry and Chocolate*. That was just such a paradigm shift. I actually marched in a May Day parade, in Havana, Cuba, in 1995, with an LGBT [Lesbian, Gay, Bisexual, Transgender] contingent!

Virginia Eubanks: Do you still identify as a socialist?

Barbara S.: I do. I recognize fully the limitations of capitalism. Capitalism is a system for the profit of a few, to build wealth for the few, the 1 percent, and it has no real investment in, or concern about who that damages or hurts or exploits. No matter how it's prettied up—social missions of corporations and what have you—capitalism doesn't address the bottom line, the root causes of poverty and exploitation.

In this country, the consequences of capitalism are obscured, by and large, except in our poor inner city and rural communities, where there is a huge amount of poverty. This nation should be asking questions, "Why are there so many poor people in the most wealthy and prosperous country on earth?" We have an economic system that does not have the capacity to make sure that all have their basic needs met. Capitalism does not do that.

"Capitalism is a system for the profit of a few, to build wealth for the few, the 1 percent, and it has no real investment in, or concern about who that damages or hurts or exploits. No matter how it's prettied up— social missions of corporations and what have you—capitalism doesn't address the bottom line, the root causes of poverty and exploitation."

Poverty is itself a form of violence. Socialism in its highest form is a system that makes sure that every person is able to have their basic needs met, and that the people who do the work benefit from that work. But the kind of socialist society that I think would be ideal has never existed. Socialism that has existed up until now has been infected by, and affected by, militarism, violence, patriarchal rule, racism, and xenophobia. All kinds of isms! I don't want anybody to think that I'm talking about some place on earth right now, that I'm thinking, "Wouldn't it be great if we were just like *them*." But I think we really have to examine our economic relationships and figure out why it's not working.

Virginia: You want to make sure that people don't confuse your support for socialism as an economic system with socialism as practiced by totalitarian states that are not democratic.

Barbara S.: That's absolutely correct. I'm interested in socialist democracy, which I would think would encompass feminist and anti-racist ideology and policies as well. Human experience is a work in progress. We never get there, because we're humans. But we can certainly aspire. We can certainly build our dreams and our visions and our work with some principles.

Alethia Jones: How did class dynamics manifest within Black feminist organizing?

Barbara S.: In Combahee there were some tensions around who had gone to college, graduate school, who was involved in academic or intellectual work versus those who were not. I always found that really painful, because you could not assume that any Black person's education was without sacrifice. There were no guarantees that they would ever be in that position of being able to take advantage of higher education. So instead of beating up on people for managing to flip the script that white supremacy determined for them, it seems better to say, "You know, we could always use some more sharp minds." Not that smartness and education are an absolute match. Even to this day I find it painful. People would attack others because they had done something that I consider entirely positive: grab an education out of a system that prefers you not get one. Literacy was forbidden to enslaved people of African heritage. High prices were paid when people made that effort. It was painful for me to be put down for something that was so valued and hard won. Having class consciousness is important. If you have a class analysis, you hopefully can function [so as] not to be detrimental to the lives and opportunities of people who have had fewer opportunities than you.

Alethia: What does it mean to be "politically conscious"? Some would say that being a Black woman is consciousness enough. Don't we live feminism every day? Do we have to declare being feminists?

Barbara S.: Consciousness means you are doing self-examination and analysis of the circumstances and the situations that you experience and face, and the factors and forces that shape your existence and your political and social status, economic status, too. It really means you're examining and looking at, not just *being*. That's what's so fascinating about a Black feminist analysis: we knew that because of our material conditions and our social/economic/racial/gender status that we had experienced things and issues that would be pathways to consciousness if we chose to look at them and examine them in that way.

Unexamined oppression is just really unexamined oppression. Usually, you find in oppressed communities a higher level of consciousness because they understand the system is not working for them. We have a lens of not taking stuff at face value and going along with the propaganda that our society puts forth as "This is the United States and everybody can succeed. All you have to do is work hard. Blah, blah, blah, blah." We have lived experiences and examples of someone who did all the right things and still ended up in a very difficult and challenging set of circumstances. Our objective status gives us an avenue and a pathway to consciousness.

I think consciousness, though, comes into being through collective dialogue. It's probably not possible to be fully conscious if the only person who you ever ran your ideas by was yourself. That gets into political organizing and movements. It's not enough just to have the markers of identity that would say logically, this person would be really very sharp about what's going on in relationship to power and oppression—stereotyping, prejudice, bigotry, violence, terrorism, et cetera. For example, Clarence Thomas and Condoleezza Rice are both smart but lack this type of political consciousness. Rice took her life growing up in a cauldron of racism and racial terrorism in Birmingham, Alabama, and jumped right over to the people who were privileged and who dominate the rest of us with their conservative philosophy. I really feel that consciousness is about self-examination and analysis, collective dialogue to really try to figure out what in the world *is* going on. "Why is it this way? What can we do about it?"

Alethia: So Black feminism is for everyone. It is a political stance and a political choice.

It may originate in the experience of a particular people or a particular body, but anyone can arrive at a Black feminist analysis through logic, sensitivity, and study of history.

Where do you think that kind of movement-driven collective dialogue is happening today?

"So Black feminism is for everyone. It is a political stance and a political choice."

Barbara S.: There are always people who are very alert and who have such a profound sense of justice that whatever their generation, whatever their life experiences or status, they are going to try to find out "What's going on here?" It may not look like the movements that were so instrumental and so fundamental in my growing-up years, but they are doing that.

I'm thinking about what happened in the Middle East in the winter and spring [of 2011]. Certainly in Egypt that was an example of people just speaking truth to power until the regime actually was forced out and change came. There are always people who are fighting for justice in different ways; you always have that tendency.

Black Feminist Organizing Tactics

Black feminism existed as a lived political practice that blended sharp structural analysis with strategic grassroots action. In a 1984 speech delivered in Boston at the progressive, interfaith feminist organization the Women's Theological Center (now known as Women Transforming Communities), Smith conveys the interwoven nature of theory and practice in movement building. She articulates how the gendered nature of violence makes a race-only framework insufficient as an analytical tool and directly connects this multilayered perspective to a local effort to resist the silencing and murder of Black women. The resulting community-wide effort to resist violence and institutional neglect led to an innovative approach, captured here in a pamphlet drafted by Barbara, refined by Combahee members, produced by the Collective, widely distributed to women and men, and ultimately translated into Spanish. Inspired by these past efforts and strategies, activist and academic Terrion Williamson extends this approach into the new media age to resist the murder of Black women and girls that sadly continues to this day. As the discussion with Kimberly Springer shows, Combahee's interlocking oppressions approach remains a critical tool for analyzing the cultural and political contexts of these tragedies.

"Black Feminism: A Movement of Our Own"
Barbara Smith ([1984] 1997)

... It is important to note that the historical impetus and inspiration for the contemporary Black Women's Movement—which began as early as the '60s, with Black women critical of sexism in the Civil Rights movement and Black power organizations—came out of the whole history of our people in this country and in Africa. The names of Harriet Tubman and Sojourner Truth are constantly invoked as our Black feminist foremothers, but thousands upon thousands, if not millions, of Black women in the nineteenth and twentieth centuries explicitly devoted their lives to the examination and eradication of the oppression of Afro-American women. In the introduction to *Home Girls* (Kitchen Table: Women of Color Press, 1983), I wrote: "I am convinced that Black feminism is on every level organic to Black experience." All of us, as Black feminists, have been called names—"traitors to the race"—and have been told that we're dividing the race, etc., because "Black issues are racial issues solely." ...

This point cannot be made too strongly, because there has been such a tendency in the Black community to dismiss feminism, even when it is practiced by Blacks, and led by Black women, as only applicable to the white race—even though sexual oppression, of course, cuts across all races and cultures with disastrous and violent results. One reason that this disavowal has been possible is that there has been such a dearth of accurate information about what grassroots, radical women's groups, including groups of women of color, have done. If the only thing I knew about feminism was what I read in [a] magazine, I would think it was irrelevant and a waste of my time, too. But as a Black feminist and a lesbian, I have access to information about—and I experience—the crucial work that progressive feminists are doing. As I wrote in *Home Girls*:

> I have often wished I could spread the word that a movement committed to fighting racial, sexual, economic, and heterosexist oppression, not to mention one which opposes imperialism, anti-Semitism, the oppressions visited upon the physically disabled, the old and the young, at the same time that it challenges militarism and imminent nuclear destruction, is the very opposite of narrow. I always felt that Black women's ability to function with dignity, independence and imagination in the face of total adversity—that is, in the face of white America—points to an innate feminist potential. To me, the phrase "act like you have some sense," probably spoken by at least one Black woman to every Black child who ever lived, says volumes about keeping your feet on the ground and your ass covered. Black women as a group have never been fools; we couldn't afford to be.

We come from a tradition of struggle, and so it is only natural that women in our particular groups would be take-care-of-business kinds of people. (I think this extends to all women of color, not just Afro-American women.) We have always faced sexual oppression, always faced racial oppression, always faced economic oppression. Certain conditions came into existence in the late 1960s that a Women's Movement—a resurgence of a Women's Movement—grew in this country. And with it came the blossoming of the feminism of women of color. But Black feminism is not a new concept.

"I always felt that Black women's ability to function with dignity, independence and imagination in the face of total adversity—that is, in the face of white America—points to an innate feminist potential."

Why do we need Black feminism? . . . [A]s women of color we face all the [multiple oppressions] that they put out there. We found that if we were going to combat it, we were going to develop a kind of politics that would meet all those "isms." It was difficult—still is difficult—for many people to cope with the idea that sexual politics affects the lives of women of color. The fact that Third World men could possibly be oppressors as well as oppressed is a very difficult admission, and there have been many open debates and confrontations about it. But we are beginning to understand that you can be an oppressor and oppressed simultaneously, and that it's nothing new. The question is, "What are you going to do about that fact?" Feminists of color have also been threatening to our communities because we expect people to change. Once you figure out that all these things are occurring and ruining people's chances for better lives and freedom, then you have to change—but nobody likes to do that, and it's been difficult for people of color to understand, particularly when the Women's Movement has been portrayed as white. That's one of the reasons for making explicit Black feminist or Third World feminist statements. Sometimes people ask me, "Why do you have to say you're a feminist?" or "Why do you have to say you're a lesbian?" I try to explain that if I don't say it, then nobody *knows* why I have the particular commitment that I do. They won't know why I view political reality the way I do. I was lots of things before I was a feminist. I was an activist. I certainly was Black before I was a feminist. Feminism is something I claim because I claim it in the name of Black women.

One of the reasons I can do that is that most of the organizing I have done around sexual politics has been with other women of color, particularly other Black women; I never had the experience, say, of being in NOW [National Organization for Women] for five years and then having to dispense with the whole thing. In 1973, the National Black Feminist Organization had its first regional conference in New York, and my sister Beverly and I went to it. It changed our lives to be in a room with so many Black women who, in 1973, were saying that they were feminists; in 1984, there are still many women who won't say it. It was an incredible experience, and a lot of our work since then has been with other Third World women. We worked on very broad-based and far-reaching issues, particularly in the Combahee River Collective, and I would like to be more explicit about some of the things I feel most embodied what we meant and what I mean by Black feminism.

I'm thinking in particular of 1979, when twelve Black women were murdered in Boston in less than six months. If you lived in Boston at the time, I'm sure you remember the murders. If not, you probably never even knew they happened; they got no media coverage because, after all, they were only Black women. I speak all over the country, and when I'm talking about feminism and organizing, I often talk about the murders, because for me that was a pivotal time, in some ways the culmination of everything I had done, learned, tried to do until then. And I have found in going across the country that Black women are being murdered in droves and waves and epidemics all over: in Columbus, Ohio, at least three Black women have been murdered in the last few months. They always try to say that the murders are not connected, but when it always happens to a Black person who also always happens to be female and probably lives in a poorer section of the city, how can they not be connected? They are logically connected. . . .

When the murders were first talked about, in January or February, they were discussed solely as racial crimes. By April, six Black women had been murdered, and there was a march in the South End to the sites where some of them had been found, followed by a rally. The speakers talked about race, but no one said a damn thing about the fact that sexual violence is the name of the game, and that it's global. It doesn't matter what the context is: if you're a woman, you're bound to suffer from it. I'm sure you know how many regimes all over this globe are practicing fascism, and whenever you read about cases of torture, disappearance, or political imprisonment, and the victim is a woman, you know that part of that torture is sexual violence. And where do the military and right-wing forces get that idea—could it be because rape is a national pastime?

I left that demonstration really upset, because I knew that it was six Black women who'd been killed and that I and all my friends were potentially the next victims—there was more happening than just racial politics or class politics. So the Combahee River Collective wrote a pamphlet about how sexual violence connects to racial violence and economic exploitation, and listing things to do to protect yourself. It was the first published, tangible thing that came out about the murders that people could use. It was the first thing that did not dismiss the murders or imply that these women deserved to die because "they might have been prostitutes or runaways."

We printed 2,000 of the pamphlets at first, and they were gone almost immediately. (Even some of you who were involved in that work may not know that at least 30,000 were distributed by the time we were finished: we kept going back to the printer.) The pamphlet was originally printed in both English and Spanish because we assumed, as Black feminists, that our concern was not just with Afro-American, English-speaking people. . . . We wanted every woman to feel some kind of solidarity and some kind of protection. And there were many other activities around the murders besides the pamphlet; it was a coalition. I saw people sitting together in rooms who I didn't think would ever have anything to do with each other. . . .

This organizing embodied the kind of work that I feel is most important. It was a coalition effort that got at a bottom-line issue—murder—and dealt with a feminist issue, sexual violence. I always feel the need to honor it, particularly when I'm standing on the very soil on which it happened. Those of us who lived through it should always respect ourselves for the work we did, for showing power and resistance instead of lying down and taking it. . . .

What kinds of things are we doing now as Black feminists? Given that we're affected by every kind of oppression, every kind of "ism" that affects Third World women and Third World people, you can imagine the range of our work. One of the things that has happened in recent years is the building of Third World women's institutions, like Kitchen Table: Women of Color Press, the Third World Women's Archives in New York City, the Black Women's Health Project in Atlanta, the Black women's self-help groups in Washington, D.C. . . . Institution building is absolutely crucial, because we don't know what we think until we ask ourselves, don't know what we need until we ask ourselves. We have to sit down and communicate. . . . That's why we need autonomous institutions and why we're building them.

But we are not separatists. That's a common misconception about feminism . . . that because we say we're Black and female we must be separatists. We know, like anyone with common sense, that our fate is tied up with all the people of our race, men, women, and children. It's important for me to always try to express that, because I am a lesbian and have been stereotyped as such. Because I was Black before I was a feminist, Black before I knew I was a lesbian. I do not see cutting off the people who fought those battles. We are all locked together, and many Third World men understand exactly what I mean. I have great respect for our families, for our people. Black feminism is not separatism; it's about autonomy.

What about the future? One of the things that I have been most enlivened by is the fact that it is no longer strictly a Black feminist movement that I am a part of, but a Third World feminist movement. Not only am I talking about sisters here in the U.S.—American Indian, Latina, Asian American, Arab American—I am also talking about women all over the globe. I was fortunate enough to go to London twice this year for book fairs. We were talking about women's politics, not just publishing, and although we had never met one another, we basically agreed that we needed to talk about sexual, racial, class, anti-imperialistic, anti-militaristic politics. I think Third World feminism has enriched not just the women it applies to, but also political practice in general. For instance, the first time I heard the phrase "rainbow coalition" was when I went to the second National Third World Lesbian and Gay Conference in Chicago in 1980, which was called "A Unified Rainbow of Strength." We were talking about rainbows then; it was not just media hype. We influenced the politics of other movements, like the Jesse Jackson [presidential] campaign [of 1984], because we believed in coalitions before other people did.

"Black feminism is all about making a place on this globe that is fit for human life."

I feel our work is cut out for us, as always. We are in a huge mishmash created by mad people at the top, and we're constantly trying to rectify the situation. I see the process of rectification as what Black feminism is all about: making a place on this globe that is fit for human life.

If we do that, then we will have done a whole lot, particularly if that means that the new society we create respects people like you and me.

This speech originally appeared in the feminist newspaper *Sojourner* in December 1984 under the title "Barbara Smith on Black Feminism." It is reprinted in Karen Kahn and Robin Morgan, eds., *Frontline Feminism 1975–1995: Essays from Sojourner's First 20 Years* (San Francisco: Aunt Lute Books, 1997).

"Who Is Killing Us," Terrion Williamson (2012)

On April 1, 1979, 1,500 people gathered in the streets of Boston to memorialize the lives of six black women who had been murdered within a two-mile radius of each other beginning in January of that year. By May the number of victims would rise to twelve. During the memorial march, Sarah Small, the aunt of the fifth victim, Daryal Ann Hargett, posed a simple question, but one with serious and long-lasting reverberations:

"Who is Killing Us?"[3]

Small's question was critical because in its asking it formulated a theory of the social—a black social—that refused to allow victims to remain individual, that

[3] Jaime M. Grant, "Who's Killing Us?" in *Femicide: The Politics of Woman Killing*, ed. Jill Radford and Diana E. H. Russell (New York: Twayne Publishers, 1992), 145–60.

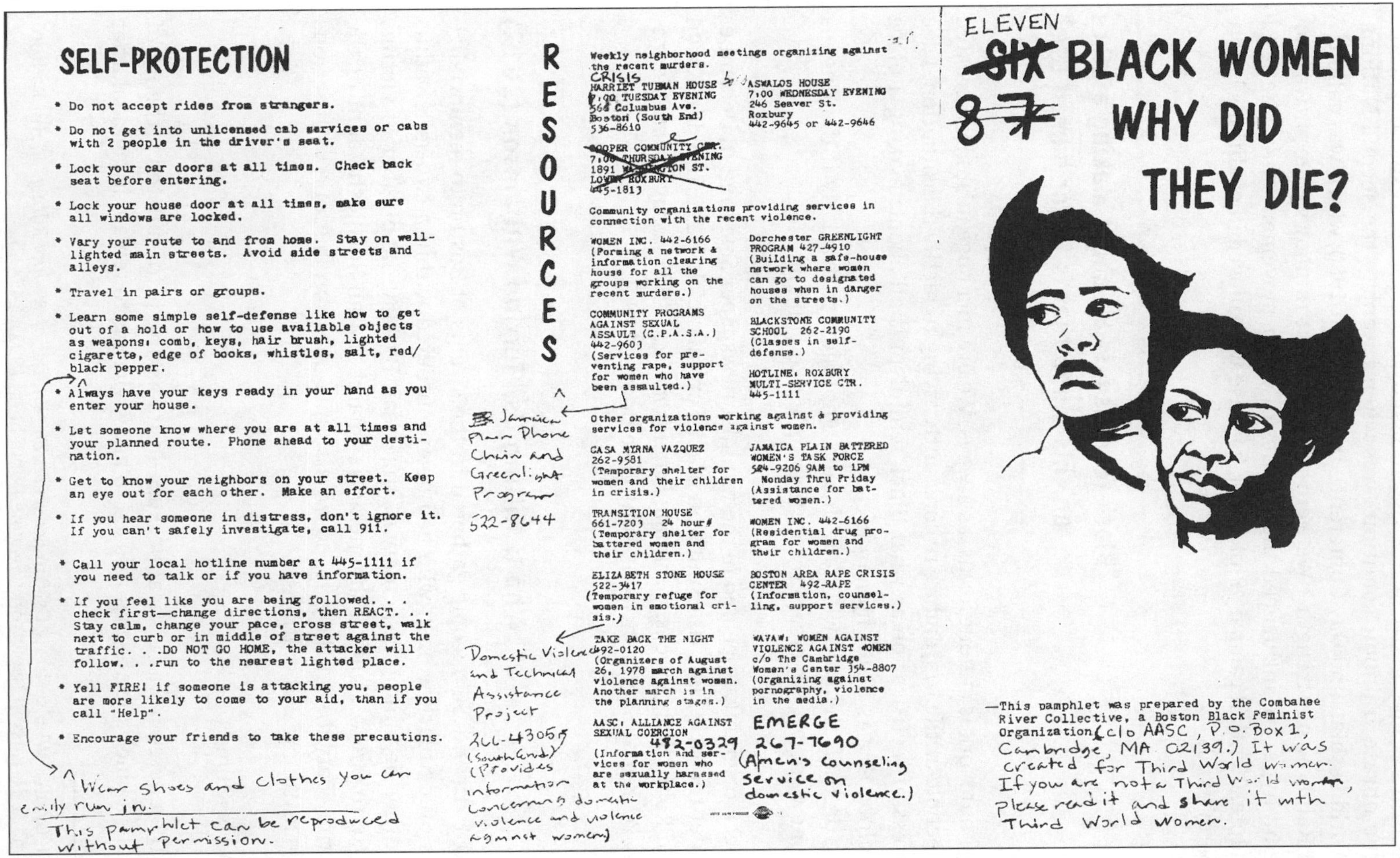

ELEVEN ~~SIX~~ BLACK WOMEN
8 ~~7~~ WHY DID THEY DIE?

SELF-PROTECTION

- Do not accept rides from strangers.
- Do not get into unlicensed cab services or cabs with 2 people in the driver's seat.
- Lock your car doors at all times. Check back seat before entering.
- Lock your house door at all times, make sure all windows are locked.
- Vary your route to and from home. Stay on well-lighted main streets. Avoid side streets and alleys.
- Travel in pairs or groups.
- Learn some simple self-defense like how to get out of a hold or how to use available objects as weapons: comb, keys, hair brush, lighted cigarette, edge of books, whistles, salt, red/black pepper.
- Always have your keys ready in your hand as you enter your house.
- Let someone know where you are at all times and your planned route. Phone ahead to your destination.
- Get to know your neighbors on your street. Keep an eye out for each other. Make an effort.
- If you hear someone in distress, don't ignore it. If you can't safely investigate, call 911.
- Call your local hotline number at 445-1111 if you need to talk or if you have information.
- If you feel like you are being followed. . . check first—change directions, then REACT. . . Stay calm, change your pace, cross street, walk next to curb or in middle of street against the traffic. . .DO NOT GO HOME, the attacker will follow. . .run to the nearest lighted place.
- Yell FIRE! if someone is attacking you, people are more likely to come to your aid, than if you call "Help".
- Encourage your friends to take these precautions.

Wear shoes and clothes you can easily run in.

This pamphlet can be reproduced without permission.

RESOURCES

Weekly neighborhood meetings organizing against the recent murders.

CRISIS
HARRIET TUBMAN HOUSE
7:00 TUESDAY EVENING
566 Columbus Ave.
Boston (South End)
536-8610

ASWALOS HOUSE
7:00 WEDNESDAY EVENING
246 Seaver St.
Roxbury
442-9645 or 442-9646

~~COOPER COMMUNITY CTR.
7:00 THURSDAY EVENING
1891 WASHINGTON ST.
LOWER ROXBURY~~
445-1813

Community organizations providing services in connection with the recent violence.

WOMEN INC. 442-6166
(Forming a network & information clearing house for all the groups working on the recent murders.)

Dorchester GREENLIGHT PROGRAM 427-4910
(Building a safe-house network where women can go to designated houses when in danger on the streets.)

COMMUNITY PROGRAMS AGAINST SEXUAL ASSAULT (C.P.A.S.A.)
442-9603
(Services for preventing rape, support for women who have been assaulted.)

BLACKSTONE COMMUNITY SCHOOL 262-2190
(Classes in self-defense.)

HOTLINE: ROXBURY MULTI-SERVICE CTR.
445-1111

Jamaica Plain Phone Chain and Greenlight Program
522-8644

Other organizations working against & providing services for violence against women.

CASA MYRNA VAZQUEZ
262-9581
(Temporary shelter for women and their children in crisis.)

JAMAICA PLAIN BATTERED WOMEN'S TASK FORCE
524-9206 9AM to 1PM
Monday Thru Friday
(Assistance for battered women.)

TRANSITION HOUSE
661-7203 24 hour#
(Temporary shelter for battered women and their children.)

WOMEN INC. 442-6166
(Residential drug program for women and their children.)

ELIZABETH STONE HOUSE
522-3417
(Temporary refuge for women in emotional crisis.)

BOSTON AREA RAPE CRISIS CENTER 492-RAPE
(Information, counseling, support services.)

Domestic Violence and Technical Assistance Project
266-4305
(South End)
(Provides information concerning domestic violence and violence against women)

TAKE BACK THE NIGHT
492-0120
(Organizers of August 26, 1978 march against violence against women. Another march is in the planning stages.)

WAVAW: WOMEN AGAINST VIOLENCE AGAINST WOMEN
c/o The Cambridge Women's Center 354-8807
(Organizing against pornography, violence in the media.)

AASC: ALLIANCE AGAINST SEXUAL COERCION
492-0329
(Information and services for women who are sexually harassed at the workplace.)

EMERGE
267-7690
(Men's counseling service on domestic violence.)

—This pamphlet was prepared by the Combahee River Collective, a Boston Black Feminist Organization (c/o AASC, P.O. Box 1, Cambridge, MA 02139.) It was created for Third World women. If you are not a Third World woman, please read it and share it with Third World women.

Figure 3.1: "Eleven Black Women: Why Did They Die?" pamphlet. The Combahee River Collective's methodology—close scrutiny of the lived experiences of those most oppressed—is evident in a widely circulated pamphlet that protested Boston's nonresponse to the increasing number of murdered Black women and girls in 1979. *(continues)*

ELEVEN

8 7≠# BLACK WOMEN

Recently 8 young Black women have been murdered in Roxbury, Dorchester and the S. End. The entire Black community continues to mourn their cruel and brutal deaths. In the face of police indifference and media lies and despite our grief and anger, we have begun to organize ourselves in order to figure out ways to protect ourselves and our sisters, to make the streets safe for women.

We are writing this pamphlet because as Black feminist activists we think it is essential to understand the social and political causes behind these sisters' deaths. We also want to share information about safety measures every woman can take and list groups who are working on the issue of violence against women.

In the Black community the murders have often been talked about as solely racial or racist crimes. It's true that the police and media response has been typically racist. It's true that the victims were all Black and that Black people have always been targets of racist violence in this society, but they were also all women. Our sisters died because they were women just as surely as they died because they were Black. If the murders were only racial, young teen-age boys and older Black men might also have been the unfortunate victims. They might now be petrified to walk the streets as women have always been.

When we look at the statistics and hard facts about daily, socially acceptable violence against women, it's clear it's no "bizarre series of coincidences" that all six victims were female.* In the U.S.A. 1 out of 3 women will be raped in their lifetimes 1 woman is beaten by her husband or boyfriend every 18 seconds; 1 out of every 4 women experiences some form of sexual abuse before she reaches the age of 18 (child molesting, rape, incest) 75% of the time by someone they know and 36% of the time by a family member; 9 out of 10 women in a recent survey had received unwanted sexual advances and harassment at their jobs.** Another way to think about these figures is that while you have been reading this pamphlet, a woman somewhere in this city, in this state, in this country has been beaten, raped and even murdered.

*Boston Globe, April 1, 1979, p. 16.
**Statistics from the paper "Grass Roots Services for Battered Women: A Model for Long Term Change" by Lisa Leghorn. Available from the U. S. Commission on Civil Rights, Washington, D.C.

[handwritten: statement is, when this pamphlet was originally written at the beginning of April, six Black women had been murdered. One month later the number is eleven.]

These statistics apply to all women: Black, white, Latino, Asian, Native American, old young, rich, poor and in between. We've got to understand that violence against us as women cuts across all racial, ethnic and class lines. This doesn't mean that violence against Third World women does not have a racial as well as sexual cause. Both our race and sex lead to violence against us.

One reason that attacks on women are so widespread is that to keep us down, to keep us oppressed we have to be made afraid. Violence makes us feel powerless and also like we're second best.

The society also constantly encourages the violence through the media: movies, pornography, advertisements and disco songs ("Put Loves Chains Back On Me"). Boys and men get the message every day that it's all right even to hurt women. What has happened in Boston's Black community is a thread in the fabric of violence against women.

Another idea that has been put out in this crisis is that women should stay in the house until the murderer(s) are found. In other words Black women should be under house arrest. (Remember that three of the fifth women were found dead in their own apartment.) If and when they catch the murderers we still won't be safe to leave our houses, because it has never been safe to be a woman alone

[handwritten: During this time, a white woman was also murdered and her body found in her own apartment.]

WHY DID THEY DIE?

in the street. Staying in the house punishes the innocent and protects the guilty. It also doesn't take into account real life, that we must go to work, get food, pick up the kids at school, do the wash, do errands and visit friends. Women should be able to walk outside whenever they please, with whoever they please and for whatever reason.

WE WILL ONLY HAVE THIS RIGHT WHEN WOMEN JOIN TOGETHER TO DEMAND OUR RIGHTS AS HUMAN BEINGS TO BE FREE OF PHYSICAL ABUSE, TO BE FREE OF FEAR.

[handwritten: But free the men]

The last idea we want to respond to is that it's men's job to protect women. At first glance this may seem to make sense, but look at the assumptions behind it. Needing to be protected assumes that we are weak, helpless and dependent, that we are victims who need men to protect us. On the other hand, as women in this society we are definitely at risk as far as violence is concerned but WE HAVE TO LEARN TO PROTECT OURSELVES. There are many ways to do this: learning and following common sense safety measures, learning self-defense, setting up phone chains and neighborhood safehouses, joining and working in groups that are organizing against violence against women are all ways to do this.

The idea of men protecting us isn't very realistic because many of us don't have a man to depend upon for this—young girls, teen-agers, single women, separated and divorced women, lesbians, widowed women and elderly women. And even if we do have a man he cannot be our shadow 24 hours a day.

What men can do to "protect" us is to check out the ways in which they put down and intimidate women in the streets and at home, to stop being verbally and physically abusive to us and to tell men they know who mistreat women to stop it and stop it quick. Men who are committed to stopping violence against women should start seriously discussing this issue with other men and organizing in supportive ways.

We decided to write this pamphlet because of our outrage at what has happened to 6 black women and to 1000s and 1000s of women whose names we don't even know. As Black women who are feminists we are struggling against all racist, sexist, heterosexist and class oppression. Many of us have have hopes of ending this particular crisis and violence against women in our community and identify all of its causes, including sexual oppression.

Figure 3.1: Thirty thousand pamphlets were distributed in Spanish and English, but the final count could be more because anyone could photocopy it. Here, we have reproduced a working draft of the pamphlet to show the living, breathing, on-the-ground organizing that took place as the numbers of murdered women increased. As far as we know, this is the first time that this version has been published.

made racialized gender violence a community concern and not just a "woman's issue," and that made the lives of black women the focal point of a collective "us" that included black men and boys. But Small's question had even further implications.

Among the marchers that spring day was Barbara Smith, a founding member of the Combahee River Collective, which just two years earlier had published "The Combahee River Collective Statement," a document that has since become foundational to black feminist thought and women of color organizing. Smith was outraged that most of the speakers at the march were men whose most immediate response to the crisis was to tell black women they needed to remain indoors for their safety and to rally other men to "protect" their women, while never actually addressing the gendered nature of the murders.

Following the march, Smith and other members of the Collective produced and began distributing a pamphlet entitled "Six Black Women: Why Did They Die?" in which they argued the importance of recognizing the role of sexual violence in the deaths of the murdered black women. They made clear that it was not just race and not just gender but race *and* gender that had made those women especially vulnerable, stating that what had happened in Boston was "a thread in the fabric of violence against women." For the Collective, "protecting" black women meant that black men needed to collectively check their own physical, emotional, and verbal assaults on black women, particularly since it most often turns out to be black men who are the instigators of violence against black women—even in serial murder cases.

Thus while some community advocates were primarily concerned with linking the murders of the Boston women to larger histories of racial oppression, the Collective intervened to ensure that the women's murders were recognized as the effect of intersecting oppressions and that advocating on behalf of those women and women like them meant working to end racism, sexism, heterosexism, classism, and all other forms of discrimination, simultaneously. It is within this context that Mrs. Small's question became significantly more than a concern about the identities of individual perpetrators. That is, "who is killing us" bordered on the rhetorical; it was not just a question but the beginnings of a declarative statement that was continued by the work of the Collective and other community advocates who were dedicated to exposing the structural, social, and political forces behind the violence against black women.

But let's be clear, given that the social and economic conditions that lead to violence still exist, the concern over who is killing us, *all* of us, is as important today as it was in Boston thirty-plus years ago. And while the violence against us continues to take on various forms—the Prison Industrial Complex, healthcare disparities, educational disadvantages, the list goes on—and must undoubtedly continue to be challenged, the deaths and disappearances of black women and children that continue to occur at (what should be) alarming rates must also become more of a priority in our struggles for social justice. According to the National Crime Information Center, thousands upon thousands of black people, most of them women and children, are reported missing each year. And the serial murders of black women continue. In just the past ten years black women have been the targets of serial killers in at least seven U.S. cities, including Detroit, MI, Los Angeles, CA, Cleveland, OH, Jacksonville, FL, Rocky Mount, NC, and Peoria, IL.[4]

Although vitally important, this is not simply a matter of figuring out the identities of those individuals who prey on the vulnerable. Rather, the concern over who is killing us must be, first and foremost, about dismantling the originary conditions of that vulnerability.

And we know that those "conditions" have to do with the fact that historically the lives of black people generally, and black women and children in partic-ular, have been of little consequence to the national public—unless, of course, they are being used for political expediency in debates around welfare, crime, cultural pathology, and the like. This is made evident at least in part by what has sometimes been referred to as "missing white woman syndrome"—the dispropor-tionate coverage of young, attractive, and often middle-class white women who go missing—and the dearth of coverage of missing and mutilated black people in national and local media. But advocacy around those lives is also tragically absent from the agendas of many black political and social organizations.

"The concern over who is killing us must be, first and foremost, about dismantling the originary conditions of that vulnerability."

In January 2012, the television network TV One in partnership with the Black and Missing Foundation began airing *Find Our Missing*, a ten-part series meant to serve as a corrective to the national media landscape and to bring attention to the stories of missing black women, men and children. Hosted by S. Epatha

---

[4] For example: Shelly Andre Brooks was charged with murdering seven black women in Detroit between 2001 and 2006 and convicted of two of the women's deaths in March 2007. In May 2007, Chester Dewayne Turner was convicted of the murders of ten black women in Los Angeles that occurred over an eleven-year period and he was charged with the murders of four additional women in February 2011. Anthony Edward Sowell was sentenced to death in August 2011 after being convicted of murdering eleven black women between 2007 and 2009 in Cleveland, Ohio. Paul Durousseau, who was originally charged with killing six black women in Jacksonville, Florida and one in Columbus, Georgia between 1997 and 2003, was convicted of the death of one of his victims in September 2007. In a still unsolved case, between 2006 and 2009 ten black women either disappeared or were found dead in Rocky Mount, North Carolina under similar circumstances. And, in 2006 Larry Dean Bright, the only white perpetrator named in all the aforementioned cases, was convicted of killing eight black women between 2003 and 2004 in Peoria, Illinois.

Merkerson, most known for her sixteen-year stint as Lieutenant Anita Van Buren on the police drama *Law & Order*, the show was complemented by social media and online content that provided information on additional missing persons cases and other social justice issues. Of the twenty people featured over the course of the series, nine were women, six were girls between the ages of two and fifteen, three were boys between the ages of two and twelve, and two were men. Tia Smith, one of the executives in charge of production at TV One, said the intention of the show was to represent a full spectrum of black Americans who are declared missing, and that the hope was not just that it would fill in the gaps in media coverage of disappeared black people, but that it would also serve as a "clarion call for activeness and community involvement."

Tia Smith also noted that the individual cases featured on *Find Our Missing*, which was produced for TV One by Tower Productions, were selected for their potential to be compelling and to "pull at the heart strings of people." That is to say, they wanted to ensure that people watched the show because they felt moved by the stories of the people who are featured. While this logic makes sense for a cable network concerned both with remaining economically viable and appealing to the widest possible audience, we must remain mindful that our own sense of justice is not so limited. Ultimately, those of us who are invested in saving our lives can little afford to pick and choose whom we save. For if we are not just as concerned about the prostitute woman who may have become the target of a serial killer as we are the honor student who disappeared while walking home from her afterschool job, we risk simply reproducing the same conditions we otherwise seek to eliminate.

Whatever its shortcomings, the premise of *Find Our Missing*—that missing black people are "ours" and should be of concern to us all—is testament to the bold recognition of a collective "us" made by Sarah Small at that Boston rally convened for six murdered black women in 1979, as well as the radical ideology outlined by Barbara Smith and the Combahee River Collective more than thirty-five years ago. An ideology that is best summed up in one of the most well-known and powerful declarations made in the Combahee River Collective Statement:

> If Black women were free, it would mean that everyone else would have to be free since our freedom would necessitate the destruction of all systems of oppression.[5]

Ultimately, the collective pronouns engaged by those and other pioneering black feminist thinkers were used not to deny the diversity of black experience or

---

[5] Combahee River Collective, "Combahee River Collective Statement," in *Home Girls: A Black Feminist Anthology*, ed. Barbara Smith (New York: Kitchen Table: Women of Color Press, 1983), 278.

to revel in some fictive black utopia, but in the service of the making of a black social space that recognizes the freedom of black women, *all* black women, from violence and terror as the condition of possibility for universal freedom.

Terrion L. Williamson is assistant professor of English and African American and African Studies at Michigan State University and holds a JD from the University of Illinois at Urbana–Champaign. Originally written in 2012 as an article for the blog *The Feminist Wire*, it was specially adapted for this collection.

Interview with Kimberly Springer

Kimberly Springer: I wanted to talk about the organizing that Combahee did with CRISIS around the murders of Black women in Boston. Can you talk a bit about that project? What's really key about that organizing is that you not only talked about what women could do to protect themselves, you talked about the social and political causes of the crimes. I don't think people even do that today, sometimes.

Barbara: That was really out of the box. It really was. To give some context, early in 1979, several young women's bodies, some of them teenagers, were found in garbage bags near the Stride Rite shoe factory in the South End in Boston. That began a series of murders, some of which were connected, during that season, January or February of 1979 into May of 1979.

The first story about the murders appeared on the page of the *Boston Globe* where the racing results were. In other words, buried in the back of the newspaper. People in the Black community in Boston were up in arms. You have to remember, we had gone through the horrors of the school desegregation crisis in 1974. And in the mid-1970s, we were also constantly dealing with police brutality. There were all kinds of things that were going on, outright racial hate activity. There was a high school football player who was shot on the football field in Charlestown, just for playing football while Black. Permanently paralyzed. There was a Black young man, Ted Landsmark, who was beaten at Government Center. Using what? An American flag. A big heavy flag with a heavy pole.[*]

So we had been through a lot in Boston. I lived at that time in Roxbury, an almost entirely Black community near the Jamaica Plain border. When I used to go to the subway, the Egleston station, I saw KKK graffiti on walls. It was serious. It was completely and utterly serious.

So when the murders of Black women started to happen a few years later, they were immediately understood as racial crimes. But it was only Black women who

---

[*]This moment was captured in the iconic Pulitzer Prize–winning photograph "The Soiling of Old Glory," April 5, 1976. Landsmark, a young thirty-year-old Black man, was a practicing attorney on his way to a meeting. The attackers broke his nose.

were being murdered. There was a rally around the time that the number had gotten to six, on a Sunday, and a march through the South End neighborhood. The primarily male speakers at that rally and march asserted that we needed to find a man to be with us at all times to walk with us, and to not leave the house. Completely unrealistic stuff. No one had an analysis of violence against women.

I went home after this rally and I was just *steaming*. I was absolutely steaming. How the crimes were being defined was not accurate, nor were the solutions useful for everybody. We didn't want to be under house arrest, nor did every single Black woman have access to a Black male bodyguard, essentially. I started writing, that night, the draft of what became "Six Black Women: Why Did They Die?" I called a few members of the Combahee River Collective and I literally read what I had written to them over the phone and asked, "What do you think about it?" And they said, "Fine, great. Go with it."

We had a wonderful resource in Boston at that time called Urban Planning Aid. They helped community groups organize by offering technical assistance, including the laying out of written materials: pamphlets, flyers, et cetera. I called them the next day, and they agreed to help with the layout. We offered an analysis in the three inside panels. Then we had the list of resources and organizations you could contact and then also things that you could do to be safe. Commonsense safety tips that women had come up with about how do you avoid being the victim of sexual assault and physical violence. And we called it "Six Black Women: Why Did They Die?"

By the end of the week, we had photocopied our first printing.

We eventually did about thirty thousand. We had several different versions. We quickly translated it into Spanish. We also did a version that had all the information that I described—the cover, the "What you can do to be safe," and the organizations—but the only thing that was inside was Ntozake Shange's poem "With No Immediate Cause." Those were the three versions of the pamphlet. Eventually the pamphlet was typeset and not photocopied but printed.

That was a great example of how, having a Black feminist organization and a Black feminist analysis, we actually could do something with the reality that was in front of our face, which was that Black women were getting murdered right and left. Telling people to stay home until it stopped happening wasn't going to really work.

Kimberly: How did working with CRISIS come about?

Barbara: Many, many people were very, very upset about what was going on. There was a wonderful Black woman named Marlene Stephens whom we met because we had done a lot of work around reproductive rights and reproductive freedom with the Committee to End Sterilization Abuse and the Abortion Action Coalition. We met Marlene when we had organized some Black women's health nights at the Blackstone Community School.

We did as much publicizing of the events as we could, and we met women whom we didn't know, definitely women who were not Black lesbian feminists. But we were talking about basic health issues. Marlene and my sister Beverly and Demita and I, we all got to be friends with each other. We'd do other things that weren't Black feminist stuff. For example, when there was a block party or a street festival or whatever in the South End, I'd bring a pot of something I had made to our table. We would do stuff together in the community that was not specifically focused on a very narrow or singular feminist agenda. I don't think feminism is narrow, I'm saying we did stuff outside of what would be in the Black feminist playbook.

When the murders started happening, we were dialoguing with each other as friends about how upset we were. Marlene and other women in the South End decided they would form their own group, CRISIS, and we worked together. One night we were working on posters for a demonstration the next day, and a woman was murdered like that very day. So we were in the midst of organizing around this violence and heard that another woman was murdered.

"One night we were working on posters for a demonstration the next day, and a woman was murdered like that very day. So we were in the midst of organizing around this violence and heard that another woman was murdered."

At that meeting, there were some people who decided to come out of their face and be really homophobic. It was just one of those moments that was like, "Oooooh, SHIT. Okay. What's going to happen next?!" Marlene, she got up and she responded and it was just stellar. She said, "I know Beverly. I know Barbara. I know Demita. They're my friends." She basically laid out all the things that we were doing that were valuable. It wasn't a long oration or anything, but she basically said that these are people who you need to *not* be attacking and to actually respect. It was such a moment. It wasn't solidarity because somebody wrote it down somewhere and said, "You should act like this, you should believe this, you should do this." It was a solidarity that we were building through practice.

Kimberly: So it's that legacy of coalition work. In the late 1990s or early 2000s, the disappearance of Black women and girls wasn't being taken as seriously as the disappearance of white women and girls. The work that Combahee did helped us have a Black feminist analysis of that. It made disparities in media coverage very apparent. The thousands of women who are missing in Ciudad Juárez, there is that kind of political and social analysis happening there. But I was also thinking about, in Cleveland, the Black women who were disappeared and murdered earlier this year. It didn't seem like that kind of analysis had carried over. Why do you think the analysis carries over in some contexts, but not in others?

Barbara: You need to have actual organizations that are focused upon these issues. The reason that we were able to mobilize in Boston is that CRISIS was not the only organization that came out of the organizing. There was the Committee for Women's Safety; there was the Support Group for Women's Safety. The organizing we had done around the murders formed a basis for some of the coalitions that worked so effectively on Mel King's second mayoral campaign.* The reason I think the analysis and the response diminishes or disappears is because we don't have these organizations, these little cells of radical women of color, to keep that stirred up and to keep that consciousness uppermost and going.

Building Linkages across Difference

This section shares how Black feminists supported others struggling to genuinely pursue the path of unlearning oppression and learning liberation. "Face-to-Face, Day-to-Day" was penned by a multiracial group of Black, white, and Jewish feminist activists and educators as a guide to conducting consciousness-raising (CR) sessions on racism. Black feminist groups, like the Combahee River Collective, were safe spaces for Black women to voice their experiences of—and build their resistance to—living in a racist society, including addressing internalized racism. This document captures an early cross-racial effort that supported white women to do this hard work among themselves. Created in 1979, it was mimeographed and passed around for years before being published in All the Women Are White, All the Blacks Are Men, But Some of Us Are Brave *in 1982. This document reflects a key moment in multiracial movement building and prompts us to ask, "What kind of spaces do movement builders create today?" Following this is a dialogue between Barbara and Laura Sperazi that conveys the courage and generosity that truth telling around race and gender requires. Both documents demonstrate the feminist dedication to creating tools that people can use to practice the art of building a better world.*

"Face-to-Face, Day-to-Day—Racism CR [Consciousness Raising] Guidelines for Women's Groups"

Tia Cross, Freada Klein, Barbara Smith, and Beverly Smith (1979)

On April 4, 1979 four women met together to discuss consciousness-raising guidelines for women's groups that are working on the issue of racism. All of us—Tia Cross, Freada Klein, Barbara Smith, and Beverly Smith—had had experiences as white and Black women thinking and talking about racism with white women's groups, or participating in ongoing racism groups ourselves. . . .

---

*Mel King is a Black progressive leftist activist in Boston who ran for mayor in 1983 under the slogan of the Rainbow Coalition.

We feel that using consciousness-raising to explore our racism is particularly useful and appropriate. It is a feminist form based upon the ways that women have always talked and listened to each other. It provides a place of validation and support for our feelings as well as the emotional support we need to change. The CR format encourages personal sharing, risk-taking and involvement, which are essential for getting at how each of us is racist in a daily way; and it encourages the "personal" change that makes political transformation and action possible. The Women's Movement has begun to address racism in a way in which no previous movement has, because we have a growing understanding that our racism often manifests itself in how we interact with other women. Doing CR acknowledges that how we feel can inhibit or lead to action, and that how we actually treat people does make a difference.

Theoretical and analytical comprehension of the political and historical causes of racism is essential, but this understanding on an intellectual level doesn't always help to make face-to-face meetings with women of color real, productive or meaningful. We need both a political understanding of racism and a personal-political understanding of how it affects our daily lives. Many women start doing CR about racism because they are already confronting it in other areas of their lives and need a place to explore what is happening. CR about racism is not merely talk, talk, talk, and no action, but the essential talking that will make action possible. Doing CR is based upon the fact that as a person you simply cannot do political action without personal interaction.

We also want to stress, however, that these guidelines are not instant solutions. You cannot spend fifteen minutes on each topic and assume that you're done. Racism is much too complex and brutal a system for that. The absence of language to explore our own racism contributes to the difficulty and is in itself part of the problem. Only one term, "racism," exists to describe the range of behavior from subtle, nonverbal daily experiences to murders by the Ku Klux Klan. "Racism" covers individual acts and institutional patterns. But this stumbling block of language presents another theme to explore, not a reason to give up. CR is just one step in the whole process of changing the legacy of oppression (based upon difference) that white-male rule has imposed on us.

Actions can grow out of the CR group directly. For example, the group can find out about and publicize the resources which exist in their area, such as other CR groups, study groups, Third World women's groups, and coalitions of Third World and white women. The group can compile reading lists about Black women, racism, and white women's antiracist activity. It can spread the word about the CR process through writing articles, and by giving workshops and talks. It can also compile its own CR guidelines. The legacy of racism in this country is long. It will take a great deal of time and ongoing commitment to bring about change, to alter the insidious and deep-rooted patriarchal attitudes we learn from the time we are children. It is important for women to show other women what is possible. . . .

I. Early Memories/Childhood Experiences

1. When were you first aware that there was such a thing as race and racial differences? How old were you? Recall an incident if you can. How did you feel?
2. What kind of contact did you have with people of different races? Were they adults, children, playmates?
3. How did you experience your own ethnic identity?
4. How did you first experience racism? Who did you learn it from? What did it mean to you? How did it function in your perception of yourself? How did it make you feel? How did it affect you in relationship to other people?
5. When did you first notice yourself treating people of color in a different way?
6. When were you first aware that there was such a thing as anti-Semitism? How old were you? Recall an incident. How did you feel?

. . .

II. Adolescence/Early Adulthood

1. What kind of messages did you get about race as you entered adolescence? How did who your friends were change?
2. Discuss the connections between coming of age sexually and racial separation. (When the four of us discussed being a teenager one woman pin-pointed the sexual-racial dichotomy by saying, "It's about who you can't date!")
3. If you went to integrated schools what messages did you get about Black people in general and about Black males specifically?

. . .

5. How did different groups of students get along in your school? Were you aware of divisions by race and class? How did it feel?
6. How were different groups of students treated by teachers and the school administration?

. . .

III. Becoming a Feminist/Racism in the Women's Movement

. . .

3. How does your class background affect your racism and making connections with women different from yourself? What are the barriers you have to over-come to connect?
4. How do you see yourself as different from a Black woman? How do you see yourself as the same?

. . .

6. Discuss different values you think white and Black women have around child-rearing, clothes, food, money, upward or downward mobility.

7. Each week the group has the "homework assignment" of noticing racist situations—things each member sees, hears, or reads. Begin each session by sharing the things you've noticed.

8. Discuss what happens when you call another white woman on her racism. What are your fears? How does it feel to do this?

9. Discuss the ways in which white women lower their standards for being feminist for Black and other Third World women. Do you find yourself "hiding" your feminism in a situation where there are Third World people? Are you afraid to confront a Black woman's anti-feminism?

10. Discuss issues that the Women's Movement has worked on which might be considered racist, because they do not touch the lives of women of color. Discuss feminist issues which are classist. Discuss feminist issues that cut across racial and class lines, touching the lives of all women. Which of all these issues have you worked on or considered a priority?

11. In what way does being a Lesbian connect to the whole issue of racism between white and Black women? What kinds of racism have you noticed in all women's social situations, at bars and at cultural events? In what ways can shared Lesbian oppression be used to build connections between white women and women of color?

"Breaking the Silence: A Conversation in Black and White"

Laura Sperazi (1978)

From the original: On January 22, Adrienne Rich, feminist poet and author of *Of Woman Born* spoke about separation and racism in the Women's Movement. The event was a benefit for *The Turning Point*, a magazine published by women prisoners at the Massachusetts Correctional Institute at Framingham. As Rich described the liberal guilt and the ignorance of our common history that divides Black and white women, I felt like some old rusty armor I wear had begun to fall apart. For two days afterward, I thought about little besides racism: the ways I learned it. The ways I practice it. I finally decided to write an article about the event to give myself a chance to think through the issues more clearly and to communicate some of the ideas Adrienne Rich had presented.

I called Barbara Smith to ask if she'd be interested in expanding a comment she made that night. She said that it was an historic event for the Women's Movement in Boston. She had helped to arrange the presentation and Adrienne Rich had been deeply influenced by an article by Barbara. We are continually creating possibilities for each other.

Barbara and I agreed to meet for lunch and to have not so much an interview ("I don't like people to pick my brain," she said) as a dialog. What could be said if a Black woman and a white woman sat down together to talk about race?

—L. Sperazi

Laura: I've been thinking about shame and ignorance as components of racism. They are related but I'll start with shame. What I found I had to overcome that night that Adrienne Rich spoke was my own sense of shame about admitting difference. Now where does that shame come from? Why is it that I should feel ashamed?

Barbara: Ashamed that you're white? Or that you're not Black?

Laura: Ashamed that I feel difference. That I don't know you. That there is something I would have to ask to know you better.

Barbara: I think shame is a much more honest term to describe what has gone on in this country historically. White people don't like to admit they don't know everything. Knowledge is power, and white people are supposed to know everything. Though clearly there are groups of people in this country who show they don't know anything about certain experiences or certain approaches to humanity. I really feel that's the level of arrogance out of which people operate that is a component of racism. Which is not just "I don't like Black people" but "I don't understand them." How to overcome it? Well, to be in touch with people who can tell you something about it. That's the bottom line.

Laura: But somehow you have to account for historical reality as well as individual consciousness. I can say to myself—where is this coming from? And there are things that as an individual I can own. But then historically, we pretend that the Civil Rights Movement had a beginning, a middle, and an end just like any good story. . . . But it's just not true. Racism is alive and well. If we understand that historically we've barely budged, then individual shame needn't be so great. . . .

Barbara: [W]e are talking about the subtleties and depth of racism. . . . Black people and white people in this country have always been at each other's throats. It was set up that way. And the most obvious level of racism and racial interaction is the death level. But there are multitudes of experiences that are much more like what people really experience on a day-to-day basis . . . those subtleties of racial interaction . . . the way this stuff gets broken down is to talk to someone who tells you what it means. I've been thinking a lot about my relationship with white women recently and even as a Black woman I take for granted a certain amount of distance and difference, too. But you see, I'm tired of that.

Laura: Do you feel a reluctance on the part of white women to reach out?

Barbara: I do. But it's complicated. I'm always changing. I'm not the person I was a year ago. I'm certainly not the person I was four years ago. I'm much more open. . . . I can be guarded. I can be afraid of reaching out. . . . But someone's got to take risks. The nature of race and racism is so deep and difficult that the first indication a Black person has that the white person is alright is that the white person makes that initial leap. I can seek out any number of white people and be rebuffed. . . .

Laura: Sure. Why put yourself in that position? It took me a long time to figure that out.

Barbara: But you figured it out?

Laura: Well, I had to. I didn't want to feel left out any more at my job. I had to look at the basic ways I operate. Why was I being so shy? Why was I waiting around for someone to invite me when there was a friendship I wanted? Eventually I had to come around to seeing that a Black woman might not make the first move because she couldn't automatically trust who I am. But I face rejection, too.

Barbara: When I think of the white person's position in this situation of trying to make friendships with Black people, I never think—well, you know, the same thing could happen to a white person that could happen to me. . . .

As far as shame is concerned and how you get over it; the thing is to like who you are, whoever you are. Most white people don't necessarily have to think about this because they are the norm and we are the deviants. In other words, the process of developing self-love on the basis of ethnic identity is not something that white people have had to deal with, at least not mainstream white people.

Laura: Even as a white Italian American my relationship to white America was that of a very dark person. Oh, I was better off than some because my eyes are hazel. But I wasn't as lucky as my brother whose eyes are blue. He was just so much closer to the ideal, to "belonging." . . . I knew on some level that I'd never be beautiful. . . . This notion that America fosters cultural pluralism is so false. White people apply racist standards to each other. Separation on the basis of color, not to mention class, occurs within white groups because we're all being judged by the same ideal of whiteness. I finally learned on a human level that even "white" white people don't have answers or access to any special kind of information, although they do have access to power, privilege, resources.

Barbara: We should engrave this in clay tablets. We are talking about the norms and standards that we came up against as outsiders and how they became demystified for us. I learned the same thing. . . . I still know Black people who believe that white people know something they don't or are smarter, or whatever.

I've been giving a lot of thought to why the Women's Movement can get to the bottom of racism in this country. What happened in Houston [in 1977 at the National Women's Conference] could not have happened at a "men's convention." At the moment of the passing of the minority women's resolution, there was so much feeling about what it meant. Very different kinds of women, women who had never laid eyes on each other before, were all in the same room and they had to deal with each other. They had to. There was no choice. . . . Talk about a solidifying experience!

If every feminist was forced to sit in a room with some people she thought were her opposites for four days and just deal on that level, well, something would happen. Particularly if it were done with sensitivity and compassion. If Black mothers from Roxbury sat down with white mothers from South Boston and talked about being mothers, they'd end up laughing. Because they'd all have these stories to tell about who they are. They'd connect on that level. . . .

Laura: What you said reminds me of something that someone once said to me—one of those things you don't forget: "As a species we've yet to learn that self-hatred is a luxury we cannot afford."

"Racial politics are sexual politics. Sexual politics are racial politics. You can't divide them. To pretend that you can is bogus and unrealistic, a politics that will get you nowhere."

Barbara: I want to talk about a standard I have for being with white women. It is central for me to be able to express who I am and not have to censor any reaction that I might have around race. Race is just a day-to-day experience for me; I can see just about anything that happens in some kind of racial framework. I was trained to be able to do that in order to survive. If something happens and I see it in a racial way and they can't stand it, well, then we have nothing more to say to each other. White people can say, "I'm guilty" or "It's too heavy" when talking about racism. Well, O.K., you might be guilty and it might be heavy, but people are dying as a result of your reluctance to get to it. So get to it.

Laura: Again, I understand this dynamic in sexual terms as well. I can't even remember the number of times I've said to a man: My freedom depends on your willingness to be open to these issues. So much of what we're talking about is how sexual politics will not be clear until they are informed by racial politics. White women are cheating ourselves if we don't.

Barbara: Yes, that's right. Racial politics are sexual politics. Sexual politics are racial politics. You can't divide them. To pretend that you can is bogus and unrealistic, a politics that will get you nowhere.

The inadequacy of the Black movement, to the extent that it still exists, is that it is not dealing with sexual politics, or half of the human race. And the failure of the Women's Movement is its inability to deal with race. . . . The Civil Rights movement was a politics of vision based on love and emotion. And that really is what feminism is, too. . . . It makes me angry when I hear women today say that they're afraid of talking about themselves, their lives—to each other. On a continuum, the level of risk is just not that high.

Now, you see, I can be called arrogant or condescending or whatever for saying this. But Black people have been put down on the level of language from Day 1. "I don't like the way you talk." I'm tired of that. I'm not interested in . . . talking in a way that's pleasant or easy for white people to hear.

Laura: You're the one who's making yourself vulnerable in that situation. You're risking being real with someone. I think I've felt the same thing when I've tried to talk to a man and felt his reluctance to listen, to be open, to give up power. It's a power issue.

Barbara: The Civil Rights movement was a dialogue—an appeal to the humanity of white people to treat Black people as human. So you ask what happens when you talk and talk and no one listens? Total anger, total bitterness, and a politics that is making no effort to make connections. What happened with the Black Power movement was the cutting off of that dialogue.

It is counter to what feminism is about to cut off the dialogue. As Black feminists we are in contact with white women whether we want to be or not and as feminists we have a commitment to women. Inherent in Black feminist ideology and practice is the commitment to make links. Not out of sappy liberalism but out of reality.

Laura: When you talked about the history of the Black feminist movement in Boston, you mentioned that there was a realization that Black feminist politics and the politics of white feminists were different, even if there were coalitions around issues of extreme importance to both, like abortion. So much of the way you define Black feminism, particularly the commitment to a spiritual visionary dialogue and making connections between race, sex, and class, describes the feminism that I, as a white woman, want to practice. Can you talk some more about what you think some of the differences are?

Barbara: By definition, white feminism is not informed by a deep racial consciousness. Maybe that's obvious. But Black feminists were thinking and working on that level that white women even now have not really dealt with in a substantial way. We were practicing both racial and sexual politics not to mention increasingly anti-capitalist politics and politics that were pro-lesbian.

There is also the fact that we are not doctrinaire. . . . [T]here is no Black feminist philosopher we can read who can tell us what to do at this time. Anything we do is informed by our identity. "Identity politics" is really a very substantial concept for what we practice. In other words we practice a politics that mesh with our real physical identities.

It is also a fact that as Third World women we have a capacity to deal with other Third World women around issues of sexual politics that white women do not have. It is not necessarily "these women are racist and can't deal with Third World women." We walk into a room and there is a level of trust. We have the capacity to make our politics real to our sisters. Now that's a substantial difference. But I will say this: I think it is something white women can learn.

I've been thinking about what Black women know that white women could learn that would make what we're trying to do more viable. As a Black child I was experiencing things—as a three year old, a five year old—that white people might never have to face. I mean Black children everywhere have had to experience real bodily fear, fear for their lives that some white people have never had to experience. But white women, all women, have experienced that fear whether they conceptualize it that way or not: Violence against women, rape, murder, battering—they're real.

Laura: I think that what needs to be learned is not only our different histories as Black and white women, but also a capacity for feeling—I always get back to this. And a capacity for not being afraid.

Interview with Virginia Eubanks

Virginia Eubanks: One of the things about your life and your tradition that really resonates with me is that we are both from Southern families, but we were raised elsewhere in the North. What role do you think the American South or Southern identity has played in your life, in your work, in the way you think about things?

Barbara Smith: When I talk about the value of having been raised by Southerners, I am talking about traditional Black culture. I think that, because so much of African American history has been sited in the South, you just have a very different kind of take on how the world works and what the United States is all about. My upbringing was not unique, of course. Many, many African Americans in this country have Southern roots. My family was part of the first Great Migration following World War I. When I started reading African American literature—Alice Walker, Richard Wright—I found so many things that were completely familiar to me, because of having been raised by the people I was raised by.

Virginia: I feel like your methods of organizing come out of a Southern tradition, as well. This tradition of starting in terms of people's actual material conditions and needs, of a politics of home. I see a resonance between your political work and that style of organizing, which tends to be much less doctrinaire and much more based in peoples' lived, material experience.

Barbara: Indeed. What do we need to do to stay alive? How can we help other people to stay alive? How can we help other people to have some power and control over their life? How can we help everyone to realize and fulfill their gifts and their destiny? I really like the idea that I've been influenced in that way, but I always say that the Civil Rights movement was the bedrock for me, and what I saw there has stayed with me until this day.

Virginia: So much of culture in the South has been influenced by Black culture, so it's a reciprocal relationship. It's partially Southern culture and partially the

South's confrontation with the Civil Rights movement that bred a movement culture that is different from the Northeast or the West.

Barbara: You are making me think about this wonderful group of Southern lesbians—Minnie Bruce Pratt, Mab Seagrest, Cris South—they had a Southern feminist literary magazine called *Feminary*. I made real links with them, and I would visit them in Durham, North Carolina. There was something about their vision and values that very nicely matched the values of Black feminists. They struggled very significantly with racism, and did not always succeed. They tried to be racially inclusive, and did not always succeed. But at least it was on the table. They had grown up in segregation and were making a real commitment to not live the way their forefathers and foremothers had lived. That's different from the Northeastern perspective of, "Oh, we were never racist anyway." [laughs]

Virginia: There's a kind of intimacy to interracial work in the South that's different than interracial work elsewhere in the United States.

Barbara: Talking about Black people's options when I was growing up, they used to say, "In the South you can get as close as you want, just don't get too big; in the North, you can get as big as you want, just don't get too close." In the North, you might have opportunities, you might have a big job, but you were definitely not going to be intimately involved with white people. In the South, people shared land, but there weren't going to be any Black people running the show.

Virginia: Intimacy is not necessarily a good thing! Most women who are murdered are murdered by their intimate partners. Intimacy is not necessarily safe, particularly for people who lack power. But there can be a willingness to be real in that context that is different.

Unfinished Business

In a special themed issue of Souls *devoted to Black feminism, the late Manning Marable moderated presentations from speakers at an invited symposium who discussed the intersection of political activism and African American studies. Smith's essay, "Establishing Black Feminism," considers where and how Black feminism has been institutionalized and where it has not. The 1991 advertisement sponsored by African American Women in Defense of Ourselves marked a national Black feminist response to the treatment of Anita Hill, an African American attorney and academic who accused Clarence Thomas, Black conservative Supreme Court Justice nominee, of sexual harassment. The incident helped define the contemporary debate on sexual harassment. Kimberlé Williams Crenshaw's 2011 article points out that Black women are "still in defense of ourselves," identifying new modes of attack on Black womanhood and the continued need to bring principled analysis and resistance to the intersection of racism and sexism.*

"Establishing Black Feminism"

Barbara Smith (2000)[6]

The primary question I want to examine is how effective Black women have been in establishing Black feminism. The answer depends on where one looks. Black feminism has probably been most successful in its impact on the academy, in opening a space for courses, research, and publications about Black women. Although Black women's studies continues to be challenged by racism, misogyny, and general disrespect, scholarship in the field has flourished in the decades since *Home Girls* was published.

Not only is it possible to teach both graduate and undergraduate courses focusing on Black and other women of color, but it is also possible to write dissertations in a variety of disciplines that focus on Black women. Academic conferences about Black and other women of color regularly occur all over the country, and sessions about Black women are also presented at annual meetings of professional organizations. Hundreds if not thousands of books have been published that document Black women's experience using the methodologies of history, the social sciences, and psychology. In the academy, at least, Black women are not nearly as invisible as we were. It is important to keep in mind, however, that discrimination continues to affect Black women academics' salaries, opportunities for promotion, and daily working conditions.

When we search for Black feminism outside the academy and ask how successful have we been in building a visible Black feminist movement, the answer is not as clear. . . . In 1983 the feminist movement as a whole was still vital and widespread. Although the media loved to announce that feminism was dead, they had not yet concocted the 1990s myth of a "postfeminist" era in which all women's demands have supposedly been met and an organized movement is irrelevant. Reaganism was only a few years old, and it had not yet, in collaboration with an ever more powerful right wing, turned back the clock to eradicate many of the gains that had been made in the 1960s and 1970s toward racial, sexual, and economic justice. Now, much as in the beginning of this century, the end of the twentieth century is a time of lynchings, whether motivated by racism as in Jasper, Texas; by homophobia as in Laramie, Wyoming; by misogyny as in Yosemite, California; or by a lethal mix of hatreds as in Oklahoma City and Littleton, Colorado. . . .

There are specific factors that make Black feminist organizing even more difficult to accomplish than activism focused on other political concerns. Raising issues of oppression within already oppressed communities is as likely to be met

---

[6] Reprint of the preface for the second edition of Barbara Smith, ed., *Home Girls: A Black Feminist Anthology* (New Brunswick, NJ: Rutgers University Press, 1983, 2000), pp. xiii–xvii. Smith read excerpts from this preface at the Black Feminism Symposium.

with attacks and ostracism as with comprehension and readiness to change. To this day most Black women are unwilling to jeopardize their racial credibility (as defined by Black men) to address the reality of sexism. Even fewer are willing to bring up homophobia and heterosexism, which are of course inextricably linked to gender oppression.

Black feminist author Jill Nelson pointedly challenges the Black community's reluctance to deal with sexual politics in her book *Straight, No Chaser: How I Became a Grown-up Black Woman*. She writes:

> As a group, Black men and, heartbreakingly, many Black women, refuse to acknowledge and confront violence toward women, or, truth be told, any other issue that specifically affects Black women. To be concerned with any gender issue is, by and large, still dismissed as a "white woman's thing," as if Black men in America, or anywhere else in the world, for that matter, have managed to avoid the contempt for women that is a fundamental element of living in a patriarchy. Even when lip service is given to sexism as a valid concern, it is at best a secondary issue. First and foremost is racism and the ways in which it impacts Black men. It is the naïve belief that once racism is eradicated, sexism, and its unnatural outgrowth, violence toward women, will miraculously melt away, as if the abuse of women is solely an outgrowth of racism and racial oppression.[7]

. . . Both Black men and women have used the term "endangered species" to describe Black men because of the verifiable rise in racism over the last two decades; yet despite simultaneous attacks on women, including Black women who are also subjected to racism, Black women are often portrayed as being virtually exempt from oppression and much better off than their male counterparts. It is mistaken to view Black feminism as Black "male bashing" or as a battle between Black women and men for victim status. . . .

Twenty years ago I would have expected there to be at least a handful of nationally visible Black feminist organizations and institutions by now. The cutbacks, right-wing repression, and virulent racism of this period have been devastating for the growth of our movement, but we must also look at our own practice. What if more of us had decided to build multi-issued grassroots organizations in our own communities that dealt with Black women's basic survival issues and at the same time did not back away from raising issues of sexual politics?

Some of the things I think of today as Black feminist issues are universal access to quality health care; universal accessibility for people with disabilities;

---

[7] Jill Nelson, *Straight, No Chaser: How I Became a Grown-up Black Woman* (New York: G. P. Putnam's Sons, 1997), 156.

quality public education for all; a humane and non-punitive system of support for poor women and children, i.e., genuine welfare reform; job training and placement in real jobs that have a future; decent, affordable housing; and the eradication of violence of all kinds including police brutality. Of course, violence against women; reproductive freedom; equal employment opportunity; and lesbian, gay, bisexual, and transgender liberation still belong on any Black feminist agenda.

"Twenty years ago I would have expected there to be at least a handful of nationally visible Black feminist organizations and institutions by now. The cutbacks, right-wing repression, and virulent racism of this period have been devastating for the growth of our movement, but we must also look at our own practice. What if more of us had decided to build multi-issued grassroots organizations in our own communities that dealt with Black women's basic survival issues and at the same time did not back away from raising issues of sexual politics?"

Since the 1980s few groups have been willing to do the kind of Black feminist organizing that the Combahee River Collective took on in Boston in the 1970s, which was to carry out an antiracist, feminist *practice* with a radical, anti-cap-italist analysis. It is not surprising that Black feminism has seemed to be more successful in the more hospitable environment on campuses than on the streets of Black communities, where besides all the other challenges, we would also need to deal with the class difference among us.

To me Black feminism has always encompassed basic bread-and-butter issues that affect women of *all* economic groups. It is a mistake to characterize Black feminism as only relevant to middle-class, educated women, simply because Black women who are currently middle class have been committed to building the contemporary movement. From my own organizing experience I know that there are working-class and poor Black women who not only relate to the basic principles of Black feminism but who live them. I believe our movement will be very much stronger when we develop a variety of ways to bring Black feminism home to the Black communities from which it comes.[8]

In the present, women of color of all races, nationalities, and ethnicities are leaders in labor organizing, immigration struggles, dismantling the prison industrial complex, challenging environmental racism, sovereignty struggles, and

---

[8] A new anthology, *Still Lifting, Still Climbing: African American Women's Contemporary Activism*, edited by Kimberly Springer (New York: New York University Press, 1999), provides an excellent overview of Black women's activism since the Civil Rights era.

opposition to militarism and imperialism. Black feminists mobilized a remarkable national response to the Anita Hill–Clarence Thomas Senate Hearings in 1991. Naming their effort "African American Women in Defense of Ourselves," they gathered more than sixteen hundred signatures for an incisive statement that appeared in the *New York Times* and in a number of Black newspapers shortly after the hearings occurred.

"It is not surprising that Black feminism has seemed to be more successful in the more hospitable environment on campuses than on the streets of Black communities, where besides all the other challenges, we would also need to deal with the class difference among us."

Black feminists were centrally involved in organizing the highly successful Black Radical Congress (BRC), which took place in Chicago in June 1998. This gathering of two thousand activists marked the first time in the history of the African American liberation movement that Black feminist and Black lesbian, gay, bisexual, and transgender issues were on the agenda from the outset. A Black feminist caucus formed within the BRC before last June's meeting and is continuing its work. Black feminists have also been active in the international struggle to free the political prisoner Mumia Abu-Jamal, who is currently on death row in Pennsylvania. The Millions for Mumia mobilization, which took place in Philadelphia on April 24, 1999, included a huge Rainbow Flags for Mumia contingent. This effort marked a first for significant, planned participation by the lesbian, gay, bisexual, and transgender community in a militant antiracist campaign. . . . Twenty years ago we most likely would not have been present, let alone part of the leadership of these two events. The success of these coalitions and others also indicates that there are some Black men who work as committed allies to Black feminists.

Within the lesbian, gay, bisexual, and transgender movement itself, Black lesbian feminists have been extremely active in the Ad Hoc Committee for an Open Process, the grassroots group that has successfully questioned the undemocratic, corporate, and tokenistic tactics of the proposed gay millennium rally in Washington in 2000. . . .

Although the Black feminist movement is not where I envisioned it might be during those first exciting days, it is obvious that our work has made a difference. Radical political change most often happens by increments rather than through dramatically swift events. Indeed, dramatic changes are made possible by the daily, unpublicized work of countless activists working on the ground. . . .

"African American Women in Defense of Ourselves,"

Elsa Barkley Brown, Deborah K. King, and Barbara Ransby (1991)

Black feminists work in many contexts to end all systems of oppression. They also push back and educate when Black women are denigrated, which occurred on a national scale during the U.S. Senate hearings to appoint Clarence Thomas to the Supreme Court. Law professor Anita Hill's allegations of sexual harassment led to her vilification in the mainstream media which spurred the founding of African American Women in Defense of Ourselves, who published this now famous statement.

The statement ran as an advertisement in the Sunday, November 17, 1991 issue of the New York Times, *accompanied by 1603 signatures of Black women. It also appeared in six Black newspapers: the* Atlanta Inquirer, *the* Chicago Defender, *the* City Sun *(New York City), the* Spotlight *(Washington, D.C.), the* Los Angeles Sentinel, *and the* Sun-Reporter *(San Francisco). The cost of the ads—more than $50,000—was raised by Black women and their allies in a few short weeks after Anita Hill's testimony before the Senate Judiciary Committee on October 11, 1991.*

As women of African descent, we are deeply troubled by the recent nomination, confirmation and seating of Clarence Thomas as an Associate Justice of the U.S. Supreme Court. We know that the presence of Clarence Thomas on the Court will be continually used to divert attention from historic struggles for social justice through suggestions that the presence of a Black man on the Supreme Court constitutes an assurance that the rights of African Americans will be protected. Clarence Thomas' public record is ample evidence this will not be true. Further, the consolidation of a conservative majority on the Supreme Court seriously endangers the rights of all women, poor and working-class people and the elderly. The seating of Clarence Thomas is an affront not only to African American women and men, but to all people concerned with social justice.

We are particularly outraged by the racist and sexist treatment of Professor Anita Hill, an African American woman who was maligned and castigated for daring to speak publicly of her own experience of sexual abuse. The malicious defamation of Professor Hill insulted all women of African descent and sent a dangerous message to any woman who might contemplate a sexual harassment complaint. We speak here because we recognize that the media are now portraying the Black community as prepared to tolerate both the dismantling of affirmative action and the evil of sexual harassment in order to have any Black man on the Supreme Court. We want to make clear that the media have ignored or distorted many African American voices. We will not be silenced. Many have erroneously portrayed the allegations against Clarence Thomas as an issue of either gender or race. As women of African descent, we understand sexual harassment as both. We further understand that Clarence Thomas outrageously manipulated the legacy of lynching in order to shelter himself from Anita Hill's allegations. To deflect attention away from the reality of sexual abuse in African American women's lives, he trivialized and misrepresented this painful part of African American people's history. This country, which has a long legacy of racism and sexism, has never taken the sexual abuse of Black women seriously. Throughout U.S. history Black women have been sexually stereotyped as immoral, insatiable, perverse; the initiators in all sexual contacts—abusive or otherwise. The common assumption in legal proceedings as well as in the larger society has been that Black women cannot be raped or otherwise sexually abused. As Anita Hill's experience demonstrates, Black women who speak of these matters are not likely to be believed.

In 1991, we cannot tolerate this type of dismissal of any one Black woman's experience or this attack upon our collective character without protest, outrage, and resistance. As women of African descent, we express our vehement opposition to the policies represented by the placement of Clarence Thomas on the Supreme Court. The Bush administration, having obstructed the passage of Civil Rights legislation, impeded the extension of unemployment compensation, cut student aid, and dismantled social welfare programs, has continually demonstrated that it is not operating in our best interests. Nor is this appointee. We pledge ourselves to continue to speak out in defense of one another, in defense of the African American community and against those who are hostile to social justice no matter what color they are. No one will speak for us but ourselves.

Reprinted with permission of the authors.

"Black Women Still in Defense of Ourselves"
Kimberlé William Crenshaw (2011)

One of the lasting images of the Anita Hill/Clarence Thomas controversy was the photograph of the "Boxer rebellion," the all-female Congressional delegation marching up the steps to the Senate to demand that it investigate credible claims of sexual harassment. Outside this frame, and perhaps more compelling, are the stories of when each of these women realized that intolerably destructive dynamics of power were being normalized or even defended by colleagues, spouses, friends, and elected officials. Every woman who was prompted into action by Anita Hill has a moment like this. . . .

In the days following the hearings, the *New York Times* printed an op-ed by Orlando Patterson that speculated that Thomas may well have said the things Hill described but nonetheless justified Thomas's denial, arguing that Hill's complaints came out of the "white, upper-middle-class work world," whereas Thomas's behavior was really just courtship, if you looked at it from a "Southern working-class" and especially black perspective. Frustrated, three black feminists—Elsa Barkley Brown, Deborah King, and Barbara Ransby—gave birth to a manifesto that captured the rage of thousands of black women . . . called "African American Women in Defense of Ourselves" (AAWIDO).

That manifesto still stands among black feminists as one of the most poignant moments of our own truth-speaking against feminist and antiracist mobilizations that frequently ignored our very existence. In this episode, the histories of feminism and antiracism were put into opposition, rendering Anita Hill a raceless figure that could represent either the puritanical sexlessness of white feminism or the universal figure of female oppression. Within the African American community, arguments that sexual harassment was a product of white sexual discourse and that lynching symbolized the essential character of racist terror in effect erased black women from the picture.

But sexual harassment had been a common experience of black women's work life since they arrived in America, and it was black women plaintiffs who first comprehended that sexual abuse at work was discrimination. At the same time that the image of lynching came to capture racial terror, against which African Americans revolted, the unpunished rape and abuse of black women across the South was in fact the rallying point for advocates like Rosa Parks, who built an infrastructure that grounded the Civil Rights movement. Black women's intersectional experiences of racism and sexism have been a central but forgotten dynamic in the unfolding of feminist and antiracist agendas.

While this anniversary brings attention to many positive developments prompted by Anita Hill's courageous testimony, the trajectory of the issues raised by AAWIDO—indeed, even the historical memory that it occurred—is not nearly as robust. The conditions that prompted these black women to fashion their own podium twenty years ago have continued to generate new defensive imperatives. Cast as the "nappy-headed ho's" of the Imus debacle,* the simple-minded reverse racism of the Shirley Sherrod affair,† the irresponsible defaulters in the subprime scandal, the illegitimate stay-at-home moms in the welfare debate, the carriers of badly parented miscreants in crime reports, and the mules, enablers, and co-conspirators who make up the fastest growing casualties in America's endless war on drugs—black women still find themselves defending their name, often alone, sometimes against friends and usually against predictable foes.

The legacy of AAWIDO today is the attention it draws to the damaging convergence between the rhetorics of neoconservatism and a non-feminist antiracism. At the core of conservative social policy about race are old ideas that link racial inequality to non-traditional family formation and its attendant culture of poverty. Marginalized in this frame are structural and historical forces that limit the upward trajectory of scores of African Americans no matter how closely they stick to a male-centered script of family and individual responsibility. And while foundations, legislative committees, advocacy groups, and others rightly address crises facing black men and boys, their mistaken assumptions that such interventions will simply trickle down to black women and girls obscures the gendered structures of race, romance, and work that contribute to the inequalities that stretch across black communities nationwide.

Kimberlé Williams Crenshaw is professor of law at University of California–Los Angeles and Columbia University.

Interviews with Kimberly Springer, Virginia Eubanks, and Alethia Jones

Kimberly Springer: In your article in *Souls* in 2000, you lamented the lack of a national Black feminist organization. Do you still feel like there's a need for a national organization?

---

*On April 4, 2007, radio "shock jock" and host of MSNBC's Imus in the Morning, Don Imus, commented on the previous night's basketball game by referring to the Rutgers University women's basketball team as "nappy-headed hos" during his Imus in the Morning show, contrasting them to the "cute" (i.e., white) girls of Tennessee State. Based on public outcry, he was promptly fired. By December, Imus was back on the air distributed by ABC Radio and RFD-TV.

†In 2010 conservative blogger Andrew Breitbart released excerpts of a video of Shirley Sherrod, a Black woman and political appointee in the U.S. Department of Agriculture, giving a speech at a NAACP event where she appeared to justify discrimination against whites. She was condemned by the NAACP as racist and quickly fired. However, unedited video showed Sherrod making the opposite point and that Breitbart had engaged in deliberately misleading editing. The Obama administration apologized to Sherrod and offered her a new position in the government, which she declined.

Barbara: I don't keep up with movements, so I couldn't really tell you exactly what's going on with the women's movement as a whole. I do know that there's Ella's Daughters and the Crunk Feminist Collective—that's Brittney Cooper, Robin Boylorn, Susana Morris—which is primarily online. They are scholar-activists and very much immersed in hip hop. INCITE! and SisterSong are also other examples of women of color organizing that is national in scope around particular feminist issues. SisterSong organizes around women of color reproductive health and INCITE! around violence against women of color. I don't know if this is a time for national organizations or not. I think it's a time for organizing. Combahee never intended to be a national organization. But we wrote the statement and it circulated globally. We were a local organization whose words and work had national and international impact.

Virginia: People talk about the "mainstreaming" of feminism. Often what they mean is that those concepts, those approaches, those analyses, have become so much a part of our mainstream institutions that specifically feminist institutions are no longer needed. While working on this book I realized how many institutions supported the work you did in the 1970s and 1980s—feminist bookstores, women's presses, women's unions, women's schools, all of these kinds of things. Many of those institutions are gone now. The Women's Building here in Albany is one of only two left in the country, for example. There are only a handful of women's bookstores left. What does it mean to be doing feminist organizing now, without so many institutions? Do you think these institutions closed because they were no longer needed?

Barbara: I wouldn't say that these institutions are no longer needed, especially to the degree that we lost them. There's always a need for alternative options and alternative resources and institutions for those who are not necessarily well-served by the mainstream. If a bookstore—there were even women's restaurants!—health centers, if those kinds of things *can* be maintained, they are always of great value to those who are able to participate in them. But it's very, very hard in reactionary times to maintain these kinds of things.

Even nowadays, in the electoral political work I'm involved in, people will talk about the Comprehensive Employment and Training Act of 1973 (CETA), which was government funding for people to do useful work in communities. Places like women's centers would have positions funded by CETA, and that drove a lot. It was a source of funding that allowed people to do some things, like anti-poverty and community health work, which now would be a lot more difficult to fund, because there's no support for it.

Times have changed. The post–World War II era was an economic boom time in the United States, and that had positive impact on lots of different communities and people, not necessarily just the ruling class or the 1 percent. When I went to college, for example, it was possible to live an alternative lifestyle and also survive. Rents had not gone through the roof. If you lived collectively, you could actually function and spend time doing the work you found most important and most fulfilling. If you were fortunate enough to go to college, and many could during that period, you were not graduating with tens of thousands of dollars in student loans. Now, a student leaving college with my same demographic background would have emerged from college in *tens* of thousands of dollars of debt. I went to school on complete scholarship, had work-study jobs, and owed very, very little in loans, for both undergraduate and for graduate school. It was hard to pay them off, given that I wasn't at a full-time, professionally paid job, but there were more options. This filters down into whether you can actually start a women's bookstore or restaurant in today's economic and political climate. There were Black and other people of color institutions that were being built during that period, as well. Then we went through the Reagan era, and it was like, "All bets are off!" Everything dries up.

The publishing industry, in particular, went through a lot of changes during the time that I was involved. First there were the chain stores: Walden Books and B. Dalton. Then those transformed into the big box stores: Barnes and Noble and Borders. Now we see that there's only one of those left—Barnes and Noble.

I think it's a shame that we lost so many institutions. It would have been nice if we could have kept a third of them, or half of them, as opposed to having lost virtually all of them.

Virginia: There's a purpose that the institutions that have survived have served in holding open a space where movement can happen. What you do in the down times, when there isn't intense social movement organizing going on, is work and work and work to keep up with what *is* happening, to keep opening the space where that can happen, so when the movement energy comes, you're on the crest of that wave and you are situated on the inside, able to help people out. You can't do that after the fact.

Barbara: I've always said that, too.

You have to keep your organizing going and your activism going because you have to wait for that next big leap forward, that next great chance to make a difference. There are some of us who are lifers, who as long as we are alive, we are going to be working to make this a better society and a better world. That's something that makes activism and organizing for justice exciting—you don't know what's around the corner. You can't predict.

Alethia: How do you see Black feminism living today?

Barbara: Recently, I have seen a vibrant Black feminist response to the Republican "war on women." Black women in elected office who are a generation or two younger than me had a very different path, which was not necessarily in movements, but they have this consciousness around women's issues and they're fierce. I see them on MSNBC, these elected representatives from Ohio and Texas who are completely breaking down the importance of reproductive freedom and issues around violence against women. They have bedrock understandings of what these issues are and are in a position to mobilize around our rights, because they are elected officials. That's a very uplifting and positive manifestation.

"You have to keep your organizing going and your activism going because you have to wait for that next big leap forward, that next great chance to make a difference.... That's something that makes activism and organizing for justice exciting—you don't know what's around the corner."

Recently, Roland Martin commented on his weekly show, *Washington Watch*, on Jay-Z's announcement that with the birth of his daughter he would no longer refer to black women as b****es. Martin said, "You should have come to this a lot sooner." He said, "Yes, all well and good, now you have a daughter, you don't think it's right to denigrate women." He just broke it down. And of course millions of people heard this Black man say, "You should have given up on this so much longer ago than when your beautiful wife had your beautiful, female baby." He was absolutely right, and he was building consciousness about how all women, and all Black women in particular, should be valued. It should not take the entrance into your life of your own child to make you think about that being the case. I loved that.

Alethia: Was Roland Martin having a Black feminist moment?

Barbara: Absolutely! And I think what's so compelling about it is that he is a man. So, a brother talking to a brother and saying, "Yeah, you may think this is impressive; I'm not impressed. Because you never should have had those kinds of attitudes and words coming out of your mouth."*

Kimberly: In the popular press there's a cyclical declaring that feminism is dead. More recently, there has also been a trend to talk about generational divisions. But it's mostly among white feminists; they don't really talk about Black feminists. Is there something about the way that the history of Black feminism is conveyed to Black women that might mitigate those kinds of generational schisms?

Barbara: There's an interesting thing that I've observed about white people

---

*In February 2012, CNN suspended Roland Martin indefinitely after the gay rights organization GLAAD argued that tweets he sent during the Super Bowl were homophobic. Martin subsequently apologized, saying, "I'm disheartened that my words would embolden prejudice," and met with GLAAD at their Los Angeles office. For a full chronicling of events and coverage in multiple outlets, see www.glaad.org/rolandsmartin/.

in relationship to generational stuff. What I saw during the 1960s was an age of rebellion and just really pushing the envelope and dispensing with all received traditions and knowledge. Everything was up for grabs, for critique and discussion.

One of the things that I experienced at that time was that my white age peers were rebelling against their families of origin. They became political radicals, they became revolutionaries, they became hippies and countercultural people in response to, and in rebellion against, what they experienced in their families of origin. I didn't get the sense that Black young people of the same age at that time were doing the same thing. We may have had disagreements with what we thought was important versus what they thought was important. But we did not see our families as being the problem.

"The people that I would say I'm rebelling against are those who are satisfied with the status quo, whatever their race, gender, sexual orientation."

For one thing, our families were not aligned with the power structure. So, when young white people in the 1960s looked at their families, they thought, "I have got to reject all of that!" I think that when Black people looked at their families, they saw units of struggle. They knew how hard it had been for their families to provide for them, to keep them safe, to do all the things that they did to get them to adulthood.

Most of the Black activists I know, women or men, lesbian or straight, it's not our families that we saw as the problem. The divides are around politics and class. The people that I would say I'm rebelling against are those who are satisfied with the status quo, whatever their race, gender, sexual orientation.

Those are the people that I have issues with, because I don't believe that the status quo is really serving most of the people in this country, and around the globe.

We make alliances with those with whom we share a political vision and commitments to humane action. That's who we make alliances with, and that's not based upon biology. What do you think?

Kimberly: I was wondering if I was romanticizing Black feminism. But it seems like different generations of Black feminists have been very good about passing the torch and about empowering younger generations to do that work. I just wanted a sort of confirmation of whether or not that was true.

Barbara: I think that's true. We come from a tradition that is born out of our history and our culture. Some people object to the slogan of the National Association of Colored Women, "Lifting as we climb," as elitist. I think it depends on how you look at it. Because to me, it's just simply saying, if you are lucky enough to have gotten a few little perks out of the system at incredible cost, you are supposed to pass it along.

Kimberly: The slogan isn't "Lifting once we've gotten there." [laughter]

Barbara: Exactly, exactly. To me, it's a slogan that says something about struggle. That you have a responsibility to try to spread it around; there is accountability. I think that's our tradition as Black feminists, and if we have been better at forming alliances and working with those who are younger than ourselves, it's part of that tradition.

Traditionally, and even now, there is a lot of respect for older Black people. There are people in Albany who will not call me Barbara, they call me Miss Barbara, no matter how many times I say, "You can call me Barbara!" I just did a story reading hour for elementary school kids at the public library on Monday, and I introduced myself as Miss Barbara, and there was Miss Lisa, and Mister Kenneth. Old fashioned, I'm old fashioned. [laughs]

Kimberly: Well, thank you Miss Barbara. [laughter]

4

Building Black Women's Studies

What I want to do . . . is lead everyone to examine *everything* that they have ever thought and believed about feminist culture, and to ask themselves how their thoughts connect to the reality of Black women's writing and lives. I want to encourage in white women, as a first step, a sane accountability to all the women who write and live on this soil. I want most of all for Black women and Black lesbians somehow not to be so alone. This last will require the most expansive of revolutions as well as many new words to tell us how to make this revolution real.

—Barbara Smith, "Black Women Writers and Feminism:
Toward a Black Feminist Criticism," in Juliette Bowles, ed.,
In the Memory and Spirit of Frances, Zora and Lorraine:
Essays and Interviews on Black Women and Writing

This chapter covers Barbara's efforts, in collaboration with many others, to create, validate, and institutionalize Black women's studies. The core belief behind this work was, and is, that Black women's lives are important, valuable, and worthy of careful study and theorizing. Smith's poetic, polemic declaration that "All the Women Are White, All the Blacks Are Men, But Some of Us Are Brave" didn't just explain the vital need for Black women's studies, it reflected the lessons of Smith's lived experience and the hopes she cherished through her struggles for social, political, and economic justice for all people.

From the outset, Smith was acutely aware of the mutually reinforcing, but fraught, connections between political movements, theoretical developments, and academic institutionalization. Black women's studies rejected the distinction between theory and practice, the separation of university departments from social movements, and the preference for "academically interesting" questions over life-saving ones.

This chapter captures key moments as Black feminism becomes institutionalized in higher education. It also traces some of the struggles and paradoxes of moving our four pillars—identity politics, coalition building, intersectionality, and multi-issue politics—into academia, not always an easy or comfortable fit. The dynamic, collaborative, concrete modes encouraged by Black women's studies have not always sat easily with mainstream academic models of truth, rigor, and objectivity. Identity politics challenges the idea that the best knowledge comes from a neutral, objective observer. Coalition building demands that scholars reach across disciplinary barriers to concentrate on real-world problems and issues rather than narrow professional specializations. Intersectionality requires the enormous intellectual sophistication needed to analyze social conditions on multiple levels simultaneously. Multi-issue politics reminds those inside the academy to recognize their role in fostering—or suppressing—progressive social change and their need to be accountable to those outside of universities.

Despite these challenges, Black women's studies has succeeded in both creating institutions dedicated to the study of Black women's lives and in challenging mainstream women's studies to recognize and correct its myopic focus on white, middle-class women. A cursory search will now reveal not just a handful of courses and anthologies in Black women's studies but a plethora of academic majors and minors, professional journals, conferences, centers, symposia, and graduate programs. Black women's studies, "more than a notion" in the 1970s, is thriving today.

The primary interview in this chapter is with friend and colleague, Beverly Guy-Sheftall, the founding director of the Women's Research and Resource Center and Anna Julia Cooper Professor of Women's Studies at Spelman College. She has authored, coauthored, or edited many generative texts within African American and women's studies, including *Sturdy Black Bridges: Visions of Black Women in Literature* (Doubleday, 1980), *Gender Talk: The Struggle for Women's Equality in African American Communities* (Random House, 2003), *I Am Your Sister: Collected and Unpublished Writings of Audre Lorde* (Oxford University Press, 2011), *Still Brave: The Evolution of Black Women's Studies* (The Feminist Press, 2009), and *Who Should Be First: Feminists Speak Out on the 2008 Presidential Campaign* (State University of New York Press, 2010).

More Than Academic

Black feminist activism and African American women's literature were both key drivers in the creation of Black women's studies as an academic discipline. The documents in this section track how scholars, writers, and organizers in the 1970s and 1980s identified key inaccuracies and omissions in mainstream knowledge and suggested techniques and strategies for producing research and scholarship that would save Black women's lives. "Doing Research on Black American Women" is an early attempt to guide students away from conventional scholarly approaches that often reinforced negative stereotypes rather than uncovering truth. This short memo is the earliest printed instance of the famous phrase "All the Women Are White, All the Blacks Are Men, But Some of Us Are Brave," which later became the title of the first collection explicitly dedicated to building Black women's studies.

An original introduction for that book, the essay "The Politics of Black Women's Studies," nicely captures the often-unacknowledged ties between social movements and scholarship and speaks to the intellectual, spiritual, and political task of pursuing scholarship tied to liberation. The fiction, poetry, and plays produced by African American women in the United States since the 1700s provided raw material for the early insights of Black women's studies. Powerful works such as Ann Petry's The Street, *Toni Morrison's* Sula, *Audre Lorde's* Between Ourselves, *and Ntozake Shange's* For Colored Girls Who Have Considered Suicide When the Rainbow Is Enuf *articulated inchoate ideas, analyses, experiences, and longings. In "'Beautiful, Needed, Mysterious'"—a review of Toni Morrison's* Sula *published in one of the leading African American theoretical, cultural, and political journals of the 1960s and 1970s,* Freedomways—*Smith celebrates Morrison's vivid prose, capturing why and how literature is fertile ground for cultivating a field of study based on the rich truths embedded in Black women's lives.*

"Doing Research on Black American Women, or; All the Women Are White, All the Blacks Are Men, But Some of Us Are Brave"
Barbara Smith (1975)

"You ask about 'preoccupations.' I am preoccupied with the spiritual survival, the survival *whole* of my people. But beyond that, I am committed to exploring the oppressions, the insanities, the loyalties, and the triumphs of black women. In *The Third Life of Grange Copeland*, ostensibly about a man and his son, it is the women and how they are treated that colors everything. In my new book *In Love & Trouble: Stories of Black Women*, thirteen women—mad, raging, loving, resentful, hateful, strong, ugly, weak, pitiful, and magnificent, try to live with the loyalty to black men that characterizes all of their lives. For me, black women are the most fascinating creations in the world."
—Alice Walker, *Interviews with Black Writers*,
ed. John O'Brien (New York: Liveright, 1973), 192

"Fascinating" as Black women are, there are as many unexplored questions about Black women's lives as there are people to ask them. Less is known about this group, whose identity encompasses membership in two oppressed castes, than is known about either of these castes separately. Black studies and research focuses almost exclusively on Black men and women's studies and research focuses almost entirely on white women. Black women, whose experience is unique, are seldom recognized as a particular social-cultural entity and are seldom thought to be important enough for serious scholarly consideration. This invisibility, however, means that the opportunities for creative research are infinite. Since there are no "experts" on Black women's lives (except those of us who live them), there is tremendous freedom to develop new ideas, to uncover new facts. . . .

Despite the fact that *everything* has yet to be verified and written, it is important to keep your topic manageable and specific. Instead of trying to get to the bottom of the myth of Black matriarchy, for example, why not investigate instead Black women's attitudes towards child-rearing or observe their actual child-rearing practices, as influenced perhaps by their class backgrounds. Another way to get at the matriarchy question might be to trace out the origins of the term "mama" as it is used about Black women on the street, in music and in sexual encounters. You might find out more about matriarchy by looking at portrayals of Black family life in poetry and fiction than you would in surveying thousands of statistics.

Imagination is the key. To do this kind of research you must look at what exists, find what is available to you and use it. Books by Black women authors are the richest written source, because in the creation of the work, we can assume that little has stood between the Black woman and the telling of her story. At least the distance between her truth and the end result is not as great as that between the truth of Black welfare mothers, for example, and the white male researcher who interprets and records it. Black women's literature can be approached in many more ways than as just pieces of written art. History, sociology, psychology, and economics are inherently available in these works.

Unfortunately, many of the most valuable works by Black women are out of print and therefore unavailable. (This unavailability and the policies and attitudes of publishers, reviewers, and readers that cause it would itself be a fine topic to research.) There is obviously a huge amount of work to be done and each person who attempts to do a part of it with sensitivity and insight is making a contribution to more than scholarship. You are working quite tangibly towards the freeing of all of our lives.

"The Politics of Black Women's Studies"
Gloria Hull and Barbara Smith (1982)

Merely to use the term "Black women's studies" is an act charged with political significance. At the very least, the combining of these words to name a discipline means taking the stance that Black women exist—and exist positively—a stance that is in direct opposition to most of what passes for culture and thought on the North American continent. To use the term and to act on it in a white-male world is an act of political courage.

Figure 4.1: Barbara Smith at the Berkshire Women's History Conference in 1978. This picture hangs in the Williston Library on the Mount Holyoke College campus with the following inscription: "Barbara Smith (1969): Writer, Scholar and Editor; a founder of Kitchen Table: Women of Color Press. Author of 'Toward a Black Feminist Criticism,' co-author of *Yours in Struggle: Three Feminist Perspectives on Anti-Semitism and Racism*, and [the] editor of *Home Girls: A Black Feminist Anthology*. Recipient of an Outstanding Women of Color Award in 1982." Reprinted with permission.

Like any politically disenfranchised group, Black women could not exist consciously until we began to name ourselves. The growth of Black women's studies is an essential aspect of that process of naming. The very fact that Black women's studies describes something that is really happening, a burgeoning field of study, indicates that there are political changes afoot which have made possible that growth. . . . The political position of Black women in America has been, in a single word, embattled. The extremity of our oppression has been determined by our very biological identity. The horrors we have faced historically and continue to face as Black women in a white-male dominated society have implications for every aspect of our lives, including what white men have termed "the life of the mind." That our oppression as Black women can take forms specifically aimed at discrediting our intellectual power is best illustrated through the words of a "classic" American writer.

In 1932 William Faulkner saw fit to include this sentence in a description of a painted sign in his novel *Light in August*. He wrote:

> But now and then a negro nursemaid with her white charges would loiter there and spell them [the letters on the sign] aloud *with that vacuous idiocy of her idle and illiterate kind*.[1] [Italics ours]

Faulkner's white-male assessment of Black female intellect and character, stated as a mere aside, has fundamental and painful implications for a consideration of the whole question of Black women's studies and the politics that shape its existence. Not only does his remark typify the extremely negative ways in which Afro-American women have been portrayed in literature, scholarship, and the popular media, but it also points to the destructive white-male habit of categorizing all who are not like themselves as their intellectual and moral inferiors. The fact that the works in which such oppressive images appear are nevertheless considered American "masterpieces" indicates the cultural-political value system in which Afro-American women have been forced to operate and which, when possible, they have actively opposed.

The politics of Black women's studies are totally connected to the politics of Black women's lives in this country. The opportunities for Black women to carry out autonomously defined investigations of self in a society which through racial, sexual, and class oppression systematically denies our existence have been by definition limited. As a major result of the historical realities which brought us enslaved to this continent, we have been kept separated in every way possible from recognized intellectual work. Our legacy as chattel, as sexual slaves as well as forced laborers, would adequately explain why most Black women are, to this day, far away from the centers of academic power and why Black women's studies

---

[1] William Faulkner, *Light in August* (New York: Modern Library, 1932), 53.

has just begun to surface in the latter part of the 1970s. What our multilayered oppression does not explain are the ways in which we have created and maintained our own intellectual traditions as Black women, without either the recognition or the support of white-male society.

The entry entitled "A Slave Woman Runs a Midnight School" in Gerda Lerner's *Black Women in White America: A Documentary History* embodies this creative, intellectual spirit, coupled with a practical ability to make something out of nothing.

> [In Natchez, Louisiana, there were] two schools taught by colored teachers. One of these was a slave woman who had taught a midnight school for a year. It was opened at eleven or twelve o'clock at night and closed at two o'clock a.m. . . . Milla Granson, the teacher, learned to read and write from the children of her indulgent master in her old Kentucky home. Her number of scholars was twelve at a time and when she had taught these to read and write she dismissed them, and again took her apostolic number and brought them up to the extent of her ability, until she had graduated hundreds. A number of them wrote their own passes and started for Canada.[2]

This document illuminates much about Black women educators and thinkers in America. Milla Granson learned to read and write through the exceptional indulgence of her white masters. She used her skills not to advance her own status, but to help her fellow slaves, and this under the most difficult circumstances. The act of a Black person teaching and sharing knowledge was viewed as naturally threatening to the power structure. The knowledge she conveyed had a politically and materially transforming function, that is, it empowered people to gain freedom.

Milla Granson and her pupils, like Black people throughout our history here, made the greatest sacrifices for the sake of learning. As opposed to "lowering" educational standards, we have had to create our own. In a totally antagonistic setting we have tried to keep our own visions clear and have passed on the most essential kind of knowledge, that which enabled us to survive. As Alice Walker writes of our artist-thinker foremothers:

> They dreamed dreams that no one knew—not even themselves, in any coherent fashion—and saw visions no one could understand. . . . They waited for a day when the unknown thing that was in them would be made known; but guessed, somehow in their darkness, that on the day of their revelation they would be long dead.[3]

---

[2]Laura S. Haviland, *A Woman's Life-Work, Labors and Experiences* (Chicago: Publishing Association of Friends, 1889; copyright 1881), 300–301; reprinted in Gerda Lerner, ed., *Black Women in White America: A Documentary History* (New York: Vintage, 1973), 32–33.

[3]Alice Walker, "In Search of Our Mother's Gardens," *Ms.* (May 1974): 64–70, 105.

The birth of Black women's studies is perhaps the day of revelation these women wished for. Again, this beginning is not unconnected to political events in the world outside university walls.

The inception of Black women's studies can be directly traced to three significant political movements of the twentieth century. These are the struggles for Black liberation and women's liberation, which themselves fostered the growth of Black and women's studies, and the more recent Black feminist movement, which is just beginning to show its strength. Black feminism has made a space for Black women's studies to exist and, through its commitment to all Black women, will provide the basis for its survival.

The history of all of these movements is unique, yet interconnected. The Black movements of the 1950s, '60s, and '70s brought about unprecedented social and political change, not only in the lives of Black people, but for all Americans. The early Women's Movement gained inspiration from the Black movement as well as an impetus to organize autonomously both as a result of the demands for all-Black organizations, and in response to sexual hierarchies in Black- and white-male political groupings. Black women were a part of that early Women's Movement, as were working-class women of all races. However, for many reasons—including the increasing involvement of single, middle-class white women (who often had the most time to devote to political work), the divisive campaigns of the white-male media, and the movement's serious inability to deal with racism—the Women's Movement became largely and apparently white.

The effect that this had upon the nascent field of women's studies was predictably disastrous. Women's studies courses, usually taught in universities, which could be considered elite institutions just by virtue of the populations they served, focused almost exclusively upon the lives of white women. Black studies, which was much too often male-dominated, also ignored Black women. . . .

Because of white women's racism and Black men's sexism, there was no room in either area for a serious consideration of the lives of Black women. And even when they have considered Black women, white women usually have not had the capacity to analyze racial politics and Black culture, and Black men have remained blind or resistant to the implications of sexual politics in Black women's lives.

Only a Black and feminist analysis can sufficiently comprehend the materials of Black women's studies and only a creative Black feminist perspective will enable the field to expand. A viable Black feminist movement will also lend its political strength to the development of Black women's studies courses, programs, and research, and to the funding they require. Black feminism's total commitment to the liberation of Black women and its recognition of Black women as valuable and complex human beings will provide the analysis and spirit for the most incisive work on Black women. Only a feminist, pro-woman perspective that acknowledges the reality of sexual oppression in the lives of Black women, as well as the oppression of race and class, will make Black women's studies the transformer of consciousness it needs to be.

Women's studies began as a radical response to feminists' realization that knowledge of ourselves has been deliberately kept from us by institutions of patriarchal "learning." Unfortunately, as women's studies has become both more institutionalized and at the same time more precarious within traditional academic structures, the radical life-changing vision of what women's studies can accomplish has constantly been diminished in exchange for acceptance, respectability, and the career advancement of individuals. This trend in women's studies is a trap that Black women's studies cannot afford to fall into. . . .

Black feminist studies . . .lead us to look at familiar materials in new and perhaps initially frightening ways, but ways that will reveal truths that will change the lives of living Black women, including our own. Black feminist issues—the real life issues of Black women—should be integral to our conceptions of subject matter, themes, and topics for research.

That politics has much to do with the practice of Black women's studies is perhaps most clearly illustrated by the lack of positive investigations of Black lesbianism in any area of current Black scholarship. The fact that a course in Black lesbian studies has, to our knowledge, yet to be taught has absolutely nothing to do with the "nonexistence" of Black lesbian experience and everything to do with fear and refusal to acknowledge that this experience does in fact exist.[4] Black woman-identified women have existed in our communities throughout our history, both in Africa and in America. That the subject of Black lesbianism and male homosexuality is greeted with fearful silence or verbalized homophobia results, of course, from the politics of institutionalized heterosexuality under patriarchy, that is, the politics of male domination. . . .

An accountable Black women's studies would value all Black women's experiences. Yet for a Black woman to teach a course on Black lesbians would probably, in most universities, spell career suicide, not to mention the personal and emotional repercussions she would inevitably face. . . . It is important for Black women teaching in the white-male academy always to realize the inherently contradictory and antagonistic nature of the conditions under which we do our work. These working conditions exist in a structure not only elitist and racist, but deeply misogynist. Often our position as Black women is dishearteningly tenuous within university walls: we are literally the last hired and the first fired. Despite popular myths about the advantages of being "double-tokens," our salaries, promotions, tenure, and general level of acceptance in the white-male "community of scholars" are all quite grim. The current backlash against affirmative action is also disastrous for all Black women workers, including college teachers.

As Black women we belong to two groups that have been defined as congenitally inferior in intellect, that is, Black people and women. . . . Our credibility as

---

[4] J. R. Roberts, *Black Lesbians: An Annotated Bibliography* (Tallahassee, FL: Naiad, 1981) contains over three hundred entries of books, periodicals, and articles by and about Black lesbians and provides ample material for developing a variety of courses.

autonomous beings and thinkers in the white-male-run intellectual establishment is constantly in question and rises and falls in direct proportion to the degree to which we continue to act and think like our Black female selves, rejecting the modes of bankrupt white-male Western thought. Intellectual "passing" is a dangerously limiting solution for Black women, a non-solution that makes us invisible women. It will also not give us the emotional and psychological clarity we need to do the feminist research in Black women's studies that will transform our own and our sisters' lives.

Black women scholars must maintain a constantly militant and critical stance toward the places where we must do our work. We must also begin to devise ways to break down our terrible isolation in the white-male academy and to form the kinds of support networks Black women have always formed to help each other survive. We need to find ways to create our own places—conferences, institutes, journals, and institutions—where we can be the Black women we are and gain respect for the amazing depth of perception that our identity brings.

To do the work involved in creating Black women's studies requires not only intellectual intensity, but the deepest courage. Ideally, this is passionate and committed research, writing, and teaching whose purpose is to question everything. Coldly "objective" scholarship that changes nothing is not what we strive for. "Objectivity" is itself an example of the reification of white-male thought. What could be less objective than the totally white-male studies which are still considered "knowledge"? Everything that human beings participate in is ultimately subjective and biased, and there is nothing inherently wrong with that. The bias of Black women's studies must consider as primary the knowledge that will save Black women's lives.

"'Beautiful, Needed, Mysterious': Review of *Sula* by Toni Morrison"
Barbara Smith (1974)

While I was reading *Sula* the second time, my grandmother, who was 87, died. In one way her death was expected, since she was old and ill, but in many other ways it was not. I have been made familiar with the reality of loss several times since my mother died when I was 9, but I have never grown used to it.

My grandmother's funeral was brief and restrained, except when a woman I did not know sang in a worn and quavering voice, "What a Friend We Have in Jesus." The song made me think of my grandmother herself, singing the same words and many others throughout my childhood. It brought back *Church* and how important it had once been to me simply because it was so vitally important to the women who brought me up. I wondered about my grandmother's faith and whether the heaven she had believed in so deeply was there for her. I hoped that it was and imagined all the women in my family, now gone, greeting her with joy in a secure realm where Black spirits dwell.

Reading *Sula* at a time when I was doing so much remembering was comforting and right, because Toni Morrison remembers and recreates our lives so extremely well. Among many other things, she knows about the matters of death and faith that had been puzzling me. She writes of the funeral of a child:

> As Reverend Deal moved into his sermon, the hands of the women unfolded like pairs of raven's wings and flew high above their hats in the air. They did not hear all of what he said; they heard the one word, or phrase, or inflection that was for them the connection between the event and themselves. For some it was the term "Sweet Jesus." And they saw the Lamb's eye and the truly innocent victim: themselves. They acknowledged the innocent child hiding in the corner of their hearts, holding a sugar-and-butter sandwich. That one. The one who lodged deep in their fat, thin, old, young skin, and was the one the world had hurt. Or they thought of their son newly killed and remembered his legs in short pants and wondered where the bullet went in. Or they remembered how dirty the room looked when their father left home and wondered if that is the way the slim, young Jew felt, he who for them was both son and lover and in whose downy face they could see the sugar-and-butter sandwiches and feel the oldest and most devastating pain there is: not the pain of childhood, but the remembrance of it. [Morrison 2004: 65]

Morrison is a virtuoso writer. The music and paintings she makes with words stun the reader's senses at the same time that they convince her of their totally natural rightness. She constantly achieves what critic Stephen Henderson calls the "mascon" image: "*a massive concentration of Black experiential energy* which powerfully affects the meaning of Black speech, Black song, and Black poetry."[5] These images are emblematic of the unique social-cultural heritage of Afro-American life and have deeply resonant associations for those who have experienced them first hand. Morrison's exquisite language and subject matter embody Black experience in a way rarely achieved by Black novelists, except for masters like [Zora Neale] Hurston and [Jean] Toomer.

As significant as her rootedness in Black life, is the fact that her perspective is undeniably feminine. As in her first novel, *The Bluest Eye*, central to the work is the relationship between young Black girls, in this case Sula and Nel who are both 12 in 1922. Although Nel comes from a home that is rigidly respectable and Sula from one that is permissively free, they mesh immediately because they are both lonely and both dreamers. Morrison explains:

> So when they met, first in those chocolate halls and next through the ropes of the swing, they felt the ease and comfort of old friends. Because each had discovered years before that they were neither white nor male, and that all

---

[5] Stephen Henderson, *Understanding New Black Poetry* (New York: Morrow, 1973), 44.

freedom and triumph was forbidden to them, they had set about creating something else to be. Their meeting was fortunate, for it let them use each other to grow on. [Morrison 2004: 52]

The girls share everything: games, hopes, fears and terrors until Nel marries Jude at age 17. Morrison explains that ". . . greater than her friendship [for Sula] was this new feeling of being needed by someone who saw her singly." If Nel needs to care for someone, her future husband needs very much to be cared for. His expectations succinctly define the traditional role of wife. Morrison writes:

The more he thought about marriage, the more attractive it became. Whatever his fortune, whatever the cut of his garment, there would always be the hem— the tuck and fold that hid his raveling edges; a someone sweet, industrious and loyal to shore him up. And in return he would shelter her, love her, grow old with her. . . . The two of them together would make one Jude. [Morrison 2004: 83]

The image of a woman as "hem," existing to complete a man to the exclusion of her own needs is chilling, but accurate in terms of many women's lives.

Nel chooses [a] conventional path of home and babies, while Sula leaves their small town for education and adventure. Ten years later she returns to raise havoc and inspire hatred in the Black people of the Bottom. Although Morrison says that she is "classically evil," I think that it is her unsettling nonconformity in a provincial place and time which makes her seem so wrong. Morrison explains that "she lived out her days exploring her own thoughts and emotions, giving them full reign, feeling no obligation to please anybody unless their pleasure pleased her." The reasons Morrison offers for Sula's numerous sexual encounters seem even closer to the source of her supposed wickedness.

In a way, her strangeness, her naiveté, her craving for the other half of her equation was the consequence of an idle imagination. Had she paints, or clay, or knew the discipline of the dance, or strings; had she anything to engage her tremendous curiosity and her gift for metaphor, she might have exchanged the restlessness and preoccupation with whim for an activity that provided her with all she yearned for. And like any artist with no art form, she became dangerous.

Sula is frightening because racial and sexual circumstance has determined that she will have no way of expressing her brilliant inner fire, yet she absolutely refuses to settle for the "colored woman's" lot of marriage, child-raising, labor and pain. I can verify the validity of Morrison's analysis. Having grown up in a family of talented women who worked as teachers in the segregated schools of the South and as domestics in the white kitchens of the North, I saw first hand the demoralizing effects of stymied intelligence and creativity. The people of the Bottom hate Sula with good reason because she is a living criticism of their dreadful lives of resignation.

To me, the only case of true wickedness is Sula's casually sleeping with Nel's husband, who then takes the opportunity to desert his wife and their three children. The betrayal of the act itself is surpassed by Sula's inability to comprehend why she might have left him alone in the name of friendship. She retorts to Nel's accusations: "I didn't kill him, I just fucked him. If we were such good friends, how come you couldn't get over it?" Her bizarre insensitivity is consistent with her character, but I find it nearly unbearable. Morrison very skillfully gives the sympathetic reader a "last straw" so that she too will share the town's hatred and fear.

When Sula dies at age 30, the community falls on evil times. Morrison implies that her abrasive presence served a definite cathartic purpose for a people with so few hopeful possibilities.

The novel ends with Nel's discovery some 25 years later that the gray ball that had hovered just outside her field of vision since Jude left was not despair for him, but instead regret for the loss of Sula. Morrison writes:

> "All that time, all that time, I thought I was missing Jude." And the loss pressed down on her chest and came up into her throat. "We was girls together," she said as though explaining something. "O Lord, Sula," she cried, "girl, girl, girlgirlgirl."

The link between Black women who share each other's lives is strong. Morrison knows *and* feels this. She has made a book for us that is beautiful, mysterious, and needed. I have only touched the surface. I loved it. Read it for yourself.

Interview with Beverly Guy-Sheftall

Beverly Guy-Sheftall: We met for the first time at those Modern Language Association [MLA] Status of Women in the Profession meetings. When I talk about the evolution of Black feminism, I talk about all of us who came out of English programs: not history, not sociology, but English.

Barbara Smith: Oh yes! English is the bomb as far as I'm concerned. Unlike the other disciplines, English literature had primary sources from the beginning. Other fields had to create primary sources and do original research, [but] we already had our primary documents, which was the writing of women. So we were a jump ahead. Certainly in those days, and even now, literary studies are the bedrock of any college curriculum. The MLA Commission on the Status of

Women was really a catalytic organization for starting women's studies in the United States. And I was the first *being* of color on the commission.

Beverly: Do you also think that those of us who went into English then were more progressive politically?

Barbara: I don't know that we all were. I would attribute the progressive perspectives of women who were academics at that time to the fact that they were doing it in the context of vibrant social and political movements. To come out as a PhD ready to teach these days, what do you have in the larger society that is indicating to you that struggle is important? History drives people's consciousness and creates what people think is possible.

Beverly: We were Civil Rights movement people.

Barbara: Exactly. Exactly. We had that consciousness whether we had gone into the women's movement or not. When I was growing up the coolest people on earth were the students who were just a few years older than I, who were down South in the belly of the beast and in very, very dangerous circumstances working for our freedom. Those were the people I looked up to.

Beverly: Academia is where Black women's studies is most institutionalized. What do you think accounts for the flowering of Black women's studies and the ways it has been embraced on lots of college campuses?

Barbara: You and Judy Gebre-Hewitt coming to visit me in the late 1970s and us finding each other—as we did through the Modern Language Association, through the National Women's Studies Association—that networking was extremely important.

One of the things that was true for me when I lived in Boston, from '72 through '81, is that there were a number of other young Black women who were able to find each other during that period. We started having these Black women's salons, as we called them. It was very alert, very innovative, and very courageous young Black women, most of whom were working on advanced degrees, who began to have dialogue about what might be possible in the realm of Black women's studies. I think of Helen Stewart, Claudia Tate, Nellie McKay, Andrea Rushing, Hortense Spillers, and Cheryl Gilkes. I can't remember all the names, unfortunately. People who became real pillars of building Black women's studies in their particular fields. We actually all were in one geographic location. When you look back at earlier Black women's history there was a, I think it was called, The Black Women's Intelligence Society or something.

Beverly: The Afric-American Female Intelligence Society of Boston [founded in Boston in 1832].

Barbara: Yes! There's a history of Black women coming together around our concerns and our issues in Boston. So we were just a part of the continuum. I think *But Some of Us Are Brave* was also a catalyst, as we intended it to be, because it was one of the first books that really said—Black women's studies exists and it is a legitimate academic pursuit. We had the articles, we had the syllabi, we had the beautiful photographs from the Library of Congress or the National Archives. I will never forget us doing that photographic research. In order to do it, Akasha Hull and I had to wade through all these racist "Negro photographs" [chuckles]. We were looking at some of the most scurrilous, racist stuff you could possibly look at as we tried to pull out these beautiful images of Black women.

Brave really was a catalyst. Then we had the presence of mind to do a grant to try to begin to institutionalize Black women's studies. I think of the deeply felt need of Black women in the academy to do work that was relevant to our existence, things that were of most concern to us! As years went on, we continued to network. There were other academic professional associations that began to have programming concerning Black women's studies. The Association of Black Women Historians, with Darlene Clark Hine. That was critical. And so was Rosalyn Terborg-Penn.

Beverly: And Sharon Harley.

Barbara: Yes, and Mary Helen Washington's anthologies which came out before *But Some of Us Are Brave*, those were extremely important. These were collections of short stories. I think the first one was *Black-Eyed Susans*. Then she did *Midnight Birds*. There was also a huge amount of creativity going on in the arts, some of it literary art, among Black women. This is also the period that Ntozake Shange's theatrical poem *For Colored Girls* came out. Michele Wallace's book, *Black Macho and the Myth of the Superwoman*. All around us there were guerrilla actions, some of which took the form of a piece of art, a dramatic performance, a theater piece, or a book, an article, a film. We were seeing more and more reflections of ourselves. The artistic realm cross-pollinated with the academic realm and the political realm.

Black feminist organizing built a political environment in which one could assert the importance of this work and not necessarily just lose everything— one's sanity, one's job, one's status, one's credibility. We were building a real-life context in which Black women could, if not be free, at least be free to express what we needed to express.

A few weeks ago I attended a symposium at the University of Alabama on Black women as public intellectuals. It's just so clear to me that we now have a third generation. We have the second generation, which is probably women in their forties, maybe even in their fifties, and then we have the generation of people who are either still in school or who have recently graduated. So it really has spread.

Beverly: And that generation, unlike us, has been much more impacted by the field of women's studies. These are women's studies undergraduate majors and minors and women who received PhDs in women's studies.

Barbara: Which, of course, we couldn't do!

Beverly: That means that Black women's studies will live on.

Barbara: It's institutionalized now. It used to surprise me, ten or fifteen or twenty years ago, when I would be on a campus and I would ask someone, "So what are you studying?" "Oh, I'm doing my dissertation on Black women's studies." Or I would ask, "What discipline are you in?" And they'd say, "Oh, gender studies, Black women's studies." It's just amazing. We really have been successful.

Beverly: Washington University is in the process of doing a faculty search in women and gender studies for a person who does Black feminist theory. That would have been unimaginable twenty years ago.

"That's why we love history and that's why we also love struggle because sometimes we can actually see that our commitments and effort have blossomed into what we wish them to be."

Barbara: At the University of Alabama, it isn't women's studies and ethnic and Black studies, it's one department, which is the Department of Gender and Race Studies. That *is* unique, particularly when you think of it as the place where Governor Wallace stood in the schoolhouse door [and famously declared, "Segregation now, segregation tomorrow, and segregation forever."]. How did we get from that to this? It's such a progressive configuration to have race and gender studies taught under one umbrella.

That's why we love history and that's why we also love struggle because sometimes we can actually see that our commitments and effort have blossomed into what we wish them to be.

Beverly: I am not sure that there is as much political organizing associated with Black women's studies [today]. I think that's what we have to keep vigilant about, making sure that it isn't only in the academy or our teaching courses and students getting graduate degrees. I hope this generation of Black women's studies people will be as involved in activism.

Barbara: I think that's a real question. But people are shaped by the historical period. So if you are living in a period of reality TV, who are our heroes these days? They are not necessarily people who are speaking out politically and working for justice. You're affected by what you think is valuable.

I see the Crunk Feminist Collective as in the historical continuum of our kind of work. My impression is that a lot of the women involved with Crunk feminism are younger Black women academics who are a part of the hip hop generation and who are also feminists. Because of the new ways of being in contact with each other technologically, they can communicate without necessarily being in the same place. My impression is that many of them are individually involved in political work but not necessarily the collective itself, like Combahee was.

Beverly: They [the younger generation] spend a lot of time on the computer as opposed to interaction or as opposed to organizing. I'm amazed. I'm a recent and reluctant Facebook person. You can sit there every night and if you add Twitter, Facebook, YouTube, you'd never leave your desk. Of course, the argument could be that you could organize online.

Barbara: Not exactly. Place-based organizing has a certain kind of impact that other kinds of organizing might not have. There's nothing that matches place-based organizing for really *figuring it out*. The bottom line of effective organizing is changing power relationships. Without place-based organizing, it is very hard to strategize around how to change our relationships, undermine vested-interest privilege, get to justice, if no one ever sits around a table or a room and is able to say, "Okay, these are the things that we know. These are the things that they're trying to put on us. These are the things that we find unacceptable. These are the resources we have. That's a person over there who I think is probably going to be able to help us." How do you ever have those conversations if you are not *with* someone in order to do that?

Beverly: I think Black women's studies flowered because these were friend-ships and relationships. People actually knew each other and spent time with each other in person.

Barbara: Everything's about relationships. That's what it means to be a human being. We're a part of that post–World War II generation, the baby boom. We were part of the Civil Rights generation, and having that kind of a background, that's what pushed us forward. We knew that we were not in school just so we could do for ourselves. We were very clear that we were fortunate. We were clear that people were oppressed, including ourselves. We were clear that we had respon-sibilities to push the movement and justice forward. It was not about being the hottest person in your field. No! We have work to do.

Beverly: And we weren't focused on tenure. We weren't even focused on job security.

Barbara: Right. I'm looking at [the] Audre [Lorde poster] on your wall. I heard Audre say so many times, "I am here. I'm a Black feminist lesbian mother warrior poet. I am here doing my work. Are you doing yours?" That's it, that's it.

There are people who are under the illusion that racism and white supremacy are just not so bad anymore. But those of us who can put together now with then, we understand that continuum and how much work we still have to do.

Beverly: One of the things that I remember from the recommendations from *But Some of Us Are Brave* was that we should form a Black feminist university. When I think about this space [the Women's Research and Resource Center at Spelman], which we call a radical Black feminist space, I see this space as having evolved as a result of the work in *Brave* and the work of Black feminists like you.

Barbara: That's a beautiful testament.

Beverly: We were not able to create very many spaces inside of colleges and universities, but this I think is one physical manifestation of the kinds of things that we wanted. One of the things that Black women's studies is doing now is becoming more global. I think we were very U.S. focused, even though some of the women who were involved with Combahee were not from the United States, or even all African American. If you think about the evolution of Black women's studies since 1982, there are more disciplines, not just humanities scholars, a global reach and a broader disciplinary span.

Barbara: We have a huge diaspora. It's very important we understand that this is global. In the context of Kitchen Table: Women of Color Press, we used to get correspondence from people all over the world. That was just phenomenal to think that our books had traveled that far and that people in other countries actually were moved by things that we were doing.

Beverly: We need a history of Black feminism. We don't really have a history of the evolution of Black feminism since the sixties. In addition to Kimberly Springer's work on Black feminist organizations [*Living for the Revolution*], we also need a broader history of Black feminism, which includes Black women's studies in the academy as well as the work that Faith Ringgold was doing in the feminist art movement.

Barbara: That would bring in the theater and the poetry, just everything. One of the people we haven't mentioned is Toni Cade Bambara, because her book, the anthology called *The Black Woman*, was really the first.

Beverly: We have an annual Toni Cade Bambara Conference, which is a way to keep her legacy alive. Toni Cade often doesn't get talked about in this narrative, because she didn't belong to any Black organizations. . . . I also want people to write their memoirs, people like you and Gloria [Akasha] Hull. What do you see as the future direction of Black women's studies?

Barbara: I would love to see it become further institutionalized. We need to have at least another women's studies major at a historically Black college.

Beverly: Morgan State University is working on an undergraduate program in women's studies. Howard University has a graduate certificate, but they don't have an undergraduate program. Howard would be the one that we would think of since it's the major research institution we have.

Barbara: There's now recognition that research about Black women and other women of color is academically credible and valid, and that it also is something that deserves publication. Most of the university presses and mainstream trade presses that do serious work understand that this is something that is of value and has a readership. And then there's a popular side. I keep thinking about Oprah. Has Oprah had impact on understandings about Black women's lives? Because she's the one Black woman that everybody knows.

Beverly: There are beginning to be some critical anthologies on Oprah finally;[*] it is a good thing that she will go under the scholarly microscope. There's more

---

[*]For example, Trystan T. Cotten and Kimberly Springer's *Stories of Oprah: The Oprahfication of American Culture* (Jackson: University Press of Mississippi, 2010).

popular culture scholarship in Black women's studies than was the case in the very, very beginning. Also more on quilts and more on Black women's crafts and folk culture. There is Black feminist science studies with Evelynn Hammonds's work, and lots of work on HIV/AIDS, like Cathy Cohen's. It's a very provocative, compelling field.

Barbara: We're probably in the mid-beginnings of that. Let's hope that fifty and one hundred years from now that there will be people doing Black women's studies research, teaching it, writing about it, and saying, "Well, that was back at the dawn of time when those women did it, but we still think it's valuable." I hope that it never gets swept under the rug or disappears. There are basic academic fields that everyone thinks you can't be educated without having access to most of them, Black women's studies belongs there. You can't really be an educated person without it.

"Irrevocable Acts": Navigating Dangerous Waters

There are dangers inherent in path-breaking work. Often pain, misunderstanding, and attack are the immediate rewards; accolades and acknowledgment occur, if ever, much later in the process. In her speech delivered at the 1978 Institute for the Arts and the Humanities (IAH) National Conference of Afro-American Writers at Howard University, Smith was joined by June Jordan, Sonia Sanchez, and Acklyn Lynch on a "Black Women Writers and Feminism" panel (full conference proceedings available in Bowles 1979). Smith shared a work of truly groundbreaking scholarship by reading from her essay, one of the first published pieces of Black feminist literary criticism, "Toward a Black Feminist Criticism," which was originally published in 1977 in the feminist journal Conditions: Two. *The essay—and her talk—was for her "the irrevocable act of being out in print, for the first time." The transcript of audience reactions that follows reveals the intense personal and professional risks that Barbara repeatedly exposed herself to in living her truths. Thirty-five years later, Barbara tells us that the dialogue that followed her speech is still painful to read.*

"Black Women Writers and Feminism: Toward a Black Feminist Criticism"
(Bowles 1979)

I operate in a context in which two words are always received positively. Those words are feminism and lesbianism and that is an assumption under which I will deliver my talk.

First I'd like to talk about the motivation for writing the kind of criticism that I write, which is Black feminist criticism. The motivation is primarily from my politics as, of course, a Black feminist. Black feminism means that I am or have been committed to both the Black and Women's Movement and the freedom struggles which they embody. I am also a radical as opposed to a liberal reformist. I am also an activist as opposed to an ivory tower intellectual. My activist credentials usually don't come up. You don't put them on a vitae but I have spent a huge amount of time doing political work from the time that I was a teenager. I think that's very important because I think it shows you the kind of literary work I am also trying to do.

The result of these commitments is a dynamic model of scholarship as opposed to the static model of scholarship. I always try to honor in my work and my life the Black female tradition out of which I come.

To answer the question, "What kind of scholarship or criticism is this?," the word that comes to my mind is "responsible," criticism having integrity and honesty; truth-telling as a major function for both fiction and the criticism of it. Another key word is "integrated." Thus Black feminist criticism is an integrated analysis just as the practice of Black feminism is an integrated politics. In the most basic terms, we see Black feminism as a politics which is anti-capitalist, anti-sexist, anti-heterosexist and of course, anti-racist, so you can see how it is an integrated analysis, and these are the things that inform the writing and the thinking I do.

One of the assumptions of women's studies is that it is non-hierarchical in the way that it is conveyed. The process is exceedingly important in that it is a collective way of learning, that every woman's experience is valid. I teach in a Black feminist manner. I see it as a very vital way to address reality and intellectual and political and spiritual questions. I am also committed to what I think of as the development of Black women's studies in this country. There is a huge amount of activity going on in this area—many courses, more every day, being taught; some things beginning to be written.

"The comparing and ranking of oppression is insupportable in any case, and it is something that I, and the Black feminists who I respect, never do."

My writing is based upon the inherently political nature of any written cultural expression. Its function is propaganda, whether that be to prop up patriarchy, capitalism and racism or more rightly to destroy these. In other words, I don't think that the situation of Black women writers is divorced from the political situation in which we live.

I think another thing that is very important to stress today is that sexual politics are as real in Black women's lives as racial politics, and are also as real as the politics of class. To deny this is to just deny facts. That's the first level of denial, just the denial of facts.

I think there has been, and probably still is, the assumption in the Black community that sexual oppression either does not exist for Black women, and, even more infuriatingly, that it is lightweight in comparison to racial oppression. The comparing and ranking of oppression is insupportable in any case, and it is something that I, and the Black feminists who I respect, never do.

You know, we are not about saying, "This is more important and if you don't believe this, you are benighted." It is a matter of saying, "Yeah, they really have got us by the neck here." We live in a capitalist patriarchy that is racist; we live in a heterosexist patriarchy which oppresses lesbians and gay men; and that's just facts.

[Measuring] how much pain a person is suffering, which is what the ranking of oppression is about, is really a meaningless undertaking. When you're dead, you're dead. The oppression of women of all colors and the very real violence and death which is the result of this oppression has been hidden, fragmented and individualized. In other words, the ways that Black women are brutalized and oppressed and killed are not the massive ways [in which] we have always been oppressed as Black people. If you think about the urban insurrections of the 1960s and the Civil Rights movement where, of course, white racist violence was visited upon people—those were very quantifiable kinds of oppression because on television you saw masses of Black people having their heads beaten. But the way that women are brutalized and killed [appears] individualized. If the accounts were given of this kind of violence every night on the evening news, you would begin to see that this kind of violence has the proportions of a war, a war against womankind.

Rape, incest, battering, pornography, and murder are, because of the Women's Movement, beginning to be understood as the average, common, and widespread political phenomena they actually are. They're beginning to be seen as politically significant manifestations of the political system of patriarchy that is male rule. I think it is important to make some kind of statement about the differences between the patriarchy of the white male ruling class which, of course, is a very small portion of white men on the planet, and the sexist and sometimes misogynistic practices of men who are not white.

In other words, you can be a sexist whether you are a member of the ruling class or not and this is very important to understand. We live under patriarchy and, as a subject people, have had that violent and bitter ideology inculcated into us just as we have been inculcated with other kinds of self-hatred and destructive ideas. So, I am not saying we invented sexism but I am trying to say that being Black does not excuse us in the practice of it.

The intersection of racial and sexual oppression as they affect Black women has yet to be looked at, acknowledged and struggled against, with the life and death intensity they require, by the Black community. The denial of this reality does not make it any less real, only more difficult to [address]. A dimension of this unwillingness to acknowledge what is really there . . .is the fact that the misogyny of Black men, the hatred of women and the consequent violence against them, has yet to be looked at in the Black community or most particularly, in its culture. The Richard Wrights, LeRoi Joneses, Ed Bullinses, and Ishmael Reeds who destroy Black women in their works are legion, and nobody dares mention how they, not us, are threatening the very fabric of Black life.

Feminism requires the changing of behavior, not just structures, and this is, of course, why I think it has been so threatening, not just to the Black community but to the world . . .it's not about going over there to the White House or to the Capitol and saying we want these rights, we want these laws changed. It's about that too, but even more essentially, it is about the changing of values, behaviors, and interactions—these are much more difficult to address than any piece of paper, any law on the book or any congressman or president. In other words, feminism does not just require political change in the world out there. It requires political change on the part of men and women.

Black feminist scholarship requires that not just Black women's lives be looked at, but that there be an entire re-evaluation of Black culture and thought. In other words, Black feminist literary criticism in particular would also have to re-evaluate Black male cultural expressions and rewrite history in this light.

I am going to read now from my essay, "Toward a Black Feminist Criticism," and it is dedicated to all my sisters, especially Beverly and Demita:

> I do not know where to begin. Long before I tried to write this I realized that I was attempting something unprecedented, something dangerous, merely by writing about Black women writers from a feminist perspective and about Black lesbian writers from any perspective at all. These things have not been done. Not by white male critics, expectedly. Not by Black male critics. Not by white women critics who think of themselves as feminists. And most crucially not by Black women critics, who, although they pay the most attention to Black women writers as a group, seldom use a consistent feminist analysis or write about Black lesbian literature.
>
> All segments of the literary world—whether establishment, progressive, Black, female, or lesbian—do not know, or at least act as if they do not know, that Black women writers and Black lesbian writers exist. The conditions that coalesce into the impossibilities of this essay have as much to do with politics as with the practice of literature.
>
> At the present time I feel that the politics of feminism have a direct relationship to the state of Black women's literature. A viable, autonomous Black feminist movement in this country would open up the space needed for the exploration of Black women's lives and the creation of consciously Black

woman-identified art . . .and I would add that redefinitions of the goals and strategies of the Black cultural and political movement would also contribute to the creation of that space. . . .

I think the fact that I've been invited to talk here today is a step in the direction that I am talking about. When I was called to speak here in January, I realized that it was the first time that I had been invited to come anywhere by the Black cultural community to do anything. . . . Black lesbians have existed during all of the Howard Black writers' conferences that there have been. The fact that they have not been mentioned, of course, does not necessarily mean that they are not here, and were not there. Of course, that's not just the history of the Howard writers' conferences. I use that as an example because that's where we're sitting at the present time, but we have existed throughout history.

The role that criticism plays in making a body of literature recognizable and real hardly needs to be explained here. The necessity for non-hostile and perceptive analysis of works written by persons outside the "mainstream" of white/male cultural rule has been proven by the Black cultural resurgence of the 1960s and 1970s and by the even more recent growth of feminist literary scholarship. For books to be real and remembered they have to be talked about. For books to be understood they must be examined in such a way that the basic intentions of the writers are at least considered.

Because of racism, Black literature has usually been viewed as a discrete subcategory of American literature, and there have been Black critics of Black literature who did much to keep it alive long before it caught the attention of whites. Before the advent of specifically feminist criticism in this decade, books by white women, on the other hand, were not clearly perceived as the cultural manifestation of an oppressed people.

It took the surfacing of the second wave of the North American feminist movement to expose the fact that these works contain a stunningly accurate record of the impact of patriarchal values and practice upon the lives of women, and more significantly, that literature by women provides essential insights into female experience. And speaking about the current situation of Black women writers, it is important to remember that the existence of a feminist movement was an essential precondition to the growth of feminist literature, criticism, and women's studies, which focused at the beginning almost entirely upon investigations of literature.

The fact that a parallel Black feminist movement has been much slower in evolving cannot help but have impact upon the situation of Black women writers and artists and explains in part why during this very same period we have been so ignored. There is no political movement to give power or support to those who want to examine Black women's experience through studying our history, literature, and culture. There is no political presence that demands a minimal level of consciousness and respect from those who write or talk about our lives.

Finally, there is not a developed body of Black feminist political theory whose assumptions could be used in the study of Black women's art. When Black women's books are dealt with at all, it is usually in the context of Black literature, which largely ignores the implications of sexual politics.

When white women look at Black women's works they are of course ill-equipped to deal with the subtleties of racial politics. A Black feminist approach to literature that embodies the realization that the politics of sex as well as the politics of race and class are crucially interlocking factors in the works of Black women writers is an absolute necessity. Until a Black feminist criticism exists we will not even know what these writers mean. . . . Not only are books by Black women misunderstood, they are destroyed in the process.

I am not going to read the section of the essay which follows this last point. What I did was just take a few examples from my files of ways that books by Black women have been talked about by white males, Black males and white women, all, of course in a very disturbing, derogatory fashion and the fact that these examples were so easily available to me, it's not like I had to go to the library or anything, I think indicates the difficult and embattled position we are in culturally and politically.

In a recent interview the notoriously misogynist writer Ishmael Reed comments in this way upon the low sales of his newest novel: "But the book only sold 8,000 copies. I don't mind giving out the figure: 8,000. Maybe if I was one of those young female Afro-American writers that are so hot now, I'd sell more. You know, fill my books with ghetto women who can do no wrong. . . . But come on, I think I could have sold 8,000 copies by myself."[6]

The politics of the situation of Black women are glaringly illuminated by this statement. Neither Reed nor his white male interviewer has the slightest compunction about attacking Black women in print. They need not fear widespread public denunciation since Reed's statement is in perfect agreement with the values of a society that hates Black people, women, and Black women.

Finally, the two of them feel free to base their actions on the premise that Black women are powerless to alter either their political or their cultural oppression and just to show you that this was not a fluke, this year in another Boston newspaper, Reed was interviewed again and he outdid himself in those comments. In a libelous attack on another Black woman, he called Margo Jefferson, who is an editor at *Newsweek*, a Creole, house feminist, you know, light-skinned, all of these things that one has so much to do with, I mean, so much control over— how you come out looking. And he was just very negative about her. He gave us

[6] John Domini, "Roots and Racism: An Interview with Ishmael Reed," *Boston Phoenix*, April 5, 1977, 20.

enlightening comments about history—that people have been fucking for 50,000 years without using dildos. I am not embarrassed to quote it, because I didn't say it, I just wanted you to know the kinds of things that are being put out in the name of righteousness.

A convincing case for Black feminist criticism can obviously be built solely upon the basis of the negativity of what already exists. It is far more gratifying, however, to demonstrate its necessity by showing how it can serve to reveal for the first time the profound subtleties of this particular body of literature.

Before suggesting how a Black feminist approach might be used to examine a specific work, I will outline some of the principles that I think a Black feminist critic could use. Beginning with a primary commitment to exploring how both sexual and racial politics and Black and female identity are inextricable elements in Black women's writings, she would also work from the assumption that Black women writers constitute an identifiable literary tradition. The breadth of her familiarity with these writers would have shown her that not only is theirs a verifiable historical tradition that parallels in time the tradition of Black men and white women writing in this country, but that thematically, stylistically, aesthetically, and conceptually Black women writers manifest common approaches to the act of creating literature as a direct result of the specific political, social, and economic experience they have been obliged to share. The way, for example, that Zora Neale Hurston, Margaret Walker, Toni Morrison, and Alice Walker incorporate the traditional Black female activities of rootworking, herbal medicine, conjure, and midwifery into the fabric of their stories is not mere coincidence, nor is their use of specifically Black female language to express their own and their characters' thoughts accidental. The use of Black women's language and cultural experience in books by Black women *about* Black women results in a miraculously rich coalescing of form and content and also takes their writing far beyond the confines of white/male literary structures. The Black feminist critic would find innumerable commonalities in works by Black women.

Another principle which grows out of the concept of a tradition and which would also help to strengthen this tradition would be for the critic to look first for precedents and insights in interpretation within the works of other Black women. In other words she would think and write out of her own identity and not try to graft the ideas or methodology of white/male literary thought upon the precious materials of Black women's art.

What I am trying to say here is that there is no need to prove that Black women writers are heavy by going to the Northrop Fryes, and whoever the rest of those people are, to try to show that. I think that we have enough material within our own frame of reference to be able to talk about ourselves.

Black feminist criticism would, by definition, be highly innovative, embodying the daring spirit of the works themselves. The Black feminist critic would be constantly aware of the political implications of her work and would assert the connections between it and the political situation of all Black women. Logically developed, Black feminist criticism would owe its existence to a Black feminist movement while at the same time contributing ideas that women in the movement could use.

Black feminist criticism applied to a particular work can overturn previous assumptions about it and expose for the first time its actual dimensions. At the "Lesbians and Literature" discussion at the 1976 Modern Language Association convention, Bertha Harris suggested that if in a woman writer's work a sentence refuses to do what it is supposed to do, if there are strong images of women and if there is a refusal to be linear, the result is innately lesbian literature. If you listen to those definitions, it also seems very familiar because it sounds a lot like what Black literature has always done.

As usual, I wanted to see if these ideas might be applied to the Black women writers that I know and quickly realized that many of their works were, in Harris's sense, lesbian. Not because women are "lovers," but because they are the central figures, are positively portrayed, and have pivotal relationships with one another. The form and language of these works are also nothing like what white patriarchal culture requires or expects.

I was particularly struck by the way in which Toni Morrison's novels *The Bluest Eye* and *Sula* could be explored from this new perspective.[7] In both works the relationships between girls and women are essential, yet at the same time physical sexuality is overtly expressed only between men and women. Despite the apparent heterosexuality of the female characters, I discovered in rereading *Sula* that it works as a lesbian novel not only because of the passionate friendship between Sula and Nel but because of Morrison's consistently critical stance toward the heterosexual institutions of male-female relationships, marriage, and the family. Consciously or not, Morrison's work poses both lesbian and feminist questions about Black women's autonomy and their impact upon each other's lives. . . .

Morrison is constantly critical of family and marriage. Sula is an outcast because of the fact that she doesn't conform. She doesn't do what she's supposed to do, which is to lead the conventional life of the town. . . . It is the fact that Sula has not been tamed or broken by the exigencies of heterosexual family life which most galls the others: "Among the weighty evidence piling up was the fact that Sula did not look her age. She was near thirty and, unlike them, had lost no teeth, suffered no bruises, developed no ring of fat at the waist or pocket at the back of her neck" (115).

In other words she is not a domestic serf, a woman run down by obligatory childbearing or a victim of battering. Sula also sleeps with the husbands of the town once and then discards them, needing them even less than her own mother did for sexual gratification and affection. The town reacts to her disavowal of

---

[7] Toni Morrison, *The Bluest Eye* (1970 reprint ed., New York: Pocket Books, 1972, 1976) and *Sula* (New York: Alfred A. Knopf, 1974).

patriarchal values by becoming fanatically serious about their own family obliga-
tions, as if in this way they might counteract Sula's radical criticism of their lives.

Sula's presence in her community functions much like the presence of lesbians
everywhere to expose the contradictions of supposedly "normal" life. The opening
paragraph of the essay "The Woman-Identified Woman" has amazing relevance
as an explanation of Sula's position and character in the novel. It asks:

> What is a lesbian? A lesbian is the rage of all women condensed to the point
> of explosion. She is the woman who, often beginning at an extremely early
> age, acts in accordance with her inner compulsion to be a more complete and
> freer human being than her society—perhaps then, but certainly later—cares
> to allow her. These needs and actions, over a period of years, bring her into
> painful conflict with people, situations, the accepted ways of thinking, feeling
> and behaving, until she is in a state of continual war with everything around
> her, and usually with herself. She may not be fully conscious of the political
> implications of what for her began as personal necessity, but on some level
> she has not been able to accept the limitations and oppression laid on her by
> the most basic role of her society—the female role.[8]

Well, the limitations of the *Black* female role are even greater in a racist
and sexist society, as is the amount of courage it takes to challenge them. It
is no wonder that the townspeople see Sula's independence as imminently
dangerous. . . . *Sula* is an exceedingly lesbian novel in the emotions expressed,
in the definition of female character, and in the way that the politics of heterosexuality are portrayed.

The very meaning of lesbianism is being expanded in literature, just as it is
being redefined through politics. The confusion that many readers have felt about
Sula may well have a lesbian explanation. If one sees Sula's inexplicable "evil"
and nonconformity as the evil of not being male-identified, many elements in the
novel become clear. The work might be clearer still if Morrison had approached
her subject with the consciousness that a lesbian relationship was at least a
possibility for her characters and a positive possibility.

Obviously Morrison did not intend the reader to perceive Sula and Nel's relationship as inherently lesbian. However, this lack of intention only shows the
way in which heterosexist assumptions can veil what may logically be expected
to occur in a work. What I have tried to do here is not to prove that Morrison
wrote something that she did not, but to point out how a Black feminist critical
perspective at least allows consideration of this level of the novel's meaning.

In her interview in *Conditions: One* Adrienne Rich talks about unconsummated

---

[8] New York Radicalesbians, "The Woman-Identified Woman," in *Lesbians Speak Out* (Oakland,
   CA: Women's Press Collective, 1974), 87.

relationships and the need to reevaluate the meaning of intense yet supposedly non-erotic connections between women. She asserts: "We need a lot more documentation about what actually happened: I think we can also imagine it, because we know it happened—we know it out of our own lives."[9]

Black women are still in the position of having to "imagine," discover, and verify Black lesbian literature because so little has been written from an avowedly lesbian perspective. The near nonexistence of Black lesbian literature which other Black lesbians and I so deeply feel has everything to do with the politics of our lives, the total suppression of identity that all Black women, lesbian or not, must face. This literary silence is again intensified by the unavailability of an autonomous Black feminist movement through which we could fight our oppression and also begin to name ourselves.

In a speech, "The Autonomy of Black Lesbian Women," Wilmette Brown comments upon the connection between our political reality and the literature we must invent:

> Because the isolation of Black lesbian women, given that we are superfreaks, given that our lesbianism defies both the sexual identity that capital gives us and the racial identity that capital gives us, the isolation of Black lesbian women from heterosexual Black women is very profound. Very profound. I have searched throughout Black history, Black literature, whatever, looking for some women that I could see were somehow lesbian. Now I know that in a certain sense they were all lesbian. But that was a very painful search.[10]

Heterosexual privilege is usually the only privilege that Black women have. None of us have racial or sexual privilege, almost none of us have class privilege; maintaining "straightness" is our last resort. Being out, particularly out in print, is the final renunciation of any claim to the crumbs of "tolerance" that non-threatening "ladylike" Black women are sometimes fed.

I am convinced that it is our lack of privilege and power in every other sphere that allows so few Black women to make the leap that many white women, particularly writers, have been able to make in this decade, not merely because they are white or have economic leverage, but because they have had the strength and support of a movement behind them. . . .

This essay for me is the act of being out in print, for the first time. I see it as an irrevocable act. . . . As Black lesbians we must be out not only in white society but in the Black community as well, which is at least as homophobic. . . . A community which has not confronted sexism, because a widespread Black feminist

---

[9] Elly Bulkin, "An Interview with Adrienne Rich: Part I," *Conditions: One* (April 1977): 62.

[10] Wilmette Brown, "The Autonomy of Black Lesbian Women," manuscript of speech delivered July 24, 1976, in Toronto, Canada, 7.

movement has not required it to, has likewise not been challenged to examine its heterosexism. Even at this moment I am not convinced that one can write explicitly as a Black lesbian and live to tell about it.

Yet there are a handful of Black women who have risked everything for truth. Audre Lorde, Pat Parker, and Ann Allen Shockley have at least broken ground in the vast wilderness of works that do not exist. Black feminist criticism will again have an essential role not only in creating a climate in which Black lesbian writers can survive, but in undertaking the total reassessment of Black literature and literary history needed to reveal the Black woman-identified women that Wilmette Brown and so many of us are looking for.

Just as I did not know where to start, I am not sure how to end. I feel that I have tried to say too much and at the same time, left too much unsaid. What I want this essay to do is lead everyone who reads it to examine *everything* that they have ever thought and believed about feminist culture and to ask themselves how their thoughts connect to the reality of Black women's writing and lives. I want to encourage in white women, as a first step, a sane accountability to all the women who write and live on this soil. I want most of all for Black women and Black lesbians somehow not to be so alone. This last will require the most expansive of revolutions as well as many new words to tell us how to make this revolution real. I finally want to express how much easier both my waking and my sleeping hours would be if there were one book in existence that would tell me something specific about my life. One book based in Black feminist and Black lesbian experience, fiction or non-fiction. Just one work to reflect the reality that I and the Black women whom I love are trying to create. When such a book exists then each of us will not only know better how to live, but how to dream.

"Black Women Writers and Feminism Question & Answer Session"
(Bowles 1979)

From the original: In what was probably the first[11] national discussion among blacks on issues of sexual politics as they relate to the writing produced by black women in the '70s, the participants on the IAH writers conference panel, "Black Women Writers and Feminism," responded to comments from the floor. . . .

—J. Bowles

Frances Welsing: We have a major challenge today to really understand the dynamics that produce the kind of discussion we heard this morning. The thing that I think is happening is that we're in some ways moving in the direction of

---

[11] *Black Scholar* devoted the May–June 1979 issue to "The Black Sexism Debate."

further alienation from one another, men from men and women from women. None of us, male or female, would be here were it not for 50 percent contribution from the man and 50 percent from the woman. [applause]

For me to love myself 100 percent, I have got to love and respect the contribution that has come from my mother. I don't care if my father was a dog, and he wasn't, but if he was, I would have to come to terms with what left him in that condition.

If we understand something about the dynamics of racism, we will understand that it necessitates the alienation of, not only one group from another, but it necessitates the alienation of the male from the female. [applause]

The thing that is on us, the thing that comes down, like right now, is that about 40 percent of our families are single parent families which means that the husband and the wife, because of the pressures that are on them, have been alienated from one another and children cannot grow up seeing Black men and Black women respect each other.

I think that the issue of homosexuality is a very important one. I am glad that the last sister [Barbara Smith] spoke and what I heard from her plea is: don't reject me, whatever form I'm in. I mean, that's all our pleas—don't reject me because of the texture of my hair, because of the color of my skin, because of my sexual orientation.

I am seeing, as a psychiatrist, what I call an epidemic in the direction of bisexuality and homosexuality within the male population and we're having a smaller epidemic in terms of females turning to one another for support because male-female relations have been so attacked and so alienated that you can't find friends unless you're relating to someone of the same sex.

Now, we have got to look at that in terms of what is happening right now and not just see it in a limited perspective of what is happening in one life, but looking at the dynamic down the road for three or four generations. If we endorse—and when I say this, please, anybody bisexual or homosexual do not take offense, I embrace you also, because you have established your position—but if we endorse homosexuality, then we have endorsed the death of our people. [applause]

I have been conducting a little struggle down in the Department of Welfare where the system of racism has left thousands of children up for grabs. Anybody can come and take them . . .and we are beginning to see a push where homosexuals are pleading, "We want to be able to adopt these children." And white male homosexuals say, "We want to be able to adopt Black male children."

Just speaking from the point of view of a Black woman, there are a couple of things that I think we have got to carry in our minds all the time: we are the mothers of the people on the planet. Black women brought forth everybody on the planet. Now, when we have that historic knowledge, nothing can really tear us down unless it's within our heads to be torn down. . . . The hand that rocks the cradle controls the nation. But what are . . .

June Jordan (moderator): Excuse me. I'm sorry, we only have fifteen minutes entirely; you have already taken eight of them. I'm sorry. I would just like to comment that I think the death of our people—[applause]—I think that the death of a people can be accomplished in many different ways. I haven't heard anybody here today talking against motherhood or talking against having children. What I have heard people talking about is about self-love and self-respect and if we cannot allow that . . .then I say we are already dead as a people.

I would like to take a couple more comments.

Woman in audience: Since there are not enough men, especially Black men, for everyone to have one, I'd like to ask the panel, what alternatives there are to either polygamy, sharing men, or lesbianism, having relationships with women?

Barbara Smith: I don't at all subscribe to the theory that the reason that our people become lesbians or homosexuals is because of a shortage of people of the opposite sex. I mean, that really in no way is a way of understanding the existence of lesbians and gay men throughout history.

You asked a question which I think I could answer about the future of relationships between Black men and Black women in this country. I think that the future will be very much a matter of whether the respect for relationships between Black men and women is not just maintained but is elevated. I think to pretend that there is not sexism in the Black community and misogyny, which means hatred of women, is just pretend, a lie.

That doesn't mean—I have the impression that my comments were misunderstood because of the reactions that I have seen in the audience, and I think there is no way that I can sit here and convince you that I am a Black freedom fighter, that I have a commitment to the entire Black community. I have no easy solutions for a situation that springs out of a political, social, cultural, and historical past.

June Jordan: I think it seems very clear from what sister Frances Welsing was saying—that Black people, Black men, Black women are engaging in many different forms of sexuality and I would suppose that would have to be decided on the basis of an individual, whether that is a positive or negative, whether that is something which leads to greater or lesser happiness, and I think—I want to remind you about something I said in my paper which is, I feel very uncomfortable about a discussion of sexuality in the context of a panel that is supposed to be centered on Black women writers and feminism.

I don't think that feminism is the same thing as sexuality, I don't see it that way. I wish we could grant that Black women writers and that feminism both have something enough so that we would let ourselves spend the morning focused on that, without going off. Okay?

Gayla Cook: (First part of question is not audible on tape) . . .Do you not feel it's equally important that Black women love themselves and determine their own destiny and also be heterosexual?

Smith: Oh, absolutely. Absolutely.

Cook: But why is it in your definition, because [Sula] is that way, she therefore must be lesbian?

Smith: I didn't say that. I never said that. What I was trying to talk about. . . . See, there's just too much, I think, to try to deal with here in the few minutes that we have and what I am referring to is a whole body of feminist and lesbian political theory and if you don't have that as a working framework, as a vocabulary, it's impossible to understand what I mean . . .

[Simultaneous conversation]

Clayton Riley: We've read your essay. We know what you're talking about . . .

Smith: I guess if you're familiar with the terminology, then I don't comprehend why these particular questions are being asked.

Jean Carey Bond (to Smith): In your definition of lesbianism, you seem to imply that lesbianism is, by definition, a vanguard—(Bond's remarks, from this point, are not entirely audible on tape. The thrust of her comment is to challenge the idea that lesbianism is a revolutionary act.)

Bernice Reagon: I would like to ask this question of June and Barbara: How do you respond to concerns when people talk about women beginning to talk together and study together . . .that activity is seen as being separate from the productivity and radicalness and progressiveness of Black people as a whole?

Jordan: When we as a people decided that we wanted to talk to ourselves and we wanted to eat by ourselves and we wanted to live by ourselves, white people said we were separatists. They called us all kinds of names and they tried to threaten scholarships that you otherwise might have held on campuses and so on, because you were an out-of your-mind-stoned-nationalist, and that was supposed to be bad and so on.

Well, now people are quite used to the idea of our loving each other, you know, and nobody thinks of that as any more threatening than it is. . . . I think the same kind of process can be expected to happen where women relating to each other is concerned. . . .

[T]he coming together of women [to talk and cooperate and help each other] in ways that have not previously been the case—that will probably be viewed as threatening by people who are not included in that. In other words, if any people . . .withdraw into themselves in order to gather strength and to know themselves better and other people view that in itself, *per se*, as threatening, then they probably should be threatened.

Clayton Riley: I really have to say I think you and Barbara have insulted the intelligence of everybody in this room by assuming that by asking questions we have threatened you. We are asking questions because people want to find things out. What happens is that some of us read Barbara's essay before we came here. We're not . . .(inaudible) . . .and I don't think anybody in this room has attempted to threaten anybody on the stage and your assumption that if people raise questions from the floor, it should be interpreted as an attempt to threaten . . .(inaudible).

Jordan: Clay, that's not what I said, and I'm sorry, but I don't think you were really listening carefully. I haven't said anybody has threatened anybody here at all.

(Inaudible conversation)

Smith: There are lots of reasons why I have the impression that I have, and that I still have it. The thing that made me think that perhaps the analysis was not understood is because what I was hearing is that lesbianism was not being conceived of as anything but a sexual preference choice. The basis of my article is an understanding of lesbianism and lesbianism/feminism, most particularly, as a political theory, a political fact and a political way of moving.

I wanted to say to the woman who asked a question about avant-gardism and Black lesbian/feminism: just as the weighing and comparing of oppressions is offensive to me, I also find vanguardism to be offensive, because it doesn't get anybody anywhere [to be] more revolutionary than thou. What I was trying to say is that if you are a Black lesbian feminist activist and anti-capitalist, anti-imperialist with consciousness that means that you have a lot of stuff going for you.

In other words, if you're a Black lesbian who does not take anti-racist stances, I mean, clearly that is not advancing our struggles. What I was merely trying to say is that an incorporation of an understanding of sexual politics is a revolutionary stance.

Interview with Beverly Guy-Sheftall

Beverly Guy-Sheftall: Speaking of attacks, at an Institute of the Black World conference, I was on a panel of Black feminists talking about *But Some of Us Are Brave*, and it was one of the most menacing experiences I've had. One of the first questions was, "Are you all lesbians?" And then we were just demonized. Pilloried!

Barbara Smith: I [had a similar experience when I] spoke at Howard at a National Black Writers Conference. I think I was invited by E. Ethelbert Miller to speak. It was the first panel on Black women's anything that they had ever had at the National Black Writers Conference, so when I got the call, I was honored. But one of the things I asked was, "Who is going to be on the panel? And can you invite another person to be on the panel who shares this perspective, that is looking at Black women's literature from a feminist perspective?" I mentioned Gloria—now Akasha—Hull. I think I mentioned Alice Walker, too. And they did not invite anyone else.

It was in the afternoon, the conference was running late, and I made a big mistake. I had not eaten enough for breakfast. So by the time we did our panel, not only was I perhaps a bit tired, I was really hungry. Hungry enough that what happened subsequently seemed to be more difficult to deal with. It was basically an attack.

I read excerpts from "Toward a Black Feminist Criticism." I also had written some specific remarks for a Black audience, because the piece had been written for *Conditions*, which was a primarily white lesbian feminist literary journal that was very anti-racist in its perspective. I wanted to say some specific things aimed at the Black community and Black writers. The first comment was from [Black psychiatrist] Dr. Frances Cress Welsing and she basically said, "I feel sorry for the sister. It's too bad that you're a lesbian, because homosexuality will be the death of the race." So that was where it began.

"We were able to assert that it was important to . . .build community, institutions, do research, publish and teach . . .and we did it with a spirit of joy and vitality! It did take a lot of courage, just like the book title says. It was more than a notion to assert that Black women's lives were valuable."

Audre was there, Cheryl Clarke was there. I think Akasha was there. My sister was there, I believe. A number of us had come because I thought if they are not going to have anybody on the panel, I'm at least going to have people who are supportive [in the audience]. The atmosphere was so hostile, so volatile. Nothing was said by *anyone* because it was *that* vicious. With Dr. Welsing's remarks—it was at Cramton, a very large auditorium, and it was full—people were off and running. And because I was so hungry, I actually felt weak. After it was over, I was devastated.

When I went to the back of the auditorium there was a Black male literary critic who wrote for mainstream publications like the *New York Times*. I was saying to him how horrible this experience had been, how devastating it was, how bad I felt. You know what he said to me? He said, "At least you weren't lynched." What could prompt a Black person to say to another Black person, "Well, at least you weren't lynched"?!

Beverly: Goodness gracious. Everywhere I go I say to young Black feminists how hard it was to be a Black feminist *in* the Black community at that point. It was unbelievable.

Barbara: It was. Yet we were able to assert that it was important to do, build community, institutions, do research, publish and teach, all the things that we did. And we did it with a spirit of joy and vitality! It did take a lot of courage, just like the book title says. It was more than a notion to assert that Black women's lives were valuable, and then beyond valuable, that they deserved the level of research; academic, intellectual scrutiny; and analysis that other people's lives got by default. We titled the book as we did because we really wanted to put that level of courage and struggle front and center.

Beverly: When Judy Gebre-Hewitt and I came to Emerson College [in Boston] in 1979 or 1980, you were the first person that we talked to. The Women's Center [at

Spelman] was just an idea, we weren't even really founded. In addition to talking about the center, we were interested in curriculum. You shared your syllabus with us, and also Alice Walker's Black Women Writers syllabus, which she had been teaching at Wellesley. That course was most associated with anything that we would think of as Black women's studies at that point.

Barbara: I don't think that there was anything else. Ora Williams, who was in literature as well, had done this bibliography of writing by Black women. That was one of the first resources we had. She got really attacked for having done that.* Now, we can't even imagine getting attacked for doing a bibliography. But that's really the way it was.

Beverly: Do you remember that faculty development workshop at Spelman Women's Center, for mostly Black women who work at HBCUs [historically Black colleges and universities]? Do you remember how the workshop broke apart, erupted, and descended into toxicity, just because we brought a bibliography that included a book on lesbianism? They asked if we were promoting lesbianism.

Barbara: We had a grant from the Fund for the Improvement of Post-Secondary Education [FIPSE] to do faculty development of Black women's studies on historically Black college and university campuses. That was a very bold move. I think that it was really Pat Bell-Scott who came up with that idea. In that period we wanted to figure out how we could use the publication of *Brave* to push forward and broaden the reach of Black women's studies. The first one was here [in Atlanta], right?

Beverly: Right. It was all faculty from Black colleges and I think all women, about twenty-five of them. What we thought was going to be a very supportive, wonderful environment to talk about Black women's studies with mostly Black women at historically Black colleges—I was stunned at the hostility. And it was around sexuality. When the material was passed out and there was that [reaction about lesbianism], we never were able to get them back.

But it was after that meeting that Pat and I started talking about *SAGE*, about starting a journal. I don't think that, since then, I have ever been in a space that was more hostile. Even when I've gone to workshops where there are racist white people and you are trying to talk about race. It was unbelievable.

---

*In her introduction to *A Bibliography of Works Written by American Black Women*, Ora Williams quotes some of the reactions of her colleagues toward her efforts to do research on Black women. She writes:

> Others have reacted negatively with such statements as, "I really don't think you are going to find very much written," "Have 'they' written anything that is any good?" "I wouldn't go overboard with this woman's lib thing." When discussions touched on the possibility of teaching a course in which emphasis would be on the literature by Black women, one response was, "Ha, ha. That will certainly be the most nothing course ever offered!" (Smith, 1982: 163)

The bibliography was originally published in the College Language Association Journal in 1972. It was expanded into a book-length version published in 1973 and then revised and expanded in 1978.

Barbara: By the time we held the second one at Wellesley, the dynamic had really turned around. The participants had clearly done some work and most of them were open to discussing the inclusion of Black lesbian experience in teaching Black women's studies.

I think we've made some strides. But we are still living in a time of great racism and great homophobic attacks, such as the student at Rutgers* who was driven to suicide because of, not just the homophobia of his roommate, but the moral idiocy of that roommate. If only he'd been assigned another roommate he would be alive. If only.

Beverly: The Women's Center has a LGBTQ [Lesbian, Gay, Bisexual, Transgender, Queer] project on Black college campuses, and as negative as they are, the suicides have given us a little window. Because Black people who normally would have just said, "Oh, who cares?," the suicides of those young gay people have been a wake-up call. It really says homophobia is real hate, like racism. That's been a very hard argument to make.

Barbara: Hate crimes are rampant. Youth suicides among LGBTQ young people are disproportionately high. That's something that people within movements have been aware of for some time.

Beverly: So here we are, this is the year 2010 and Spelman's still the only Black college with a women's studies major. Fortunately there are some Black colleges who are working on majors and having minors, but still no other Black colleges with a major.

Barbara: This is such a flagship. Who wouldn't want to have this depth of research, the writing and teaching, so that all of our students on these historically Black campuses could become enlightened? Why wouldn't you want to do that?

Truth Telling in the Academy

In "Racism and Women's Studies," Barbara delivered a keynote address at the very first annual conference of the National Women's Studies Association in 1979. Her comments go to that most sensitive of spots where the personal, political, and professional coincide. In an ongoing effort to upend assumptions that convey the presumed "place" of non-mainstream women, Barbara forged ahead by speaking unflinchingly and courageously to stimulate a more thoroughgoing approach to radical liberation.

---

*Barbara is referring to the death of Tyler Clementi, an eighteen-year-old student at Rutgers University who jumped to his death from the George Washington Bridge on September 22, 2010, after his college roommate, Dharun Ravi, used a webcam to spy on him while he was kissing a male friend. Ravi, who broadcast the webcam footage to other dorm residents, was convicted of harassment and sentenced to thirty days in prison.

"Racism and Women's Studies"
Barbara Smith (1980)

Although my proposed topic today is Black women's studies, I have decided to focus my remarks in a different way. Given that this is a gathering of predominately white women and given what has occurred during this conference, it makes much more sense to discuss the issue of racism: racism in women's studies and racism in the Women's Movement generally.

"Oh no," I can hear some of you groaning inwardly. "Not that again. That's all we've talked about since we got here." This of course is not true. If it had been all *we* had talked about since we got here, we might be at a point of radical transformation on the last day of this conference that we clearly are not. For those of you who are tired of hearing about racism, imagine how much more tired we are of constantly experiencing it, second by literal second, how much more exhausted we are to see it constantly in your eyes. The degree to which it is hard or uncomfortable for you to have the issue raised is the degree to which you know inside of yourselves that you aren't dealing with the issue, the degree to which you are hiding from the oppression that undermines Third World women's lives. I want to say right here that this is not a "guilt trip." It's a fact trip. The assessment of what's actually going on.

"Feminism is the political theory and practice that struggles to free *all* women: women of color, working-class women, poor women, disabled women, lesbians, old women, as well as white, economically privileged heterosexual women. Anything less than this vision of total freedom is not feminism, but merely female self-aggrandizement."

Why is racism being viewed and taken up as a pressing feminist issue at this time and why is it being talked about in the context of women's studies? As usual the impetus comes from the grassroots, activist Women's Movement. In my six years of being an avowed Black feminist I have seen much change in how white women take responsibility for their racism, particularly within the last year. The formation of CR [consciousness-raising]* groups to deal solely with this issue, study groups, community meetings and workshops, articles in our publications, letters in newspapers, and the beginning of real and equal conditions between Third World and white women are all phenomena that have begun to really happen and I feel confident that there will be no turning back.

---

*For more on consciousness-raising, see Sarachild (1978), Shreve (1990), and Morgen (2002). Also see the CR guidelines in Chapter 3.

The reason racism is a feminist issue is easily explained by the inherent definition of feminism. Feminism is the political theory and practice that struggles to free *all* women: women of color, working-class women, poor women, disabled women, lesbians, old women, as well as white, economically privileged heterosexual women. Anything less than this vision of total freedom is not feminism, but merely female self-aggrandizement.

Let me make it clear at this point before going any further something you must understand: white women don't work on racism to do a favor for someone else, to solely benefit Third World women. You have got to comprehend how racism distorts and lessens your own lives as white women, that racism affects your chances for survival too and that it is very definitely your issue. Until you understand this no fundamental change will come about.

Racism is being talked about in the context of women's studies because of it being raised in the Women's Movement generally, but also because women's studies is a context in which white and Third World women actually come together, a context that should be about studying and learning about all of our lives. I feel at this point it's not only about getting Third World women's materials into the curriculum, although this must be done. This has been happening and it's clear that racism still thrives, just as the inclusion of women's materials in a college curriculum does not prevent sexism from thriving. The stage we're at now is having to decide to change fundamental attitudes and behavior, the way people treat each other. In other words, we're at a stage of having to take some frightening risks.

"A major roadblock for women involved in women's studies to changing their individual racism and challenging it institutionally is the pernicious ideology of professionalism. . . . I always cringe when I hear *anyone* describe themselves as 'professional,' because what usually follows is an excuse for inaction, an excuse for ethical irresponsibility. It's a word and a concept we don't need because it is ultimately a way of dividing ourselves from others and escaping from reality."

I'm sure that many women here are telling themselves they aren't racist because they are capable of being civil to Black women, having been raised by their parents to be anything but. It's not about merely being polite: "I'm not racist because I do not snarl and snap at Black people." It's much more subtle than that. It's not white women's fault that they have been raised for the most part not knowing how to talk to Black women, not knowing how to look us in the eye and laugh *with* us. Racism and racist behavior is our white patriarchal legacy. What is your fault is making no serious effort to change old patterns of contempt. To look at how you still believe yourselves to be superior to Third World women and how you communicate these attitudes in blatant and subtle ways.

A major roadblock for women involved in women's studies to changing their individual racism and challenging it institutionally is the pernicious ideology of professionalism. The word "professionalism" covers such a multitude of sins. I always cringe when I hear *anyone* describe themselves as "professional," because what usually follows is an excuse for inaction, an excuse for ethical irresponsibility.

It's a word and a concept we don't need because it is ultimately a way of dividing ourselves from others and escaping from reality. I think the way to be "successful" is to do work with integrity and work that is good. Not to play cutthroat tricks and insist on being called "Doctor." When I got involved in women's studies six years ago and particularly during my three years as the first Third World woman on the Modern Language Association Commission on the Status of Women, I quickly began to recognize what I call women's studies or academic feminists. Women who teach, research, and publish about women but who are not involved in any way in making radical social and political change, women who are not involved in making the lives of living breathing women more viable. The grassroots/community Women's Movement has given women's studies its life. How do we relate to it? How do we bring our gifts and our educational privilege back to it? Do we realize also how very much there is to learn in doing this essential work? Ask yourself what the Women's Movement is working on in your town or city. Are you a part of it? Ask yourself what women are living in the worst conditions in your town and how does your work positively affect and directly touch their lives? If it doesn't, why not?

The question has been raised here whether this should be an activist association or an academic one. In many ways this is an immoral question, an immoral and false dichotomy. The answer lies in which emphasis and what kinds of work will lift oppression off of not only women but all oppressed people: poor and working-class people, people of color in this country and in the colonized Third World. If lifting this oppression is not a priority to you then it's problematic whether you are a part of the actual feminist movement.

There are two other roadblocks to our making feminism real which I'll mention briefly. First, there is Third World women's anti-feminism which I sometimes sense gets mixed up with opposition to white women's racism and is fueled by a history of justified distrust. To me racist white women cannot be said to be actually feminist, at least not in the way I think and feel about the word. Feminism in and of itself would be fine. The problems arise when we must define a responsible and radical feminism for ourselves and not assume that bourgeois female self-aggrandizement is all that feminism is and therefore attack feminism wholesale.

The other roadblock is homophobia, that is anti-lesbianism, an issue that both white and Third World women still have to deal with. Need I explicate in 1979 how enforced heterosexuality is the extreme manifestation of male domination and patriarchal rule and that women must not collude in the oppression of women who have chosen each other, that is, lesbians? I also wish I had time here to speak about the connections between the lesbian-feminist movement, being woman-identified, and the effective anti-racist work that is being done by many, though not all, lesbians.

In conclusion, I'll say that I don't consider my talk today to be in anyway conclusive or exhaustive. It has merely scratched the surface. I don't know exactly what's going on in your schools or in your lives. I can only talk about those qualities and skills that will help you to bring about change: integrity, awareness, courage, and redefining your own success.

I also feel that the Women's Movement will deal with racism in a way that it has not been dealt with before in any other movement—fundamentally, organically, and non-rhetorically. White women have a materially different relationship to the system of racism than white men. They get less out of it and often function as its pawns whether they recognize it or not. It is something that living under white male rule has imposed on us and overthrowing racism is the inherent work of feminism and by extension feminist studies.

Interview with Virginia Eubanks

Virginia Eubanks: In "Racism and Women's Studies," the speech you gave at the very first National Women's Studies Association (NWSA) Annual Conference in 1979, you say, "The question has been raised here whether this should be an activist association or an academic one. In many ways, this is an immoral question, an immoral and false dichotomy." Can you say a bit more about what you mean when you say that?

Barbara Smith: Why would we divide academic from activist feminism? It was activism that made it possible for women's studies to exist.

"It was activism that made it possible for women's studies to exist."

All of the oppression and injustices that faced women were front and center. So how could we say, "Oh, we only want to talk, write, and teach about what's happening, but if there's an opportunity to support the opening of a battered women's shelter in our town, we're not going to do a thing about it." That's immoral. You always have to have that mentality of, "How do my ideas and my understanding about these problems, how do we bring that to bear in real time, in real people's lives, who are facing them?" It's not just something that we read about.

Virginia: What was important about the link between grassroots and academic feminists in your experience?

Barbara: Well, the fact that everything made sense! It didn't feel so contradictory to be involved in teaching. During my early years, I would do Black feminism at night and teach Black women's literature in the morning. Everything was of a piece. The books I was discovering and loved, we talked about them in the Combahee River Collective. People read them, not because they were taking a course but because they were great books. There was real synergy, real coherency between the political organizing and the academic work. It was exciting. It was really exciting.

Virginia: So by keeping action and knowledge together, it made it easier to be whole?

Barbara: Well, that's what we say in the introduction to *But Some of Us Are Brave*, that the knowledge most worth having is the knowledge that will save Black women's lives. And we were perfectly serious about that.

Virginia: It's not just that connections to grassroots movements makes you a more effective force for social justice—I also think *not* having that connection makes you dumber. All the great concepts of women's studies: intersectionality, reproductive justice, environmental justice, prison abolition, all this stuff comes from frontline grassroots work.

Barbara: Right. [The real world] makes you really sharp. There's a tradition of course of intellectual-activists . . .it's not like we are the only people who ever did that. We were part of a tradition of people who were both deep thinkers and people who had to make change in their own times and in their own lives. There are people who are still doing it—they may not be the best known, but the combination is really important.

Virginia: I see the Combahee River Collective, and your own intellectual and political work from this period, as developing a very complex but very understandable system for doing analysis and action together—praxis—centered on four things: identity politics, intersectionality, multi-issue politics, and coalition building. Identity politics and intersectionality have been taken up very vigorously in women's studies. Yet, these other two ideas—multi-issue politics and coalition building—have not been taken up as successfully. Why do you think that intersectionality and identity politics have been taken up so successfully within the field, while this idea of multi-issue politics and coalition building has not been as successful?

Barbara: I think that's pretty obvious in the content of the categories. The two that people have not taken up are the ones that require action. With action sometimes comes sacrifice, putting yourself on the line. The two things that are not so popular are the ones that require actually getting your hands dirty, doing the work, and being in the trenches and working for change. Obviously, by focusing upon the simultaneity of oppressions and identity politics, you don't actually have to do any work with other humans to get to a point of transformation and change. You can talk about those things, and you can utilize those concepts in your activism. But the two others are dead up about organizing.

5

Building Kitchen Table Press

An early slogan of the women in print movement was "freedom of the press belongs to those who own the press." This is even truer for multiply disenfranchised women of color who have minimal access to power, including the power of media, except that which we wrest from an unwilling system. On the most basic level, Kitchen Table Press began because of our need for autonomy, our need to determine independently both the content and conditions of our work, and to control the words and images that are produced about us.

> —Barbara Smith, "A Press of Our Own" (1989)

Writing is crucial to movement building. Before the digital era of blogs, e-mail, Facebook, and Twitter, social networks circulated information by distributing books, journals, anthologies, pamphlets, fliers, and posters via independent bookstores, community centers, and conferences. Then and now, publishers play a critical role linking writers and audiences. They affect what stories are available to us and—as a result—help to define the horizons of our dreams.

Kitchen Table: Women of Color Press (KTP) was one of the first independent women of color presses in North America.[*] Cofounded by Barbara, Audre Lorde, Cherríe Moraga, Hattie Gossett, Myrna Bain, Mariana Roma-Carmona, Rosario Morales, Ana Oliveira, Alma Gómez, Helena Byard, Susan Yung, Rosie Alvarez, and Leota Lone Dog, it was a conscious effort to build an institution to fill critical gaps in the social, historical, creative, and intellectual apparatus of the Black and Third World feminist movements. The decision to create KTP in 1980 required an absolute devotion to finding, publishing, and selling the written works of women of color. The decision to publish the books they wanted to see represents a bold and daring move fraught with incredible risks, rewards, and sacrifices. As a women of color press, Kitchen Table cultivated alliances across race, ethnicity, and national origin. It was a crucial piece in a web of connections, bound by the printed word, which fueled and fostered movement building.

---

[*] Third Woman Press, founded by Norma Alarcón, began as a journal in 1979 and supports the writing of Chicanas, Latinas, and other women of color writers.

This chapter illustrates the rewards and perils of building institutions that challenge, and provide alternatives to, the status quo. In this case, Kitchen Table published only written work by and about women of color from around the world. As anti-assimilationist counterparts to the U.S. fixation with the "melting pot," alternative institutions like Kitchen Table create vibrant counterpublics, which don't simply withdraw from mainstream life but agitate and organize to push the boundaries of public discourse. As feminist political theorist Nancy Fraser argues (1997: 82), these counterinstitutions provide spaces where marginalized and exploited groups articulate their own unique contribution to U.S. life, culture, and politics, and in doing so, contribute to emancipatory social change.*

The writing of Alice Walker, Toni Morrison, and Zora Neale Hurston, virtually unknown in the 1970s and widely read and hailed as genius today, is a case in point. As Barbara writes in "Our Stories: Women of Color,"

> Increased interest in the writing of women of color did not come about because above-ground media and critics decided to single out a few best-selling authors. It resulted from a grassroots movement of women of color— including teachers, researchers and feminist activists—who have been working for years to discover, support and create artistic works that accurately reflect our experiences in a white-male dominated system. (p. 145, in this volume)

The hard work and dedication of innumerable feminist organizations and individuals who built alternative journals, scholarly institutions, bookstores, community schools, and presses paved the way for Black women's writing to enter the mainstream. Ironically, their success often also spelled their undoing. Once these small, underfunded, and understaffed alternative institutions established the market for women of color writing, they suddenly found themselves competing with larger mainstream presses and bookstores with devoted marketing budgets and large distribution networks that now targeted specialty ethnic markets.

The central interview in this chapter is with Matt Richardson, once a Kitchen Table: Women of Color Press staffer, now a professor and writer. Matt has been a feminist activist and writer for over twenty years and is the author of *The Queer Limit of Black Memory: Black Lesbian Literature and Irresolution* (Ohio State University Press, 2013). He has published extensively on Black sexualities, the U.S. Black Transgender experience, and feminist theory. The interview captures how building KTP forged links among women of color around the world, raised the visibility and viability of political work, and provided crucial public spaces for recording and validating the lives, struggles, and joys of feminists of color.

---

*For more on subaltern counterpublics, see Nancy Fraser, *Justice Interruptus*. She describes subaltern counterpublics as "parallel discursive arenas where members of subordinated social groups invent and circulate counterdiscourses, which in turn permit them to formulate oppositional interpretations of their identities, interests, and needs" (1997: 81).

Black in Print

The stories of women of color have always been written but are often maddeningly difficult to find. Novels, plays, and poetry collections were constantly in and out of print, creating an unpredictable situation that made it impossible to assign them in college courses, read for review, or even suggest to friends. "Black Women and Publishing" marks the first time the Modern Language Association (MLA), the foremost professional body devoted to promoting the study of literature, validated criticisms that had previously been ignored by the publishing industry. Barbara's appointment to the MLA Commission on the Status of Women in the Profession led to highly productive years for changing the institutional landscape and bringing intellectual attention to the lives of Black women and women of color. The longevity of Kitchen Table: Women of Color Press refuted the oft-repeated claim that writings by women of color had no audience. Published four years after KTP's founding, "Our Stories: Women of Color" documents the hunger for stories and themes that spoke to the energy and creativity of lives that refused to be limited by the oppressive structures determined to silence them.

"Black Women and Publishing"
Modern Language Association Commission on the Status of Women in the Profession (1976)

There are two reasons why the black woman writer is not taken as seriously as the black male writer. One is that she's a woman. Critics seem unusually ill-equipped to intelligently discuss and analyze the works of black women. Generally, they do not even make the attempt; they prefer, rather, to talk about the lives of black women writers, not about what they write. And, since black women writers are not—it would seem—very likeable—until recently they were the least willing worshipers of male supremacy—comments about them tend to be cruel.
—Alice Walker in *Interviews with Black Writers*,
ed. John O'Brien (New York: Liveright, 1973), 201

In a few words Alice Walker has described the embattled position of Black American women writers and by extension their relationship to the American publishing industry. The works of Black women writers, unlike those of white women and Black men some of the time and of white men all of the time, have never been considered to be popular or substantial, i.e., salable by trade publishers or in the case of academic publishers, intellectually significant. As shown by their lists, when a company defines Black writers or Black studies, they inevitably mean Black men and when they refer to women writers and women's studies they inevitably mean white women. The status of Black and Third World women in book and periodical publishing is as peripheral as their status in the society as a whole.

A complete analysis of the situation of non-white women in publishing, which would include consideration of the underrepresentation of those who work in publishing as well as the dearth of materials actually in print, would take a considerable amount of research. Some observations follow, however, which indicate issues that need to be discussed as well as areas in which changes might be made.

Textbooks and Anthologies

In textbook publishing, particularly literature anthologies, Black women are, for the most part, excluded. Because of the attitude already referred to that the category of women encompasses only white women, while the category of Blacks encompasses only Black males, Black women are more often than not completely left out of anthologies or are included in only token numbers. In American literature collections or collections that focus upon a particular genre, Black women are virtually invisible. . . . The lack of good anthologies devoted exclusively to Black and Third World women writers is also a problem, particularly for teaching purposes.

Scarcity of Titles

Very few titles by Black and Third World women are generally available. It was impossible to obtain figures, but it seems that there may well be as few as twenty titles by Black and Third World women brought out by all the major trade publishers in any given year. It is difficult to get a sense of how much is actually being produced since the few books that do come out are not widely promoted or reviewed. Books such as Toni Morrison's *The Bluest Eye* (Holt, Rinehart and Winston) remain comparatively unknown.

How Books Are Reviewed

When books by Black women are assigned at all, they are almost never given to another Black woman to review. The obvious order of preference, and this is true of all review assignments not just books concerning Black women, is white men, white women, and Black men. There have been several glaring examples of damaging and incongruous reviews of books by Black women in recent years, e.g., Sara Blackburn's review of Toni Morrison's *Sula* (Knopf) in *The New York Times Book Review*, 30 December 1973, and the superficial assessment of Gayl Jones' novel, *Corregidora* (Random House), last fall by a bevy of male journalists in mass circulation periodicals. When Black women's books are reviewed, they are far too often approached as sociological phenomena as opposed to serious works of literature or scholarship. This issue involves more than the debate over whether one has to be a member of the same group as an author to be qualified to review her or his book, although as Alice Walker states in the case of Black women "this argument seems convincing." It also has important bearing on the employment status of Black women writers in periodical publishing as well as their status as freelance writers, to whom many reviews are assigned.

Out of Print Titles/Reprints

The titles that manage to get published seem to go out of print faster and are less regularly available than books by other groups, including Black men. Persons who conduct courses in Black women writers literally do not know what they will be able to teach until the first week of class, when they find out from the bookstore which books are out of stock or out of print at that particular time. Examples of fine books that are either completely or frequently unobtainable are Zora Neale Hurston's *Their Eyes Were Watching God* (Fawcett), Ann Petry's *The Street* (Pyramid), and Toni Morrison's *The Bluest Eye* (Pocket Books).

Even more distressing than the disappearance of fairly contemporary works are the vast numbers of books that never go into paperback editions at all and are therefore completely unavailable for individual reading or classroom use. The titles in this category are legion but notable examples are the works of Zora Neale Hurston, Jessie Redmon Fauset, Frances E. W. Harper, and Dorothy West. The unavailability of these works also inhibits the expansion of research in the area of Black women's studies, since these works have much historical as well as literary value.

Academic Publishing

Another roadblock to research is the lack of a body of scholarship concerning Black women, particularly Black women writers. There is only a handful of book length critical studies of Black writers, either male or female. The only places where research on Black writers [is] regularly published are the few Black scholarly and literary journals. Women's publications are notably neglectful in their coverage of Black women and the conventional scholarly journals do not have any coverage at all.

Conclusions

In conclusion two points need to be stressed. First, there is the interconnect-edness of the different areas of publishing as they affect the situation of Black women writers and scholars. One cannot, for example, write a critical article on a specific Black woman writer if her books are not available. The critical article that is never written will of course never appear in a journal or anthology. One cannot assign a book to a class if its existence is not known, because no one has bothered to review it. One cannot include representative selections by Black women writers in an anthology if one has never even heard their names (the case with most compilers of anthologies) because, among other reasons, all their books went out of print twenty or thirty years ago.

The second point is that there is a readership and therefore a market for works by Black women. There are many more Black women teaching at the college level now than at any other time in history. There are more Black students on college campuses, more women students with an interest in studying about women, and also a proliferation of Black and women's studies courses and departments. Many Black women are beginning to teach . . . courses on Black and Third World women, and usually they have to search high and low for materials. If publishers become more aware and responsive to the needs of Black women scholars and general readers, the result cannot help but be advantageous to all concerned.

The Modern Language Association Commission on the Status of Women urges that publishers take seriously the need to be more fully representative of American women in their publishing endeavors.

> Jean Perkins, Co-Chairperson, French, Swarthmore College
> Gloria De Sole, Co-Chairperson, English, Skidmore College
> Joan Hartman, English, Staten Island Community College, CUNY
> Leonore Hoffmann, English, Youngstown State University
> Ellen Messer-Davidow, English, University of Cincinnati
> Kittye Delle Robbins, French, Mississippi State University
> Deborah Rosenfelt, English, California State University, Long Beach
> Cynthia Secor, English, Higher Education Resource Services, Mid-Atlantic
>   Region
> Barbara Smith, English, Emerson College

"Our Stories: Women of Color"
Barbara Smith (1984)

In 1973 I taught one of the first courses in the USA on Black women writers.[1] The most frequent reaction I got whenever I mentioned the course to somebody, or used the term Black women writers, was a blank stare. Black literature was what Black men wrote. Women's literature was what white women wrote. Thanks to sexism and racism, the writing of Black women and of other women of color was invisible.

---

[1] The term "Black" is specifically used here to refer to people of African origin, including Afro-Americans and Afro-Caribbeans. The terms "women of color" and "Third World women" are used interchangeably to refer to American Indians, Latina, Asian American, and Black women in the USA and to women from Third World countries all over the globe.

More than ten years later, the term "Black women writers" is much more likely to strike a responsive chord. Toni Morrison has appeared on the cover of *Newsweek*. Alice Walker has received the Pulitzer Prize. But increased interest in the writing of women of color did not come about because above-ground media and critics decided to single out a few best-selling authors. It resulted from a grassroots movement of women of color—including teachers, researchers, and feminist activists—who have been working for years to discover, support, and create artistic works that accurately reflect our experiences in a white-male dominated system.

In 1984, writing by Afro-American women constitutes nothing less than a literary renaissance and more and more writing by other U.S. women of color—American Indian, Latina, and Asian American—is also available. It is not possible in this limited space to explore even a fraction of the major themes prevalent in this writing, but I would like to mention several general topics that many, though not all, of these writers address.

A fundamental concern of writing by women of color is the exploration of what it means to be female *and* a person of color *and* economically oppressed *and* officially or unofficially colonized *and*, in some cases, Lesbian, in a society that is hostile to every aspect of one's identity. . . . [This concern] is cited by the editors of *Cuentos: Stories by Latinas* in their introduction to the very first collection of short stories by Latinas written from an explicitly feminist perspective.

> Particularly for so many Latinas who can no longer claim our own country, or even the domain of our own homes—barely holding *la tierra* below our feet— we need *una literatura* that testifies to our lives, provides acknowledgment of who we are: an exiled people, a migrant people, *mujeres en lucha*. [Gómez, Moraga, Romo-Carmona 1983: vii]

Work which incorporates autobiographical elements is a tradition of all oppressed writers, because our stories are continually ignored and dismissed. The necessity for this kind of writing is particularly critical for women of color who encompass multiple "unacceptable" identities within one skin.

A unique capacity of Third World women writers is the way in which they integrate concern with external political forces with scrutiny of the internal politics in our communities that also keep us oppressed. Third World women writers do not hesitate to explore such issues as the pressure on us to assimilate and to deny our cultures; sexual abuse at home; or the gulfs within our groups caused by differences of color and class. Nor are they reluctant to define these problems as being political and as worthy of struggle as the more traditional "isms."

Another sign of transformation from the early 1970s until now is that much more writing by women of color is physically available. When I first began teaching Black women writers, major texts such as Zora Neale Hurston's *Their Eyes Were Watching God*, Ann Petry's *The Street*, and Toni Morrison's *The Bluest Eye* were constantly kept out of print by commercial publishers. Currently, commercial houses publish a token number of works by women of color, usually by Afro-American women, but it is the alternative presses that are producing the most politically vital and risk-taking work by women of color in the USA—particularly writings by Lesbians of color. Progressive Third World Lesbians have been at the forefront of all the political organizing and writing which has helped provide the context for *all* women of color to express themselves both artistically and politically. . . .

The founding in 1981 of Kitchen Table: Women of Color Press—the first publisher in North America* committed to producing and distributing the work of Third World women of all racial/cultural heritages, sexualities, and classes—was partially motivated by our need, as Third World Women, to have complete control over both the content and the production of our words—control which is usually not available even when working with feminist and alternative publishers. . . .

Although commercial publishers claim that work by women of color, especially by Lesbians, does not sell, the experience of Kitchen Table and other alternative presses indicates quite the opposite. By targeting those readers most likely to be interested in such work . . . anthologies such as *This Bridge Called My Back*, *But Some of Us Are Brave*, and *Home Girls* have sold in multiples of 10,000 and the audience for these titles is far from saturated.

The organizing of women of color in the USA is of course linked to Third World women's organizing globally, including the incredible work done by the Black Women's Movement in Britain. The forthcoming special issue of *Feminist Review* entitled *Many Voices, One Chant: Black Feminist Perspectives*, edited by Gail Lewis, Pratibha Parmar, Val Amos, and Amina Mama, and plans for the new Black women's press in London, Black Womantalk, indicate that women of color in Britain have a similar need for and are finding the means to create autonomous cultural resources. The writing and publishing of women of color represents one of the most exciting and politically significant cultural phenomena during this period. Although not nearly enough writing is yet available, as a result of a global movement of women of color our invisibility is finally a thing of the past.

Interview with Matt Richardson

Barbara Smith: I was destined for publishing. Our junior high school, Alexander Hamilton Junior High School, had a school newspaper that was printed—wasn't typed or mimeographed—that came out once a semester, and you could take journalism courses. So I first was exposed to galleys in the ninth grade.

We had a wonderful journalism teacher whose name was Miss Virginia Follin. Had it not been the 1950s and sixties, she might have been a professional

---

* At the time this claim was made, those associated with Kitchen Table Press were aware of *Third Woman*, which was based in Bloomington, Indiana, when it was founded in 1979 and later moved to Berkeley, California, in 1987. Because *Third Woman* began as a journal focused upon writing by Latinas, it did not have as broad a focus as Kitchen Table.

KITCHEN TABLE: Women of Color Press

Spring 1987 Catalogue

New releases by
Angela Y. Davis, Barbara Omolade, and Mila D. Aguilar

KITCHEN TABLE: Women of Color Press,

founded in 1981, is the only publisher in the U.S. committed to publishing and distributing the writing of Third World women of all racial/cultural heritages, sexualities, and classes.

Home Girls: A Black Feminist Anthology,
Barbara Smith, Editor.

Fiction, poetry, political analysis, and essays by 34 contributors bring together a decade of Black feminist writing and organizing. "In terms of teaching, sharing, curing, healing and liberating, *Home Girls* is one of the most important books in the history of Black women's writing." —Alice Walker
$13.95 paper, $30.95 cloth, 5½ x 8½, 400 pages. ISBN 0-913175-02-1

This Bridge Called My Back: Writings by Radical Women of Color, Cherríe Moraga & Gloria Anzaldúa, Editors.

WINNER OF THE 1986 BEFORE COLUMBUS FOUNDATION AMERICAN BOOK AWARD.
This classic collection of writings by Native American, Asian American, Latina, and African American women reflects "an uncompromised definition of feminism by women of color in the United States." 35,000 in print.
$9.95 paper, $28.95 cloth, 5¼ x 8¼, 261 pages. Illus. ISBN 0-913176-03-X

Cuentos: Stories by Latinas Alma Gómez, Cherríe Moraga & Mariana Romo-Carmona, Editors.

A collection of thirty stories by Latinas from the U.S. and Latin America which breaks "la cultura de silencio" by depicting the myriad unrecognized ways Latinas have resisted colonization both in the flesh and in the spirit. *Cuentos* includes selections in Spanish and English.
$7.95 paper, $16.95 cloth, 5½ x 8½, 248 pages. ISBN 0-913017-01-3

Narratives: Poems in the Tradition of Black Women
by Cheryl Clarke.

A gallery of incisive, specific portraits of Black women, whose lives, as June Jordan states, are "honestly perceived with a clearly hard-working respect and without affectation." Clarke considers her Black, Lesbian, and feminist identities to be "the filter of her imagination," in a work which points to a courageous new African American women's poetry for the 1980s.
$5.50 paper, $14.80 cloth, 5½ x 8½, 52 pages. Illus. ISBN 0-913175-00-5

Figure 5.1: Kitchen Table: Women of Color Press spring 1987 catalogue. Six years after its founding, Kitchen Table: Women of Color Press had developed an impressive and diverse list of titles by and about Third World women of all racial/cultural heritages, sexualities, and classes.

journalist. But because the only thing they let women do on most newspapers in those days was the society columns, I think she decided she'd rather do journalism with students on the high school level than be writing society gossip. She took it completely seriously. She ran our newspaper like it was a newsroom. She did not play. And I *loved* it. I loved every minute of it.

Sometimes she would take us down to the *Cleveland Plain Dealer* printing plant [that printed our school paper], and that was really fun. It was beginning to end: first you write it, then you type it, then it gets sent to the printer, then you get galleys back, then you do your layout, and then you took that layout down to the printer. It certainly helped when I became a publisher myself. It's in my blood, you know?

My dream has also been to be a writer, to write and be published. Because of my involvement in the women's movement, in the early 1970s, I was beginning to do that by the time I left graduate school. I had already coedited *Conditions: Five*, I was working on *But Some of Us Are Brave*, and I was also getting my work published in the myriad women's periodicals being published at the time.

I had also audited Alice Walker's course in Black women's literature at the University of Massachusetts, Boston. I wasn't teaching during that particular period, but I said to myself, "The next time I teach, I'm going to teach Black Women Writers." It could have been a fanciful assertion to say that, because it was 1972! But it just so happened that I heard about a job at Emerson College. The chair of the department was a wonderful woman, and besides the usual English composition courses and things like that, she asked, "What else would you like to teach?" And I told her. And that's how I got to teach Black Women Writers.

In those early days it was almost impossible to get a consistent set of books for a course. When I was teaching at Emerson College and my sister lived in Brooklyn, I remember asking her to go to the publishers of Ann Petry's *The Street*. I had contacted them, and they said they had some copies lying around, but the book was out of print. She literally brought me a shopping bag full of Ann Petry's *The Street* so that I could teach it. You never knew from one semester to another what you could teach, because they kept the books out of print or the books kept going out of print. I think now that resource of solid publication is one that we have built.

Matt Richardson: What were you writing at that point?

Barbara: Mostly book reviews. Beverly, my sister, was working at *Ms.*, and the review of Alice Walker's *In Love & Trouble* that they had assigned and received back was not one that they could use. They needed somebody to write a review *immediately*, and I turned out to be that person. So, that was really great, that my first publication was in what was becoming a major national magazine.

Matt: Had you come out at this point?

Barbara: I came out in '74/'75. In the early seventies, I was beginning to publish work, doing book reviews and things like that—not always for women's periodicals, either—I wrote some stuff for *Freedomways* and other publications. But by '74/'75, I was in the thick of it in Boston.

Matt: How did you get to do *Conditions: Five [The Black Women's Issue]*?

Barbara: In Boston, there were many wonderful bookstores [that carried journals like *Conditions*]. That's how I found *Amazon Quarterly*. Of course, I had that trepidation of going up to the counter with this lesbian magazine. What was someone going to think? But I purchased it, started reading it, and there's Audre Lorde's name! I knew who Audre was because I was familiar with Broadside Press, a groundbreaking Black publishing operation out of Detroit. I knew that Audre was an important writer in the Black Arts movement, and then I open *Amazon Quarterly*, and it's like, "Could it be?!" That was really exciting.

That may be how I found out about *Conditions* magazine. There were also women's schools at that time, grassroots community schools started by feminists in the Boston area, and I took a writing workshop with this wonderful person, who happened to be Adrienne Rich's sister, Cynthia Rich! So, that's how I met Adrienne, and it also might be how I found out about *Conditions*.

Adrienne told the editors of *Conditions* that they should contact me to see if I would write something for them. It was an extremely important new lesbian feminist literary publication; it had articles that were very thoughtful, loads of book reviews, short stories, poetry. They sent me a letter asking if I wanted to write something for the magazine about African American women writers. But the letter was written as if there was such a thing as a critical mass of Black women's literature [and literary criticism]. So I said, "Well, I can't write a very specific article. I need to really write something that is going to try to make some attempt to define the field, and what the challenges of the field are."

And that's how I wrote "Toward a Black Feminist Criticism." It was an attempt to say, "Okay, this is how we get left out of what is called 'women's literature' and what is called 'Black literature.'" Then of course I did that reading of Toni Morrison's *Sula*, looking at it as a lesbian novel. I don't know if I'd even think to do that today! After that, they asked if I would like to do an entire issue devoted to Black women writers, which became *Conditions: Five, The Black Women's Issue*. You can see now how graduate school was becoming . . .

Matt: . . . fading . . .

Barbara: . . . into my rear view mirror. [laughs] I always like to do things with other people, collaborate. So Lorraine Bethel and I ended up doing that together. But now it's not in print. That was really the basis of my doing *Home Girls*, because I wanted to preserve the writing that was in *Conditions: Five* in book form.

Matt: When did you start *Home Girls*?

Barbara: I think it was '81. The history of that book was interesting. It was a Kitchen Table: Women of Color Press book, but it was originally supposed to be published by Persephone Press.

Matt: Now, *This Bridge Called My Back* had already been published by Persephone? Were you with Cherríe [Moraga] at this time? You were living in New York?

Barbara: We moved to New York City in the summer of 1981 because we had already had discussions in 1980 with Audre Lorde, Hattie Gossett, and other people who lived in New York City, about starting some kind of publishing *something* for women of color. Audre and I were talking on the phone about her upcoming visit for a poetry reading in Boston on Halloween 1980, and she said, "Barbara, we really need to do something about publishing." I said, "Yeah. We sure do." We had both experienced special issues, and Third World women's issues, and working with white women's presses. Sometimes those experiences were positive, and sometimes not so positive. Whatever they were, we were not controlling the process or the outcomes or the product.

Myrna Bain, Hattie Gossett, Kate Rushin, and others who lived in Boston decided to meet when Audre was in town. From the very beginning, we were clear that it was going to be a press for women of color, not just for women of African heritage. So, there were people of different nationalities and ethnicities at that meeting. That was really the beginning of Kitchen Table.

It soon became apparent that the real energy for the press, and people who were willing to work on it, were in New York City. So, Cherríe and I moved here.

Matt: So what was that like, as Cherríe was working on *Bridge* and you were working on *Home Girls*?

Barbara: She wrote me a letter about working on a collection, because she had read *Conditions: Five*. I was so unaware—she talked about Brown women, and I just thought, "Oh, well that's just another way of saying Black women." I didn't realize that she was actually talking about Latina women, Chicana women!

Cherríe decided to work with Persephone on *Bridge*, which was coedited with Gloria Anzaldúa. I learned a lot during that period, because I had the opportunity to visit their offices and see how a press ran, what the elements were of getting a book from its manuscript stage to its production and then publication stage. Things were very different then because there was no desktop publishing.

In order to get a book done, you had to have a graphic designer and a typesetter. The typesetter played a very important role, as did your graphic designer, because that determined what your book would look like. Persephone was very good at graphic design; their books looked beautiful and had really compelling visuals.

Matt: Now, were you working on *Brave* at the same time? When did you decide to go with Feminist Press?

Barbara: That was a decision that was made some years before. I was on the Modern Language Association Commission on the Status of Women. Florence Howe, cofounder of the Feminist Press, was one of the original members of the MLA Commission, and several of our publishing projects were going to be published by the Feminist Press. I was in my twenties at that point, and for someone in graduate school to suddenly have access to credible publication was a great opportunity. It was nice to be working on a book that had a home once it was completed.

Gloria (Akasha) Hull came onto the commission during that time, and we then began to collaborate. Florence thought it would be good for us to have someone with a social science or other disciplinary background and introduced us to Patricia Bell-Scott, who became our third coeditor. That book took quite a few years. I articulated that I wanted to work on a book on Black women's studies sometime in the mid-seventies, and I think it was released in early '82.

Matt: How would you characterize what it was like to work with Persephone and Feminist Press?

Barbara: Challenging. Feminist Press does such remarkable publishing, and it makes such an important contribution. Very, very, very important. There are not very many women's presses left. And that was one of the oldest, if not *the* oldest, and it still continues. So that is wonderful.

But we had to fight them for the title of *But Some of Us Are Brave*. We actually got an attorney to help us through the process of getting the book into reality. The book is dedicated to our attorney, Beverly Towns Williams. [laughs] A lot of people don't know that! We were very fortunate to find a wonderful Black woman attorney who did everything for us pro bono.

I had come up with this title—*All the Women Are White, All the Blacks Are Men, But Some of Us Are Brave*—and I was using it for presentations I was doing about Black women's studies on various college campuses. One day, in a conversation with Cherríe, we were trying to puzzle out the naming of the book. She said *that's* the title. That's the title. People *love* that title. They love it to this day.

Matt: It's a great title.

Barbara: When the 2008 presidential electoral campaign was going on, and there was all that madness around white women versus Black men, there were some wonderful articles that came out. One writer in particular cited us and said, I'm thinking of that title today because it's so relevant to what we're seeing before us, those innate divisions. There was a lot of racism that came out during that campaign, and a lot of sexism, too.

Matt: So then, some of those complications, were they replicated at Persephone?

Barbara: Persephone had a different dynamic. Persephone did really good publishing, but they declared bankruptcy a few weeks before *Home Girls* was supposed to be published. Many people don't know that *Home Girls* was originally going to be a Persephone Press book. A lot of decisions had been made, the cover had been designed, and it was already typeset. And then I got a letter, while I was at the Millay Colony for the Arts in Upstate New York, saying that they were going bankrupt and the publication of my book was indefinitely suspended. Needless to say, I almost had a nervous breakdown. I got on a train and I went down to New York. We had a Kitchen Table Press meeting, and we immediately said that we would take it as a Kitchen Table Press title, but then there was an issue of getting the rights to it.

So similarly to the struggle for *But Some of Us Are Brave*, a lawyer helped me get my book. In this case, it was a dear friend from college, Ellen Wade, who lived in Boston. We had a meeting in a downtown Boston skyscraper with the two principals of Persephone, and they brought the materials. All I wanted was the stuff. I didn't care about anything else, but I wanted the typesetting. To have to re-typeset a three- hundred-page book—so expensive! I literally got my book in a couple of shopping bags, and I took my shopping bags with *Home Girls* in it back down to New York. [laughs]

Matt: Can you say anything about your part in the decision to make *Bridge* a Kitchen Table Press book?

Barbara: When Persephone stopped publishing there were a number of us who were caught up in that, who had titles that had already been published by them, or who had books that were on the verge of being published. Each of us had to figure out what to do. Fortunately, most of us were in communication with each other, so people could talk about different decisions.

I think Audre's *Zami* was originally a Persephone book. Michelle Cliff was involved because her novel, *Abeng*, had been published by Persephone. Elly Bulkin had edited these wonderful anthologies of lesbian poetry and fiction. I think Elly's books actually ended up going out of print.

Home Girls was on the verge of being published by them. *This Bridge Called My Back* had been published by them. So everyone had to work to get their book to another home. And just as Kitchen Table saved *Home Girls*, and brought it into the light of day, publishing *This Bridge Called My Back* was a natural kind of way of keeping that book in print.

By the time I started having contact with Persephone, we were already talking about starting Kitchen Table. Because Kitchen Table was in its gestation period, I was really very observant and very curious when I got to visit their office. I'd say, "What's that?" and "How do you do this?" It was really by happenstance, but I did get to see how a successful publisher did the work that it did: laying out a book cover, for example. I was able to bring some of that experience to Kitchen Table. One of the things I liked most about them is that their books looked good. I used to tell my wonderful coworkers, including you, "It costs just as much money to produce an ugly book as it does to produce a pretty book, and we're going to do pretty books."

Matt: Yes. I do remember you saying that.

Barbara: It's really about images on paper. It doesn't cost any more to choose a beautiful typeface than it does to choose a clunky, average, dull typeface. But you have to have an eye for it. Remember when I redesigned the cover of *Seventeen Syllables*? That was our first four-color cover. It was gorgeous. We entered it into a professional book binders/book design association competition, mainstream books were being judged right along with ours, and we got first prize in our category!

I particularly enjoyed working on *Seventeen Syllables* by Hisaye Yamamoto and *Desert Run* by Mitsuye Yamada. I loved working on those books. I always tell people that my favorite parts of being a publisher—there were two—one was publicity, promotion, and marketing; the other was graphic design. Those were the two things I really, really liked.

Our Books Were Lifelines

"A Press of Our Own" surveys the birth and growth of Kitchen Table: Women of Color Press and describes how a "movement press" consciously fostered social change by attending conferences, marches, meetings, and gatherings, and bringing hard-to-find voices to enthusiastic audiences. Moreover, the multiple oppressions shared by women of color helped the press to forge a genuine multiracial alliance against shared injustice.

"A Press of Our Own: Kitchen Table: Women of Color Press"
Barbara Smith (1989)

If anyone had asked in 1980 whether books by women of color could sell or if a press that published only work by and about women of color could survive, the logical answer would have been "no," especially if the person who answered the question was part of the commercial publishing establishment. Even fewer than seven years ago, writing by American Indian, African American, Latina, and Asian American women was barely noticed by literary and academic establishments, let alone by the general reading public.

> ## "Starting a press for women of color in 1980 may have defied logic, but it was one of those acts of courage which characterize Third World women's lives."

Since the early 1970s, however, a small but devoted group of feminist activists, teachers, and writers, many of them Black women, have been working to make visible the writing, culture, and history of women of color. It was their work, not Madison Avenue's, that laid the political and ideological groundwork for Kitchen Table: Women of Color Press and also for the current 1980s renaissance of writing by Black and other women of color.

Starting a press for women of color in 1980 may have defied logic, but it was one of those acts of courage which characterize Third World women's lives. In October 1980, Audre Lorde said to me during a phone conversation, "We really need to do something about publishing." I totally agreed and got together a group of interested women to meet Halloween weekend in Boston when Audre and other women from New York were in town to do a Black women's poetry reading.

It was at that meeting that Kitchen Table: Women of Color Press was born. We did not arrive at a name or announce our existence until a year later, but at that initial meeting we did decide to be a publisher for all women of color, although there were only women of African American and African Caribbean descent in the room. This was one of our bravest steps since most people of color have chosen to work in their separate groups when they do media or other projects. We were saying that as women, feminists, and lesbians of color we had experiences and work to do in common, although we also had our differences.

A year later, we were officially founded and chose our name because the kitchen is the center of the home, the place where women in particular work and communicate with each other and because we wanted to convey the fact that we are a kitchen-table, grassroots organization, begun and kept alive by women who cannot rely on inheritances or other benefits of class privilege to do the work we need to do.

Given the odds, why were we so strongly motivated to attempt the impossible? An early slogan of the women in print movement was "freedom of the press belongs to those who own the press." This is even truer for multiply disenfranchised women of color who have minimal access to power, including the power of media, except that which we wrest from an unwilling system.

On the most basic level, Kitchen Table Press began because of our need for autonomy, our need to determine independently both the content and conditions of our work, and to control the words and images that are produced about us. As feminist and lesbian of color writers, we knew that we had no options for getting published, except at the mercy or whim of others, whether in the context of alternative or commercial publishing, since both are white-dominated. . . .

We have always considered the Press to be both an activist and a literary publisher, because we are equally committed to producing work of high artistic quality that simultaneously contributes to the liberation of women of color and of all people. We do not simply publish a work because it is by a woman of color, but because it consciously examines the specific situations and issues women of color face from a positive and original perspective. . . .

We have always defined our target audience as people of color, not solely women of color or lesbians of color, but the entire gamut of our communities. This reflects a perception about audience that differs from that of other women's presses, who can more logically define women as their priority constituency since white, Christian, middle-class women do not share an oppressed identity and status with their white male counterparts. The history and everyday reality of women of color have been shaped at least as much by racism as by sexism, and racism of course affects all the members of our race or nationality group; women, children, and men of every age, sexual orientation, and economic status. The Press's goal of informing and educating about crucial and often difficult issues, especially those that are close to home, also determines how we see our audience. . . .

Because we have a commitment to publishing feminist and lesbian writing, coalescing with our communities can be difficult and even painful, but the longer the Press exists, the easier it becomes to share our work in these contexts and we have been met with increasing interest and understanding. Books have proven a powerful vehicle for challenging sexism and heterosexism in Third World communities, perhaps because they provide something concrete for a reader to relate to and can elicit a potentially thoughtful response as the result of the one-to-one interaction between the reader and the writer's words. . . .

The Press's work is international both because of our foreign distribution and also because the issues addressed in our publications make connections with and are inspired by the global movement of Third World women, who in turn recognize our existence as supportive of their struggles. Sister Vision Press in Toronto, Black

Womantalk Press in London, and Kali [for Women] in New Delhi are three sister presses run by women of color which started after Kitchen Table.

Because Kitchen Table is the only publisher for women of color* in the United States, and one of a handful of feminist of color organizations with national visibility, we function not only as a press, but as a resource network for women of color worldwide. We must cope daily with the stresses of tokenism, of being the only one, for example, having to handle an inconceivably large and far-reaching correspondence. Although Kitchen Table is the only resource of its kind for women of color, some white women still do not comprehend the need to have at least one press of our own. Sometimes white women academics who are doing research on women of color, usually in Third World countries, ask if they can submit manuscripts to us. At workshops, when I discuss the numerous barriers to women of color getting into print, white women have asked me, "What about white women who can't get published?," implying that our policy of only publishing material by and about women of color is somehow discriminatory. Racism and traditional power dynamics die hard. Until this society completely transforms itself, and justice for all people prevails, there will undoubtedly be a need for a Kitchen Table: Women of Color Press.

In fact, I can foresee the Press existing in a revolutionary society, although by that time it would undoubtedly not be the only one.

Recently, I have begun to acknowledge that the Press does indeed play an important role in making political change. When we began I was hesitant to confuse our cultural and ideological work with grassroots organizing and activism. Having done a great deal of the latter, I believed it was inaccurate to view the cultural work of the Press as identical to the grueling work of directly taking on the power structure around issues such as economics, housing, education, jobs, racial violence, violence against women, and reproductive rights.

After seven years I have started to see things differently, perhaps because I have had time to experience the difference it makes for women of color to control a significant means of communication, to have a vehicle for shaping ideology which serves as a foundation for making practical social and political change. Consider, for example, if Kitchen Table and other independent feminist presses did not exist, the writing of lesbians of color would be virtually unavailable, since with only two exceptions (Audre Lorde's poetry and Anne Allen Shockley's fiction) commercial publishers do not print the works of "out" lesbians of color. And yet it is this same body of writing that has been most incisive in defining sexual politics in communities of color and inspiring the feminist organizing of women of color of all sexual orientations.

Kitchen Table: Women of Color Press is a revolutionary tool because it is one means of empowering the society's most dispossessed, who also have the greatest

---

* See earlier notes in this chapter on Third Woman Press.

potential for making change. After seven years our work has only begun. We have been able to come this far because we have not been afraid to defy white male logic, which will always tell us no, when our hearts and spirits tell us *yes!*

Interviews with Matt Richardson, Barbara Ransby, and Kimberly Springer

Matt Richardson: What was the first Kitchen Table book?

Barbara Smith: That's always a question mark. The first one that we intended was *Cuentos: Stories by Latinas*—that was to be our first publication. Cheryl Clarke had self-published *Narratives: Poems in the Tradition of Black Women*, but she asked us to distribute and market it, and to do publicity and promotion. So that was the first book that we ever worked on that we were sending out to review publications and alerting the bookstores, et cetera. We sold out of that book very, very quickly. So Cheryl decided that the next printing would be done by Kitchen Table Press. It was out there before *Cuentos* was. So the first book that

The Spanish translation and adaptation of
This Bridge Called My Back
Writings by Radical Women of Color
edited by *Cherríe Moraga and Ana Castillo*

This classic collection of writings by Native American, Asian American, Latina, and African American feminists in the U.S. has been translated into Spanish and adapted for a Latin American readership. Containing poetry, essays, and personal narrative, with a new introduction by Cherríe Moraga and several new contributions by Latina writers, *Esta puente, mi espalda* makes vivid the connection between third-world women in the U.S. and in the third world.

ESTA PUENTE, MI ESPALDA

268 páginas. Contiene 37 ilustraciones, incluso fotos de las escritoras, fotos históricas, y dibujos originales. 5¼" × 8". Includes an index. Published in autumn 1988 by Ism Press. LC 88-13483. Printed on acid-free paper. Contains Cataloging-in-Publication data.

Paperback . . . . ISBN 0-910383-19-7 . . . . $16.
Hardcover . . . . . . ISBN 0-910383-20-0 . . . . $16.

FORMA DE SU PEDIDO

☐ Envío _____ ejemplar(es) de *Esta puente* . . . @ $10.00 . . . . $_____
☐ Envío _____ ejemplares (5 o más ejemplares) @ $8.00 . . . . $_____
Adjunto por franqueo: $1 por uno, 25¢ por cada libro adicional . . . . $_____
Residentes de California agregen 6.6% de impuesto (66¢ por ejemplar) . . . . $_____
Cuenta total . . . . $_____

Name
Nombre _____

Address
Dirección _____

City
Ciudad _____

State and Zip
Estado y Zona Postal _____

Remitan su cheque o giro postal a:
Ism Press, Inc.
P.O. Box 12447

editado por *Cherríe Moraga y Ana Castillo*

Esta puente, mi espalda

Voces de mujeres tercermundistas en los Estados Unidos

The Spanish translation and adaptation of
This Bridge Called My Back:
Writings by Radical

Figure 5.2: Announcement of *Esta Puente, Mi Espalda*, the Spanish-language translation of *This Bridge Called My Back*, 1988. Kitchen Table Press, the publisher of the classic anthology, worked closely with ISM Press to support the publication and distribution of this translation.

had "Kitchen Table: Women of Color Press" on it was actually *Narratives*, but our intent was that *Cuentos* was going to be the first one.

Matt: Was Kitchen Table a collective?

Barbara S.: That was what was said on the piece of paper. [laughs] I have to say that because there were a lot of collectives in that era, and often they were not truly collective. We had a commitment to people having non-hierarchical roles and relationships, but it can be very difficult, particularly if you are running what is essentially a business, to operate in that way. We did consider ourselves to be a collective, and there were a number of women who were involved in those early days.

Kitchen Table: Women of Color Press books 1983–1992

Narratives: Poems in the Tradition of Black Women, by Cheryl Clarke (1983)

Cuentos: Stories by Latinas, edited by Alma Gómez, Cherríe Moraga, and Mariana Romo-Carmona (1983)

Home Girls: A Black Feminist Anthology, edited by Barbara Smith (1983)

This Bridge Called My Back: Writings by Radical Women of Color, 2nd Edition, edited by Cherríe Moraga and Gloria Anzaldúa (1984)

A Comrade Is as Precious as a Rice Seedling: Poems, by Mila D. Aguilar (1984)

Desert Run: Poems and Stories, by Mitsuye Yamada (1988)

Seventeen Syllables, by Hisaye Yamamoto (1988)

Healing Heart: Poems, 1973–1988, by Gloria T. Hull (1989)

Camp Notes: And Other Poems, by Mitsuye Yamada (1992)

The Freedom Organizing Pamphlet Series

1. *The Combahee River Collective Statement* ([1977] 1985)
2. *Apartheid U.S.A.*, by Audre Lorde, and *Our Common Enemy, Our Common Cause: Freedom Organizing in the Eighties*, by Merle Woo (1985)
3. *I Am Your Sister: Black Women Organizing Across Sexualities*, by Audre Lorde (1985)
4. *It's a Family Affair: The Real Lives of Black Single Mothers*, by Barbara Omolade (1985)
5. *Violence against Women and the Ongoing Challenge to Racism*, by Angela Y. Davis (1985)
6. *Need: A Chorale for Black Women Voices*, by Audre Lorde (1991)

Matt: Do you remember some of the names of the people who were involved in the collective in these early years?

Barbara S.: Hattie Gossett, Myrna Bain, Audre [Lorde], Cherríe [Moraga], Mariana Roma-Carmona, Rosario Morales, Ana Oliveira, Alma Gómez, Leota Lone Dog, Rosie Alvarez, Susan Yung, and Helena Byard. I think those are the core people. People lived in different places geographically, so they might not be coming to meetings, but they were editing books or whatever.

Matt: How were you making a living at this time?

Barbara S.: I always had teaching to fall back on. I taught at Barnard when I lived in New York City. I had a lot of speaking engagements in those days, so there were many years when I made the majority of a modest living doing that, primarily on college and university campuses. When I first moved to Albany I taught a short course for the School of Social Work at NYU. I commuted down to do that. I had a job working at Hobart and William Smith Colleges. I was a visiting professor at the University of Minnesota in the fall of 1986. So you can see, not long-term jobs. It was very hard to balance all of that.

Matt: You would try to do press business in between all of that?

Barbara S.: Generally, I would try to teach on Tuesday and Thursday, and travel on Mondays and Thursdays. We didn't have the technology that you have now. Now, somebody would just send something via e-mail and you'd look at it, and sign off. But the only way to make those decisions in those days was to be there physically. I remember going up and down that highway twice a week, just so I could sign off on a design, so things could get to the printer.

Matt: What was the impetus around the Freedom Organizing pamphlet series?

Barbara S.: The United Nations Women's Conferences that were happening in the seventies and eighties. The first one we were involved with was in Nairobi, Kenya, in 1985, and that was really exciting because Black women in the United States, who had not necessarily gravitated toward the women's movement or to women's issues, got very excited about an international women's conference in the Motherland. So there was a lot of organizing, a lot of NGOs formed specifically to get ready for this experience of this international women's conference.

During International Women's Year [1977] in the United States, there was a major national women's conference in Houston. I participated as a delegate. Before the Nairobi conference, we were going to one of those planning pre-conferences, I believe it was at Morgan State University, a historically Black university in Maryland. I wanted to bring the Combahee River Collective Statement, because it really lays out Black feminist politics so clearly. I had gotten many copies of it photocopied, and I was literally up in the Kitchen Table office until far too late into the night, collating, stapling, getting these copies of the statement ready to take to this conference. And I thought, "Wait a minute! This is crazy! You have something called a press! Kitchen Table: Women of Color Press! Why in the world are you sitting up here working with photocopies? You could actually publish this as a pamphlet and be done with it, and you would never have to sit doing this ridiculous thing again!" I also liked the idea of having something that was affordable and explicitly for organizing. That's why it was called the Freedom Organizing pamphlet series.

Nancy Bereano, at Firebrand Press, was going to be publishing pamphlets as well, and she and I were talking about how to produce these pamphlets so they didn't disappear on the bookshelf when you turned them spine out. She came up with the idea of putting a button on the cover of the pamphlets. That meant that they had to be displayed face out! So we both did pamphlets near the same time that had a button affixed to them, and it got them a lot more visibility. It also made real the fact that this is about organizing. Not only is it about organizing, we're going to give you a button to wear that expresses something that the pamphlet covers.

Barbara Ransby: I've been thinking about Kitchen Table Press lately. It made such a powerful mark and still serves as both inspiration and a model. I was just with a friend who has been working with Barnard's Women's Center, and they've started this "New Feminist Solutions" pamphlet series. And what does that remind me of?

Barbara S.: The Freedom Organizing pamphlets?

Barbara R.: Yes! Which we loved, and used. If you're organizing and you want to do a teach-in, or a study group, and people don't want to read a

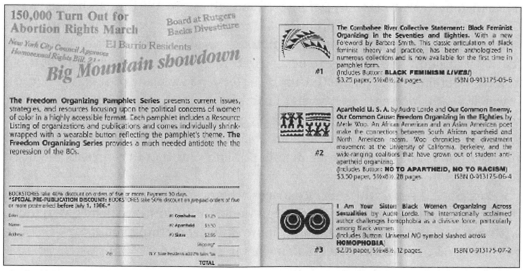

Figure 5.3: 1986 Kitchen Table Press brochure featuring the Freedom Organizing pamphlet series. As a movement press, Kitchen Table published short, concise pamphlets dedicated to pressing contemporary issues, penned by some of the greatest writers of the generation, including the Combahee River Collective, Audre Lorde, Angela Y. Davis, Barbara Omolade, and Merle Woo. Attached to each pamphlet was a button for readers to wear.

three hundred–page book, we had these beautiful, succinct, provocative, clear pamphlets. Then you had your little button on there, so if you read this and you're in agreement, put the button on. It was a great model for that kind of engaged intellectual work, which didn't have the name "public intellectual," "engaged scholarship," all the things that have some currency now, without the substance. That was a model for that!

The pamphlet didn't compromise the complexity of the ideas, either. Some pamphlets could kind of talk down to people, "Let's have some bullet points." There was a richness about them that I certainly always appreciated.

Barbara S.: That was one of the things about Kitchen Table that made it unique. We were not just a women's press, we didn't just do literary publishing, and we didn't just do political publishing, or academic publishing. We did *all* of it. We also were very much involved with, and supportive of, progressive organizing that was going on during that period. For example, when we were still located in New York City we were involved with Art against Apartheid. We wanted to be on the scene where important things were going on.

Barbara R.: In Ella's Daughters, we talk about political quilting, which is something that I see as being different than coalition building: supporting, connecting, convening, bringing together. Sometimes you don't have to be visible in doing that, but you bring together different organizing traditions and different people working around different issues. I think of your work, both personally and as part of Kitchen Table, as being very much a model for that. When we did African American Women in Defense of Ourselves,[*] in 1991, in response to the Clarence Thomas–Anita Hill situation, we made these ads [for the *New York Times* and other newspapers]. You were a signatory and a supporter, but you also called [us] up and said, "This is going to be a poster. We need a historical record of this." You connected us to Syracuse Cultural Workers and we made it. It was generous, it was forward-looking, and it's what I think of as political quilting. What does it mean to take this action and to make it bigger than it would be otherwise, to give it permanence? I appreciated that, but I was also taking notes and learning that this is the way that you mark a campaign or an event that in ten years might be forgotten otherwise.

Barbara S.: People still walk into places, wherever they are, and see that poster. A couple of years ago, a Muslim American woman, via Gloria Steinem, got in touch with me, because they were thinking about doing something similar in response to the horrific beheading of a Muslim woman in Buffalo, New York.[†]

---

[*] See our discussion of African American Women in Defense of Ourselves in chapter 3.

[†] The woman Barbara mentions is Aasiya Hassan, who was beheaded by her estranged husband, with whom she had started a television network dedicated to challenging stereotypes of Muslim people. Aasiya Hassan had filed for divorce six days before the murder. Muzzammil "Mo" Hassan was convicted of second-degree murder in 2011 and sentenced to twenty-five years to life.

Kimberly Springer: Why did you put this "Black Feminism Lives" button on all of the Combahee River Collective pamphlets?

Barbara S.: Because it's true!! [laughs] We wanted to make sure that people understood that this is real, this is ongoing, this is vital and viable. This is important. All of the Freedom Organizing pamphlets had buttons. It was also a marketing idea.

> ## "Kitchen Table: Women of Color Press had really high editorial standards and a love for the written word. And it also had a love for justice. That's what made it unique."

Kimberly: Very shrewd! I went on the hunt for the one with the button on it!

Barbara S.: Indeed. Kitchen Table was a movement press. It had high literary standards, but it was very connected to organizing. So, it was the perfect thing for us to do. Buttons are connected with movements.

Matt: Is there anything that you'd like to say about your time at Kitchen Table that we haven't talked about?

Barbara S.: One of the things that I always say, that I think is really important, is that Kitchen Table wasn't just a press. It did not function just as a press; it functioned as a beacon. It was a resource for women of color and very often lesbians of color, not just in this country, but around the globe. One of the reasons it was so hard to get everything done is because the expectations were not purely publishing expectations.

We were a literary publisher that produced books to a very high standard at the very same time that we had a strong political perspective about what the work was, what was important for us to prioritize and to do. We combined two streams of alternative publishing in this country: literary publishing and political publishing.

Particularly when we were down in New York City, we were engaged with people who were involved in the Central American Solidarity movement, in the anti-Apartheid movement. There was a Latin American book fair that used to happen in New York City, we prioritized that. There was an Asian American book fair, we worked that.

Another very important thing we did was to distribute books that were published by other independent presses. Some thought that that was not cost-effective. But we wanted to be able to use the platform of Kitchen Table to get the word out about other worthwhile projects, even if we did not publish them.

Kitchen Table was autonomously run by women of color. It was not solely a press; it wasn't just literary; it wasn't solely political. It had really high editorial standards and a love for the written word. And it also had a love for justice. That's what made it unique.

Matt: I remember, even in the early nineties, there was a lot of political work that we did, both locally in Albany, but also we went to Cleveland and did some work around . . .

Barbara S.: . . . homophobic attacks.

Matt: . . . all these anti-gay initiatives that were kind of virally running around the country, and we would go to activist conferences and do workshops. There was just so much political organizing work that happened in the press as well. We haven't talked about Kitchen Table Press's presence in Albany. What do you remember of the anti-gay initiative that was circulating in Albany in the early 1990s?

Barbara S.: What I remember is that we had an organization called the Feminist Action Network (FAN), and that was the time when that film, *Gay Rights, Special Rights*, was rearing its ugly little head all over the country. The film that was made by severe right-wing organizations, like Focus on the Family, as a kind of an insurgent way of dealing with the issue of homophobia in general. They wanted, of course, to popularize a homophobic agenda, and they thought, cleverly, that the way to do it was to get Black religious people, and Black people in general, on board. That's what that film was designed to do.

We were aware of that happening nationally. That was around the time of Audre's death, around 1992. Holding Our Own, the women's foundation in Albany, started an Audre Lorde funding initiative, which required that two organizations collaborate with each other in order to get the funding, to encourage collaboration and coalition. At FAN, we discussed doing something around this homophobic juggernaut and working with our local NAACP.

We had worked previously with the NAACP when the Ku Klux Klan came to Albany, in 1991.[*] The Martin Luther King birthday celebration was not that old at that time. They were targeting the Martin Luther King birthday celebration across the country, and they let it be known that they were going to be on the steps of the State Capitol. So we formed a really good coalition effort to protest that and really take the wind out of their sails. So when I asked the president of the NAACP, whose name was Anne Pope, she was very open to doing something together.

Then we began to do the work of, "Alright, so what are we going to do in Albany to push back against these homophobic attacks?" We did things like bringing religious leaders together. We did some stuff with the Metropolitan Community Church. One of the big things that we did was to organize a concert with Lavender Light, which is the people-of-all-colors LGBT [Lesbian, Gay, Bisexual, Transgender] gospel choir from New York City. We wanted to get some of the church choirs from Albany to also participate. Ultimately, we were not that successful, because I think people really got cold feet and we got mixed messages. The day of, we had a wonderful performance, but we didn't

---

[*] For an overview of the counter-actions against the Klan rally in Albany, see Sack (1991).

get that kind of buy-in from the church community. Ironically, of course, some of the people we were dealing with from those churches were themselves gay. So . . . [laughs] . . .

Matt: [laughs] I'm shocked!

Barbara S.: Yes! Shocked, just shocked! [laughter] But we were doing a lot of things to try to put these issues out there. We also raised the issue of AIDS in the Black community. We got support, again from Holding Our Own, to do work on AIDS in the Black community. That was back in probably 1989/'90, when there was little discussion in the Black context about what was going on with this very frightening epidemic. Now there is at least one Black organization focused on AIDS in Albany, and it has participation of people of various sexual identities and orientations. So we did make some progress there.

Matt: I remember I did a writing workshop for women with AIDS as well, and a writing group for women of color. Also, I remember a campaign against an anti-gay initiative in Albany. You and I both participated in canvassing, going around, walking around in the Black community . . .

Barbara S.: I don't remember that!

Matt: You don't? The right wing had actually walked around in Black communities, and given people information that said, "Did you know that homosexuals want your rights? They want to have the same rights that you do, but they make twice as much as you do." Remember all this?

Barbara S.: *No!* Maybe it was so traumatic I had to forget! [laughs]

Matt: There was a report that came out by "Overlooked Opinions," in the *Wall Street Journal*, that said that gays made so much money.

Barbara S.: Oh, yes. I do remember that.

Matt: They used that information to go around to the poor Black communities in Albany and say, "Look. These are the people who want to have the same rights that you do, but they are super privileged." They'd say, now you need an anti-gay initiative to protect your rights in this city. A whole bunch of different organizations came together to try to deal with this, but it was the eleventh hour when the white lesbian and gay establishment kind of turned to Black people and said, "Help." I don't know if you remember, because you were instrumental in trying to figure out how to . . .

Barbara S.: . . . so it wouldn't be the disaster that it was going to be if we were not involved.

Matt: The reason why I brought it up in this context is because what happened in Albany was threatening to happen in Cleveland as well.

Barbara S.: Indeed, indeed. With *Gay Rights, Special Rights*, the right wing was making a very concerted and strategic effort to get Black congregations and Black people generally involved in their homophobic campaigns. In Cleveland, the minister of the church that my sister and I had attended as children was one of the main people who was putting out this crazy stuff. It was just unacceptable. They were using the Black newspaper. I think there was a Black ministers' statement. We really wanted to do something to counter the madness, and because of our involvement with the National Gay and Lesbian Task Force, and other elements coming together, we were able to at least have some dialogue with people, LGBT people of color in Cleveland, Black LGBT people specifically. I really appreciated the fact that you were involved. Because you are an activist, and you know how to do that stuff, and we had worked together in Albany. It was great to take that somewhere else, particularly someplace called home.

Matt: It was amazing for me, that trip.

Barbara S.: Kitchen Table was an amazing platform for doing that kind of activist work. People knew where to find us. Most of this history was before people had PCs, not to mention Twitter and Facebook and all that. How do you find that one outpost where feminists, lesbians, all kinds of people are welcome? We were never separatist, so we always had wonderful relationships with gay men of color, like Joseph Beam, who was one of my closest friends, and Essex Hemphill. I was involved with the National Coalition of Black Lesbians and Gays, I was on their board. If you look at some of our catalogues, you will see books by Black gay men listed. We really were a meeting place of the word for people all over the world.

Matt: You organized a statement with Essex around race and queer publishing at the OutWrite Conference, I think it was like 1992? 1991? Before I ever got involved with Kitchen Table Press, I was there at that OutWrite Conference in Boston when that statement that you and Essex did was circulated, and that was pretty amazing.

Barbara S.: Yes, indeed, indeed. Actually, there's another one of those Joe Beam and I did at one of the National Black Writers Conferences hosted by Medgar Evers College (City University of New York). We challenged the Black literary establishment around their homophobia. That was hot! [laughter]

Matt: There was so much! Kitchen Table Press did so many different kinds of work. . . . It was crucial to me, absolutely. It was part of my development as a scholar, activist, and a writer to do that work at Kitchen Table Press. The poster of Audre that I see everywhere, I was there when we did that! I still have that poster from the I Am Your Sister Conference, above my computer in my home. Also, I still have the African American Women in Defense of Ourselves statement. Those posters were amazing . . .

Barbara S.: Sometimes I'll go into places far away, and there will be one of those posters. It's just delightful, really delightful.

Matt: Would you have liked to publish more fiction, more non-fiction? Where would you have wanted to take it?

Barbara S.: Both. Absolutely both. I think the anthologies played such an important role and still do. I wish we could have done more publishing. We did the best that we could under our circumstances. We didn't publish that many books over the lifetime of the press, but each book really seemed to make quite a difference.

Matt: Do you want to say anything about your decision to no longer be the publisher of Kitchen Table Press?

Barbara S.: It was fifteen years! From 1980, when we first started talking, until 1995. I was just ready to do other things. It was really important to make that decision. We had a transition team process, and we did try to settle the press in a good environment in Brooklyn. It was time for me to move on. Kitchen Table was more than a chapter in my life [laughs], but it was just time for me to do other things. It was very, very challenging to do it.

Matt: Did you write when you were at Kitchen Table? Did you get a chance to do any of your own writing?

Barbara S.: Not very much, no. In 1998, Rutgers University Press published a collection of my essays, *The Truth That Never Hurts: Writing on Race, Gender, and Freedom*. There's only one piece in that book that was new, "A Rose," and it was mostly focused on my Kitchen Table Press experience. I also worked on *The Reader's Companion to U.S. Women's History*, which was a trade reference book that I coedited with with Wilma Mankiller, Gwendolyn Mink, Marysa Navarro, and Gloria Steinem.

Before we finish, there is another thing that I would like to say. You, Matt Richardson, contributed so much to the vitality of Kitchen Table, to the success of Kitchen Table, to the meaning of Kitchen Table. I really felt that you loved the press so much, the way that I loved the press, and you were so excited to be involved with it. And you know, you were younger than I was. [laughter]

Matt: I was very little. Twenty-one or something!

Barbara S.: You had such commitment, such brilliance—that's the only word I can think of, brilliance—about what we were involved with together. We shared the perspective that you can't change things just by writing and reading about them. You were a great person for me to get to know and to work with at Kitchen Table during those years.

Matt: Thank you! I did love Kitchen Table Press dearly. I *loved* getting up in the morning and going to work. I did. Thank you so much for your mentorship, and your continued mentorship in print over the years. I could go back to your work over and over again, I teach it over and over again, and it is still groundbreaking material. The book that I'm just finishing up now* is the first Black lesbian monograph that is full-length literary criticism of works by Black women who identify as lesbians from around the diaspora. It's the only one, and I could not have even conceptualized of such a project without you, without the work you did before I ever even got to Kitchen Table Press. So, I thank you so much.

---

*Matt Richardson, *The Queer Limit of Black Memory: Black Lesbian Literature and Irresolution* (Columbus: Ohio State University Press, 2013).

The Cost of Independence

The elitist indifference of mainstream publishers fueled the founding of many independent presses. Sadly, feminist institutions could also be a vehicle for transmitting the racism and classism that pervades society. This dialogue among women of color publishers, published in the feminist newspaper Sojourner, *captures some of the hope and heartbreak of working with white feminists and publishers, and of pursuing a radical vision in a capitalist economy.*

"Packing Boxes and Editing Manuscripts: Women of Color in Feminist Publishing"
Sojourner Editorial Collective (1993)

> *From the original*: Each year, the American Booksellers Association (ABA) holds a multimillion-dollar trade convention that nearly all book publishers attend in order to market their books directly to booksellers. The day before ABA starts, nearly all the feminist and lesbian publishers gather for a day-long business meeting to discuss professional concerns and to network with other independent women's presses. The following conversation took place on May 28, 1993, in Miami Beach, Florida, the day after the women's publishers meeting. Participating in the discussion were: Martha Ayim and Deborah Barretto of Women's Press in Toronto, Canada; Jamie Lee Evans of Aunt Lute Books in San Francisco, California; and Mattie Richardson, Barbara Smith, and Lillien Waller of Kitchen Table: Women of Color Press in Albany, New York. The original dialogue was much longer and lasted about an hour and a half. A seventh participant asked that her remarks be deleted from this dialogue.
>
> —*Sojourner*

Deborah: Throughout the day I got more and more distressed about the way the meeting was going. We noticed that a few white women dominated the meeting and the women of color in the room didn't say much. It became increasingly difficult just to sit there. We had to do something about this. . . .

Barbara: I have to say, this meeting has always been the worst day of the year, as far as I'm concerned, for me as the publisher of Kitchen Table: Women of Color Press. Having been in that room as many years as I have been, and having been the only woman of color, has been just really a soul-destroying experience. There have been so many changes in women's publishing since the second wave of the Women's Movement began in the U.S. I think women come to these meetings now primarily as professional publishers, not as feminist activists who see publishing as a means to inspire other women and strengthen the movement.

Martha: It was important for me to be a part of this dialogue because yesterday's women's publishers meeting was so much about silencing. Silencing totally contradicts everything that I believe in as far as my commitment to feminist publishing. Feminism is not about taking up space that ought to be shared among a group of human beings. And yesterday, it came down to that level of racism. . . . I needed to hear what the other women of color in that room were feeling and thinking. As soon as we did get together, I started to feel human again.

Jamie: The white women had no self-consciousness at all about what they were doing. They weren't embarrassed by the fact, maybe not even aware of the fact, that they were the only ones speaking all day. Like we've said, it was painfully clear to us that we were silent, that we weren't speaking. . . . I wanted to respect the work that my sisters have done, of color and white, through their years in publishing. I know that it's not been easy. . . . But that balance between appreciating and respecting the longevity and the hard work that has gone into the women-in-print movement, and being disgusted at the lack of consciousness and respect for other women in the room, especially women of color, really collapsed, especially when the comment, "Edit books, don't pack cartons," was made. . . .

Jamie: I just thought, "How many of us have the luxury of making a statement like that?" And how can this woman not see the obvious classism, racism, and elitism in her comment? . . . It's been a long time since I've been in a room with white feminists who've been behaving so badly.

Lillien: I can't ever really recall a time when I was in a room filled with white feminists when they weren't behaving badly, frankly. Because, unfortunately, just like you were saying before, Jamie, it was as though we were not there. For them it was about acquisition. It was all about gimme, gimme more, how can we be white/feminist/lesbian versions of the big boys at Simon and Schuster and Random House? . . . There was absolutely nothing on the agenda about how we as a "feminist publishing movement" can aid each other. All of the women's presses serve different purposes and have different specific goals, but the ultimate goal should be liberation on all fronts.

Jamie: I was really struck by how so many publishers were speaking in "me" phrases. Everything was, "Well, I did this, I did that. My press this." There was no collective feeling at all. . . .

Mattie: I thought it was interesting that, during the entire day, no one mentioned the readers of the books in any way, shape, or form. We are here to provide material for women so that they go on in their daily lives with some sense that they deserve to exist in this world. The whole concept of that meeting was greed. "How can I get money?" Nobody ever said anything about the women we are supposed to be out there serving.

Barbara: I really felt the need to do something positive after a day of such degradation and feelings of frustration and powerlessness. This conversation is a rare and unique opportunity. There's never been a dialogue by feminist-of-color publishers. We've never done anything like this for our sisters to read because there haven't been very many of us. . . . I think that the politics of what's going on in women's publishing reflect the politics of the Women's Movement and the politics of the U.S. as a whole, which of course have been swinging ever rightward since 1980 or so, if not before. It's a real challenge to do the kind of work that we do in this context. But we are committed to doing it, and we're going to continue to do it regardless of the obvious gaps in understanding and responsibility of white women who are involved in the same kind of work.

Mattie: Every day is a struggle at Kitchen Table because we work with so few of the technological advances that other independent presses, including feminist presses and Black presses, take for granted. For example, we don't have a copy machine or a laser printer. We do without, but we still put out the best [books] we can.

Barbara: And that's why I have tried to keep Kitchen Table alive through the greatest adversity I've ever experienced in my life, really. My life would have been entirely different had I not become involved in Kitchen Table. You know what I'm saying?

Lillien: You don't get paid.

Barbara: Be that as it may, it's really important for women of color to have something. And as little as we have at Kitchen Table, I'll kid with our interns and volunteers and with Mattie and Lillien, and say, "It's a crazy place, but it's our place." Nobody can come in there and tell us how to do zip. Because the thing is, it's ours. So what if it's three little rooms on the first floor of a cracker-box house in the ghetto? Who cares? . . .

Lillien: [Our books] have an impact on feminist movement, they make a difference in the lives of women of color. . . . We get out a book a year. But I'll tell you something, ten years from now, people will still be reading Kitchen Table books; twenty years from now, thirty years from now, they'll still be ordering them for their classes. . . .

Barbara: The fact is that if we walked around ABA and looked at all the big multinational corporations, we would see more books by people of color than ever before, usually men. We're the ones who opened up the trend. The irony is that we can hardly make it from week to week financially. . . .

Jamie: In terms of multicultural work, people of color work, and work around racism, it's not because they like us that they're publishing us. Random House and the big publishers . . . walk down the aisles at ABA and see what we're doing; then they publish something just like it. They're stealing from us.

Barbara: Exactly. And sometimes . . . our authors end up going to them.

Mattie: The same dynamic holds true for some of the feminist presses that we tolerated in that room yesterday. Not all of them, some of them actually have a vision of inclusion, a vision of antiracist work in their publishing. Some of them, though, were upset that the "multicultural trend" was over, and, now, what they gonna do with all these books they can't sell?!

Martha: This situation parallels the gay "trend" that white women were complaining about yesterday.

Barbara: The gay white male publishing trend?

Martha: Yes. They were, rightfully, angry that some mainstream publishers pick up gay material as a trendy, lucrative market, that mainstream publishers are not publishing this material because they care about it. Yet this is exactly what is happening in white women's presses. When I see white women with no respect for their women of color colleagues and no representation of women of color [on staff], I find the fact that they publish women of color immediately suspect.

Mattie: Yeah, it was clear that our lives didn't make any difference to them. . . . They're not really dealing with the women who read the books; they're dealing with lining their pockets. . . .

Deborah: I think it's been really important for me personally to see so many more women of color being published. I know that before I worked for Women's Press, I didn't know anything about publishers, [except] Sister Vision, because they were a Black women and women of color press. I thought, "Wow, there is a press that is actually publishing women like me." It was like a lifeline really.

Martha: Even if white women's presses publish a lot of work by women of color, the fact that they don't hire women of color ignores questions of appropriation and power. We need to ask, who is evaluating and editing women of color's words? Even if white women's presses get outside women of color readers to read these manuscripts, the absence of women of color at such presses remains an issue.

I want to pick up on what you said earlier, Lillien, about the impact that women of color writing has made. Women of color have been vocal for a long time, but having access to publishing . . . has played a crucial role in our becoming a force that can no longer be ignored. When the writings of women of color are shared, so many people are inspired by it and recognize themselves in it. Definitely, for me, reading other women of color's words has given me so much strength. It is critical that we find a way to keep producing this work, to keep our presses alive. . . . All of us together have got to find a different way to do that.

Interview with Matt Richardson

Matt Richardson: What was the collective's relationship to other feminist presses?

Barbara Smith: We had wonderful help and support from other presses. There were women in print conferences that were held periodically. That was where we announced the birth of Kitchen Table, and we also did some significant fundraising. We got stories about the creation of KTP in several major national women's periodicals like *off our backs* and *Sojourner* without having to call or send letters or press packets.

There were other periodicals: *Sinister Wisdom*, *Conditions*, *Amazon Quarterly*, *The Second Wave*. There was a great synergy. And I can't forget the bookstores! We had so many women's bookstores all over the country at that time.

One of the people who was most supportive during that period is Judith McDaniel. She and her partner started an important feminist press called Spinsters Ink, and she came down to meet with us at the Kitchen Table office to talk about particular things; she had a wealth of knowledge and information. I remember her giving us things, too, like a scale for UPS. Really, really, really helpful and supportive. Nancy Bereano, who may have been with The Crossing Press at that time, and later created Firebrand Books, was also very helpful.

In the fall of 1981, we invited some of the white women's presses to a meeting at Audre's home on Staten Island to talk about starting Kitchen Table, and to ask them for their advice. We wanted to ask them should we become a for-profit business, or should we be a not-for-profit? That was an interesting discussion! Persephone was a for-profit business. Other presses were not-for-profit. The women from *Conditions* were probably at that meeting as well. It got contentious.

At that time, there were tensions in the women's movement around issues of anti-Semitism and racism. There were a lot of really difficult things going on among Jewish women and women of color. Cross-accusations: "Oh, you're anti-Semitic." "Well, you're racist." There were some really painful dynamics that affected people who we really liked and admired as they grappled with those issues of identity and political commitment.

Audre was so important in the things I am describing, because she was so clear in her politics, and really did not suffer fools gladly. It was great to have her as a friend and as a mentor in many ways. She had been through similar things already in the context of the Black Arts movement. When certain things would happen in the women's movement, she would be like, "Oh yeah. This feels very familiar." It was great to have her insights about all that was going on.

Matt: Was the Kitchen Table Press collective all lesbian?

Barbara: Hm. No. I had to think, but no, it was not. Audre was really a pillar, and stayed with the press for quite a while until her health made it difficult for her to continue with that. Cherríe and I were really very much committed to the press during those early years. Ana Oliveira, Betty Powell, Karen Sebastian, Mirtha Quintanales, and Sonia Alvarez are the names I can remember, but a number of people who were really committed didn't live in the New York City area.

Matt: What was some of the reasoning behind moving the press to Albany in 1986?

Barbara: I just did not want to live in New York City any longer. I wanted to live somewhere where getting to New York City was not difficult, but that wasn't as expensive. It was kind of an arbitrary decision. Judith McDaniel had recently moved there from further upstate, and I just thought, "Okay. Albany. That'll work." I never thought I would be there for the rest of my life.

Matt: Can you say a little bit about what went into the decision for the press to follow you to Albany?

Barbara: It was because of my level of commitment. By that time, Audre was no longer involved, Cherríe was no longer involved. It had been challenging times. It just seemed like the logical thing to do. And also, I found a person in Albany who really was committed to the press, a wonderful friend of mine named Lucretia Diggs.

Lucretia was probably in her late sixties at the time I met her. She was such a remarkable individual, and so, so instrumental in us surviving those early Albany days. When the press first moved there, we really were in dire straits. We were never rolling in dough, but we were always able to do what we needed to do, including making trips to conferences and conventions like the American Booksellers Association and the National Women's Studies Association. But at the time I moved the press to Albany, we had virtually no resources. And we built it back up.

Matt: What were some of the things that you didn't like about publishing?

Barbara: The editorial work. We were always understaffed, and we always got far more manuscripts than we could ever publish, far more manuscripts than we ever could adequately read. That really bothered me. The workload was humongous, and I always felt that I wasn't doing enough. The volume was just too much. That was my major frustration, not being able to do everything and respond to everything that people sent.

I feel badly until this day about the letter that never got answered, the phone call that didn't get returned. We just didn't have the capacity. Not only were we reaching a national audience, we heard from people all over the world. We got letters from Japan, from the United Kingdom, from France, from Central and South America. Lots of people knew what we were doing. We heard from people in India—there were presses that were being formed, like Kali for Women in India, Sister Vision in Canada, there were wonderful presses in London and in the United Kingdom. There were international women's book fairs that were happening during that period. It was exciting. It was fascinating, but it was a lot to have to handle without capacity.

Matt: What about the financial struggle? Personal and for the press?

Barbara: Our books did very well, particularly *This Bridge Called My Back* and *Home Girls*. Those were our two strongest-selling titles. We did very well in general, as far as getting our books out and getting them to their audience. Because they were well done and well edited, a lot of our success was because of course adoptions. But, as I said, we were never rolling in dough. Printing bills are some really big bills!

I don't think I was very good at business, either. That was not my motivation. We successfully ran a press that made a difference, but the financial struggles were significant.

I never had any aspirations to have a lot of money. I just wanted to be able to support myself. There was teaching, and there were speaking engagements. It was just making the decisions that one needed to make in order to do what one was passionately committed to. And for fifteen years, that was Kitchen Table: Women of Color Press.

6

Building Multi-Issue Movements

As a person of color, a lesbian, and a feminist, I've spent a great deal of energy refusing to let others pit the various elements of who I am against each other. I always maintain that these elements only seem to be in opposition in this particular time and place, under U.S. capitalism, whose functioning has always required that large groups of people be economically, racially, and sexually oppressed, and that these potentially dissident groups be kept divided from each other at all cost.
—Barbara Smith, "Blacks and Gays: Healing the Great Divide" (1993)

In four decades of building movements for liberation, Barbara brings her whole self—Black, female, lesbian, working class, radical—and refuses to leave any part at the door. Barbara consistently extends a loving challenge to leaders in the Civil Rights; feminist; and lesbian, gay, bisexual, transgender, and queer (LGBTQ) movements to expand their conception of justice. Oppressions and liberations must be addressed in the same way they are experienced—simultaneously. A narrow focus on one form of oppression often ignores how race, gender, and class hierarchies leave entire segments of our communities excluded from full representation and participation in democratic life.

This chapter explores the demanding, yet joyful, work of building coalitions and multi-issue political agendas. To build multi-issue movements means approaching political organizing in a way that consciously and strategically connects particular issues to the overall struggle for social and economic justice. Often, this requires simultaneous attempts to eliminate the economic injustice, racism, sexism, and homophobia in society to open the path to transformative change. To be genuinely anti-racist, anti-sexist, and pro-justice entails a political analysis and commitment to creating new ways to be inclusive, transparent, and accountable, which requires building coalitions. As Bernice Johnson Reagon famously argued in "Coalition Politics: Turning the Century," "You don't go into coalition because you just *like* it. The only reason you would consider trying to team up with somebody who could possibly kill you, is because that's the only way you can figure you can stay alive" (Reagon 1983: 356–57). Coalition-building forces groups out of the "safe little rooms" they build for themselves, and, if you are doing it successfully, can make you feel like you are going to die. But it is also the only way to win inclusive, transformative campaigns for social justice.

This chapter demonstrates how a sophisticated understanding of identity politics and the analysis of multiple, interlocking oppressions that centers Black feminist politics provide resources for truly effective multi-issue organizing and coalition-building. Barbara's writings and practice consistently illustrate how key choices by movement-builders—to choose the easy one-issue target, to leave an important but potentially difficult player out of the coalition, to fall back on top-down leadership styles, or to accept assimilation rather than fight for larger social change—can replicate hierarchies of privilege in their organizations and strategies, and limit their vision for creating a just and peaceful world.

The primary interviews for this chapter were conducted by Barbara Ransby and Joo-Hyun Kang. Barbara Ransby is a historian, writer, and longtime political activist who has published dozens of articles and essays in popular and scholarly venues. She is most notably the author of an award-winning biography of Civil Rights activist Ella Baker, entitled *Ella Baker and the Black Freedom Movement: A Radical Democratic Vision* (University of North Carolina, 2003), and of *Eslanda: The Large and Unconventional Life of Mrs. Paul Robeson* (Yale University Press, 2013). She is the director of both the Gender and Women's Studies Program and the campus-wide Social Justice Initiative at the University of Illinois at Chicago and professor of history, African American studies, and gender and women's studies. She is also the cofounder of the Black feminist network Ella's Daughters and the second editor in chief of *Souls*, a critical journal of Black politics, culture, and society.

Joo-Hyun Kang is an activist fighting for racial/gender justice, self-determination, and LGBTST (Lesbian, Gay, Bisexual, Two-Spirit, and Transgender) liberation. Formerly affiliated with Astraea Lesbian Foundation for Justice, the Audre Lorde Project, and Kitchen Table: Women of Color Press, she currently directs Communities United for Police Reform, which is leading a movement to end discriminatory and abusive policing practices in New York, including the NYPD's stop-and-frisk policy. She is a licensed acupuncturist.

Forging Coalitions: Fighting Homophobia, Racism, and Classism

The articles and interviews in this section convey the inspiration, trepidation, pain, and success embodied in Barbara's efforts to have Black Lesbian, Gay, Bisexual, Transgender, and Queer (LGBTQ) members fully and openly accepted in the African American family and in the LGBTQ movement. The articles cover the years 1985 to 2000 and succinctly capture hard-earned lessons from decades of sustained activism. "Soul on Hold" and "Blacks and Gays" squarely take on prejudices within the African American community, while "Where Has Gay Liberation Gone?," a chapter in Homo Economics, *argues against a political strategy that uses claims of "unity" to marginalize the issues of gays and lesbians who are not white, not Christian, and not professional middle class. Since the LGBTQ movement emerged in the 1970s, there have been five gay rights marches on Washington, D.C. (1979, 1987, 1993, 2000, and 2009). In "Will People of Color Pay the Price?," Barbara joins fellow activists to critique the top-down methods and narrow single-issue focus of the planners of the Millennium March. Fighting for LGBTQ rights requires joining coalitions to address the economic exploitation, police violence, and racial discrimination that many LGBTQ people face. In "Organizing in Albany: Justice for Diallo," Smith lends her voice to those who condemned a heinous case of police brutality to support the family of Amadou Diallo, a young African immigrant who was shot forty-one times by police. In interviews with Joo-Hyun Kang and Kimberly Springer like-minded colleagues discuss multi-issue, multiple-oppressions frameworks for effective organizing. We include two letters to the editors of local newspapers that Barbara wrote to express public support of a high-profile billboard campaign promoting the health of Black gay men. We end the section with an article from* Colorlines *magazine that describes innovative LGBTQ grassroots organizing where activists, especially in the U.S. South, pursue broad-based campaigns that connect across generations, classes, and races, and operate outside of 501(c)3 funding structures. Their vibrant multi-issue organizing strategies reject the narrow strictures of a rights-only agenda. Full inclusion, it turns out, is both ethically sound and strategically effective.*

"Soul on Hold"
Barbara Smith (1985)

Twenty years ago, I met Fannie Lou Hamer. I'd just graduated from high school in Cleveland. My sister, Beverly, and I were very active in the Congress of Racial Equality, and I met Mrs. Hamer at a party following a rally she'd addressed. Mrs. Hamer was sitting in a chair in the middle of the basement room and people were going up to pay their respects. She looked like the women in my family. She was stout, wore a wig, and had trouble with her legs (in her case because of the beatings she'd taken in jail). Even then I knew she was one of the most important people I would ever meet.

I didn't come out as a lesbian until ten years later. Since then, I've often reflected on what it would have been like to be an openly gay person in the Civil Rights movement. Reading Hamer's early statement supporting equal rights for women, long before most Black women dared to make the connection, I suspect her politics would have encompassed me as a lesbian. After all, it was the open-hearted spirit and hard work of older, poor Black women that made the movement possible. But the few known homosexuals in the movement—James Baldwin, for example—did not demand recognition of their homosexuality, and I'm sure there would have been no place for me as an openly lesbian activist.

One of the major barriers for lesbians and gay men was, and remains, black religious institutions. Traditionally an inspirational and organizing tool in the Black community, the church has almost always taken a stand against homosexuality. This condemnation naturally causes great pain among the large numbers of Black lesbians and gay men who want to maintain religious ties, which are also ties to family, culture, and home. That lesbians and gay men can be found in every Black church in this country—even in the pulpit—is hardly a well-kept secret. Yet, Blacks and other people of color pretend that homosexuality is a "white disease," and brand gay people in their communities as "white-minded." Many Black people still consider homosexuality a sin, an illness, a crime, or worse, tantamount to renouncing membership in the race.

Because of our shared status as outcasts, the Black community often shows great tolerance for members who do not conform to white social, sexual, and legal conventions. But for gay people, that tolerance is only extended if we stay closeted, "play it, but don't say it." Peaceful co-existence between Black homosexuals and heterosexuals is bought at the exorbitant price of our silence. The same sisters and brothers to whom racial passing would be anathema expect Black lesbians and gays to pass as straight and endure similar devastation to the spirit.

"Peaceful co-existence between Black homosexuals and heterosexuals is bought at the exorbitant price of our silence. The same sisters and brothers to whom racial passing would be anathema expect Black lesbians and gays to pass as straight and endure similar devastation to the spirit."

Many of the current generation of Black gay activists came through the Civil Rights and Black Power movements, and we see our situation in political terms. Just as we refuse to accept racist assaults, we also refuse to bow to attacks upon our sexuality, which is as crucial to our identities as race. The development of Third World lesbian and gay organizations, closely tied to the growth of Third World feminism, has prompted volatile debate about homosexuality in the Black community after years of no talk at all.

One of the stormiest confrontations occurred in 1983, during the fight to have a lesbian or gay speaker at the 20th Anniversary March on Washington.

Congressional Representative Walter E. Fauntroy, national director of the march, polarized the situation when he reputedly equated gay rights with "penguin rights." Fauntroy later denied this statement, but also asserted that the march "would not be an aggregation of single-issue groups" and insisted that including proponents of abortion or gay rights might be "interpreted as the advocacy of abortion or the gay lifestyle." The very march being commemorated only added Black women—like Fannie Lou Hamer—to the speakers' roster at the last moment.

Then as now, the organizers' concept of coalition building was shortsighted. As another movement veteran, Bernice Johnson Reagon, has written, "You don't go into coalition because you just like it. The only reason you would consider trying to team up with somebody who could possibly kill you, is because that's the only way you can figure you can stay alive. . . . There is an offensive movement that started in this country in the '60s that is continuing. The reason we are stumbling is that we are at the point where in order to take the next step we've got to do it with some folk we don't care too much about. And we got to vomit over that for a little while. We must just keep going" [Reagon 1983].

The fact that 17 out of 20 members of the Black Congressional Caucus, including Fauntroy, are co-sponsors of national gay rights legislation is ironic, but not contradictory. As supporters of social justice whose consciences were shaped by the Civil Rights movement, these politicians may recognize that gay people face discrimination. Yet, they also believe the stereotype that all gays are white men. What they—like the Black population in general—have yet to grasp is how many of their brothers and sisters are also gay.

It took action by seven of Fauntroy's Black lesbian and gay constituents to turn the tide in that speaker controversy. Three days before the march, a group attempted to meet with Fauntroy in his office. When he failed to appear, they refused to leave until four of them were arrested. As a result of the sit-in (a pointedly appropriate tactic), an 11th-hour decision was made to permit Black lesbian poet Audre Lorde to speak briefly at the rally. The march's organizers, including Coretta Scott King, Fauntroy, and the Rev. Joseph Lowery, called a press conference and spoke as individuals in support of the federal gay Civil Rights bill. It was the first major public recognition by the Black Civil Rights establishment that our movements are related.

But gains on that side are being offset on another: gay white racism is as divisive as Black homophobia. The new professional profile of the proper gay activist assumes that gay equals white, reflecting growing conservatism in the white gay movement. For example, the National Gay and Lesbian Task Force (NGLTF), which lobbied heavily for gay inclusion in the 20th Anniversary March, refused to endorse this past spring's April Actions in Washington for domestic justice and against intervention in Central America and apartheid in South Africa. NGLTF's decision reflected the narrow scope of a white-oriented agenda, which favors assimilation over larger social change.

The failure of gay as well as Third World and feminist groups to adequately address our concerns has spurred autonomous organizing by gay men and lesbians of color. For the first time, we are stating unequivocally that coalitions fail when individuals must meet a white, male, heterosexual standard. Just as one of the goals of the Civil Rights movement was to get white people to believe we were actually human, at least human enough to use the same bathrooms and water fountains, homosexuals have to convince many heterosexuals that we are likewise human.

For me and many other Black lesbians and gay men, the Civil Rights movement is where it all began. It was where we learned that ethical and spiritual as well as political transformations were possible because we experienced the changes within ourselves. So, we expect no less a transformation from our own communities, both Black and gay. As Reagon says, "You can't tell me that you ain't in the Civil Rights movement. You are in the Civil Rights movement that we created, that just rolled up to your door. But it could not stay the same, because if it was gonna stay the same it wouldn't have done you no good. Some of you would not have caught yourself dead near no Black folks walking around talking about freeing themselves from racism and lynching. So by the time our movement got to you it had to sound like something you knew about. Like if I find out you're gay, you gonna lose your job" [Reagon 1983].

This spring a friend, Suzanne Pharr, arranged for me to speak at Philander Smith, a historically Black college in Little Rock [Arkansas]. Suzanne, who is white, lives across from Central High School, the scene in 1957 of one of the cruelest battles to end segregation. Daisy Bates, president of the National Association for the Advancement of Colored People at that time, was a guiding force throughout the fight. When I was in Little Rock, I met Mrs. Bates, and just as when I met Mrs. Hamer, I knew I was in the presence of greatness. This time, however, I would not be left wondering whether my lesbianism would be acceptable to an important Civil Rights figure. Mrs. Bates came to hear me speak about being a Black woman, a writer, a lesbian.

Needless to say I was shaking inwardly even more than I usually am before I come out in public. In many ways, I owe my life to people like Mrs. Bates and Mrs. Hamer, and the thought that they might disapprove of me because I'm a lesbian is shattering. But I came armed with a number of lesbian titles from Kitchen Table: Women of Color Press and ready to talk about Jesse Jackson's inclusion of lesbians and gay men in his Rainbow Coalition. I also explained how being out has given me the strength and peace of mind to continue being political, and also to write. How there was a time during the height of Black power and Black nationalism when I doubted that I'd ever be politically active again, since I in no way fit their macho definition of Black femaleness. I know of too many gay people who were lost to the cause when movements made them pariahs. When I looked up from my notes I was relieved to see nods and even smiles. Later, Mrs. Bates had me sign her copy of my anthology, *Home Girls*. It was the feeling of acceptance that only your family can give.

"Blacks and Gays: Healing the Great Divide"
Barbara Smith (1993)

In 1993, it has been declared that two essential aspects of my identity are at war with one another. As a person of color, a lesbian, and a feminist, I've spent a great deal of energy refusing to let others pit the various elements of who I am against each other. I always maintain that these elements only seem to be in opposition in this particular time and place, under U.S. capitalism, whose functioning has always required that large groups of people be economically, racially, and sexually oppressed, and that these potentially dissident groups be kept divided from each other at all cost.

For the first time, however, the relationship between the African American and gay communities is being widely debated both within and outside of movement circles, and surviving as a Black lesbian or gay man has become that much harder. Catalysts for this discussion have been gay leaders' cavalier comparisons between lifting the military ban [on gays serving in the military] and racially desegregating the armed forces following World War II, and the decision by the NAACP and other Black Civil Rights organizations to speak out in favor of lesbian and gay rights and to support the March on Washington [for Lesbian and Gay Rights in 1993]. Those decisions have met with protests from some sectors of the Black community and have also spurred the debate.

Ironically, the group of people who are least often consulted about their perspectives on this great divide are those who are most deeply affected by it: Black lesbian and gay activists. Contradictions that we have been grappling with for years, namely, homophobia in the Black community, racism in the gay community, and the need for both communities to work together as allies to defeat our real enemies, are suddenly on other people's minds. Because Black lesbians and gays are not thought of as leaders in either movement, however, this debate has been largely framed by those who have frighteningly little and inaccurate information.

Thanks in part to the white gay community's own public relations campaigns, Black Americans view the gay community as uniformly wealthy, highly privileged, and politically powerful, a group that has suffered nothing like the centuries of degradation caused by U.S. racism. Rev. Dennis Kuby, a Civil Rights activist, states in a letter to the *New York Times*: "Gays are not subject to water hoses and police dogs, denied access to lunch counters, or prevented from voting." But most Blacks have no idea that we are threatened with the loss of employment, housing, and custody of our children, and are subject to verbal abuse, gay bashing, and death at the hands of homophobes. Kuby's statement also does not acknowledge Black lesbians and gays who have been subjected to all of the racist abuse he cites.

Because we are rendered invisible in both Black and gay contexts, it is that much easier for the Black community to oppose gay rights and to express homophobia without recognizing that these attacks and the lack of legal protections affects its members.

The racism that has pervaded the mainstream gay movement only fuels the perceived divisions between Blacks and gays. Single-issue politics, unlike gay organizing that is consciously and strategically connected to the overall struggle for social and economic justice, do nothing to convince Blacks that gays actually care about eradicating racial oppression. At the very same time that some gays make blanket comparisons between the gay movement and the Black Civil Rights movement, they also assume that Black and other people of color have won all our battles and are in terrific shape in comparison with gays.

"Single-issue politics, unlike gay organizing that is consciously and strategically connected to the overall struggle for social and economic justice, do nothing to convince Blacks that gays actually care about eradicating racial oppression."

In a December 1992 interview in the *Dallas Voice*, lesbian publisher Barbara Grier stated: "We are the last minority group unfairly legislated against in the U.S." Grier's perception is, of course, inaccurate. Legislation negatively affecting people of color, immigrants, disabled people, and women occurs every day, especially when court decisions that undermine legal protections are taken into account.

In 1991, well before the relationship between the gay community and the Black community was a hot topic, Andrew Sullivan, editor of *The New Republic*, asserted the following in *The Advocate*, "The truth is, our position is far worse than that of any ethnic minority or heterosexual women. Every fundamental civil right has already been granted to these groups. The issues that they discuss now involve nuances of affirmative action, comparable pay and racial quotas. Gay people, however, still live constitutionally in the South of the '50s. . . ."

Sullivan's cynical distortions ignore that quality of life is determined by much more than legislation. Clearly, he also knows nothing about the institution of slavery. Joblessness, poverty, racist and sexist violence, and the lack of decent housing, health care, and education make the lives of many "ethnic minorities" and "heterosexual women" a living hell. But Sullivan doesn't care about these folks. He just wants to make sure he gets what he thinks he deserves as a powerful white male.

Lesbians and gay men of color have been trying to push the gay movement to grasp the necessity of anti-racist practice for nigh onto 20 years. Except in the context of organizing within the Women's Movement with progressive white lesbian feminists, we haven't made much progress.

I'm particularly struck by the fact that, for the most part, queer theory and politics, which are so popular, offer neither substantial anti-racist analysis nor practice. Queer activists' understanding of how to deal with race is usually limited to their including a few lesbians or gay men of color in their ranks, who are expected to carry out the political agenda that the white majority has already determined, and/or sleeping with people of color.

> **"I'm particularly struck by the fact that, for the most part, queer theory and politics, which are so popular, offer neither substantial anti-racist analysis nor practice."**

This month Lesbian Avengers from New York City will travel to several states in the Northeast on what they are calling a "Freedom Ride." Lesbians of color from Albany, New York pointed out that the appropriation of the term is offensive because the organization has no demonstrated involvement in anti-racist organizing and has made no links with people of color, including non-lesbians and gays in the communities they plan to visit. Even when we explained that calling themselves "Freedom Riders" might negatively affect the coalitions we've been working to build with people of color in Albany, the group kept the name and simply made token changes in their press release.

The Right Targets Communities of Color

These divisions are particularly dangerous at a time when the right wing has actually targeted people of color with their homophobic message. As white lesbian activist Suzanne Pharr points out in "Racist Politics and Homophobia" (*Transformation*, July/August 1993):

> Community by community, the religious Right works skillfully to divide us along fissures that already exist. It is as though they have a political seismo-graph to locate the racism and sexism in the lesbian and gay community, the sexism and homophobia in communities of color. While the Right is united by their racism, sexism, and homophobia in their goal to dominate all of us, we are divided by our own racism, sexism, and homophobia.

The Right's divisive strategy of enlisting the Black community's support for their homophobic campaign literally hit home for me in June. A Black lesbian who lives in Cleveland, Ohio where I grew up, called to tell me that a group of Black ministers had placed a virulently homophobic article in Cleveland's Black newspaper, *The Call and Post*.

Entitled "The Black Church Position Statement on Homosexuality," the ministers condemn "HOMOSEXUALITY (including bisexual as well as gay or lesbian sexual activity) as a lifestyle that is contrary to the teachings of the Bible." Although they claim to have tolerance and compassion for homosexuals, their ultimate goal is to bring about "restoration," i.e., changing lesbians and gays back into heterosexuals in order "to restore such individuals back into harmony with God's will." . . .

The ministers also held a meeting and announced their goal to gather 100,000 signatures in Cleveland in opposition to the federal gay and lesbian Civil Rights bill, HR431, and to take their campaign to Detroit and Pittsburgh. A major spokesperson for the ministers, Rev. Marvin McMickel, is the minister of Antioch Baptist Church, the church I was raised in and of which the women in my family were pillars. Antioch was on a number of levels one of the most progressive congregations in Cleveland, especially because of the political leadership it provided at a time when Black people were not allowed to participate in any aspect of Cleveland's civic life.

McMickel states, "It is our fundamental, reasoned belief that there is no comparison between the status of Blacks and women, and the status of gays and lesbians." He explains that being Black or female is an "ontological reality . . . a fact that cannot be hidden," whereas "homosexuality is a chosen lifestyle . . . defined by behavior not ontological reality."

By coincidence, I met Rev. McMickel in May when Naomi Jaffe, an activist friend from Albany, and I did a presentation on Black and Jewish relations at the invitation of Cleveland's New Jewish Agenda. Antioch Baptist Church and a synagogue co-sponsored the event. My cousin had informed me that McMichol had just stepped down as head of the NAACP. Naomi and I were struck by his coldness to us throughout the evening. This was in sharp contrast to the kind reception we received from both the Black and Jewish participants, most of whom were elder women. We guessed that it was because of his homophobia and sexism. Little did we know at the time how right we were.

When I first got news of what was going on in my home town I was emotionally devastated. It would have been bad enough to find out about a major Black-led homophobic campaign in any city in this country, but this place wasn't an abstraction, it was where I came from. It was while growing up in Cleveland that I first felt attracted to women and it was also in Cleveland that I grasped the impossibility of ever acting upon those feelings. Cleveland is a huge city with a small town mentality. Now I was being challenged to deal with homophobia, dead up, in the Black community at home.

I enlisted the help of NGLTF [National Gay and Lesbian Task Force] and Scot Nakagawa, who runs their Fight the Right office in Portland, Oregon, and of members of the Feminist Action Network (FAN), the multi-racial political group I belong to in Albany. Throughout the summer we were in constant contact with people in Cleveland. . . . We had several meetings, primarily with Black lesbians, but found very few people who were willing to confront the severe threat right in their midst.

Most of the women we met even refused to acknowledge the seriousness of the ministers' campaign. We had been warned that remaining closeted prevented activism, but we also found a deep reluctance to deal with Black people in Cleveland's inner city, because of both closeting and class divisions. Cleveland's white lesbian and gay community had never proven itself to be particularly supportive of anti-racist work, and racial segregation seemed to characterize the gay community, just as it does the city as whole.

I cannot say that our effort to support a visible challenge to the ministers in Cleveland was particularly successful. The right wing's ability to speak to the concerns and play upon the fears of those it wishes to recruit; the lack of visionary political leadership, locally and nationally, among both Black and white lesbians and gays; and the difficulty of countering homophobia in a Black context, especially when it is justified by religious pronouncements, make this kind of organizing exceedingly hard. But we had better learn how to do it quickly and extremely well if we do not want the Christian right wing to end up running this country.

Since returning from Cleveland we have been exploring the possibility of launching a nationwide petition campaign to gather at least 100,000 signatures from Black people who support lesbian and gay rights. One Black woman, Janet Perkins, a heterosexual Christian who works with the Women's Project in Little Rock, Arkansas has already spoken out. In a courageous article entitled "The Religious Right: Dividing the African American Community" (*Transformation*, September/October 1993), Perkins calls upon the ministers in Cleveland and the entire Black church to practice love instead of condemnation. She writes:

> *These African American ministers fail to understand they have been drawn into a plot that has as its mission to further separate, divide, and place additional pressure on African Americans so they are unable to come together to work on the problems of the community* . . . [italics original]. What is needed in our community is a unity and bond that can't be broken by anyone. We must see every aspect of our community as valuable and worth protecting, and yes, we must give full membership to our sisters and brothers who are homosexual. For all these years we have seen them, now we must start to hear them and respect them for who they are.

This is the kind of risk-taking and integrity that makes all the difference. Perkins publicly declares herself an ally whom we can depend upon. I hope in the months to come the gay and lesbian movement in this country will likewise challenge itself to close this great divide, which it can only do by working toward an unbreakable unity, a bond across races, nationalities, and classes that up until now this movement has never had.

"Where Has Gay Liberation Gone?
An Interview with Barbara Smith"
Amy Gluckman and Betsy Reed (1997)

Amy Gluckman and Betsy Reed: What connections do you see between . . . gay oppression and our economic system, and issues of class?

Barbara Smith: I think that's really a very complicated issue. I often say that, unlike racial oppression, lesbian and gay oppression is not economically linked, and is not structurally and historically linked, to the founding of this country and of capitalism in the United States. This country was not founded on homophobia; it was founded on slavery and racism and, before that, prior to the importation of slaves, it was founded on the genocide of the indigenous people who lived here, which also had profound racial consequences and rationales. . . . As with all groups, I think that our economic system has the most implications for lesbians and gay men when their class position makes them vulnerable to that economic system. So in other words, it's not that in general being lesbian or gay puts you into a critical relationship to capitalism, it's that a large proportion of lesbians and gay men are poor or working class, but of course they're completely invisible the way the movement's politics are defined now.

So much of this society is about consumerism. As long as lesbians and gay men are characterized as people who have huge amounts of disposable income and who are kind of fun and trendy . . . probably capitalism can incorporate them. If they begin to think about how extending lesbian and gay rights fully might shake up the patriarchal nuclear family and the economic arrangements that are tied to that, then that might be the point at which capitalists would say, "Well no, I don't think we can include that."

Amy and Betsy: Right-wing organizations have used inflated income information about gays and lesbians to try to drum up homophobia, which is almost a direct appeal to people's economic frustration. As an organizer, have you encountered that?

Barbara: What they say is that these people do not qualify as a disenfranchised group because look at their income levels, as if the only way you could be disenfranchised is by income or lack of access to it. When they tell the untruth that all of us are economically privileged, of course that fans it. I can't say that I have personally seen that myth being picked up. When I come into contact with straight people, it's usually Black people. And it's usually around Black issues.

I don't know that the economic thing is such an issue for heterosexual Black communities; I think it's the moral thing. It's not so much that those white gays are rich, it's that those white gays are sinners, they're going against God. And they're also white, so they must be racist. And if you are a Black lesbian or gay man, then you must be a racial traitor. Those are the kinds of things that I hear, not so much that they're so rich. But I think there's an assumption on the part of most people of color that most white people are better off than we are anyway. It's an assumption that in some cases is accurate and in some cases is a myth that is perpetuated to keep people apart who should be in solidarity with each other because of class. It's a myth that keeps people away from each other, because there are some real commonalities between being white and poor and being of color and poor.

> **"I care about everyone who is under siege. . . . I care about all people who are not getting a fair shake, who are not getting an equal chance to fulfill their maximum potential and to live without fear and to have the basic things that every human needs: shelter, clothing, quality health care, meaningful and fairly compensated work, love and caring and freedom to express and to create, all those things that make life worth living. How limited would my politics be if I was only concerned about people like me!"**

Amy and Betsy: Can you say more about the links that you see between racism and gay oppression?

Barbara: All of the different kinds of oppression are tied to each other, particularly when it comes to the kinds of repression and oppression that are practiced against different groups of people. When you look at a profile of how people who are oppressed experience their oppression, you see such similar components: demonization, scapegoating, police brutality, housing segregation, lack of access to certain jobs and employment, even the taking away of child custody. They have done that to poor women of color and to poor women from time out of mind. . . . Our enemies are the same. That to me is the major thing that should be pulling us together. . . . My own experience [is] as a person whose [Black and lesbian] identities [are] linked. I think that the clearest answers come from those of us who simultaneously experience these oppressions. . . . Of course, I am concerned about these issues because in my own life and experience I know what struggle is about, I know what oppression is about, and I have seen and experienced suffering myself.

That's not the only reason I am an activist, though. I care about everyone who is under siege. Some people think that because I'm so positively pro-Black and because I speak out against racism at every turn, that I don't really care if white people are suffering. Quite to the contrary. I care about all people who are not getting a fair shake, who are not getting an equal chance to fulfill their maximum potential and to live without fear and to have the basic things that every human needs: shelter, clothing, quality health care, meaningful and fairly compensated work, love and caring and freedom to express and to create, all those things that make life worth living. How limited would my politics be if I was only concerned about people like me! Given who I am as a Black woman and a lesbian and a person from a working-class home who is a socialist opposed to the exploitation of capitalism, well maybe that isn't so narrow. But what if I only cared about other Black lesbians? I would be sitting on the head of a pin.

The systems of oppression really do tie together. The plans and the strategies for oppressing and repressing our various groups are startlingly similar, and a society that is unjust, it's like cancer. . . . You can't contain it. It poisons the body politic of the society as a whole, and therefore you can't have singular solutions.

Amy and Betsy: One of the arguments people make for single-issue activism is that the gay community is too diverse to agree on an entire multi-issue agenda. They say, "We'll never get anywhere if we have to agree on everything else, so we're just going to work on one thing that we do agree about."

"If gay rights were put in place tomorrow, my behind would still be on fire."

Barbara: That's LCD politics—lowest common denominator politics. What they don't take into account, though, is the dehumanization and the disempowering of those of us for whom a single issue isn't going to get it. They pretend that it's unifying, but it's not. I'm a lesbian, but what if I'm concerned about the fact that in the state of New York, from now on they're going to be fingerprinting welfare recipients. That bothers the hell out of me. You see, I could have been one, and I could be one still. . . . Whether I ever am [on welfare], I know right from wrong. I may be a lesbian, but I may be very concerned about the fact that my children don't have decent schools to go to, and with school lunch programs being cut, they won't have anything to eat when they get there.

If gay rights were put in place tomorrow, my behind would still be on fire.

I would still be in ultimate danger here, because racism is still in the saddle. And so is class oppression, and so is sexual oppression. So getting a middle-of-the-road, mainstream gay rights agenda passed, how's that going to stop me from being raped? How's that going to help me not get breast cancer? How is it going to help the environment not get poisoned? How is it going to help the children of my community to have a chance for a decent life?

"Will People of Color Pay the Price? A Statement by People of Color in Support of the Ad Hoc Committee for an Open Process"*

Ted Beck, Mandy Carter, Chandra L. Ford,
Kara Keeling, and Barbara Smith (1999)

People of color have taken the leadership in raising the very first clear and decisive objections to the process involved in planning the Millennium March on Washington (MMOW) since the day that rally was announced. We have continued to raise substantive criticisms of the MMOW, taking it as an opportunity to denounce the way that the mainstream lesbian, gay, bisexual, and transgendered (LGBT) movement demands that we neglect our race, gender, class status, and other matters of passionate concern in order to carry out their narrow agenda.

The events surrounding the MMOW are symptoms of problems that are prevalent in the mainstream white-led LGBT movement. As people of color, we suffer disproportionately from the lack of diversity among those in positions of leadership in the mainstream movement because we have no one at the table to represent us. At the 1998 meeting between five white people at which the decision to "march" on Washington was made, not only were there no people of color present, but there was no youth, bisexual, transgendered, or union representation (to name a few of our rich, diverse community).

Such blatant disregard for the needs and interests of entire segments of our community is not only indefensible, it also prohibits any possibility of realizing the types of substantial social, economic, and political change needed to make our lives better. When we raised concerns about this process, these white-led organizations, which exert tremendous influence in the national LGBT movement, moved ahead with planning the march anyway, stating that the march was a done deal because, without consulting those very LGBT people they claim to represent, they had already spent money on the event.

In an effort to silence our criticisms, they then plugged people of color onto the board of directors of the MMOW. . . . But, far from addressing our concerns, this gesture raised a new set of problems which are also typical of the movement as a whole: Because the majority of the forces that affect us as people of color both within the LGBT movement and in the larger American society are structural, mere reform will not address them.

Putting people of color on the board of directors of an organization whose lack of democracy is itself the problem does not address the underlying issues. It is simply putting a band-aid over an oozing, infected sore. It does not change

---

* A subsequent version of this statement was written by Mandy Carter, Kara Keeling, Barbara Smith, and Diana Onley-Campbell, dated March 29, 2000, and accessible at www.newyorkslime.com/ahc/poc-statement-f.html.

the content of the MMOW; the sore remains infected. People of color in positions of leadership can only represent the interests of people of color within a context that demands their accountability. Because there are many political differences among us, even as people of color, it is not wise to assume that by simply being a person of color, one is automatically acting in the best interest of people of color.

"People of color in positions of leadership can only represent the interests of people of color within a context that demands their accountability."

No efficient channels of accountability currently exist on the national level. Those national organizations we have created to be our faces and voices have, by and large, made no effort to hear our concerns and act on our behalf. On its web site (available only to those with the resources to have Internet access), the MMOW presents its target population to potential sponsors as the "affluent and loyal gay/lesbian market" and makes no effort to disclose the terms of its contracts, including deals made with sponsors and the ultimate fate of the demographic and personal information it collects from and about participants. Evidently, the MMOW is banking on the "affluent," predominately white male, elements of our community. If marching on Washington is a political action, what will a 99.9% white audience on the mall in D.C. achieve for us as lesbian, gay, bisexual, two-spirited, transgendered (LGBTST) people of color?

The white-led gay organizations have failed to address issues of dire and immediate concern to LGBTST people of color. Because we realize that these issues cannot be separated from those the mainstream movement incorrectly presents as specific to homosexuality, many of us simultaneously devote our time and energy to fighting against police brutality, racist violence, violence against women, environmental racism and environmental destruction, and fighting for reproductive freedom, economic justice, and many other critically important causes.

"Any issue concerning oppression, domination, or exploitation, whether it is of one person over another, one group over another, one culture over another, is an altogether 'queer' issue. Our liberation cannot be won without that simple recognition."

The MMOW debacle has forced us to closely examine the current direction of our movement. As people of color, we have always raised crucial questions concerning the processes and assumptions that conspire to silence us and make us invisible. Any issue concerning oppression, domination, or exploitation, whether it is of one person over another, one group over another, one culture over another, is an altogether "queer" issue. Our liberation cannot be won without that simple recognition. Until the white-led mainstream LGBT movement grasps this point, we will pay the price.

We call on the LGBTST community as a whole to join us in our call for an open process within the LGBTST community. We also invite LGBTST people of color to continue working towards our own self-sufficient and multi-issued LGBTST people of color movement and community.

"Organizing in Albany: Justice for Diallo,"
Barbara Smith (2000)

From the original: When the trial of the police officers who murdered Amadou Diallo was moved from New York City to Albany, N.Y., activists in Albany immediately organized. Barbara Smith, Black lesbian-feminist writer, thinker, socialist and revolutionary, has been involved in the Capital Region Justice for Diallo Committee. In the days before and after the shocking verdict, Feb. 25, exonerating the four New York City cops who murdered Amadou Diallo, she reflected on the meaning of the trial, the verdict, and the organizing around it.

—*News & Letters*

The verdict makes me feel like, once again, my life as a Black person isn't worth anything in this society. There are two parallel worlds in America: the world of clueless white people, and the world of Black people. The murder of Amadou Diallo is about race, but not the way the press said the case was "racialized." The white power structure is absolutely oblivious to the racial nature of this case. The true race content is that the police consider every Black person a dangerous criminal, and that Black people are right to fear for their lives in this society. I think Amadou Diallo was terrified that night. But the police couldn't even read that as a possibility: they just saw his race, assumed he was dangerous, and started shooting.

"If police can shoot an unarmed person 41 times and it's not murder, then what is murder? From the change of venue, to the unbelievably inadequate prosecution, to the judge's rulings limiting the evidence—the entire criminal justice system came together to protect these officers from answering for their crime. When you look at how quick that same system is to put young people of color in prison, we are convinced there is a double standard by race in this country." That's what Vickie Smith, a spokesperson for Capital Region Justice for Diallo Committee, said in our press release.

"Lesbian feminists of color ... virtually invented multi-issue political organizing in the late 20th century."

The positive in the picture is in our organizing here in Albany around the case, which provides a dynamic example of lesbian feminists of color—who virtually invented multi-issue political organizing in the late 20th century—putting our politics into practice. The fact is that there has been lesbian-of-color leadership around this issue. Vickie Smith was one of the first to get word of the change of venue from lesbians and gays of color who were active around the Diallo case in New York; we immediately helped form the coalition, Capital Region Justice for Diallo Committee.

It marks a new day in some ways that we as lesbians of color are being recognized as proactive on an issue—police brutality—that is not driven solely by sexuality or gender. Every Diallo rally has had speakers making connections between issues that concern LGBT (lesbian-gay-bisexual-transgender) people of color and people of color in general. These mark real and practical challenges around homophobia, because we are there on the ground doing the work on an issue that matters to everybody.

This is creating a real context for dialogue in the Black community here around issues of sexuality. This doesn't mean there has been no homophobia in the organizing; there has been, and we've been the targets. But I'm pleased that we've been able to expand the definitions of what LGBT work looks like. We also had a youth day with participation from the Audre Lorde Project in Brooklyn [a center for LGBT people of color].

What does all this mean? Police brutality is the leading edge of repression, showing us where white supremacy is and what crimes it is capable of. Every community I've visited lately, and all across the country, I notice more and more police brutality being reported. The gunning down of an unarmed 14-year-old in Hartford is ruled "justifiable homicide." In Providence, an off-duty Black police officer went to help other officers who were in pursuit of suspects; his "fellow" officers, including one who had been in the same cadet class with him, shot him dead. All they saw was his race, and his race meant to them that he was a dangerous criminal. This is what a recent issue of the excellent magazine *Colorlines* referred to as "domestic militarization" of communities of color.

I'm struck by how pandemic it is. Activists in Seattle have been trying to get a civilian police review board. We are trying to do the same thing in Albany.

We've had people dying "mysteriously" in custody and many examples of police misconduct and brutality. The fight against police brutality is a cutting edge issue for all communities that are fighting racism.

The question now, after the verdict, is: what do we do next? Here in Albany, we did an excellent job of organizing in the Capital Region Justice for Diallo Committee. We brought people and communities together who had never worked together before. The struggle continues.

Interviews with Joo-Hyun Kang and Kimberly Springer

Joo-Hyun Kang: What was it like to be out as a Black lesbian in the 1970s? What made you come out in that period?

Barbara Smith: Oh, because I was a lesbian. I mean, I *was* a lesbian. I had lesbian feelings since I was a teenager undoubtedly. It wasn't just like a notion or a whim. It was like this hidden and very painful reality that I knew and couldn't speak to and didn't believe I would ever be able to, because there was no context in which it felt safe to do so.

Joo-Hyun: What was your support to be able to do so?

Barbara: The women's movement. The fact that I was meeting women who identified as lesbians and who were very well integrated and who were not miserable about it. Who were, in fact, excited! It was so challenging to come out in that period, and also so dynamic. It was both very scary and very exciting, especially in the years just after Stonewall occurred. I came out less than a decade after Stonewall occurred. The spirit of Stonewall was still very much in place. I remember being in Boston after coming out and going to a demonstration against Anita Bryant and her homophobic manifesto coming out of Florida.* It was just so exciting to be involved in what was actually the lesbian and gay *liberation* movement at that time.

Joo-Hyun: You were coming out in the context of so many of the key artists and cultural workers, thinkers, and public intellectuals that influenced my generation. How did you meet Audre Lorde?

Barbara: We met at a Modern Language Association convention in New York City. I was on the Modern Language Association's Commission on the Status of

---

* Barbara is referring to Bryant's campaign against a 1977 ordinance in Dade County, Florida, which would have prohibited discrimination on the basis of sexual orientation. Bryant became the leader of a coalition called Save Our Children and coauthored a book with Bob Green called *At Any Cost* (Bryant and Green, 1978). Bryant's argument was that homosexuality endangered children, and because homosexuals could not have children themselves, they were trying to recruit or molest straight people's children. Her campaign was successful, and the anti-discrimination ordinance was overturned.

Women in the Profession, which was a key organization in building women's studies in this country. It was a funded commission, so we had these wonderful events that we would plan because we had to organize programming for the annual national convention. It was kind of like a wish list. "Who do you want to see at this year's MLA?" "Oh, Judy Grahn, and Adrienne Rich, Audre Lorde, June Jordan."

So many people whose names are kind of legendary now. We would all just be in a room sometimes together. I knew Sapphire, Joan Gibbs, who started a magazine called *Azalea* with her partner, the first Black lesbian literary magazine. *Azalea* would have these Black lesbian writers' conferences down in New York City. We would all be there. I met Cheryl Clarke at a socialist feminist conference in Yellow Springs, Ohio in 1975.

Audre also did great work internationally. She traveled a great deal. Then, of course, *This Bridge Called My Back* was a revolutionary intervention for letting women of color, not just in this country but also globally, know that we had a right to exist. We had our own perspective, our own politics, our own agendas . . .

Joo-Hyun: You, Audre, and so many of the women of color, especially lesbian women of color during that period, were so influential on all of the social justice movements in the United States, and around the world, in terms of having a multi-issue vision.

"Lesbian women of color during that period were so influential on all of the social justice movements in the United States, and around the world, in terms of having a multi-issue vision."

When I think about a lot of the work the more progressive social justice organizations around the country are doing, most of them are trying to integrate more multi-issue work, whether it's within the women's movement or whether it's within environmental justice, or LGBT. They talk about "intersectionality" now, but I've always traced the intersectionality dialogue to your writing, including the Combahee River Collective Statement.

Barbara: The Combahee River Collective Statement, and the work of the Combahee River Collective, was so groundbreaking, because we grasped that concept early on. I think it's because we were really genuinely pulling the analysis out of our lived experience. We had a perspective that wasn't just a feminist women's movement mainstream perspective, nor was it just a lesbian perspective. We had also our roots in the Left, Black movements, and peace movements.

Joo-Hyun: So much of what gets called the "social justice movement" now is under the umbrella of nonprofits. A lot of them are doing really important work that makes a difference in people's daily lives, and some of them also organize. But during the seventies it wasn't the same. It was before the landscape of political work, justice work in the United States was transformed by this massive growth of formal non-profit organizations, governed by IRS tax codes and regulations.

Barbara: Absolutely. The 501(c)3-ing of the movement, as they say.

Joo-Hyun: What are the rays of hope around organizing and movement-building you see in this country?

Barbara: I think that immigrant rights is one of the most critical struggles in this nation at this time. It is indicative of where our politics are, and it will probably play out in our next major election cycle, the presidential campaign of 2012. These are movements that have great integrity, are in the tradition of working for justice, and are doing so on a multi-issue, grassroots level.

Joo-Hyun: How about work for prisoners' rights and justice for political prisoners?

Barbara: We had the first statewide prisoner justice conference here in Albany recently. I was working for New Yorkers for Alternatives to the Death Penalty at the time. I'm really glad that I went and saw that our prison abolition movement work continues. There are people who eventually want to see the prisons abolished. I also think the death penalty movement is really interesting. I didn't realize, until I went to a small conference this past summer, how conservative some of the strains of that were: everything from religious conservatives who have a kind of right-to-life perspective, to people who are pulled in [by the system] like law enforcement.

Joo-Hyun: And the anti–death penalty movement doesn't universally have abolitionist views in relation to prisons. For many, it seems specific to the use of the death penalty. It's interesting though, some of the unlikely alliances they've been able to build.

Barbara: It is. Here's an example. We had a small group discussion during the conference to talk about the issue of diversity. A person from one of the state organizations described how they had gone to a [Gay] Pride event in June and had an information table about abolishing the death penalty. One of their conservative religious supporters had called up, maybe more than one, and said they wanted to know why they had gone, and objected to their having been there.

His response to them was to say, "Well, I respect your opinion," and leave it at that. I said, "That was not what I would have said, nor do I think it's the right response," and he asked very honestly and openly what I would have said. I said, "I would have said that the reason we went to the Pride event is that the people at the Pride event are supporters of abolishing the death penalty, just as you are, and that's why we were there." Because that would have given that person who objected something to think about: Oh, so they actually oppose the death penalty, too, just as I do?

I want to tell you about something that is going on around my relationship to these issues in my local community. In Our Own Voices, an LGBT of color

Figure 6.1: In Our Own Voices billboard: "I Am Gay, and This Is Where I Pray." One of three images used on eighteen billboards in the Capital Region in 2010 as part of an organizing campaign to promote Black gay health, decrease homophobia, and encourage HIV testing, launched by In Our Own Voices. Used with permission.

organization [in Albany] that concentrates on health issues, recently launched a campaign to address homophobia. I noticed a billboard on the highway just before Christmas that said, "I am gay. And this is where I stay." And I said, "Oh, look at that. That's great." Then a couple of weeks later, I received an e-mail from the In Our Own Voices e-mail list about how the *I Am Gay* billboard campaign is being attacked by people in Schenectady, specifically by the only Black member of the Schenectady City Council. [Each campaign billboard featured one of three themes: This is where I stay. This is where I play. This is where I pray. Each included a picture of a Black gay man surrounded by people appropriate to the setting—home, basketball court, church.]

Joo-Hyun: What were they claiming as the basis for why they're attacking it?

Barbara: It's the religious stuff. A couple of black ministers, most of whom I have met in the last two years, have joined in calling for the removal of the billboards. The ministers are talking about what if a teenager . . .

Joo-Hyun: . . . or a *child* sees it?

Barbara: Exactly! There was an article in the Schenectady *Daily Gazette*, and then a few days later there was one in our Albany *Times Union*. In the Albany *Times Union* article, there was a minister who I've sat at a table talking with about how to stop the killing and the shooting [in Black communities], who was quoted as saying, "Anyone who God hates, I hate too."

In Our Own Voices asked people to write letters to the editor. I was puzzling over that and feeling every time I read another thing, "Who else could do this as effectively?" Especially when you consider that one of the people who was at the center of the homophobic response was also a council member. How great would it be to have another council member from the other city council in the city next door say something very different?

I had been reading a publication of the Southern Poverty Law Center, and it had some great quotes about how statistically LGBT people are the most likely to be the victims of hate crimes. I am reading this on Sunday, the day before Martin Luther King Jr.'s birthday and I realize, "Okay, the handwriting's on the wall. I've got to write these letters." So I stayed up all night on Martin Luther King Jr.'s birthday writing two different letters to the editor to the two different newspapers.

Joo-Hyun: It sounds like the billboards for In Our Own Voices have been a really good educational opportunity.

Barbara: It's an incredible splash. There are eighteen billboards in four different counties.

Joo-Hyun: That's so fantastic, because regardless, it's just going to bring up all this daily conversation.

Barbara: And they are funded by the New York State Department of Health. People are just bent over that! The purpose of them is to create an atmosphere in which Black gay men, in particular, will feel more comfortable about their identity, and therefore will get tested, and also will participate in safer sex.

Joo-Hyun: So it's coming out of HIV prevention strategy.

Barbara: Yes, but it's not explicit. It doesn't say you need to do so and so about HIV or whatever.

Joo-Hyun: It's addressing homophobia.

Barbara: One of the things I say in the letters is that "to my knowledge, God does not hate anybody." I talk about how for those people who are invoking religious justifications for homophobia, they might want to keep in mind that religious justifications were used for slavery. They're going to hate these letters. They are going to hate them! [laughs]

Kimberly Springer: What about the Black church? Because that's one of the questions I get about *Living for the Revolution*, my book about Black feminist organizations. Did Black feminists grow up in the church? Where does the Black church fit?

"Please Don't Fan Flames of Bigotry," Barbara Smith (2011)

The negative reactions to the "I Am Gay" billboards in Schenectady show how very much public education concerning the actual diversity of the Capital Region is needed. Unchallenged homophobia, like unchallenged racism, has devastating impact upon those who are its targets.

The billboards address the social context that contributes to the rising rates nationwide of HIV and AIDS among Black gay men who may be reluctant to be tested because of the stigma and bigotry they experience in their home communities.

The Southern Poverty Law Center, which was founded in 1971 as a Civil Rights law firm and now also monitors all types of hate group activity, reports that "Gays, or those perceived to be gay, are by far the most targeted in America for violent hate crimes . . ." The center also notes that hate speech contributes to the violence.

To my knowledge, God does not hate anybody. During a period when the nation is examining how hateful rhetoric may lead to deadly consequences,[*] it is disturbing that local civic and religious leaders would fan the flames of bigotry.

—Barbara Smith, Member, Common Council Fourth Ward, Albany, NY

---

[*] The mass shooting in Tucson, Arizona, at Congresswoman Gabrielle Gifford's Congress on Your Corner event had just occurred.

Barbara: There are Black feminists, some of them who name themselves "Womanist," who indeed have grappled with organized Black religious institutions. But that's not work that I have been very involved in except in the early 1990s when the white right wing was really targeting Black congregations to help with their homophobic agenda. They did this film called *Gay Rights, Special Rights*, and they really cynically used Civil Rights history to make a case for why Black people should be homophobic. It was horrible for those of us who are out as lesbians or gay men.

Kimberly: But I wonder if that's a side effect or a symptom of how Black feminism fails to grapple with the Black church. Have we, as Black feminists, put into place the foundation within Black churches for people who might have a progressive agenda within them, to be able to argue for Black feminist principles?

Barbara: People who are engaged in Black religious institutions have done that. For example, during that period in Albany, Holding Our Own, one of the earliest women's foundations in the country, developed the Sister-to-Sister grant initiative. It was conceived as a tribute to Audre Lorde and required that all those who applied do so with another organization, and worked in coalition with other

---

"It's a Diverse World, and That Includes Sexuality," Barbara Smith (2011)

Re: Jan. 11 article, "Critics urge removal of gay signs": I am very disturbed by the negative reactions to the billboards in Schenectady that inform the public of what they should already know—that gay people are an integral and contributing part of the community.

Those who view members of the lesbian, gay, bisexual, and transgender community as sinners and criminals—as opposed to business owners, church-goers, doctors, volunteers, members of the military, parents, teachers, and taxpayers—are very much in denial about the diversity of the world they inhabit.

Those who invoke religion to justify homophobia might consider that slavery was likewise defended upon religious grounds.

It is doubtful that anyone ever made a snap decision about their sexual orientation because they saw a billboard. Countless individuals, including teen-agers, however, have committed suicide, been viciously attacked and murdered because of societal bigotry toward their identity.

—BARBARA SMITH, Albany

The writer is a member of the Albany Common Council.

groups. I was a part of the Feminist Action Network, which was a multi-racial, multi-issue group founded to organize against racism from a feminist perspective.

We were dealing with and confronting homophobia in the Black community, and we applied for the grant with the local chapter of the NAACP. We also worked with our local Metropolitan Community Church, which is a gay, predominantly white denomination. We had the idea of inviting Lavender Light, the LGBT people of color gospel choir from New York City, to do a concert in Albany in cosponsorship with Black congregations and their choirs. We were not that successful, because at the last minute, amazingly, some of those local choirs pulled out. We were quite disappointed. But we were making the effort.

"If you're not connecting these issues with ethical commitment and integrity, you're just not doing the work. You can't be in a silo."

Joo-Hyun: You were talking about structural inequality, where the struggles are around structural issues. Where does the LGBT movement fit into that [work] these days? Or does it?

Barbara: Now that Don't Ask Don't Tell has been resolved [in 2010 when the Congress ended mandatory expulsion of gays and lesbians once their sexuality became known], the major issue is marriage. Those of us who have a radical feminist critique of marriage, patriarchy, and sexual conformity have never been that excited about that. As we know coming from the movements during the period that we did, there are people who are sex radicals and people who question the received wisdom about the *Leave It to Beaver*, Donna Reed lifestyle that many LGBT people aspire to.

Joo-Hyun: If you could redirect the agenda of the movement so that it wasn't fully on [marriage and military issues], where would you want to redirect it?

Barbara: I don't know a huge amount about what Queers for Racial and Economic Justice are doing, but it sounds like what I would be doing, if I were working in a movement context now. I always suggest that you look at the whole situation of institutionalized oppression and figure out how your work connects to that. If you're not connecting these issues with ethical commitment and integrity, you're just not doing the work. You can't be in a silo. You have to understand: How did it get this way? Why does it need to change? What does justice look like?

A two-income couple, both men (so you make more than women on the average), and you're white: that doesn't describe every queer couple. You can't be so narrow and superficial that you think the one thing you want—to get married—fixes everything. There are LGBT people at the very same moment in time who are homeless. How do we fix that?

Joo-Hyun: Zuna Institute did a national survey about a year ago, looking at the top issues for Black lesbians, and the top three included employment/ economic security, healthcare, and education. Marriage was somewhere soon after that, but it wasn't the top three. That brings home the reality that LGBT folks are facing the same bread-and-butter issues as other people across the nation.

Barbara: I bet if you ask a comparable group of [straight] people who share a class identity, [the answer would be the same]. People are not doing well these days. Economically they're not doing well. I think you would find very similar [concerns]. That's commonality. That is a moment to think, "Well, maybe we could work on that together."

Joo-Hyun: One of the things I remember was that there was a separate category about employment non-discrimination. It was separated from access to work. So the LGBT movement generally talks about employment discrimination, which is of course a real issue. But in this economy, it's kind of a non-issue if there are no jobs.

Barbara: Exactly.

"A New LGBT Politics Seeks to Marry Issues, Not Just People"
Jamilah King (2012)

In April of 2009, Alexis Pauline Gumbs and her partner Julia Wallace sat in a small conference room in Durham, N.C. Both were Southern-born, twentysomething activists with academic training—Gumbs was wrapping up a PhD in English at Duke, and Wallace had a master's degree in theology—but they weren't there to debate theories or strategize about tactics. They were at a larger annual gathering of labor and human rights organizers, and around them sat over a dozen women, all of them self-identified black lesbians, and each one at least 20 years older. The workshop session was led by Mandy Carter, a longtime LGBT activist, and Carter wanted to share only one thing: stories.

So they did. The women told decades-old stories about trips through the South with their high school basketball teams, of first loves, and of families. Gumbs, now 30, remembers being struck by each woman's bravery and overwhelmed by the sense that it was these women and their stories that laid the foundation for younger activists like herself to do the work about which she's become passionate. "It's very rare for people who are not in the same age group and who are part of the LGBT community to be together in the same space," Gumbs says. . . .

The [event] turned into the Mobile Homecoming Project, a multimedia storytelling project to uncover hidden histories. Gumbs and Wallace scour their networks to find older members of the black LGBT community, record them on video or podcasts, and sometimes host screening events that bring together people from all ages.

The project has allowed them a firsthand look at how political work is being done in the regions of the country long overshadowed by their coastal counterparts. From Selma to San Antonio, Durham to Detroit, and dozens of small towns in between, they've seen up close how circumstance and necessity have helped build bridges across issues ranging from racial discrimination and unemployment to immigration and marriage equality.

"This type of work—a patient focus on building broad and unexpected communities outside of the old gay political capitols—is starting to look like the future of LGBT politics."

This type of work—a patient focus on building broad and unexpected communities outside of the old gay political capitols—is starting to look like the future of LGBT politics. And as the debate over same-sex marriage in particular drags on, LGBT communities in places like North Carolina, Minnesota, and Mississippi are no longer cringing at it, they're setting about redefining the discussion.

Uniting Communities

This year North Carolina became a pivotal stepping stone in the fight over marriage equality. In the spring, opponents of gay marriage ginned up support to pass Amendment 1, a revision to the state's constitution that strengthened North Carolina's ban on same-sex marriages. The state's conservative swing on family law wasn't unique—29 similar amendments have already passed nationwide at the state level. But what was different in North Carolina was the broad coalition that sprung up to oppose the move.

The Protect North Carolina Families Coalition came together from over 135 activist and legal groups, community centers, university clubs, and religious institutions. They pointed out that Amendment 1 wasn't just an attack on gay marriage, but on anyone who fell outside of the conservative norm. They made their case that the law threatens domestic violence protections for unmarried women, strips legal protections away from children, and jeopardizes the pensions of senior citizens.

"It was more than a gay issue or equal rights for marriage issue," says Bishop Donagrant McCluney, the North Carolina field organizer with Southerners On New Ground (SONG), an LGBT group that was part of the coalition that opposed the amendment. "It was more about codifying discrimination in the constitution."

Though Amendment 1 eventually won at the polls, the broad coalition that opposed it signaled a more promising future for progressive politics in the state. As Kenyon Farrow wrote for *Colorlines.com* shortly after the vote, the coalition's work was a sign that activists are building a strong social justice infrastructure for the future.

SONG's Paulina Helm-Hernandez said that the group was initially reluctant to join the coalition, after having been active in previous amendment fights in which race was ignored. But it was the group's members that pushed it forward, especially its members of faith who were angry that the right was using religion to villainize members of the LGBT community.

"Our base pushed back really hard on us," says Paulina Helm-Hernandez, the group's co-director. "They said, 'We know that amendment fights may not be the most strategic thing, but they're saying we're pedophiles and we shouldn't be around children.'"

A similar story is unfolding in Minnesota. . . . According to activists in the region, these sorts of coalitions aren't just political niceties—they're necessities.

Race and LGBT Rights

The day after North Carolina passed amendment 1, President Obama made his historic endorsement of same-sex marriage, telling ABC's Robin Roberts, "I've just concluded that for me personally it is important for me to go ahead and affirm that I think same-sex couples should be able to get married." For the first time in the United States' history, a sitting president said publicly that same-sex relationships were equal to straight ones. But many in the media speculated that Obama's endorsement would infuriate black voters, who were often cast as more homophobic than the rest of the electorate. A day after the president's announcement, cultural critic Touré wrote at *Time* that black voters would punish Obama over his support of gay marriage. . . .

In reality, research has shown that black opposition to marriage equality has softened considerably. Since 2008, the proportion of African Americans favoring gay marriage has increased, while opposition has fallen almost 20 points. A recent *Washington Post–ABC News poll* found that people of color overall are more likely to support gay marriage than whites.

But for many black LGBT activists, polling misses the point entirely. Keith Boykin wrote at the *Huffington Post* challenging the assumption that blacks had suddenly grown to support gay marriage. "We didn't evolve overnight. We've been evolving for decades, even when the media wasn't paying attention." . . .

Perhaps the most symbolically important endorsement, however, came from the NAACP. On May 19, the 103-year-old Civil Rights group passed a resolution that endorsed gay marriage as a civil right.

Derrick Johnson, president of the Mississippi State Conference NAACP, said that his members supported the NAACP's position because they saw their own liberties were at stake.

"It is no coincidence that we are seeing multiple states dredge up marriage purity laws at a time when the middle class is becoming aware of growing economic inequities between the richest Americans and the rest of this nation," Johnson wrote in a statement that was released shortly after the NAACP's announcement. "Likewise, it is no accident that the issue of same-sex marriage arises at a time when a host of southern states seek to create laws restricting voting." . . .

"There was an attempt or belief that if the NAACP or others take a position in support of not codifying discrimination, that the religious base in our community would deeply oppose that. There have been attempts to create a wedge among the religious community and the Democratic Party based on morality issues—personhood, marriage equality, and abortion—and it hasn't happened."

In fact, progressive organizers have learned to use those potential wedges to their advantage. Last fall, Pro-lifers In Mississippi introduced an amendment that would have outlawed all forms of abortion, including in cases of rape, incest, or for women who face life-threatening complications. The amendment, sponsored by conservative group Personhood Mississippi, was ultimately defeated thanks to a broad coalition of constituencies that came together to oppose it.

The Costs of Change

While Southern and Midwestern activists deal with today's hot button political issues, funding—or a lack of it—has helped unite those with seemingly disparate interests.

"There hasn't been as much Left infrastructure in the South that's been built around single-issue fights," says SONG's Helm-Hernandez. "A lot of the organizations we work with that are building in the South can't really do single-issue reform work. We can't really do educational reform work without doing anti-racism work without addressing economic factors in our communities."

While that sort of hustle, as Helm-Hernandez calls it, might strain what little resources do exist, some activists think it's an important part of having the freedom to try new things.

"A lot of our infrastructure for us to do movement-building in the Southeast does not come directly out of the 501(c)3 structure," says Helm-Hernandez. . . . "People are very resistant to incorporating it because they know that it's been such a sucker of energy and resources."

To that end, Gumbs acknowledges that the Mobile Homecoming Project gets its energy from its grassroots supporters.

"Those of us who are working for liberation in the South have had to be creative and have also had the opportunity to be creative, because the kind of major funding norms that seem to govern other more metropolitan areas of the Northeast and California have not really been accessible," says Gumbs. "The Mobile Homecoming Project is completely grassroots funded. It's funded by everybody—five dollars at a time."

Whether that will be enough to support a long-term movement remains to be seen. What's clear is the coming years will see plenty of opportunities to find out, as insurgent conservatives push hard at the state level on everything from women's health to LGBT rights. Gumbs says that in her travels she's come across many people whom she calls "exiles," or Southern LGBT people who've felt the need to flee to other cities to live their lives safely and honestly. "For those of us who are here and have the privilege of being our whole selves here, the coalition-building is strengthened by how blatant the right is in attacking all of us."

Embraced by the Black Radical Congress

The Black Radical Congress (BRC) was launched in Chicago in 1998 with a historic gathering of two thousand activists representing the full spectrum of progressive and leftist ideologies and strategies for political change. Barbara's involvement in the planning and public events for the Congress marked a unique instance of Black radicals explicitly recognizing and including LGBTQ issues and participation as integral to a militant Black political agenda. In this section, we provide several historical documents from the BRC, a transcript of Barbara's dialogue at the opening event with then–graduate student Kimberly Springer and her assessment of the experience from interviews with Barbara Ransby, a key BRC organizer, and Alethia Jones, who attended. For Barbara, fighting for a society free of racism, exploitation, and violence meant fighting for freedom for the Black community, for women, and for lesbian and gay liberation simultaneously. Participation in the Black Radical Congress finally acknowledged her principled commitment to the liberation of everyone in her work against violence, police brutality, homophobia, and racism.

"The Struggle Continues: Setting a Black Liberation Agenda for the 21st Century: Call for Participation in the Black Radical Congress"
BRC Organizing Committee (1998)

Black people face a deep crisis. Finding a way out of this mess requires new thinking, new vision, and a new spirit of resistance. We need a new movement of Black radicalism. We know that America's capitalist economy has completely failed us. Every day more of us are unemployed and imprisoned, homeless and hungry. Police brutality, violence, and the international drug trade threaten our children with the greatest dangers since slavery. The politicians build more prisons but cut budgets for public schools, day care, and health care. They slash welfare yet hire more cops. The government says working people must pay more taxes and receive fewer services, while the rich and the corporations grow fat.

Black people and other oppressed people have the power to change the way things are today, but first we must unite against the real enemy.

Now is the time for a revival of the militant spirit of resistance that our people have always possessed, from the Abolitionist Movement to outlaw slavery to the Civil Rights movement of the 1950s, from Black Power to the anti-apartheid campaign of the 1980s. Now is the time to rebuild a strong, uncompromising movement for human rights, full employment, and self-determination. Now is the time for a new Black radicalism.

If you believe in the politics of Black liberation, join us in Chicago in 1998 at the Black Radical Congress. If you hate what capitalism has done to our community—widespread joblessness, drugs, violence, and poverty—come to the Congress. If you are fed up with the corruption of the two party system and want to develop a plan for real political change, come to the Congress. If you want to struggle against class exploitation, racism, sexism, and homophobia, come to the Congress. The Black Radical Congress is for everyone ready to fight back: trade unionists and workers, youth and students, women, welfare recipients, lesbians and gays, public housing tenants and the homeless, the elderly and people on fixed incomes, veterans, cultural workers, and immigrants. You!

Sisters and Brothers, we stand at the edge of a new century. The moment for a new militancy and a new commitment to the liberation of all Black people, at home and abroad, has arrived. Let us build a national campaign toward the Black Radical Congress, setting in motion a renewed struggle to claim our historic role as the real voice of democracy in this country. Spread the word: "Without struggle, there is no progress!" Now's the time!

"Dialogue between Barbara Smith and Kimberly Springer"
Democracy Now! (1998)

Kimberly Springer: You are often introduced as Barbara Smith, Black lesbian feminist activist, and some people seem to think that doesn't mean that you are involved with the Black struggle. So I wanted you to talk somewhat about your political activism.

Barbara Smith: Starting when, Kim? [laughter] How did I become politicized? I became politicized by being raised by a family of Black women who were completely unrecognized as human beings and as people with their own agency in this country and this society. Because I came of age in the 1960s, I had that rare opportunity to attend what I call "A School for Life." All we had to do during those days was to turn on the television or to read the newspaper and we saw the glaring contradictions of this society being played out in front of our faces. Sometimes you could not tell the news footage from Watts, from Detroit, from Cleveland, where I grew up, from what was going on in Saigon or in Soweto. It's

"Black Radical Congress Principles of Unity," BRC Organizing Committee (1998)

1. We recognize the diverse historical tendencies in the Black radical tradition including revolutionary nationalism, feminism, and socialism.

2. The technological revolution and capitalist globalization have changed the economy, labor force, and class formations that need to inform our analysis and strategies. The increased class polarization created by these developments demands that we, as Black radicals, ally ourselves with the most oppressed sectors of our communities and society.

3. Gender and sexuality can no longer be viewed solely as personal issues but must be a basic part of our analyses, politics, and struggles.

4. We reject racial and biological determinism, Black patriarchy, and Black capitalism as solutions to problems facing Black people.

5. We must see the struggle in global terms.

6. We need to meet people where they are, taking seriously identity politics and single-issue reform groups, at the same time that we push for a larger vision that links these struggles.

7. We must be democratic and inclusive in our dealings with one another, making room for constructive criticism and honest dissent within our ranks. There must be open venues for civil and comradely debates to occur.

8. Our discussions should be informed not only by a critique of what now exists, but by serious efforts to forge a creative vision of a new society.

9. We cannot limit ourselves to electoral politics—we must identify multiple sites of struggles.

10. We must overcome divisions within the Black radical forces, such as those of generation, region, and occupation. We must forge a common language that is accessible and relevant.

11. Black radicals must build a national congress of radical forces in the Black community to strengthen radicalism as the legitimate voice of Black working and poor people, and to build organized resistance.

hard for me to believe that anyone could be part of my generation and not be politically active and radical.

Kimberly: One of the principles of unity of the BRC is opposition to homophobia. So I wanted to ask you how easy—or difficult—has it been to incorporate lesbians, gays, bisexuals, and transgender people into the agenda of the Black movement?

Barbara: Not easy! [laughter] For the introduction, Barbara Ransby needed material from me, and I thought, "How do I get this in?" How do I say I've been involved in these major movements for human liberation, including the Black liberation struggle, including the Women's Movement, including the anti-capitalist, anti-imperialist struggle, and including the struggle against homophobia and heterosexism? I said, "Oh! I know. I'll just say I'm a lesbian. That should do it." [laughter and applause from audience] But saying it always raises the blood pressure. One of the things, coming to the BRC, I'd tell my friends, *I'm going to go to the Black Radical Congress, and I'm going to be on this opening panel with all these legendary activists of my generation, and you know what? It's the FIRST time I have ever been included in this kind of context IN MY LIFE.* [Wild, sustained applause] As I was packing and getting ready to go to the airport yesterday morning, I said to myself, "Even though it took this long to be invited, at least when I was invited, everybody knew what they were getting."

"How do I say I've been involved in these major movements for human liberation, including the Black liberation struggle, including the Women's Movement, including the anti-capitalist, anti-imperialist struggle, and including the struggle against homophobia and heterosexism? Oh! I know. I'll just say I'm a lesbian."

It has been really, really, really hard. Hard to the point of tears. Hard to the point of hearts breaking over and over and over again. I don't know what motivated me in my youth to be out as a Black lesbian in the 1970s. I really cannot tell you what motivated me in particular. And perhaps had I known all the dimensions of difficulty it would have occasioned, I would have kept my mouth shut. [laughter] However, sometimes when I have been asked that very question, I see my grandmother who raised me, who was born in 1887 Georgia, who taught us that we must always tell the truth. Telling lies was such a terrible thing, and I know you know what I mean, those of you who were raised in that way. You can't tell an untruth.

But I think that's a part of integrity, of principle, a sense of "Why not?" Then, also, a sense of community, which I have helped to build. There are two people who are gone now, who are of the ancestors, who actually did a lot of this work both with and before me, and they are Pat Parker, brilliant poet, revolutionary, and activist, and Audre Lorde, brilliant poet, writer, and revolutionary. And I was colleagues with Pat and friends with Audre for 16 years. It helped me to know that there was at least one other someone who was trying to do this at the same time that I was trying. And it feels good, as I said, to have done it the way I've done it.

Kimberly: As evidenced by the presence of so many young people here today, not everyone in my generation is cynical and jaded. What wisdom can you share with us about keeping cynicism at bay? In other words, how do you keep the faith that revolution is possible?

Barbara: One answer is that in socialism, there is an understanding that, in order to make revolution happen, you have to live as if revolution is possible always. Even if it doesn't seem to be apparent, every little action you do that is toward justice and toward freedom is going to help make that happen. This weekend we finally have come back together to say that we're tired of handouts. We're tired of rollbacks. We're tired of accommodationists. We're tired of assimilationists. We're tired of people who think that because they make a nice five- or six-figure salary, that there's no need for Black revolutionary struggle any more. [Applause]

> **"In order to make revolution happen, you have to live as if revolution is possible always."**

We have been given a moment to move. And the reason we're ready to move is because we kept alert in the meantime. And we will continue to keep alert. But also, it's because I am Black. That's a part of it, too. If anyone had asked in 1682 or 1751 or 1799 or 1801, would Black people in this country ever be free, the answer would have been "Hell, no." And yet, on paper (and it really is on paper), we are by law no longer enslaved. So to me, if I can come from that tradition of struggle, there's a lot we will be able to do.

Kim, how did you get involved in political activism? How did you become radicalized?

Kimberly: My parents are subversives and they don't know it. [laughter] My father works at the Rochester Products Plant for General Motors in Grand Rapids, Michigan, and my mother worked for Michigan Bell. They had different literature on the table that my father would get with his union membership.

I don't think he knew I was reading it. Also, my mother would show me slides and things to supplement my education at home, to sort of make up for the things I wasn't getting at school, films about Langston Hughes and the Black Arts movement. Though it was the early 1970s, and everybody in my house had an Afro, that didn't necessarily mean that we were particularly radical or involved with the Movement.

Then when I went to the University of Michigan, I met people like Barbara Ransby and Tracye Matthews and Kim Smith, and others, who showed me that I didn't have to assimilate. I was already in the place where I needed to be, and there was work to be done there. As we can see from the rollbacks in affirmative action, particularly on the West Coast, we are not safe. I feel like it is my duty to think of ways that we can make it better for others after us. [Applause]

Barbara: Kim also has been in contact with me in the last few months because she wants to interview me for her dissertation, which is on the building of the Black feminist movement. And I really would like you to share more with everyone here about why you chose that topic, and what you think you'll be finding.

Kimberly: One of the main reasons I chose to work on a history of Black feminist organizations was because I didn't see too many other Black feminists around me. I saw women of your generation who I looked up to, but yet it seemed like there was a distance between you and I. So I thought to bridge that distance by studying the organizations and also figuring out what happened to Black feminist organizations. What were the strengths and weaknesses of those, and how can we carry them into the future? But another reason I chose it: one of my advisors asked me why I wanted to do this particular dissertation on Black feminists, and to be quite honest, I told her because I want to prove that I am not wrong. That it is possible to be a Black woman and to be a feminist or a Womanist; whichever label you choose, the work needs to be done.

Interviews with Barbara Ransby and Alethia Jones

Barbara Ransby: I was on that planning committee for the Black Radical Congress in 1998, and you immediately came to our minds when we asked ourselves, "Who are the people who represent and embody the best of certain traditions of radicalism?" I remember you being surprised to be included, like it was the first time an explicitly Black feminist lesbian presence was at the table of a Black radical convening.

I think for some people, hearing you speak on a range of issues challenged a kind of parochialism on the Left that doesn't really appreciate how a Black and woman-of-color feminism always represents a broad base of radicalism. Somehow I think they had a very narrow notion of what you would speak to.

Barbara Smith: It was quite historic. I think that the particular strain or variety of Black feminism that I was fortunate to be involved with, that we created out of the Combahee River Collective, really did have a strong Left perspective. A lot of the people who were leaders in the Combahee River Collective had solid—though not necessarily pleasant—experiences in other movements. We had people who had been influenced by the Black Panthers, who were involved in the anti-war movement against the war in Vietnam, who were very sophisticated Marxists. Sharon Bourke had been involved with the Institute of the Black World and brought those perspectives to us. When we came together, we had something to grasp and something to use for analysis that wasn't what we were reading and hearing about in the white women's movement.

We were often in coalition with socialist feminists. During the early days of the second wave, there were women's unions all over the country. We had a Boston Women's Union, and it was logical that we would work with them because they had a race and class analysis. They might not have gone as far as they needed to, but at least we could have a conversation about: Why is sterilization abuse happening? Do we need to be working to end it? What is a leftist and class-race inflected analysis of reproductive freedom?

Barbara R.: Everyone at the Black Radical Congress wasn't a feminist, but I think there was an openness about bringing feminists to the table. I felt, even though there was some resistance to some of the ideas among the larger group, that that was a terrain on which I could struggle. You hadn't won, but that was a place where you could wage the struggle and be heard, as opposed to much more politically hostile circumstances.

Barbara S.: By the time the Black Radical Congress happened in 1998, the Black Left could not ignore Black feminism. It was not possible. They would seem to be simple minded and out of touch had they tried to do that. We definitely had people who were Black nationalist, Pan-Africanist, people involved in the Communist Party, which has generally, I think, been more doctrinaire. It was really interesting.

> **"By the time the Black Radical Congress happened in 1998, the Black Left could not ignore Black feminism. It was not possible."**

Barbara R.: It was a very eclectic group. The way I saw it, from a feminist point of view, was as a direct response to the Million Man March [called by the Nation of Islam] in 1995. Bill Fletcher and others convened the Black Radical Congress

Planning Committee right after that. For me, [the Million Man March was] a mass Black mobilization that celebrated capitalism and patriarchy, and there had to be a response! So what else should be at the center than voices like yours, and a Black feminist tradition that could offer a robust response? It felt quite right.

When people got to hear you and know you in that process, they would say, "She's really amazing! She's really amazing!" It reminded me of that thing that happens when articulate Black people speak, and it's like, "My gosh, she's so articulate!" Well, what do you expect? Do you expect a Black lesbian feminist to have only one party line or one cliché that she's going to use? She's got a big vision! That's why these ideas are powerful. . . .

I remember being very pleasantly surprised that you were so excited about a Black Radical Congress. Because here you were, this busy person with lots of demands on you. It was like you were waiting for it. You said, "Yes. This needs to happen. I'll come to this meeting. I'll be there on the panel." So it struck a chord with you? It was something that you felt was necessary at that moment?

Barbara S.: Well, yes! It had two of my favorite words: Black and radical. [laughs] Because I am Black and I am a radical. It was just really exciting. Our political culture is exhausting, I can't think of any other word except for exhausting. We had gone through the Reagan years and we were dealing with the Clinton era, which was a really conservative version of Democratic politics. There was a new wave of activism, a new wave of people coming together, nationally, to say that we are not really down with the status quo and the way things are. The fact that it also embraced, or at least had an open door, for feminism, for a very large Black LGBT caucus, was really powerful. There were two thousand people that attended, so it was a huge, huge meeting.

Barbara R.: It was a great moment, and in some ways, some of the best work was leading up to it. Trying to listen to each other across different ideological divides is really what defines a movement, rather than an organization. You can have an organization or a campaign, but you have a movement when there are some diverse, eclectic, different angles on a set of problems, but still a common ground. That's what we were trying to forge.

"Trying to listen to each other across different ideological divides is really what defines a movement, rather than an organization."

So there was a moment in the sun, if you will, and then I think there were attempts in several cities—New York, LA, Chicago, Atlanta—to sustain it, but it just really didn't quite sustain itself.

Alethia Jones: What was it like being defined within the Black radical political family at the BRC rather than being placed outside of it because of your politics?

Barbara: Important contributions made by a lot of women and Black feminists [were recognized], and homophobia was [seen as] something that should not be clung to. It was a historical marker, and a break point, similar to President Obama's coming out in favor of gay marriage.*

Very little has been said about the historical context of this moment at the BRC, about what went before. For example, Coretta Scott King had a press conference where she affirmed her support for Black lesbian and gay legitimacy leading up to the twentieth anniversary of the March on Washington for Jobs and Freedom in 1983. I was part of the National Coalition of Black Lesbians and Gays [formerly the National Coalition of Black Gays, based in Washington, D.C.]. Gil Gerald, who was an important leader in that organization, led the organization to pressure the planners of the twentieth anniversary march to have a speaker who was either gay or lesbian. They named specific people, like myself, Audre Lorde, and James Baldwin—creating a slate for them to choose from. They asked James Baldwin to speak, but he was unavailable. So Audre Lorde spoke. The press conference was the first time that Coretta Scott King, who was eternally great around LGBTQ issues throughout the rest of her life, made a major public statement about embracing LGBT people.

That's the context for what happened at the Black Radical Congress and for the statement that president Obama made this year. It's beautiful that the first president to speak in favor of same-gender marriage is also the first African American president. And recently the NAACP has come out in support of marriage equality.† It puts so many people back on their heels.

---

* President Barack Obama announced his official support of same-sex marriage in an interview on ABC's *Good Morning America* on May 9, 2012, saying his view had "evolved."

† The NAACP released a statement supporting marriage equality on May 19, 2012. The statement is available at http://www.naacp.org/.

7

Building Progressive Urban Politics

"How can I stick it to the man, if I am the man?" This is a most peculiar place for an unreconstructed sixties radical to be, but running for office just seemed like the next logical thing to do. . . . Every single day I find myself making delicate calibrations about how to move forward to get something accomplished, to be effective, to honor relationships, and to maintain my principles. It is extremely challenging work. I feel in some ways that being in this position is the ultimate test of my Black feminist politics, how to make them operative in the wider world, and not only in the context of movements where people hold shared beliefs.

—Barbara Smith, "Black Feminist Activism:
My Next Chapter" (2012)

From 2006 to 2013, Barbara served in elective office. Her approach to this new role highlights how movement and electoral politics can intersect. The system is broken—worldwide. Electoral politics and public policy often function as handmaidens of deep injustices and sustainers of the status quo. Can skilled movement builders working inside the "belly of the beast" make real change? This chapter journeys first into the brutal sport of electoral politics, then delves into Barbara's attempts to create and support grassroots policy around policing, community violence, and education. It closes with reflections on the tensions between radical visions and difficult political constraints. As Barbara encounters the political establishment as an elected official, the quest for democratic, grassroots processes that seek and respect the community's knowledge and experience takes on a new form. In the age of Obama and Occupy Wall Street, Barbara provides a bottom-up view as a Black woman living in a neighborhood where the system's failures are vividly evident. In it, we see how Barbara marries a vision of global change with local action.

Vera "Mike" Michelson, an activist and community organizer based in Albany, New York, conducted the primary interview for this chapter. Vera is involved in (among other things) SNUG/CeaseFire, an anti-violence community-driven effort to reduce gun violence; ROOTS (Re-Entry Opportunities and Orientation Toward Success), an organization established by ex-offenders and supporters to mentor persons who were formerly incarcerated; the Underground Railroad

History Project of the Capital Region, which preserves and promotes the history of anti-slavery organizing; the Capital District's Working Families Party, which endorses and elects progressive candidates for public office and has provided leadership on multiple local political campaigns. The interview brings together two friends who share an unswerving commitment to grassroots organizing and racial justice. Vera's interview is supplemented with excerpts from interviews by Joo-Hyun Kang, Barbara Ransby, Alethia Jones, and Virginia Eubanks. We embarked on this chapter to learn how Barbara changed Albany, but we found that we also had to contemplate how Albany changed her—her strategy, her approach, her legacy.

A Movement Builder on the Campaign Trail

Political work in Albany can be difficult for those with a vision for change. Albany is the capital of New York State, but much of its political culture is defined by one fact—it is home to the longest-serving mayor of any major U.S. city. Erastus Corning 2nd held office for forty-two years, outlasting even Chicago's famous machine boss Richard Daley. As a result, generations of Democratic Party functionaries have had a stranglehold on resources and decision making. This section begins with Barbara's reflections on how her work as an elected official operates as an extension of her Black feminist roots. We trace her entry into electoral politics, which occurred as part of collective efforts to stimulate community change by supporting a progressive African American candidate for district attorney. Her own efforts to run for office required learning different skills and making tough choices in order to successfully navigate mainstream politics with a marginal identity and a devotion to working across differences of identity and political perspectives.

"Black Feminist Activism: My Next Chapter"
Barbara Smith (2012)

. . . In November 2005, I was elected to the Albany Common Council. Speeches like this allow me to consider the relevance of Black feminist politics and practice to solving social problems that on the surface seem to have little to do with gender oppression, but which nevertheless disproportionately affect Black women. . . .

The Black feminist movement grew out of a desire to create political theory and practice that accurately illuminated Black women's experience and that also provided the tools to challenge the multiple oppressions we faced. Although Black feminism may seem only to address the concerns of a specific racial/gender group, it is in fact extremely inclusive and has relevance for anyone committed to working for justice. It challenges multiple systems of oppression [racism, sexism, homophobia, and class] that have impact upon those who are not of African heritage and female. Because of this, Black feminist activism has the potential to lead to major social and political change. I rely upon the lessons of Black feminism every day in the very different political arena in which I now operate. . . .

What has it been like to shift from being involved in movement organizing, to community organizing, and then to becoming an elected official? One of the jokes I told my friends on the day of my swearing-in ceremony in late 2005 was, "How can I stick it to the man, if I am the man?" This is a most peculiar place for an unreconstructed sixties radical to be, but running for office just seemed like the next logical thing to do. Although I have lived in Arbor Hill since 1987, I did not get involved in community-based organizing in Arbor Hill until 2003. I did so because of neighborhood issues, especially crime, that had direct impact upon me. Right now I'm in the midst of negotiating on a daily basis the myriad responsibilities, expectations, and paradoxes of being simultaneously an elected official and a Black lesbian feminist. . . .

One of the differences is that in movement organizing people come together because they share certain basic political principles and beliefs, for example, war cannot be justified; the rape, battering, and murder of women must be stopped; and homophobia and heterosexism in any form are always unacceptable. In community organizing, as I have experienced it, people come together because there are immediate pressing problems that need to be solved, such as the lack of decent affordable housing, no summer activities for children and youth, and the destruction of community peace as a result of crime, drugs, and violence. People who hold a range of political beliefs can actually work together to come up with solutions for these kinds of problems and may never discuss their politics per se. I have found myself doing more interesting coalition work than at any time of my life. I have also experienced more racism, sexism, and elitism than I am used to in the context of doing activist work.

Now that I am involved in government, I am constantly challenged to figure out how to work with people whose values and perspectives may be extremely different from mine, but at the end of the day we have work that must get done. I think my negotiating skills and my coalition-building skills are more challenged and perhaps sharper than they have ever been.

In the movement work I have done there is usually a recognition that each individual needs to acknowledge, understand, and negotiate her or his race, class, and gender privilege in order to be politically accountable and also in order to work effectively and respectfully with those who do not share these same privileges. This commitment does not mean that there are never conflicts or mistakes, but at least the commitment to consistently examine these differences exists. In my recent organizing, these issues of privilege are not necessarily raised, but they nevertheless operate to enfranchise some and to disenfranchise others. . . .

Every single day I find myself making delicate calibrations about how to move forward to get something accomplished, to be effective, to honor relationships, and to maintain my principles. It is extremely challenging work. I feel in some ways that being in this position is the ultimate test of my Black feminist politics, how to make them operative in the wider world, and not only in the context of movements where people hold shared beliefs.

Interviews with Vera "Mike" Michelson and Joo-Hyun Kang

The Campaign of a Lifetime

Vera "Mike" Michelson: Before you decided to run for office in 2005 you got very involved with the David Soares campaign for district attorney of Albany County. Why did you do that?

    Barbara Smith: It was the campaign of a lifetime. The campaign to elect Albany's first Black district attorney mobilized a lot of people who had not previously known each other and brought them together. It was a real grassroots effort, a David and Goliath campaign, and David won! I always tell people his victory on his primary night in 2004 was a lot more exciting to me than my own victory a year later in 2005.

    The campaign was remarkable because David Soares was running against the incumbent, who was also his former boss. In running against the Democratic Party's incumbent, he ran against a powerful political machine with a monopoly on resources and knowledge. David is of African heritage—his family comes from the Cape Verdean Islands—and he grew up in Rhode Island. He was endorsed by and supported by the Working Families Party, and he was not in any way the likely suspect to win. We worked so hard.

    Vera: David's victory was historic. In a New York City broadcast devoted to the elections, WNYC radio host Brian Lehrer said, "This is the most important race in New York State. . . . [B]y winning on Tuesday, Soares, who ran on a platform of reforming the Rockefeller Drug Laws, completed one of the most stunning upsets in New York's political history." How did you get connected to Soares and to electoral politics?

    Barbara: I have lived in Arbor Hill since 1987, and as situations and conditions in the neighborhood continued to decline, I had a lot of contact with the police over quality-of-life issues. Then, in April of 2003, I went to an Arbor Hill neighborhood meeting. Most of the people at the meeting were not people from the neighborhood, nor were they people of color! I asked myself, "What kind of an Arbor Hill meeting is this?" I knew a few people, including Beverly Padgett, my neighbor, who had recruited me to sign a public safety declaration about quality-of-life issues in the neighborhood and invited me to the meeting. I also knew Charles Touhey, a real estate developer of low- and moderate-income housing, who built my house and many others in the neighborhood. He introduced me to David Soares, who was then assistant district attorney and community prosecutor, and Chris D'Alessandro, who was then a police commander.

David and Chris were the authors of the public safety petition I had signed. They were a very visible team doing community policing by walking in the neighborhoods of Arbor Hill and the South End. David asked me to serve on the Community Accountability Board [a community-based alternative sentencing program for non-violent, first-time offenders who report to a group of local community leaders instead of city court]. I served until June 2004, when David announced that he was going to run for district attorney.

Vera, you, and I got to work closely together in the fall of 2003 when the police chief told Chris D'Alessandro to stop doing work in the community, that is, to stop attending community meetings and talking to residents. This was very distressing to people who had worked with him and who so valued that kind of access. People went to City Hall to ask the mayor to intervene. Then, in early 2004, we created the Community Coalition for Accountable Police and Government and went to the common council to ask why this valuable person, who had so much to offer, was being restricted. We had signs; we had speakers. Within hours of our testimony, Chris was suspended. Then, he was actually fired from the police department! He was the highest-ranking police officer to ever be fired from the department in such a summary manner. It was just astonishing. We continued to go to the common council on a regular basis. Every time they opened their doors, we were there. We kept the spotlight on the issue of firing someone who provided something that was very rare in our most challenged communities, someone in law enforcement who had a real commitment to the welfare of the community and whom people trusted.

So I got into the habit of going to common council meetings. One day I called the president of the common council—Helen Desfosses, who is a professor at SUNY Albany, and also graduated from Mount Holyoke College—about another matter and she began to talk to me about the upcoming election. "Is there anyone that you know in the 4th Ward who might want to run?," she asked. And then she said, "Barbara, what about you?" I responded, "Are you out of your mind?!"

Mount Holyoke women are known for being very tenacious; she would not let it drop. Every time I saw her, she would ask again. I had no experience being involved in a campaign and felt ill-suited to run for office. I had done some work on Mark Mishler's campaign, a local progressive attorney who ran for district attorney in 2000 on the Working Families Party line, and I met with him to discuss it. He said, "There is this really interesting campaign this summer and if you would like to get involved, that would be a great place for you to learn how a campaign is run." He didn't say it because David had not announced, but he had David's campaign in mind.

Vera: On primary night you and I were assigned to go to the restaurant where his victory party was going to be . . .

Barbara: . . . to be there early, as soon as the polls closed. The television was on and early returns were coming in. He was winning in the hill towns and the river towns, these places where we had never been. Our eyes were getting bigger and bigger. I'm getting goose pimples as I describe it now because the excitement kept building and building. Then people started to arrive and the poll watchers had results directly.

Vera: The energy!

Barbara: Anything that goes up against the Albany political machine and is successful is historic. David's win was historic. But the campaign was brutal. People literally went through David's trash. They uncovered things and shared them with the media. This is a one-party town—if you win the Democratic primary in September, you basically have won the general election in November. So when David won the Democratic Party's primary, there was a big unity rally a few days after the primary, and people who opposed him before supported him for the general election. But one person never endorsed David, the mayor of the City of Albany, Jerry Jennings. He was not there that day, and he was not there for David's second campaign in 2008.

Vera: You and I did a lot of immersion learning about political campaigns. You helped to coordinate the effort to ensure the involvement of the African American community.

Barbara: I did organizational work with "People of Color for David Soares" to get people mobilized. I know organizing. But I did not know about electoral organizing and getting out the vote. I met a lot of people who knew how to make things happen: Mae Saunders, president of the Tenants Council for the Albany Housing Authority; and Bill Payne, one of the first Black police officers in the City of Albany. I did anything that they asked me to do. All of these skills that I had developed outside of electoral politics—being a writer, editor, publisher, organizer—proved to be useful. As a result, I learned the steps of running for elected office, such as getting petitions signed to get on the ballot, targeted door-to-door campaigning, and working with the media. My long history in movements and the ability to conceptualize and articulate important social, economic, and political issues also made a difference in the campaigns.

Vera: There are many people who want to get involved with campaigns but don't really see or learn the "science" and details of campaigning that greatly improve the chances of winning.

Barbara: I enjoyed learning that there is an actual science to campaigning, logical steps to get your potential electorate excited and to get them out. I loved finding out that it is not just making some posters and sending out a few pieces of mail and hope, hope, hope that on election day it is going to turn out in your favor. The science of voter identification and voter contact is intriguing. The steps take a huge amount of work, like going door-to-door, phone banking, and voter contacts through a sequence of mailings. There isn't a recipe, because there are always human factors and things beyond your control, but by analyzing who voted when and where, you can identify on a map precisely where you need to get your votes. It is a logical way to cover all your bases.

Vera: What impact do you think the campaign had on the African American community, and on all of us?

Barbara: A lot of people came together that had not previously worked together, so it brought together a solid progressive base. It also electrified the Black community. District attorney of Albany County is an extremely powerful and important position. The fact that a young Black man won shifted power relationships in Albany County. For David to run, to assert that he had the right to run, the capacity and qualifications to run—and to win!—was just amazing and wonderful.

I think since the David Soares campaign, people are continually meeting each other and defining things that are important to them for the benefit of our day-to-day lives. Not necessarily the big issues or the big things. The contours of organizing as I've experienced them always have similar kinds of steps. You don't know what the outcome is going to be necessarily, but it's always about figuring out what the problem is, coming to that through collective dialogue, figuring out where the soft spots are or where the possibilities for alteration are, and then going for it. Making sure people are excited, giving them ways to connect.

Vera: Soares didn't come through the Democratic Party. He was endorsed by and supported by the Working Families Party and had the support of Citizen Action of New York. The campaign was grassroots, completely independent of the existing political structure. One of the by-products of the Soares campaign appears to be that it created a base of experienced people who could run aggressive independent campaigns. Citizen Action and the Working Families Party remain the institutional foundations, with key databases and technical know-how essential for getting signatures to get [progressive candidates] on the ballot and to get voters to the polls.

Barbara: That's right. We now had a base of volunteers available for other campaigns. A slate of progressive candidates for common council endorsed by the Working Families Party and by Citizen Action who could run and win. Some of us had never run before. Corey Ellis [who would later run for mayor], Cathy Fahey, and I had not run previously. Dominick Calsolaro was already on the council. Not only were these council candidates *not* endorsed by the established political structure, they were also bona-fide progressives.

Barbara's Run for Office

Vera: Why did you want to run for office yourself?

Barbara: I ran to continue the forward movement that we achieved with David's campaign. We need to have more than one person who is accountable and who has a solid vision about how our communities and neighborhoods can survive and thrive. I wanted to make my community better.

Vera: Yet you were reluctant to do it.

Barbara: Following David's campaign I just said, "There is no way I can do this." It's just too, too much, especially the character assassination. A few weeks after David was sworn in, Beverly Padgett e-mailed me to say, "If you run for the common council, I will be behind you every step of the way." Several other people who were politically progressive and electorally savvy also expressed support. Virtually everyone I talked to said, "Oh, yes. Oh yes." It made me reconsider.

Vera: What was your own campaign like?

Barbara: My campaign was very well organized. Many people who worked on David's campaign worked on mine. In my race, I was not considered a long shot. The seat was open because the incumbent decided to run for another office. I had one opponent in the primary who I believe had the Democratic Committee's endorsement. Her campaign was not highly visible. Nevertheless, it was hair tearing; it was still incredibly hard and exhausting work. You were there at the first meeting when we discussed my campaign. We wanted to do a very smart, practical campaign that would help me actually get elected. That's what we did.

On the common council, I represent a primarily poor and Black community in Albany, which includes Arbor Hill, and small parts of West Hill and the South End. The political dynamic of the city is reflected in the position of poor people of color and how marginalized we are. Many of the city's problems are situated in our neighborhoods, like other economically distressed communities of color across the nation, including excessive violence and school failure. Poverty and oppression create a fertile context for these conditions, sadly.

Although my district is predominantly people of color and economically challenged, it is also one of the most racially and economically diverse wards in the city. I represent all of North Albany, which is a working-class and lower middle-class residential neighborhood with a lot of businesses and industry. North Albany traditionally has been the center of Albany's Irish American community and each year holds its own Saint Patrick's Day parade in which I usually march. Another section of my district has some of the most expensive homes in the entire city.

Joo-Hyun Kang: Were you an out lesbian on the campaign trail?

Barbara: When I ran for common council the first time and the second time, the fact that I am a lesbian was not on my campaign literature, nor were the issues explicit on anything written. But I was endorsed by the Empire State Pride Agenda both times. I was also endorsed the second time by the Victory Fund. Those endorsements were on my literature.

Joo-Hyun: Was that a conscious, strategic decision?

Barbara: Yes, we talked about it. Because I really wanted to win. I wanted to be successful, and I was running to represent a district that includes Arbor Hill, a primarily Black and economically challenged neighborhood, which is also where

I live. I knew that in order to be successful there, I shouldn't give fodder for a negative attack. We talked about it very seriously. We decided that we wouldn't lead with that.

There was a gay elected official who was a member of the county legislature at that time. He and I got together to talk about my running, and he said, "You absolutely have to come out." There were other people giving me advice—who were not from Albany—who felt that I needed to do that as well. I was very clear that that was not the way to go.

Joo-Hyun: Was that hard for you?

Barbara: It was very, very hard. I felt like, I'm betraying my roots. I felt like movement people would be so unhappy with me. I wasn't running as a queer candidate. I was running as a member of the Arbor Hill community.

Joo-Hyun: A community you'd been living in for years at that point.

Barbara: That's what it was. And when I ran for reelection in 2009, I said to people who had been involved in my campaign and who had been supportive

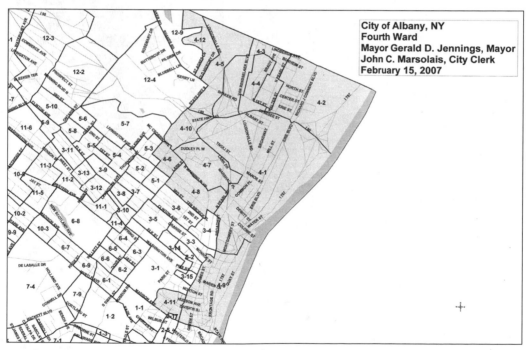

Figure 7.1: Map of the Fourth Ward of Albany, NY. This ward was represented by the Honorable Barbara Smith from 2005 to 2013. Much of her common council ward is in zip code 12210, where residents are majority people of color (46% African American, 9% Hispanic or Latino, 3% bi- or multiracial, and 2.5% Native American), 80 percent rent their homes, wages and incomes are only about half of the state average, individual poverty rates top 30 percent, and 75 percent of students in the public schools qualify for the free or reduced lunch program. Forty percent of the ward is white, and some areas are quite wealthy. Sources: www.city-data.com, www.zipdatamaps.com.

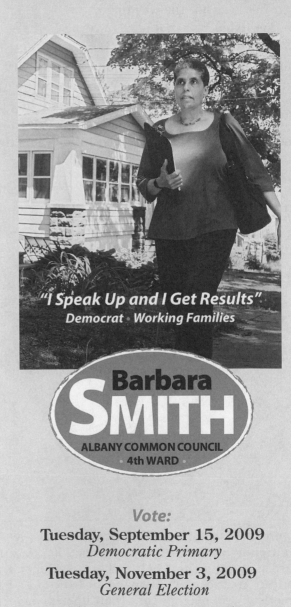

Figure 7.2: Campaign Palm Card, "I Speak Up and I Get Results," produced for 2009 reelection campaign by Friends of Barbara Smith. Photo by Drea Leanza. Used with permission.

of me throughout, that I really hope that during my second term, I'm going to have a chance to help to enlighten people more about these issues. To help them understand that the person who got their sidewalk fixed, and the tree cut down, and the cat out of the tree—and I've literally done all of these things—that this person is also a lesbian. And I was [glad] the opportunity arose around the "I Am Gay" billboards [see chapter 5].

In the Belly of the Beast

"I am not a politician!" Barbara insists. Public Servant. Elected Official. Those titles better fit her approach. Barbara navigates a world thick with politicking and heavy with the history of backroom deals. Decades of Democratic machine politics, politicians, and their decisions provide comforts for insiders and limit opportunities for outsiders. In contrast, Barbara knits together partnerships with other progressives and uses policy as a weapon for social change to create concrete improvements for people in neighborhoods where it matters most. Her top two priorities are violence—stopping it, preventing it, healing from it—and improving public education. Most of her work at committee meetings, budget hearings, and community forums is invisible as she seeks to marshal resources, cultivate a multilayered network of community members and policy experts, and alter public dialogue. We supplement the interviews in this section with flyers and photos from key community events as well as excerpts from monthly radio commentaries by Barbara in 2008 that aired on the local NPR affiliate, WAMC.

Interviews with Vera "Mike" Michelson, Alethia Jones, and Virginia Eubanks

Vera "Mike" Michelson: There is a political sea change going on in Albany and you have a lot to do with it.

Barbara Smith: Some people [in Albany] think that my involvement in political activity began with my decision to run for office in 2005. I have been politically active for decades, but I was not involved in electoral politics until now. I did not foresee when I ran for local office that I was going to be involved in sweeping, policy-driven, innovative initiatives around some of the most pressing problems in my community, but that's how it turned out.

Vera: What is the political reality in Albany?

Barbara: Albany had the longest-sitting mayor of a major city in United States history. Much longer than Richard Daley in Chicago. Erastus Corning 2nd was elected in 1941 and he died in office in 1983. We have had *three* mayors in Albany since 1941. Thomas Whalen was the mayor for a decade. Then the current mayor,

Jerry Jennings, was elected and he is in his fifth term. That describes a very, very constricted political culture. There have been some attempts to challenge that, particularly in the last election cycle, when [common council member] Corey Ellis ran for mayor. But there is a widespread assumption that the status quo will continue.

Virginia Eubanks: The organizers of the recent "A Tale of Two Cities" march explicitly argued that there's a white Albany and a people-of-color Albany, that the power extremes are vivid and obvious, and that there needs to be a space opened up where we can have meaningful discussions about what it means to have an Albany that works for all people. Do you agree that there are two Albanies?

Barbara Smith: Absolutely.

Virginia: Where do you think that comes from, politically?

Barbara: It comes from the history of the political machine here. The machine in the twentieth century has been extremely destructive to the dreams, hopes, and opportunities of those who are not part of it. Albany has such a unique history. Mayor Erastus Corning 2nd attended Yale University and was from one of the city's most prominent families. His great-grandfather, Erastus Corning, served as Albany's mayor from 1834 to 1837. Corning 2nd linked up with Dan O'Connell, who was working class, Irish, and had dropped out of school in

---

Flyer for Albany Neighborhoods First

ALBANY NEIGHBORHOODS FIRST
A Vision for Albany's Future

Albany Neighborhoods First came together in the summer of 2008. We see a diverse City, offering many exciting opportunities as the home of state government, the site of nanotechnology research, and of many other academic, economic, and cultural institutions. Newly energized work and entertainment venues in our downtown, new and rebuilt schools and libraries, and a committed, neighborhood-based constituency are the foundation of a new Albany.

Albany Neighborhoods First is committed to a City that works for everybody and that prioritizes the health and safety of our greatest assets: the vitality of our neighborhoods and the people who live in them.

To learn more about Albany Neighborhoods First and to read our entire vision statement, visit us at http://www.albanyneighborhoodsfirst.net

fifth grade. Dan O'Connell was head of Albany's Democratic Party from around 1919 until his death in 1977. It's basically the Ivy Leaguer connecting with the tough guy and they get this city in a stranglehold that we're living in to this day. The way the city operates, I sometimes call it a "thugocracy." Thuggery is just really part and parcel of how people understand power and access and privilege. It's about who you know, how much power you have, how much you can intimidate, how you frighten and force people into the positions that you wish them to be in.

The people who have been most damaged and hurt by the Albany political machine are those who have the least power and privilege, those who are the least white, the least rich, and the least male. So, there are people in this city who are not that much hurt by the machine because they have more than adequate income, they have class privilege, they have race privilege, and they may have gender privilege, too. So even though they might not like the system, it isn't necessarily damaging them on a day-to-day basis. They still get to make decisions and have power and have agency in their lives. Those of us who are far away from privilege are the most damaged by this very, very exclusionary system.

Vera: What do you think of Black political leadership in Albany?

Barbara: That's hard. The history of the Albany political machine does have an impact on Black leadership. Black elected officials often enter hidebound institutions that are exploitative and counter to freedom, liberation, and justice. Furthermore, the pace of change in these institutions has been glacial, so it may not totally be the fault of the Black elected officials, but rather a result of the nature of the county, local, state, and federal institutions that they enter. Early on in my time as an elected official, a wonderful wise person told me, "You may get frustrated at how long everything takes and how slow it is." It's true. It is incremental.

And people's aspirations are also low. When constituents call me about jobs, they are usually looking to work at the Department of General Services, which provides sanitation and infrastructure maintenance positions. Historically, those are the jobs the machine gave us. I hear people of color who have been in Albany much longer than I speak nostalgically of the days of the Corning administration, and of the very, very tight Democratic machine, because it provided material necessities and helped people. So there was a chicken in every pot, or if you needed coal, you would call up your ward leader and they would get you some coal.

Elected officials are not really any different from other people in our communities; we just have a different job description and a higher level of responsibility and accountability. No matter what the race or ethnicity of the elected official, the only legitimate reason for seeking elected office is to serve. It's a job, not a coronation. That's what I try to do—service.

Vera: Is there anything else you want to say about the current political situation?

Barbara: I think that one of the characteristics of democracy is periodic regime change. We are probably going to see that in Egypt tonight. [Egypt's president of thirty years, Hosni Mubarak, was expected to announce his resignation in a speech that night.]

Vera: So, regime change at home?

Barbara: Exactly. I would love innovative, principled, and democratic leadership in the Executive Branch in the City of Albany. I would like to see someone who is open to a community-based model of neighborhood empowerment and engagement and does not see residents as only good for votes every four years.

Cultivating Community Policing

Vera: Why did you want to chair the Public Safety Committee in your second term?

Barbara: I have been pulled into the realm of criminal justice issues and law enforcement, because these issues are really important for the community that I serve, and in which I live. There is an attribution of criminality to Black and Brown people far out of proportion to their actual involvement in crime. We have the dynamic of driving while Black, walking while Black. On the other hand, many people who live in inner-city communities, as I do, would like to live in a place where we feel safe and where people cannot get away with just anything. We live in neighborhoods where drugs are being sold, where shots are being fired, where things are being dumped.

Most people who are conscious and who live in urban settings know that violence is incredibly destructive to any future health and success of a community. You can't have gratuitous violence and have a healthy community: on a physical level, on a spiritual level, on an economic level. On no level. You just can't have it. I often find that people living in the most distressed neighborhoods are calling for things like more cameras, more police, and demands for an increasingly top-down approach. But there are other ways of looking at law enforcement to create solutions.

I was on the Public Safety Committee during my first term when there was a public outcry to change the model of policing in Albany to community policing. The existing model utilized a Strategic Deployment Unit, which used statistics to figure out where to deploy their assets and their personnel to deal with hot spots of crime. The police stayed in their cars and the people in the community did not really get to know them. The police might not address the car with no plates or the noisy house where they have parties until all hours—but instead appeared for the dramatic thing and often responded with what the community felt were storm-trooper tactics.

Vera: The new chief of police means a new direction, and more work to be done in the community.

Barbara: Exactly. There was a real outcry in different places over traditional policing tactics that came together all in a few days of each other. As a result, the mayor appointed a Selection Committee in late 2009 to evaluate candidates for a new police chief. This was unprecedented! Normally, the mayor chooses an individual and appoints him unilaterally. This new process brought in some members of the Albany public to work on that issue.* During the same period we were working with the police department to establish community policing. We also started the Albany Community Policing Advisory Committee, which still exists. We now have a Neighborhood Engagement Unit; we have officers who are assigned walking and bicycle beats all over the city of Albany; and we also have a new police chief, Steven Krokoff, who won the post with community support and organizing.

Policing is a part of the fabric of city, rural, and suburban life. There are always people who have that job of enforcing local laws, of keeping people safe, preventing crime, and [arresting] people who are breaking laws and rules of the social contract. I have learned that some of them do it with the highest commitment to service. It's a very dangerous job. Many officers could just as well turn out to be social workers or teachers because they have that kind of desire to help people.

Alethia Jones: Do you credit movement politics for changing the leadership of the police department?

Barbara: I credit people who have movement experience applying their expertise to what was not necessarily a movement intervention. Progressives from the labor movement, the women's movement, the anti-racist movement, the anti-apartheid movement, who have those kinds of experiences, bring that wonderful consciousness and expertise to bear in situations that are not necessarily classic movement initiatives. People organized and got a police chief in Albany that they felt would be positive for the entire city, and particularly for our inner-city, economically challenged communities of color. We have a very specific situation of forward-looking leadership that has made certain kinds of dialogues and certain kinds of interactions more possible. In some cases, when crimes occur, there's more willingness to give information to the police that will help solve them. That's a sign of better relations. We're a long way from

---

* In 2009 Mayor Gerald Jennings appointed a Police Chief Search Committee. Its members were: James Campbell, then-Albany County sheriff; Dale Getto, principal of North Albany Academy; Alice Green, founder and executive director of the Center for Law and Justice; the Honorable Daniel Herring, common council representative for Ward 13; Alan Lizotte, professor of criminal justice and interim dean of the School of Criminal Justice at University at Albany (SUNY); the Honorable Carolyn McLaughlin, majority leader of the Albany Common Council; Felix Perez, resource and development director, Salvation Army; Judge Larry Rosen, former Albany City and Albany County Court judge who also chaired the committee.

where we need to be. But we have actually made some progress because we have leadership who is willing to listen to voices in the community.

For me talking with a big smile on my face about having the right police team is like, "Are you crazy?" I never thought that would ever be important to me. But given that I am an elected representative in an economically challenged, predominantly Black community, the police department is very, very important.

Vera: What is your current relationship with the police department?

Barbara: My current working relationship with the Albany Police Department is really quite positive. Anthony Bruno, who is now an assistant chief, replaced Chris D'Alessandro. At first, we were wary, but he has been very congenial and open to discussion. When I met him in the spring of 2004, he said he would call me the next day to talk about our concerns. Just as he promised, he did! From that day to this, we have had a high level of accountability and also a real commitment to the community from him. I am not naïve; there are still issues between our community and the police. But I also know that we have really made some great strides.

Vera: You have expressed a lot of hope for what the police department can do when it partners with the community. As someone who has been critical of law enforcement and the criminal justice system in the past, does that present any irony for you?

Barbara: It is such a delicate and complex job to be a council member representing a community that has the kinds of issues we experience in Ward 4. On which side do you err? Do you err to the side of people who are feeling objectively oppressed, and the police are part of that dynamic? Do you turn an unseeing eye to things that in other neighborhoods would not be acceptable, quality-of-life issues like littering or spitting or sitting on the stoop or making a lot of noise?

Vera: Stoop sitting can be a really great thing for building community and camaraderie.

Barbara: But a car blaring at two o'clock in the morning, when we can reasonably assume that most people would like to be able to sleep? That's a problem. Do we say, "Oh, well it's in a Black neighborhood?" Or do we have standards so people can live their lives in peaceful enjoyment? Everyone has a right to that.

I have constituents coming to me who want me to help solve problems that the police are qualified to address. I live in a community where there is a lot of violence, where people don't feel safe, and where there's a need to have some counterbalance to those who are terrorizing our communities. There is a disproportionate amount of contact between people in poor communities of color with law enforcement. A lot of it is negative. The levels of incarceration of Black men in this country are astronomical. The United States has the largest prison population in the entire world. In our communities, so many people are incarcerated, have been incarcerated, are on probation or parole, have children who have been affected by their absence, or have family members affected by where they are.

The history of policing of Black people in this country goes back to slavery, when policing people of African heritage was an economic imperative. People who were enslaved had to be kept under control. They also had to be kept from running away. The paddy roller* relationship has been a troubled and volatile relationship from slavery on.

I always had a high suspicion of law enforcement and the police. I knew how detrimental police brutality, racial profiling, and the prison industrial complex are for our Black and Brown communities. These days, I have a better understanding of what a police officer's job is; I have a better understanding of where the police are coming from and their priorities. I see how some of them define the job, and their concern about the quality of life in our communities. But I'm not oblivious to what is actually going on in this country. Traditional law enforcement still has a very questionable, sometimes negative, role in relationship to our communities of color—as witnessed by stop-and-frisk policy in New York City.

Vera: Can you talk about SNUG?

Barbara: SNUG [GUNS spelled backwards] is a statewide initiative. We work with Trinity Alliance, which employs the people who do street outreach, violence interruption, and the other aspects of the program. [We are based on] the Chicago-based CeaseFire model, a grassroots effort started by former gang members. The idea is that people who have been involved in street activity, including a history of violence and incarceration, who know the streets but have turned their lives around and want to give back, can contribute to alleviating the crisis of violence in our neighborhoods.

They are on the front line, doing what's called "violence interruption," and also community outreach. Violence interruption involves mediation, knowing who the players are, knowing what and where things might jump off—like when different clubs close, what's going to happen after sporting events and social gatherings at the high schools. SNUG violence interrupters will be there to make sure that nothing happens that will be negative.

One of the things I like most about it is that it's a community-based organizing model. It's about getting people to not accept a culture of violence where they live. We have community responses after any violent incident in our target neighborhoods: West Hill, Arbor Hill, and the South End. After a shooting, or a stabbing, or, very tragically, a homicide, we are *required* to have a community

---

* "Paddy rollers" refers to slave patrols, groups of white men who enforced rules against slaves as well as capturing and returning escaped slaves.

"WAMC Commentary on Gun Violence," Barbara Smith, July 21, 2008

On the evening of May 29, 2008 ten-year-old Kathina Thomas was playing in front of her home in Albany's West Hill. A bullet came out of nowhere and ripped into her back. On June 10th, the day after her funeral, the police went to Albany High School and arrested a fifteen year old for her murder. In his statement he said that he thought he saw someone in a rival group of boys reach for a gun so he responded by firing a shot in their direction as they ran away. . . .

Someone has described life in Albany since Kathina Thomas's murder as similar to the aftermath of September 11th, a period of overwhelming grief and of people coming together to try to respond. Since Kathina Thomas was murdered there have been at least eight shootings in Albany, most involving youth.

What is happening in Albany is similar to what is happening in Rochester, Philadelphia, Boston, Chicago, and many other cities. Urban violence, often fueled by the drug trade, is the manifestation of deep hopelessness and the ongoing legacy of racism.

What, you may ask, does racism have to do with Black-on-Black crime? After all, the leading cause of death for African American males, ages 15 to 29, is homicide. Ninety-four percent of all homicides in which Black people are the victim are perpetrated by other Blacks. How can racial oppression be a factor when Black people are apparently victimizing each other?

In order to grasp how racism is very much implicated we must understand the context, a context of decaying neighborhoods; highly segregated, inadequate school systems; high unemployment and low-paying jobs inadequate to support families. Crime disproportionately occurs against a backdrop of poverty and although African Americans are only 12 percent of the U.S. population, they are 24 percent of the nation's poor. Intractable urban poverty, extreme disinvestment in neighborhoods where the poor reside, and disproportionate violence are twenty-first-century manifestations of the historical trajectory of slavery and racial oppression. Poverty itself is a form of violence. The concentration of crime and violence in poor Black communities is tied to decades of concentrated injustice.

In the aftermath of ten-year-old Kathina Thomas's death it is time for all in the Capital Region, whether government officials, corporate leaders, not-for-profit organizations, faith-based communities, or concerned individuals to step up and take collective action to find solutions to violence and the socioeconomic conditions that breed it.

Reprinted with permission of WAMC Northeast Public Radio.

response within seventy-two hours. One of the slogans of Chicago CeaseFire is a picture of a young child and the message on the little postcard is, "Don't shoot. I want to grow up." We chant:

"Save the babies."
"Save the children."
"Save the women."
"Save the men."

It's really not rocket science. The mechanics of it are fairly simple: have a bullhorn, have stuff to pass out, have banners, do canvassing two hours before and after to maximize your presence. What's not simple is getting people out on the corner shouting and chanting. We're managing to do that. At first we had seven or eight people, maybe ten. The last one had fifty people speaking out against violence.

"Intractable urban poverty, extreme disinvestment in neighborhoods where the poor reside, and disproportionate violence are twenty-first century manifestations of the historical trajectory of slavery and racial oppression. Poverty itself is a form of violence."

SNUG and CeaseFire are based on a public health model that says that community well-being depends upon addressing anything that compromises or undermines the health and safety of people. Do shooting and stabbing and violence undermine the health and safety of people? Yes, they do. That's why, in addition to the street-based intervention and prevention, there are four other components to the model: (1) community mobilization, (2) public education, (3) faith-based involvement, and (4) relationships to law enforcement. In Albany, we have put a series of partnerships in these areas in place.

One is a hospital-based initiative where SNUG workers go into Albany Medical Center, the region's trauma center, and interact with people who have been shot or stabbed to diminish retaliation. It took years of work to establish that relationship. Some of that work started during the Gun Violence Task Force in 2008 but accelerated once we had full-time staff.

SNUG workers communicate with law enforcement to learn where violent incidents have occurred so they can deploy violence interrupters, but they do *not* share information with the police that might lead to arrest. SNUG has the cooperation of the police department, but it is not a law enforcement program.

In addition, the model is research-based. Professors at the School of Social Welfare at the University at Albany, SUNY, are collecting data to evaluate the model's success based on hard facts and evidence. There are CeaseFire model projects around the country, but New York State's ten sites is perhaps the largest number initiated at one time in a single state.

Vera: You worked very hard to get a five hundred thousand dollar grant to get this program into operation.

Barbara: Yes, and we were successful. In summer 2008, Malcolm Smith led the Democratic minority in the Senate and advocated for funds to begin the initiative. By November of 2008, the Democrats took over the Senate majority for the first time in more than forty years, which placed him and his colleagues in a

---

SNUG rally flyer

SNUG

STOP THE VIOLENCE

Did you know someone was Shot in your neighborhood on Saturday?

SHOOTINGS ARE UNACCEPTABLE

JOIN US!!!!!!

December 22, 2010

6:30 pm

Corner of Elk St. & Quail St.

---

position to put significant resources towards this initiative. They appropriated four million dollars in the 2009 budget for ten SNUG/CeaseFire sites around the state. Albany SNUG has five hundred thousand dollars, a modest budget given the number of people that it is trying to reach, the number of people on staff, and all the things we do.

SNUG has been much more successful as far as engaging people, staying close to an innovative public health model, a grassroots way of getting people engaged and empowered. One of the reasons that people in positions of power didn't want SNUG to continue is because they sensed this percolating sense of community efficacy and desire for change. There's an instinct within the power structure that something's happening. They might not even be able to articulate it, but it's like, "No. No, no, no, no, no, no."

I am the community coordinator for SNUG, sharing the news of this model. A lot of my job is putting the right people together: Trinity Alliance, the School of Social Welfare, the neighborhood associations. We are forming some really positive networks and relationships that feel like a breath of fresh air in the city where everything has been top-down. SNUG is very much a part of my heart.

Alethia: If SNUG were a movement activity, how would it be different?

Barbara: There are organizations in Albany, particularly the United Front Youth Organization, that were having mobilizations and peace marches against violence on a regular basis. The community wasn't sitting idly by. Long before there was SNUG, people in Albany responded, except they could not do it full-time. We started the Inner City Youth and Family Coalition in 2007 following the murder in my ward of a fifteen-year-old, Shahied Oliver. He was murdered by another fifteen-year-old at a birthday party. The coalition identifies resources for youth because we believe violence happens, in part, because young people don't have enough positive things to do. There are people all over this country who live in inner-city, urban communities where there's too much violence and where violence is tearing the fabric of the community apart. On a grassroots level, in almost any urban setting, you're going to find people who are trying to figure out ways to counteract the violence. But like many, many grassroots organizations addressing violence, most of them are not staffed or funded adequately.

Alethia: How did things shift from grassroots volunteers to a full-time program?

Barbara: We didn't go to the state and say, "Could we have money to do this?" New York State came to ten sites, including Albany, and encouraged us to start anti-violence initiatives. Some of the origins lay in the Gun Violence Task Force created by common councilmember Dominick Calsolaro in response to the level of violence occurring in our city. The task force's sole responsibility was to study the problem of violence and to come up with recommendations. When I joined the council [in 2005], I became vice chair of the Public Safety Committee and was made liaison to the task force. I attended virtually all of their meetings, twice a month for a year. The task force meetings were open to the public and it hosted community forums, giving its work great visibility and impact on the community.

Then Kathina Thomas was murdered, and that really got a lot of people's attention. During that summer people were very, very distressed and really distraught with this horrible tragedy. A few days after Kathina was killed, there was a Gun Violence Task Force meeting. One member, Dr. Leonard Morgenbessor, called state senator Malcolm Smith and asked him to come to the meeting. He did, and we talked about the idea of SNUG. Later that summer, Chicago CeaseFire staff came to New York to visit various sites around the state, including Albany. Senator Smith's office contacted me to help arrange attendance of relevant community people, especially those involved in criminal justice organizations. It was standing room only, out the door!

By the end of August 2008 we formed what became the Community Coalition to Prevent Violence, and through that organization, we advocated for funding. In 2009, the coalition arranged for another CeaseFire visit, and we identified local people to go out with the Chicago CeaseFire staff, specifically people who had been involved in criminal and violent activity in the past, who knew the community and knew the streets but who had transformed their lives.

Alethia: What is the future of SNUG?

Barbara: At the current time, we are trying to get funding for the second year. The state started this, but unfortunately, they couldn't sustain it, and we are about to be shut down.

Alethia: Can it be sustained without public funding?

Barbara: It's not possible to do it without funding a staff. Organizations in Albany have done parts of what SNUG is doing, including the violence interruption and the public community mobilization. They can't sustain it because their volunteers have other jobs. You can't be out there eight hours a day or twelve hours a day when you have another job to attend to. We need to have people whose job *this* is.

Alethia: If not state funding, then what?

Barbara: We are knocking on every door. We have formed a key stakeholders committee and that is of high-level, corporate, not-for-profit, government, and educational leaders in the city. One of their functions is to figure out other, alternative ways for us to support ourselves. We have applied for federal funding twice now.

Alethia: Some might say, "The work of freeing ourselves and our communities is *our* work." The Civil Rights movement didn't happen with government funding and staff. Is that naïve?

Barbara: There were absolutely staff and organizers in the Civil Rights movement. Often they lived with people in the community, so they weren't paying rent. But there were definitely people whose full-time job it was to organize.

Alethia: But they weren't funded by the government.

Barbara: We can't afford to have just a voluntary group working to stop the incredibly profound violence that tears our communities apart. Also keep in mind that violence is a public safety issue and maintaining public safety is a key responsibility of government. The police don't necessarily do prevention; their arrest and prosecution functions occur after a crime happens. We would never say funding and delivering education should be a volunteer effort. I don't think anybody would ever say, "We don't really need hospitals. If somebody gets sick then here's a phone number to call and maybe someone will come over." SNUG is funding salaries, office space, and dedicated staff time. Community violence is too complicated, too pervasive. Problems this pervasive and detrimental need full-time interventions.

To Educate All Children

Vera: What is your assessment of public education in Albany?

Barbara: Like many urban areas, the city school district of Albany does not have a blazing record of educational success. The majority of students in the school district are Black and from families that are economically challenged. Education is absolutely critical for all of us but is particularly critical for populations and groups that do not have access to other kinds of economic stability and productivity.

Quality education is violence prevention.

By the time teenagers or people in their twenties are waving guns around, are conducting stabbings, a lot has already gone wrong. Whereas, if you are dealing with infants to pre-K, the early years of elementary school and through the educational continuum, you can make sure that people won't pick up a gun or think to stab someone. The education side is a side of possibility, of opportunity, dreams. The violence intervention and prevention side is like, "Okay. Things aren't going so great. People are trying to kill each other. Let's see if we can stop that." It's two different ends of the continuum to me. They are both necessary.

Vera: You have done a lot of work in terms of the public school system—attending school board meetings, working with the group Communities United for Quality Education.

"Quality education is violence prevention."

Barbara: We are working now to establish a "Cradle through College through Career" educational pipeline initiative, modeled after the Harlem Children's Zone. The current superintendent of the City School District, Dr. Raymond Colucciello, has been a real partner in our work to improve the quality of education in our school district. We work from a neighborhood development model; it's not just education, it's social services, health, neighborhood development, anti-poverty, all rolled into one. In Albany our emphasis has been upon building a relationship with the public schools through the Albany Family Educational Alliance, which meets regularly to involve people in the target communities: Arbor Hill, West Hill, and the South End.

Vera: How did you get connected to the Harlem Children's Zone?

Barbara: I read *Whatever It Takes: Geoffrey Canada's Quest to Change Harlem and America* [Tough 2008]. Then I wrote a letter to Geoffrey Canada to ask if we could visit. They hosted us and we learned about their model. At the same time, I contacted our congressional delegation to alert them to the possibilities around Promise Neighborhoods, a set of planning and implementation grants for school improvement and neighborhood revitalization from the federal government. The offices of our senators and congress members have been great allies on both the anti-violence initiative and this Promise Neighborhood/Harlem Children's Zone initiative. Working with the State University of New York (SUNY) chancellor's office, we applied for a Promise Neighborhood grant. We did not get it, but we ranked number 36 nationally out of 339 applicants.

Alethia: What makes the pipeline model effective?

Barbara: The basic philosophy is to get children and families from birth; don't wait for them to come unprepared to kindergarten. "Baby College" is what they have at the Harlem Children's Zone. In Albany, we have a "Baby Institute" for parents with children from ages 0–3 and parents who are expecting. Those are nine-week courses on Saturday mornings, from 9 a.m. to 1 p.m. with breakfast and lunch. Unlike regular parenting courses, the focus is on getting your child cognitively ready to engage with an academic setting and to be successful in the school environment. Beyond the regular training on safety, health, emotions, and behavior, we also teach what children need to know to succeed in pre-K and in kindergarten: for example, numbers, letters, colors, and shapes and some vocabulary, too. Parents are often unaware that their children should know this.

Alethia: It's not surprising that what is common knowledge amongst the middle and upper classes isn't common knowledge elsewhere.

Barbara: That's exactly what Geoffrey Canada says in *Whatever It Takes*. He says we want to provide for all of our kids what middle-class and upper-class families take for granted.

Alethia: Is access to a middle-class approach to education effective, especially if it is taught in ways that invalidate or ignore the students' realities? Some may feel, "Why do I have to become this other thing? Why is it being imposed on me? Why isn't my reality being acknowledged?" It's too bad that not enough teachers know, value, or respect urban inner-city life enough to use it to teach in the classroom.

Barbara: I think there's a difference between wanting your children to have better opportunities than you had and status seeking. I was raised to identify and connect to all other Black people. Education need not be about turning students into middle-class achievers who abandon the community. But we want to make sure that our kids have choices and have the capacity to take care of themselves and their loved ones. I'm not sure we're asking or wanting young people to be different than they are. We want them to have choices about what they can do in life. It's not doing young people of color a favor to thrust them into violence, drug addiction, and prison. If most of the people you grew up with are dead by the time you're twenty-five, I don't see that as a positive value.

Most people would agree that closing the achievement gap, having a quality education available for all children, and the opportunity for higher education—that these are all positive goals. People in economically depressed communities of color who are struggling for quality education for their children, for better life opportunities, and for a cessation of violence need allies. There are people who have been privileged to become educated who are not thinking about the situations that poor people of color face. That's when the educational edge becomes a problem. As long as you use the privileges, skills, and gifts that you have been fortunate enough to develop towards the liberation of the entire community, it's a plus. It really is a plus. I've almost always lived in inner-city Black communities. I've found my education to be very useful because it helps me to navigate the challenges of the world, the challenges that I face individually, and the challenges of my community.

Another approach to education is to ask, "What are you interested in?" and to expose students to experiences they have never heard of or known so they can discover their interests.

We need to have people in our school systems who can relate to our kids. We have a real dearth of teachers of color, including in Albany. Why would you believe somebody whose experience is nothing like yours? In an effective educational system, you'd have people of all ages and of various races, all of whom are focused upon that one thing: having our children succeed and fulfill their full human potential. I do think that having the voices of the elders, voices of the past, and connection to your culture and history—that's a benefit to every child.

Alethia: The public dialogue on Black poverty is so polarized between a structural analysis, which says the systems don't work given the history of oppression, exploitation, and criminalization; and an individualistic or cultural analysis, which says that it's how people behave. If they actually valued education, they would actually be much better off. How do you navigate those two poles of individual behaviors and structural failures?

Barbara: Blaming the victim is not productive. We operate from an empowerment, engagement, and leadership model. We believe that the people who know most about their communities and their children's needs are those who are living in those communities and under those conditions. By forming partnerships between people in poor Black communities—who let us know what's important—and Black middle-class allies—who have had access to formal education—we can come up with great plans for moving forward. That doesn't happen nearly often enough, but it certainly is what I would like to see.

Alethia: The system privileges the voices of those who are middle or upper class. If you are perceived as an economic failure, then the presumption is that you have nothing to offer.

Barbara: The most important thing is to create opportunities for people to access the things that will help them improve their lives. People in inner-city neighborhoods who suffer under institutionalized inequality should get to define what's important and move on it. It's very, very important that people be actors in their own lives, not just the recipients of charity.

"People in inner-city neighborhoods who suffer under institutionalized inequality should get to define what's important and move on it."

One of the reasons the Harlem Children's Zone works is because parents and community members are mobilized around their own interests and those of their children. They have voice. That's really, really important. With that kind of agency to make decisions about which way forward, you have real potential for transformation and change.

Virginia Eubanks: How has your experience in grassroots movements impacted your work on education as a public official?

Barbara: This is a time when organizing and a sense of historical roots are necessary. You always have to ask, "What's moving this? Why is it the way it is?" It's not sufficient to look at the *results* of systematic and institutionalized oppression; we also need to be looking at what caused it. It's so helpful in the kinds of things that I'm involved in now to have a structural analysis. I can assess not only what's happening right now, but why things are that way to begin with.

"There's no disconnect between chattel slavery, colonialism and imperialism, and the genocide of the people whose land we are still visitors on.... There's a direct line between those formative national experiences and where we are at the present time. Now what we have is disenfranchised, poor communities of color. We also have massive school failure."

When I look at the conditions in core Black communities in Albany, like the vacant and abandoned buildings, the lack of healthy food, violence, the lack of empowerment and massive poverty, when I see those things, I don't think, "Oh! I wonder why people in my neighborhood are so poor? I wonder why all these buildings haven't been taken care of?" I know why! It's because of systemic oppression, capitalism, and rampant vested-interest power, which doesn't see us as being worthy of anything better. The reason I'm involved in electoral politics is because conditions in my own community, where I've lived since 1987, continued to degenerate, and it was not right.

The condition of my poor Black community and of every poor Black community and Brown community in this country has everything to do with the history of white supremacy. There's no disconnect between chattel slavery, colonialism and imperialism, and the genocide of the people whose land we are still visitors on. It's not disconnected. There's a direct line between those formative national experiences and where we are at the present time. Now what we have is disenfranchised, poor communities of color.

We also have massive school failure. Again, that's not accidental. Because massive school failure for poor children of color maintains a racial status quo.

Figure 7.3: Smith at Albany rally for striking taxi workers. The 1991 demonstration supported union organizing at Albany Yellow Cab. Photo by Vickie Smith. Used with permission.

"WAMC Commentary on Education,"
Barbara Smith, November 6, 2008

... In 2006 Noelene Smith and I started the Parent Advocacy Project. Our goal was to work with family members and their children to identify the interventions and resources needed to help students have the best chance to achieve in school and to be prepared to enter college. The Parent Advocacy Project has had a measure of success, but because of the small scale of our efforts and the difficulty of obtaining funding, the impact upon the school district as a whole is frustratingly limited. . . .

As an Albany Common Council member, I believe that increasing the level of educational success in poor communities of color will go a long way to addressing the violence that undermines our neighborhoods. Sixty-eight percent of state prisoners have dropped out of high school. I was very excited to read Paul Tough's book *Whatever It Takes: Geoffrey Canada's Quest to Change Harlem and America,* which documents Canada's innovative community-driven approach to educational success. . . .

The primary goal of the nationally recognized Harlem Children's Zone is to close the achievement gap between poor children of color and their middle-class counterparts by providing them with everything that middle-class parents provide that helps their children succeed. Child-rearing practices that boost cognitive skills such as providing rich verbal input through both conversation and reading are often unknown to parents who are poor. The Zone has established a "conveyor belt" which provides the parental supports and academic programs that lead to children's academic success at every developmental stage. It is a paradigm-shifting model that works to change the values of the entire community so that they embrace education as the surest way out of poverty for their children.

. . . One day soon I want to see an Albany Children's Zone. This will require major funding as well as the empowerment of new leadership in both government and education. The current charity model cannot achieve the changes that a community empowerment, justice-building model can.

It won't be easy, but I am quite sure that giving every child a real chance for success via a quality education will be worth every penny. . . .

Reprinted with permission of WAMC Northeast Public Radio.

When I talk about school failure, I'm talking about the schools failing. I'm not talking about the students. I'm not talking about their parents. I'm talking about the institutions themselves not being adequate to the job that they purport to be doing. Most people seem satisfied with the status quo, which works to maintain white privilege and white supremacy. If the mechanism for maintaining that is massive urban school failure everywhere in this country, they're cool with that.

By the middle of the twenty-first century, the majority of people living in the United States will not be of European heritage. I hope I live to see it. People are realizing that the educational standards of our country have really plummeted since the mid part of the twentieth century, and their lack of interest in educating poor children of color is going to come back to bite them. Some are beginning to realize that the massive under-education and mis-education of poor people of color is going to actually *wreck* the United States economy because there won't be enough skilled workers. Having a bigger view, a structural analysis, an understanding of first causes helps you to see these larger dynamics. School failure—I always use the term "school failure" to put the onus where it belongs, as opposed to on individual students—failing schools disproportionately serve poor, young people of color. All of us deserve a quality education, and certainly all of our children should have that opportunity.

Radical Visions versus Reformist Institutions

In this section, Barbara steps back to look at the bigger picture. How and why do radical views matter to conventional politics? Are such views a source of frustration or hope? How does one work with institutions and individuals who do not share your assumptions or aspirations? What about Occupy Wall Street's strategy to eschew conventional politics and policy? Barbara uses her post to spur public debate and shape opinion. We share two such efforts captured in two common council resolutions she spearheaded—one on homophobia and the other on immigrant rights—that her colleagues unanimously passed.

Interviews with Alethia Jones, Vera "Mike" Michelson, Barbara Ransby, and Virginia Eubanks

Alethia Jones: What movement skills have been particularly beneficial in electoral politics?

Barbara Smith: There are a lot of them. One is recognizing collective consciousness and collective intelligence. In other words, knowing that you can't possibly figure it out all on your own, and that the way you get to a great idea is to dialogue with people who have similar concerns and a commitment to solving the problem. That's a movement perspective. It's not about the "I"; it's about the "we."

Also, power structure analysis: Where are the weak spots? Where might we be able to insert ourselves to make transformation in material conditions, or in perspective and perception? Sometimes changing people's perceptions is the first step to being able to make the material change around power and decisions. For example, one of the changes in perception [we've been able to accomplish in Albany is to help] people who are not in positions of power realize that they had something important to say, that they had a right to assert, for example, "We're not going to have somebody who was in the FBI be our police chief. It's unacceptable." Sometimes the element of surprise is really important. Showing up where you're not expected to show up, or saying what you're not expected to say.

Vera "Mike" Michelson: You have often said that if more political figures had movement experience they could be better leaders. You are now functioning in a capacity that you never imagined and it is not exactly an environment for radical politics . . .

Barbara S.: . . . but we slip a few things in there! [laughs]

Vera: What is the role of radical politics now, in these years?

Barbara S.: It's a lifeline. It's the only thing to me that makes sense. We have to have a critique, if not a practice, coming from the Left. We need that here locally and we need it at the national level. My understanding of what is fair and just for budget issues, criminal justice issues, social welfare issues, and any other issues come from my prior political experience and background.

Vera: Are you equating radical and progressive?

Barbara S.: To me radical, or leftist, is to the left of progressive. Progressives address basic bread-and-butter economic, racial, and social justice issues. A leftist critique looks at first causes and why things are the way they are. It looks at capitalism, a system designed for the profit of a few. The burning question for most of my life has been, "How can you get to anything resembling justice under a system that is inherently unjust?"

It's important to have a functional Left that raises critiques to inspire a vision of what is possible. For example, for years you worked in the anti-apartheid movement, Vera. It seemed like there was no way in the world that that regime was going to crumble.

Vera: Exactly.

Barbara S.: There had to be people worldwide, as well as in South Africa, who had the vision—a sense of hope and faith, also the incredible keen intelligence—to figure out apartheid's weaknesses, the places where if you push hard enough, you expose that what looks insurmountable is [possible to overcome]. The Left helps us believe it is possible, and at the very least to understand that what we are doing is righteous. It's the same with slavery in this country. Ending it didn't look plausible, it didn't look reasonable or easy, but there were people who said:

"We can't be doing this anymore. And we are gonna step out there." Some of those people were enslaved people themselves. We did not get slavery to end simply because so many white people were willing to give up their privileges. These are examples of what the Left can do.

Alethia: What makes a radical perspective radical? What is the difference between being radical or revolutionary versus reformist or mainstream?

Barbara S.: The word "radical" comes from "root." To be a radical is to have an understanding of the root causes of injustice, violence, and exploitation.

To think that the reason that poor people of color are poor is because they don't have the right habits or frame of mind is ridiculous. That is not legitimate history, it's not an analysis rooted in political power. Radicalism is having an understanding of the root causes for the injustices that we experience and that we wish to change. We don't fool ourselves into thinking that a good government program or a law is the be-all and end-all, because that doesn't necessarily change power relationships.

Having an international perspective often characterizes those of us who identify as radical. For example, there was a wonderful organization called Black Voices for Peace led by Damu Smith, who passed away in 2006. They did great work around these wars, particularly the wars in Iraq and Afghanistan, making great connections between state-sanctioned violence and violence in our home communities. Black Voices for Peace's slogan was something like, Peace in the Hood, Peace in the Land, Peace in the World.* In other words, peace everywhere, we fight violence everywhere and on every level.

Alethia: Some would say that radicalism is not the legitimate voice of poor and working-class people. More often, conformity, consumerism, and aspiration to capitalist accumulation is. If one seeks to be representative of the aspirations of the poor, would one move in a more mainstream direction?

"To be a radical is to have an understanding of the root causes of injustice, violence, and exploitation."

Barbara S.: No, you would not. Those things that you just mentioned are legitimate things to want, particularly if you don't have any of them or have too few of them. There's nothing wrong with having decent housing, quality schools, access to high-quality health care, economic opportunity, and sound employment. There's nothing wrong with any of those things. But in order to get there, you

---

* Now the Washington Peace Center (washingtonpeacecenter.net/pla_blackvoices). Damu Smith passed away May 5, 2006. He was also a leader of the National Black Environmental Justice Network.

need to have some radicals who are turning over the ground so that there's a possibility of that occurring.

Moderate solutions and "go along to get along" positions don't really get to points of change. The major points of change that we've seen in U.S. society and other places occur when people go for the whole thing, they "take it to the wall," so to speak. That was true of the Civil Rights and Black liberation era. If not for people being willing to sacrifice everything, including their lives and personal safety, we would absolutely not be where we are today. Moderate solutions do not really put the system on notice that something has got to change. You always need to have radical analysis and sometimes action in order to move the needle. It may result in radical incrementalism or reform, but if you don't have a radical analysis and action, you will never get to anything resembling justice for all people.

Virginia Eubanks: What do you think of Occupy Wall Street?

Barbara S.: Occupy has taken such an interesting stance in relationship to power, laying out an agenda and speaking truth to power. It's not just about cosmetic changes, it's not about a little bit of change, it's about profoundly changing relationships of power and authority and control, and perhaps even demolishing those notions so that everyone can live in freedom and with all the rights and opportunities that every creature deserves.

This historical period doesn't necessarily have big visions and big ideas that people can respond to. Occupy is in some ways peculiarly privileged. It comes from a privileged perspective. Even the fact that Occupy says, "We're not interested in electoral politics." Being able to say that and feel like it is not going to hurt you down the road, or that you are not going to lose something down the road by not engaging, that's about privilege! You don't have to worry about it because you're still going to have access. I find it fascinating. In some ways, Occupy is great, but some of the "We're not going to go there, we're not going to tell people what to do, we're not going to lay out an agenda or a plan or a program" has to do with privilege, I think.

Virginia: As much as I'm interested in, and supportive of, Occupy, "We are the 99 percent" does not a class analysis make! On one hand, it's very, very hopeful—this idea that middle-class and professional-class folks can start thinking of themselves as having some of the same problems that poor and working people have—building that kind of coalition. At this point it might be more intellectual than actual, but I do think it's important. The downside of that, of course, is this pernicious idea that we're all the same. Which is not true, and is not a valid or reasonable analysis or plan for action. I think that cross-class work is so crucial, and yet so difficult, even in times when it is clear that we have more common-alities across class than differences. That's the genius, I think, and the worst Achilles' heel of Occupy, at the same time.

Barbara S.: I think the solutions come through struggle. When you have values that recognize that everyone has an important role to play, and important gifts to

Peace and Unity Resolution

RESOLUTION OF THE COMMON COUNCIL AFFIRMING UNITY AGAINST HATE AND BIGOTRY

Resolution Number 28.31.09R (MC)

March 2, 2009

WHEREAS, the city of Albany is a highly diverse community that values its residents of all sexual orientations, genders, races, ethnicities, nationalities, ages, religions, physical abilities, and economic backgrounds; and

WHEREAS, residents of diverse backgrounds have made countless contributions as family members, workers, volunteers, and neighbors to the greatness of the city of Albany; and

WHEREAS, the city has enacted human rights ordinances to protect the rights of all of its citizens; and

WHEREAS, people of all backgrounds and faiths will come together in a peaceful community-wide vigil for unity and caring and to demonstrate unity against hate and bigotry on Thursday, March 5, 2009 on the steps of City Hall.

NOW, THEREFORE, BE IT RESOLVED, that the Common Council of the City of Albany hereby affirms that Albany is a city that is united against hate and bigotry and that respects the dignity and human rights of all.

Passed by the following vote of all the Council Members elected voting in favor thereof:

Affirmative (14) Negative (0) Abstain (0)

---

contribute to whatever your actions are, then you begin to make some progress. I go to meetings where people don't think it's important to have everybody speak once before some people speak eighteen times—they don't know about that. To me, that makes a difference. Treating people with respect and not necessarily thinking it is only the elected person or only the person with the big-paying job that has something to bring to this dialogue. Little things. Every day.

Vera: Several years into this, most people do not view you as a radical person. How do you think your constituents judge you?

Barbara S.: On a day-to-day basis, my radical politics is reflected in my understanding of things. Most days, practical issues are the focus of my work as

Immigrant Rights Resolution
RESOLUTION SUPPORTING IMMIGRANT RIGHTS
IN THE CITY OF ALBANY
Resolution Number 54.52.09R (As Amended)
Passed July 20, 2009.

WHEREAS, the recent tragedy in Binghamton, New York* has brought attention to the many challenges that immigrants face, and

WHEREAS, approximately twelve million undocumented immigrants reside in the United States, and many in our own community, and

WHEREAS, many immigrant workers are exploited with sub-standard wages and working conditions, and

WHEREAS, immigrant families, including local families, are living in constant fear of repression, jail, or deportation, and

WHEREAS, we call upon the Federal Government to develop and enforce a comprehensive immigration reform policy which promotes reunification of families, provides a path to earned citizenship, and a plan for current and future immigrant workers, and

WHEREAS, it is not the intent of this body to encourage immigrants to reside in the United States without documentation, however given that this issue exists it is incumbent on municipalities to attempt to deal with the matter as the Federal Government has failed to create a comprehensive reform policy, and

WHEREAS, many new immigrants face structural barriers to resources and services because of lack of language access, and

WHEREAS, we, the City of Albany Common Council find the above conditions deplorable and unjust, and

WHEREAS, Albany is a city built by immigrants and continues to benefit from the economic and cultural contributions of new immigrants.

NOW, THEREFORE, BE IT RESOLVED, that when an immigrant living, visiting and/or working in the City of Albany is not posing a threat to the community, the City of Albany Common Council calls on all state, federal, and local political leaders and agencies to:

---

*On April 3, 2009, Jiverly Wong, a naturalized Vietnamese immigrant, shot and killed thirteen people, critically wounded four others, and then killed himself at the American Civic Association, a small immigrant settlement agency in Binghamton, New York.

1) Refrain from all unnecessary measures to jail, detain, or deport documented and undocumented immigrants and their families living in the City of Albany;

2) Instruct public safety personnel to refrain from asking people their immigration status, which is a federal matter;

3) Support a transparent and equitable legal due process leading to citizenship for all immigrants living in our city;

4) Provide equitable language access to all city offices and services;

5) Encourage the City of Albany Commission on Human Rights to serve as a vehicle to educate the public about these issues and

6) Support a welcoming and compassionate environment for immigrants and their families within our city and its institutions.

NOW, THEREFORE, BE IT FURTHER RESOLVED, that a copy of this resolution, suitably engrossed, be transmitted to the locally elected federal, state, and county officials.

Passed by the following vote of all the Council Members elected voting in favor thereof:

Affirmative (14) Negative (0) Abstain (0)

---

an elected official. The constituents who call me are concerned about getting a street's pavement fixed. They don't really care about radical politics. There are some exceptions, like introducing the Immigrants' Rights Resolution, or being a cosponsor of Dominick Calsolaro's preemptive prosecution legislation,* or sponsoring some of the legislation around lesbian and gay rights. Specifically, I introduced legislation as a counterweight to Fred Phelps, a really reprehensible and virulently homophobic individual who disrupts funerals in the name of his crackpot, made-up religion, who threatened to visit Albany High School because it was planning a production of "The Laramie Project." My resolution was about us being a welcoming and accepting community, which the council had affirmed in previous legislation in support of LGBT rights.

Barbara Ransby: Now you're doing this great, hard work in city government. Is it a continuation in some ways, or a break?

---

* In April of 2010, Dominick Calsolaro and Barbara Smith urged the Department of Justice to review terrorism cases that they say unfairly targeted Muslims. They called for an independent panel to review cases of Muslims convicted through "preemptive prosecution," a federal law enforcement tactic of conducting sting operations against Muslims in the United States suspected of having terrorist links.

Barbara S.: I see it as a continuation. Being a member of the common council in Albany is informed by my political understandings and my political values, formed over a lifetime of movement activism. I see issues differently because I have some sense of first causes.

Barbara R.: There's an ebb and flow to where we locate ourselves in this kind of work. I often ask the question, "Where's the locus of power? If you're in a movement, are we trying to get access to people, like you, who are elected officials?" People who are elected officials, if they are good-hearted and honest—which sometimes is not the case, as we know—are looking for a base. [They ask themselves,] "Where are the people who I want to push me so that I can go in there and argue for something and have a constituency that's behind me when I do it?"

> **"When people band together to transform power relationships, when they understand that they actually hold the power because of their collective energy and talent, that's what movements are about. People get rights because they get to a point of critical mass of being fed up."**

Barbara S.: Having movement experience gives you a political analysis, particularly an analysis of power structures and relationships. You don't just take it as a given that this person has all the money, this person has intimidation, this person is white male and heterosexual and has to be the leader. When you come from movements, particularly grassroots, bottom-up movements, you don't necessarily think that way. Having been involved in the Civil Rights movement as a teenager and really seeing it as the bedrock of my political perspectives, I know very clearly that people with no identifiable privileges can transform social relationships in the biggest, baddest country in the world. If people like Fannie Lou Hamer can topple accepted notions of who is in power and who deserves to be listened to, then almost anything is possible.

It's important that I have political experience that is not limited to running for political office. I really think that's what makes it viable for me to serve as a member of the common council and to be an elected official. Having been involved in the struggle for so long, I can see wider possibilities.

Vera: You decided to run to try to heal and unify the city. Where do you think we are now?

Barbara S.: The most important thing is community empowerment. When people band together to transform power relationships, when they understand that they actually hold the power because of their collective energy and talent, that's what movements are about. People get rights because they get to a point of critical mass of being fed up.

It takes some people who are very courageous to say: Maybe if we closed down this bridge, this highway, boycotted this company, picket in front of this building, maybe people will have to pay attention and maybe something will change. We saw that constantly in the Civil Rights era, the sit-ins, the bus boycotts, the school boycotts, the voter registration drives—all the things that people did to transform power relationships.

Vera: How far away from that are we in Albany?

Barbara S.: We are getting closer. We have seen some steps, even leaps, forward. For example, the restoration of community policing and the selection of a [police] chief that many people in Albany feel positive about. It was not a top-down process. The community spoke out and it was very effective. We have networked with the school district unlike anything before in Albany. I didn't plan to make these changes in law enforcement, education, and politics before my election. I was alert, and I wanted to do as much as possible to make things better.

Vera: How do we get people to see these victories—the David Soares win, the election of progressives to the common council, the new police chief, SNUG—as the start of creating an environment that lasts? There are people in the neighborhoods who are more active now than before.

Barbara S.: But not enough. One of our weaknesses during this period is that we have not done enough community mobilization. I would love leadership development, mobilization, and community organizing to be a part of all of these different projects. For our education work, I want to see community organizers going door-to-door in neighborhoods to figure out collaborative, strategic, and appealing ways to get people on another track about what could be a better future for them and their children.

In 2008, after ten-year-old Kathina Thomas was murdered, one of the things we talked about was starting a center for non-violent organizing and non-violent change. I would like to see that, a physical place for people to come and learn to organize around their issues, from "How do I get this vacant lot cleaned up?" to "How do I reduce the level of violence in my community to some reasonable level?"

Virginia: So how do you push the horizon of what is possible, so that people can get at a radical analysis that goes to the root of the problems, and nourish hope that something different is possible? As an activist and an elected official, how do you push that horizon?

Barbara S.: I don't know that I've done a good job of that. I really wish that the results of my being in office would be an increased level of empowerment and a better understanding of how these pieces fit together. I think it is hard because there are not necessarily forums or contexts in which thoughtful conversations can be held. Everything can be so crisis-driven.

One of the things that I would really like to see happen is political education. I think you really need to have explicit opportunities for people to find out about their history, to find out what other people have done about similar problems and how they did it. Here in Albany, I don't think there is a clear conception of what a progressive justice agenda looks like because the machine has historically beaten it out of us.

Alethia: What is the state of Black organizations and organizing in the Black community in Albany?

Barbara S.: I would like to see more organizations in the city of Albany that are grassroots and founded to address issues of racial, economic, and social justice. The Center for Law and Justice is a wonderful organization and a part of the solution. It effectively focuses on the criminal justice system and is run by Alice Green, an African American woman who is the city's most dynamic activist. A Village is a very exciting and relatively new community-based organization in the South End that recently helped save a summer youth employment program from the mayor's cutbacks. The local organizations plan good events, deliver services, and have activities. But we don't have a multi-issue group, like ACORN* was or like Project South† in Atlanta that organizes around a broad social justice agenda, has a large grassroots membership base, regular meetings, and campaigns. What is missing is some strategic analysis and using these activities to push for greater justice, educate people in power, and address root causes.

Alethia: What aspects of Albany's politics need to change to make it more vibrant, more effective?

"I know enough about history and our struggle to know that when people come together, they can do what seems impossible. As Martin Luther King Jr. said, 'The arc of the moral universe is long, but it bends towards justice.'"

Barbara S.: I would add to our current city government structure an office focused solely on the eradication of poverty. It would pursue lots of different approaches, not jobs only, or training only, or better educational outcomes only, or helping families to build wealth and financial literacy. It would undertake lots

---

*The Association of Community Organizations for Reform Now (ACORN) (1970–2010) was a member-based organization in the United States with chapters in hundreds of neighborhoods that advocated for low- and moderate-income families by working on neighborhood safety, voter registration, health care, affordable housing, and other social issues. At its peak, ACORN had almost two hundred thousand members. (See www.acorn.org.)

† Project South: Institute for the Elimination of Poverty and Genocide is member based and for the last twenty-five years has worked to "dismantle systems of poverty, racism, and violence while also building community power" (www.projectsouth.org).

and lots and lots of different types of interventions. But we have no organized game plan about that, and the level of poverty in the city of Albany continues to increase. I think one-third of the population of the city of Albany is living in poverty. More than 40 percent of the children in the city of Albany are living in poverty. Completely unacceptable.

What intelligent things might we do that do not cost money, necessarily? It costs very little to raise awareness of the federal Earned Income Tax Credit, and to help people to do their taxes so they can access it. You bring millions of dollars back into impoverished communities by simply having a programmatic way of helping people receive what they are owed. That's one of the things that New York City's Center for Economic Opportunity does, but we don't have anything like that in Albany. I am interested in things that make a difference in the communities that I serve. Everything I am dealing with—the police, the schools, all the violence, everything—things *can* be done to make things better than they are now.

Vera: How do you keep going?

Barbara S.: My grandmother was born in 1887 in Georgia, about twenty years after the Civil War had ended, and she knew the worst of the worst. The Great Migration to the North is an example of the communal courage of African Americans. Living conditions, social conditions, and access to decent employment in the South were so poor. They had a huge amount of hope; it's kind of in my bloodstream. Seeing the successes—getting slavery off the books, then peonage, sharecropping, Jim Crow, lynching. I got to live through the second revolution, which was Civil Rights.

Vera: So it is hope that keeps you going?

Barbara S.: Yes. I come from political experiences, political realities where the answer to a number of questions like—Will these persons ever be free to live as full-fledged human beings? Will these people ever live in these particular neighborhoods outside of the ones they are confined to because of race? Will these people ever have jobs where they would be the supervisor of white people? Could these people ever attend major colleges and universities in this country? Could these people walk the streets and not ever be afraid of being disrespected and even physically attacked? The answer would have been, No, No, No, No!!! It's never going to happen.

I know enough about history and our struggle to know that when people come together, they can do what seems impossible. As Martin Luther King Jr. said, "The arc of the moral universe is long, but it bends towards justice."

8

"Took Root, Bore Fruit"

Legacies and Futures of a Black Feminist Life

Basic pervasive justice. Worldwide. That's what I want to see.
—Barbara Smith, interview with Alexis Pauline Gumbs (2010)

Legacies are about the future of the past. Barbara and her allies consciously acted within a longstanding tradition of African American sheroes and foremothers and added "Black feminism," a label not previously used, to that legacy. So far, we have described the rich inheritance—intersectionality, identity politics, multi-issue organizing, and coalition building, among other concepts and tactics—that Barbara's lived political practices and movement experiences offer to current social movements in the United States. But, ultimately, legacies do not center on a single individual—they are collectively built.

Traditions are lived, changed, reinterpreted, and extended by new practitioners. Barbara's work has contributed to and inspired a rainbow of movement organizing, political engagement, institution building, knowledge generation, and artistic practice. This chapter considers new directions inspired by Barbara and her allies' work. We provide five of many possible examples of political and cultural work inspired by the tradition of Black feminism. Each represents a vibrant node in a broad network of Black feminists who are making revolution: Ella's Daughters quilts together distinct, unique, and dispersed actors into a blanket of justice builders in the tradition of Ella Baker; the Black Feminist Working Group blends Black feminism and Black Power in an inspired twelve-point plan for a transformed world; UBUNTU, a grassroots group based in Durham, North Carolina, fights to end sexual assault and violence by blending local action and piercing structural analysis; the Crunk Feminist Collective shares a "Letter to Patriarchy" written in their distinct "kick ass kiss off" style. Another dimension of this legacy is captured by Dr. Ron Daniels, former presidential candidate and president of the Institute of the Black World, who offers an internationalist, class-conscious, radical analysis that links the Black struggle to Occupy Wall Street. In addition, we share letters secretly solicited by the University of Alabama's Department of Gender and Race Studies and presented as a surprise gift to Barbara during their 2010 conference Black Women as Public Intellectuals: Past, Present and Future. The three letters we include convey the genuine appreciation of women who truly understand the depth of Barbara's efforts and sacrifices.

The primary interview in this chapter is with Alexis Pauline Gumbs, a queer Black feminist troublemaker from Durham, North Carolina. Alexis is the founder of the Eternal Summer of the Black Feminist Mind educational program and the co-creator of the Mobile Homecoming experiential archive, amplifying generations of LGBTQ (lesbian, gay, bisexual, transgender, and queer) Black brilliance. She earned her PhD in English, Africana studies, and women's studies from Duke University in 2010 and is widely published in national print and online publications and scholarly journals. Her poetry appears in poetry journals *Kweli*, *Vinyl*, *Turning Wheel*, *Everyday Genius*, and in many anthologies. In her interview, this young, conscious practitioner of Black feminism engages in an intergenerational exchange with Barbara that captures the multilayered dimensions of an activist life.

Sheroes and Foremothers

One generation's battles quickly become the taken-for-granted realities of a younger cohort. But Alexis sets the tone for the entire chapter with her deep and explicit appreciation of the pathways blazed by foremothers and her passionate efforts to build and extend that legacy. We include one letter of appreciation—an original poem—by poet, writer, and professor Robin Boylorn of the University of Alabama. From Ella's Daughters we include a description of their "Seven Sisters" campaign, which embodies engaged, practical coalition building in today's Black feminist communities.

Interview with Alexis Pauline Gumbs

Alexis Pauline Gumbs: I think about Black feminism as my spiritual practice: there are sacred texts and there are ancestors, like Fannie Lou Hamer. I think of Black feminism as a sacred, political legacy, and it speaks to my spirit. I wanted to tell you about my altar that I have in my room. At home I have a mantelpiece, and on it are two large pieces of wood with quotations from the Combahee River Collective Statement that I painted on them. One says, "Our politics evolved from a healthy love for ourselves, our sisters, and our community." And the other one says, "We are ready for the lifetime of work and struggle before us."

Barbara Smith: That's giving me chills.

Alexis: Every morning when I wake up I open my eyes and I see those two statements, because they ground me, before anything else can have a chance to influence the way I'm feeling. Those are the first things. And I have *Conditions: Four, Conditions: Five, Home Girls, But Some of Us Are Brave,* and *This Bridge Called My Back* sitting up there. I often have to take them down because I'm rereading them and using them. I also have on the mantelpiece the Freedom Organizing pamphlets, like a rainbow.

It wouldn't exist at all if it weren't for the work that you have done and the way that you have done it. It's important for you to know that so many people of my generation who identify with Black feminists, they hold the work that you've done, and the work that you've done in collaboration, in this exalted place.

Barbara: That is really wonderful. That's so gratifying.

Alexis: What would you say is the Black female organizing tradition?

Barbara: If we just start with this country, and with our experience as people of African heritage, we came here under the most sordid and terrifying of conditions, that is as enslaved people, so I think that probably the organizing started on the ships.

"That people of African heritage have survived for so long in a very hostile environment shows that there was a lot of political consciousness, a lot of struggle, and a lot of underground activities that kept our race alive. I'm sure women were at the center of those activities."

One of the things that I always say about the abolition of slavery is that Black people had agency in that process. It wasn't just white people—Quakers and Northerners—coming to rescue us. Even in the worst of circumstances, Black people had agency in their own liberation. Some were fortunate enough to participate in the abolitionist movement; others weren't in organized groups. You don't survive if you don't know how to get things together, keep things going, and get things done. I think that the existence of Black people in the Americas in the present indicates organizational capacity in the past.

Alexis: A lot of the work is remembering what's come before that has been suppressed, or wasn't documented, or has been intentionally "forgotten." As a spiritual practice, this sometimes happens more on a vibrational level. There are ways that we lift up and invoke it. One of the examples that I love, and that I think about all the time, is the naming of the Combahee River Collective. I wouldn't know about the Battle of the Combahee River otherwise. How did that happen?

Barbara: There are a couple of factors. One is that I read this wonderful, short forty-page biography of Harriet Tubman and it talked about the military campaign

University of Alabama letter from Robin Boylorn

Ms. Smith,

> Reading *Home Girls* some years ago was startling.
>
> I was right at "home" with your words, with your bad self,
>
> a home girl talking about the luxury of home,
>
> and what it felt like in between those walls,
>
> around black women,
>
> surrounded by majesty and strength,
>
> being at home with yourself and going back home,
>
> and telling a story not unlike my own.
>
> You talked about leveling out oppressions,
>
> owning our experiences,
>
> embracing all of who we are.
>
> Talking all that "truth" about black girl's lives
>
> and the lies told about black girl's lives,
>
> out while I was living my black girl life,
>
> you saved me, and rescued me with your words.
>
> Thank you feels too redundant, not big enough a sentiment,
>
> so I will concentrate instead on telling you that I heard you—
>
> twenty years across your kitchen table
>
> wisdom
>
> met with deep understanding
>
> stirred within me and pushed me to do what you did,
>
> use my words to challenge, defend, protect, and tell
>
> it like it is.
>
> I gathered your memories in my own stories of home
>
> and mother wit
>
> and having "a grandmother who believed in Jesus and in sin,

not necessarily in that order"

and a mama who "believed in education and in books"

and pretty aunts who "believed in beauty"

and sass

and each other

and me.

I find myself continually coming back to feeling brave when

all of the women are white,

and feeling brave when all of the blacks are men,

and finding myself enough,

because you were enough,

and your stories, strength, and survival resonates across time.

Even though the truth hurts sometimes.

You made freedom possible because of the activism you initiated,

for women who were black and feminist and lesbians and

straight

and hurting

and those who just want to go home,

or be at home

with themselves.

Your voice echoed loud and reverberates across time.

I heard you.

I hear you.

I thank you.

—Robin M. Boylorn, PhD

she led on the Combahee River. I'd never heard about it before.* The second is that it was a very productive time in the second wave of the U.S. women's movement. White women were using the names of Black women, historical figures, right and left. Sojourner was taken! Finally, why name it after one person? Why not use something that has even more political resonance than a person's name? We could have called ourselves the Harriet Tubman Collective, but why not name it after a very specific instance of a liberation struggle and liberating action? That's how the name came about.

Alexis: That energy so resonates, that it's that energy of 750 enslaved people rallying behind Harriet Tubman and achieving their freedom.

Barbara: Right, yes! And she planned the action. My understanding is that she worked as a scout for the Union forces and she actually was military personnel. She knew the territory. In the 1970s, it was described as the only campaign in U.S. history planned and led by a woman.

Alexis: What sheroes are significant to you? In this spiritual cosmology of mine, I think of saints and different deities who represent different qualities that we aspire to. To me, Fannie Lou Hamer embodies the qualities I aspire to, or Ella Baker.

Barbara: I completely agree. Fannie Lou Hamer is a person who I always think of. One of the reasons is that I got to meet her, so she was more vivid to me. There's a passage in "Doing It from Scratch," an article about organizing that's in *The Truth That Never Hurts*, when I talk about meeting her. She was so much like the women in my family who I would go home to later that night: Southern and sturdy.† It was really wonderful to meet her.

There's a wonderful film called *Freedom on My Mind*‡ about the Mississippi freedom struggle. It includes the murders of Chaney, Schwerner, and Goodman, and the Mississippi Freedom Summer.§ They have a lot of footage of her. It's really inspiring to see her, particularly at the Democratic Convention in '64.¶ I

---

*Earl Conrad's *Harriet Tubman: Negro Soldier and Abolitionist* (New York: International Publishers, 1942).

†From "Soul on Hold," reprinted in chapter 6 of this volume:

> Because of my devotion to Black women's freedom, I will never forget meeting Fannie Lou Hamer at a basement party in Cleveland in 1965 following a rally at which she had spoken. What struck me most about her was how much she resembled the women in my family who I would return home to later that night: her southern voice, her ample figure, her difficulty walking, and her great kindness to me simply because I was young.

See also Smith (1998: 170).

‡Produced by Connie Field and Marilyn Mulford in 1994.

§In June 1964 two white (Andrew Goodman and Michael Schwerner) and one Black (James Chaney) Civil Rights workers were brutally murdered by the Ku Klux Klan while participating in Mississippi Freedom Summer, during which young people from all over the country went to the South to register Blacks to vote. The heinous crime gained international attention. The Civil Rights Act was signed later that year.

¶Hamer helped organize the Mississippi Freedom Summer and became the vice chair of the Mississippi Freedom Democratic Party, which led to her attending the 1964 Democratic

remember watching that on television. It was still such a rarity for Black people to be on television at that time, and to see a Black woman basically kicking butt in a center of power? We watched with fascination! She was remarkable, and she paid a physical price. Black woman generally have not been treated as ladies, or as people to be protected. Anything they put on a Black man, they would put on us, even more so, because of sexual abuse and rape. She had physical injuries that affected her for the rest of her life, from having been beaten when she was in jail. She was also burned out of her home.

She had a really clear sense of what was important. She inspired younger people who were around her because she was from the place where the organizing was happening. It wasn't abstract for her. She didn't make a decision, "I think I'll live in Mississippi and suffer there!" She was from there. Why do you admire her?

Alexis: So much of what you said. June Jordan wrote a children's book called *Fannie Lou Hamer*.

Barbara: Oh yes! I've read it. I have it. Did you read it as a child?

Alexis: I did. My parents were very much about children's books as a way for my siblings and I to really see ourselves. Learning about this collective story, and the steps of organizing, organizing around food. She took that step from being really abused as a child growing up and sharecropping, to really thinking about whether people have land and food, and what it really means for power, for Black people, and in a majority Black, majority agricultural place, Mississippi. I also remember watching *Eyes on the Prize* and seeing how she was not going to pretend to be calm about things that were infuriating. She was just raising her voice. And she would sing. I always got the sense that she knew how powerful she was, and she knew that she didn't have to try to fit into somebody else's definition of power.

I think that is huge in terms of qualities that I would aspire to and want to canonize. To be present to your own power despite the abuse, to not fake it, to be honest about all of those things that happened, imprisonment, the Mississippi appendectomy [involuntarily sterilization].* All of these levels of abuse, and yet, the sound of Hamer's voice and the strength of her presence carries.

National Convention to challenge the official Mississippi delegation that was all-white and anti–Civil Rights as unrepresentative of all Mississippians. The Mississippi Freedom Democratic Party drew national attention to the injustices they faced and threatened to upset the normal presidential nomination process. They were not seated as part of the delegation, but due to the controversy, the Democratic Party approved a clause in 1968 that demanded equality of representation in state delegations.

* Hamer is credited with coining this phrase by saying, "She went into the doctor for a cold and came out with a Mississippi appendectomy." Sterilization without knowledge or consent meant hysterectomies and tubal ligations performed on women of color and on women with physical or mental disabilities and others deemed unfit (illiterate, poor). The practice originated with the eugenics movement (1920s), persisted for decades, and sought to reduce the birth of "undesirables" and encourage the birth of desirable people (white, intelligent, upper class). Thirty-two states had laws allowing sterilization of those "unfit to breed," and one (North Carolina) is considering reparations. See Mustufa (2011).

"Ella's Daughters' Seven Sisters Campaign," Ella's Daughters (n.d.)

The Seven Sisters Campaign is Ella's Daughters' effort to hold up 7 vitally important organizations and areas of work and to highlight the ways in which they mirror, intersect, and overlap with one another. We also think the women, particularly young women and women of color, who are actively giving leadership, energy, and vision to these struggles are sisters we want to strengthen and nurture in any way we can.

Ella's Daughters (ED) is a network of women activists, artists, and scholars working in Ella Baker's radical democratic, grassroots tradition. We see ourselves as political quilters. Political quilting like other forms of quilt making is a woman-centered collective practice that takes patches and fragments and carefully and creatively stitches them together; producing something that is more than a sum total of its parts, something functional and artful. We want to offer our time and labor to help facilitate this movement-building work without presuming to "lead" or define or control it.

Those 7 issues/principles we are focused on in this campaign are:

1. A just peace in Palestine and Israel, and solidarity with the Palestinian people, especially the people of Gaza living under such brutal occupation. This work is being carried out by many groups that EDs work with including: www.arabjewishpartnerhsip.org and www.vivapalestina.org

2. Community-based restorative justice approaches to street violence that is killing our Black and Latino urban youth in gut-wrenching numbers. This work is being carried out by many groups that EDs work with including: www.project-nia.org

3. Support, services, and self-determination for the Black LGBTQ youth, who are often marginalized by the multiple communities to which they belong. This work is being carried out by many groups that EDs work with including: www.affinity.95.org

4. Solidarity with the long-suffering and hard-struggling people of Ayiti (Haiti) and a defense to their right to self-determination, peace, land, and resources. This work is being carried out by many groups that EDs work with including: http://www.risinginsolidarity.wordpress.com

5. An end to all forms of torture, whether perpetuated by agents of the State, local police forces, or in intimate relationships. This work is being carried out by many groups that EDs work with including: http://illinoiscat.wordpress.com

6. Rights and recognition for domestic workers in the United States and globally who are too-often under-paid, overworked to be treated with dignity and respect. This work is being carried out by many groups that EDs work with including: www.domesticworkers.org

7. Full human rights and recognition for undocumented workers and youth, and support for the leadership of young activists who self-describe as "undocumented and unafraid." This work is being carried out by many groups that EDs work with including: www.iyjl.org

Ella's Daughters network hopes to provide a community where new collaborations could be conceived.

I've transformed my living room in Durham into this Black feminist classroom—the Eternal Summer of the Black Feminist Mind. We have a wall that I painted with chalkboard paint and then I surrounded it with pictures of people who I think of as Black feminist ancestors. They are all people who are not with us right now. There are several different pictures of Fannie Lou Hamer. And several different pictures of Ella Baker.

Barbara: Oh yeah, that's the other person.

Alexis: Why Ella Baker?

Barbara: She had such an incisive analysis of race and class, and she was so accessible to people. She had a very humble way of understanding what her role was. She was one of two or so adults who were allowed to be a part of SNCC [Student Nonviolent Coordinating Committee], and the other one was Howard Zinn. I so identify with her perspective. She had to deal with sexism in the context of the movement, too.

Alexis: I'm grateful that I had a professor, Farah Griffin, who created a reading group specifically so we would read Barbara Ransby's *Ella Baker and the Black Freedom Movement: A Radical Democratic Vision*. That was the first time I had a chance to read about her incisive analysis of race and class. Also her intergenerational analysis, her way of being able to work with young people without trying to impose, and without trying to act like she should tell them what to do and they should just do it. That was huge for me because I was still a teenager when I was learning about her.

She was pushed out of different organizations: the NAACP, the SCLC [Southern Christian Leadership Conference]. She had these different ways of being too radical, or too Left, or not getting with a particular model of leadership. As somebody who has been the "too difficult," the woman-out-of-her-place, the Black woman who's too angry and too loud, in different organizations that I've been in, it was so validating. It was like, you know what? That doesn't mean that I'm not doing effective work for my people. Actually, sometimes it means that this organizing structure is trying to silence Black women.

"We don't always get the stories of people who were seen as difficult in their own time, to be an example of different ways that leadership looks."

Barbara: Yes, I think that that's a mark of honor in some ways that she was kicked out or marginalized.

Alexis: She was removed from particular positions that she had in organizations because of her politics and because of her approach. She was not into top-down leadership. I'm thankful to Barbara Ransby for writing the history, and to Joanne Grant who made the film *Fundi*, because we don't always get the stories of people who were seen as difficult in their own time, to be an example of different ways that leadership looks. She's definitely a shero. Are there other sheros that feel really significant to you?

Barbara: All of the people who got to participate in the Civil Rights movement and go down South, or were in the South already. I was just a few years younger than they. We always look up to our peers who are a few years older than us, the people who live in our neighborhoods and who come from similar places. So I really looked up to them.

Another woman I really looked up to was Lorraine Hansberry, particularly when I found out that she had written letters to the Daughters of Bilitis. Of course, Audre Lorde, whom I knew personally. I admired her greatly. It was very much a gift to know her. We did a lot of good work together. A number of us built Black feminism, but she was central in that.

The Legacy of Kitchen Table Press and Black Women's Studies

Alexis Pauline Gumbs shares how the books Kitchen Table: Women of Color Press published found their way into her life and shaped her path. Two others share the influence of KTP publications on their lives through University of Alabama letters—Lisa C. Moore, founding publisher of RedBone Press, and Sheri Davis-Faulkner, a PhD candidate at Emory University. They, too, acknowledge the legacy and the futures that KTP made possible.

Interview with Alexis Pauline Gumbs

Alexis Pauline Gumbs: One of the things we need to do is situate ourselves in historical context in relationship to this idea of your legacy. So you all were founding Kitchen Table Press in 1981. I was born in 1982. I actually always lived in a world where there was Black feminism and where there was Black feminist literature. I had the privilege of being born into that context.

Barbara Smith: There are many, many who are your age peers who know nothing about it! Black feminism has been marginalized, as far as a more widespread consciousness about it. Yet we see manifestations of its impact, even among those who don't know it ever happened.

Alexis: I didn't grow up in school learning about Black feminism, even though Black feminism existed, and even though the work to create Black women's studies existed. My mom was in a very early course in Black women's studies at SUNY New Paltz that Margaret Lewis taught. But it really took digging and persistent research to find poetry by Audre Lorde and then being able to find *This Bridge* and *Home Girls*. The fact that there was Black feminist literature in print allowed me to do that! That was what made it accessible for me to be able to find [this work] as a self-directed person obsessed with the energy of Black women in media. When I think about sacred texts, I also think about your decision to relate to publishing in a strategic way. Otherwise, it certainly wasn't going to come to women in my schools.

> **"Our books were lifelines. They traveled to places that we could not possibly go."**

Barbara: That written record is really important. That's what we understood. This was before personal computers, the Internet, texting, and all the social media. It was before all of that. So people understood that the written record was *the* record, and that's what we were involved in. And, of course, we had always been bookish. By we, I'm talking about Audre and Cherríe Moraga and people who were involved in the early days. Hattie Gossett. We loved books, we valued them. We understood how important they were. We were about creating them, too.

Alexis: I'm remembering that paragraph in the Combahee River Collective Statement that explains that because Black women are scattered all over the place, and [you had] some skills in publishing and writing, [you] identified publishing as an important way of raising Black feminist consciousness, a major way to build alignment, a place for people to recognize themselves.

Barbara: The books had such reach. The best publishers in our country, even the ones that are mainstream, the people who started them, the editors, had great vision. Our books were lifelines. They traveled to places that we could not possibly go. It was just so thrilling to get mail from people in other countries who had found Kitchen Table: Women of Color Press books.

Alexis: I am thinking about *The Politics of Women's Studies: Testimony from the 30 Founding Mothers*, about the founding mothers of women's studies. You are one of the people who is interviewed in that collection, and you say Black women's studies is my legacy.

Barbara: There are two generations, at least, following mine that have been involved in Black feminism. I'm thinking about people who are in Farah Jasmine Griffin's generation and then yours. And there's probably another one coming up. So we really do have two generations of people who have been involved in this work, and who have been affected and influenced by this work.

The reference point for us might have been in other movements like the Civil Rights, Black Power, Black Nationalist movements, Third World Liberation movements. We might have been looking at those places for how you organize something. We were very excited to find out about foremothers in earlier eras, but they were not necessarily organizing explicitly as Black feminists, although they were in their writing, and in their organizing and lives, raising Black feminist concerns. You can make a case for Ida B. Wells-Barnett, and Mary Church Terrell, and Anna Julia Cooper being Black feminists, but they weren't explicitly saying, "This is a Black feminist group," and "This is what we believe as Black feminists." They were raising Black women's issues from a perspective that was critical of sexism and traditional gender relationships. Today's contemporary Black feminist organizers have something that we didn't have, which is bona fide, explicit Black feminist foremothers to look at.

Alexis: I think that makes a huge difference. For so many other women my age who identify as Black feminists, our politicization is collective. Black punk rock movements within the United States, or different subcultural movements, Riot Grrrl, or anti-poverty organizing politicize some people. When I think about my own influences, I think that it was important to have self-identified, explicit Black feminists who were able to look at the contradictions, able to look at sexism in a Black punk movement and racism in a white punk movement, for example. To be able to be like, "Wait a minute, I'm not the first person looking at it in these ways." Now the punk movement is not the Civil Rights movement. I mean the punk movement is not people laying their lives on the line for a political set of beliefs on behalf of their people.

Barbara: We don't have any control over history. We don't have any control over when we arrive or when we leave, though we do have some impact on events. We generally don't control the big sweep. So all we can do is to be as alert as we possibly can, and to make those commitments to justice and working for the widest possible benefits for all . . .not just humanity! Animals and plants as well.

Alexis: It was huge that I made it to college; that was a big deal. It was a complete shift in my access to Black feminism. There was a strong Black women's studies presence—Farah Griffin telling me about the Kitchen Table Press Freedom Organizing pamphlets, for example—and there remains this really strong impact of saying that the experiences of Black women are a catalyst and a lens for looking at the world in a transformative way. That there's an analysis there. Do you want to talk a little bit about creating *But Some of Us Are Brave* or strategic relationships to the academy and to scholarship?

Barbara: One of the things that was really wonderful about the work that I was doing with Black women's studies in the 1970s and the '80s is that it was all connected. Teaching Black women writers, building Black feminism, trying to define Black women's studies, those things were all related to each other. I think that's what perhaps made my work unique. I was involved in movement building; I wasn't only in the academy. I was out there when Black women were being murdered in Boston. There were all these pulls between intellectual pursuits and activism. I think they work together fairly well, and that is a part of the legacy. There have always been people who combine those commitments and those priorities, and I hope I'm in that tradition.

Alexis: I remember being in the library in college, looking on the shelves and seeing the title *All the Women Are White, All the Blacks Are Men, But Some of Us Are Brave: Black Women's Studies*. First of all, the title is a poem. It's so clear; it's so true. I said to myself, "Yes, it's true, all the women *are* white." I had to pull this book off of the shelf. I didn't even know that my mom had been in one of the first Black women's studies courses until I saw the syllabus in the back. I was like, "Wait a minute, SUNY New Paltz, Margaret Wade-Lewis?" I called my mom and asked her, "Did you ever take this class with this professor?" And she had! It opened a whole conversation about the struggle for Black studies at SUNY New Paltz, and my mom's politicization. That's huge. So there are ways that the work of teaching about Black women writers, bringing the archive and the literature that existed to be looked at in an academic setting, I know it had impacts on me that I don't even know. Because I'm raised by a woman who took a Black women's studies class.

Barbara: You're a perfect example of the apple not falling far from the tree. How unique is that?

University of Alabama letter
from Lisa C. Moore

Dear Barbara Smith:

We haven't spoken in a few years; I know you've been busy with your work in Albany, and I've been busy with mine here in D.C. But thoughts of you do pop into my head often, and I am taking this occasion (surprise!) this October to send you a love letter. You do know, don't you, that without you there would be no me?

If you had not edited *Home Girls*, I would not have known I could edit *does your mama know?* I would not have known it was possible to change someone's life by publishing a book. I would not have known that she who owns the press has the power of the press. I would not have known that yes, it matters who publishes. I would not know your history of women in publishing, and which land mines to avoid, and which roads would take me in the right direction. You got me started on the path I'm on now, and I thank you wholeheartedly.

I'm reminded of a Langston Hughes story in *The Best of Simple*, titled "Banquet in Honor." Honor comes in the form of support for the living. I will continue to honor you by buying your books, recommending your books, passing on your knowledge to a young woman who may be interested in publishing.

I hope that you are taking care of your health, as I am learning I must take care of mine. Giving so much to the world is hard work. You didn't teach me to pace myself! And now this youngster, Alexis Pauline Gumbs, is showering accolades on me, while I think I'm just doing my work. But I get it; without me, there would be no Alexis, and without you, there would be no me. I get it.

I thank you for your love.

Sincerely,
Lisa C. Moore
Publisher, RedBone Press[*]

[*] RedBone Press's mission statement: "RedBone Press publishes work celebrating the cultures of black lesbians and gay men, and work that further promotes understanding between black gays and lesbians and the black mainstream."

University of Alabama letter from Sheri Davis-Faulkner

Dear Dean Barbara Smith,

The title Dean is necessary because you are to me one of the deans of Black Women's Studies. I definitely feel a kinship towards you because my mother is from Cleveland and I was born in 1974, when the CRC started meeting. Thanks to my black feminist mother, Beverly Guy-Sheftall, I have had the opportunity to grow up in a black women's studies world where I can name my experiences, I can define my worth, I can determine my work, and I can develop my normal. But I learned to do this as part of a larger political project in her Feminist Theory course at Spelman College in 1997 where I was introduced to the Combahee River Collective's "A Black Feminist Statement." The idea of scholar activism for me comes from this powerful statement, which taught me to make "the personal political" in dialogue, in action, and in solidarity with all my black sisters, with appreciation for our differences.

It continues to function as a roadmap for listening, learning, organizing, loving, and doing the work to liberate black women from violence, body-hatred, isolation, racism, heterosexism, poverty and more. Oftentimes I hear people say that we have progressed because my son's generation will never know a time when there wasn't a black male president of the United States. I know we have progressed because my son will never know a time when black women's lives are completely invisible and marginalized, because his black feminist mother knows better. I am deeply grateful for the life that your words and your work have provided for my generation. The struggle continues. . . .

A Heartfelt Thank You,
Sheri Davis-Faulkner, ABD
Emory University, American Studies
Spelman College c/o [class of] 1997

The Legacy of Combahee: Identity Politics and Interlocking Oppressions

Ideas grow and spread in often unpredictable and untraceable ways. Thinking with, about, and through multiple marginalities is one distinct and enduring contribution of Combahee's work to movement building. How Combahee did that work and the enduring importance of wrestling with the place of identity in political activism are explored in this section. As part of this journey, we include "What Sistas Want, What Sistas Believe" by the Black Feminist Working Group, who invoke Combahee's work and combine it with their own vision and elements of the Black Panther program, illustrating the vibrant creativity of next-generation Black feminism. In addition to Alexis's interview, additional perspectives come from conversations with Virginia Eubanks and Alethia Jones.

Interview with Alexis Pauline Gumbs (2010)

Alexis: The Combahee River Collective Statement is an everyday touchstone for me. But sometimes it's frustrating, because I don't think it is acknowledged as much as it should be as the source of an analysis of the impact of interlocking systems of oppression. As an analysis that [insists that] "the major systems of oppression are interlocking." That's a direct quote. Of course, it influenced Kimberlé Crenshaw's idea of intersectionality, and that is the bedrock of cultural studies and so many academic studies right now. But I'll talk about the Combahee River Collective and people are like, "What's the Combahee River Collective?" You can't find an earlier source for this type of analysis than the Combahee River Collective Statement. [When these ideas move into the academy, people sometimes forget] that movement building itself, the actual practice of doing this work, is what causes us to think in complicated ways about our lives and what they mean. The statement makes it really clear that people were willing to think about only one issue at a time. A lot of people can't do that. Black women especially can't do that.

Barbara: Indeed. It was really my sister Beverly Smith, Demita Frazier, and I who knocked that thing out. Demita talked about how we can hold more than one idea in our minds at the same time. Black feminists of that era, and of other eras, talk about [the fact that] we don't choose each day when we get up *which* we are going to be. We don't say, "Well I'm Black today," "I'm a woman today," "I'm economically oppressed today," "I'm a lesbian today." You just get up and you deal with it.

We really wanted to get to an understanding of what actual impact the different oppressions and identities had upon lived experience. There are examples, like sterilization abuse, that are perfect examples of an intersectional oppression.

Who was it happening to? Women of color in this country, in Puerto Rico, and on indigenous land in the U.S. It wasn't happening to men, not to that degree. There were other things, like the Tuskegee Experiments, that were happening to them.[*] The name of the game is abuse. Any way we can subjugate you, that's what we'll do. Any way that we can take away your life chances, your options, your opportunities, and your humanity, that's what we'll do. But there are certainly different scripts for people who have different identities within that cauldron of oppression.

> **"Movement building itself, the actual practice of doing this work, is what causes us to think in complicated ways about our lives and what they mean."**

Alexis: Combahee was organizing in Boston at a time when there was so much race hatred. Unfortunately, that has not ended or altered as much as it could have.

Barbara: The height of that was during the Boston school-bussing crisis. My twin sister, Beverly, was in Boston, at the end of August and in early September when the schools were going to be desegregated in South Boston, and she said it was like you could hear a pin drop. The city seemed poised and waiting for an explosion.

> **"Understanding your own identity and making connections with others who don't share that identity is part and parcel of the same work."**

This may be an extreme statement, but it was, in some ways, like starting Black feminism in Mississippi. At that moment, Boston was functioning like Mississippi. It had the whole New England history and the Pilgrims, and the American Renaissance people, the intellectuals at Harvard and all that. And then it had racial warfare in the streets. I dare you to be able to tell the mobs in Boston from the mobs in Little Rock [Arkansas].

---

[*] The Tuskegee Experiments refers to a U.S. Public Health Service forty-year study (1932–1972) of syphilis conducted by leaving four hundred syphilis-infected poor Black Alabama share-croppers untreated in order to learn the course of the disease. Study participants were misled about the nature of their illness, and their wives and children who became infected were not informed, even after penicillin proved to be an effective cure in 1947. See Washington (2006) for more on medical experiments on Blacks.

"What Sistas Want, What Sistas Believe:
Black Feminist Twelve Point Plan,"
Black Feminist Working Group (2011)

This document is inspired by the work and legacy of the Combahee River Collective and the Black Panther Party for Self Defense.

We are a collective of Black feminist/womanist activists who are committed to the liberation of the Black community. As Black women the conditions of our lives are created by interlocking systems of oppression. As a collective we oppose all forms of oppression and are continuously working to develop our analysis to be effective allies with other marginalized communities. We created this platform to address the misconceptions about what Black feminists/womanists believe, where our allegiances lie and what we want for the Black community. We recognize that the problems that exist within the Black community are connected to larger systems of oppression and domination. However, this document addresses those issues that disproportionately affect the Black community because this is the community that we as Black feminists identify as our homebase and foundation. We developed this statement from a place of love and not divisiveness, as we struggle along with our brothas and Black people of all genders for the safety, security, and liberation of our community. We believe that the liberation of Black women is necessary and integral to the liberation of the Black community and not separate from it.

1. WE WANT FREEDOM.
   We believe that freedom is only possible through individual and community self-determination. In order for the black community to achieve self-determination all systems of oppression must be dismantled.
2. We want a reformation of the criminal justice system, the abolition of the prison industrial complex, and the implementation of community based models of justice and accountability.
3. We want control over our reproductive health and believe it is essential to building and maintaining strong black communities.
4. We want an end to all forms of physical, emotional, and sexual violence against black children.
5 We want media to reflect the diversity of who we are, to include our voices, value our bodies and our stories.

6. We want an end to poverty and the development of an economy that benefits and provides for all people.

7. We want education for liberation that includes equitable distribution of funding, culturally relevant curriculum, community control of schools, and an end to the school to prison pipeline.

8. We want access to secure, equal, safe, affordable, and hazard free housing (public and private), community land rights, residencies of our choice, and an end to homelessness.

9. We want to live in a society where we can feel safe and protected.

10. We want an end to invisibility, violence, and homophobia towards LGBTQ people in our community.

11. We want a world where respect of the Earth's resources is central to every human society and economic system.

12. We want a Black community free of sexism and sexist oppression, where Black Women can be self-determined members of their community.

Copyright © Black Feminist Working Group, 2011. Reprinted with permission of the Black Feminist Working Group (Iresha Picot, Tiamba Wilkerson, Nuala Cabral, Ladi Sasha Jones, Darasia Shelby, Kim Murray).

Interviews with Virginia Eubanks and Alethia Jones

Virginia Eubanks: Do you think identity politics and intersectionality are still relevant to social justice organizing today?

Barbara Smith: It is probably still relevant, because we still have oppression based on perceived or actual differences in identities. How would we understand, for example, when Don Imus attacked the Rutgers basketball team, had we not done identity politics when we did it?* Because what was fascinating about how that was covered is that they talked about how he was being both sexist *and* racist. It was great, because it was accurate.

Understanding your own identity and making connections with others who don't share that identity is part and parcel of the same work. We were much more able as Black women and Black lesbian feminists to connect to others because identity politics gave us that confidence, it gave us that grounding, it made us think we were of value. We were less easy to intimidate, and because we had an analysis, we understood how the isms and the oppressions connected to each

---

* See note in chapter 3.

other. So we would be out on a picket line in front of a construction site where they weren't hiring men of color.

Our politics were complex enough that when a Black man was accused of having raped white women in a virtually all-white section of Boston during a period of Boston's history when there was racial warfare [the 1970s], we could actually speak out against violence against women at the same time that we could talk about the railroading of a Black man in a very typical scenario of being accused of a crime of sexual violence. It was a hard stand to take, and it was not a stand that white women in the movement as a whole might have understood or agreed with, but we took it. There was a complexity to what we were doing that was really, really important.

Virginia: So there's something about understanding the complexity of your own identity that makes it possible to meet other people "where they're at"?

Barbara: We were young, a number of us were lesbians, some of us had had access to great educations, and yet we were able to make links with people who lived in our neighborhoods who did not necessarily share any of these things. There were people who saw our integrity, commitment, compassion, and passion, and we made wonderful connections with different kinds of women that were just precious because they were across barriers and differences that would make people say, "Oh, those people could never get along."

Virginia: One of the things that I understand differently than I did when I started working on this project is the way that identity politics requires you to be located. Your knowledge and your action have to come from somewhere, and you have to be able to be called into account for your location.

From a real personal place, I'm a Southern white woman, raised middle-class in the suburban Northeast, who currently works with three organizations dedicated to feminist social change and economic justice. In two of the three, women of color are the majority of members, and I've been blessed to have a number of amazing women of color mentors throughout my life. But I struggled for decades to find a comfortable activist identity—particularly doing cross-class and inter-racial organizing. I dealt with a lot of guilt around my race and class privilege, which wasn't productive for my movement work.

This changed when I found an amazing legacy of Southern, white, anti-racist organizing centered on the Highlander Research and Education Center, going back to the 1930s and beyond. I found mentors, and models, and ways to understand my identity as part of a legacy of resistance and change. Letting go of racial guilt and self-blame also meant that I found empathy for my family and my people. I see identity politics as allowing you to bring your whole self, even the not-so-great parts, to movement work. But this is something people seem to have trouble understanding—that identity politics is not just about marginal identities. Do you think identity politics can be used to help white people navigate their racial identities in a positive way?

Barbara: You can't roll the tape backwards. If you are white, middle-class, male, female, straight, whatever. You can't roll it backwards. You can't say "I would prefer to come here as . . ." No. You're here. As far as we know, unless you believe in reincarnation, this is your one opportunity! [laughter] At least, you can't bank on another go. So you have to figure out what you are going to do with the hand that you are dealt.

Don't assume that because someone has what you perceive to be a lot of "politically correct" identities, they are not struggling with some of the same things that you are. That can help bridge differences. Everyone has their own particular history, story, and struggle.

> **"Identity politics can be useful for people who have privilege. You can use all these differences, these nuances, life stories, to build something that is really, really vibrant and beautiful. Something that looks like a functioning democracy, a beloved community."**

I don't like it when people who are privileged do "cultural tourism." I don't like it when white people build a fantasy about what it means to be different from themselves. At the end of the day, to me, it becomes very insulting. If you don't know about it, don't pretend. Inherent in identity politics is the idea that your location, your experience, your class, race, gender, sexuality, nationality, geographic origin, ability, age are all important. We are respectful of it. We are interested to find out what we don't know, and we don't mythologize or fantasize about who other people are.

So yes, I think identity politics can be useful for people who have privilege. You can use all these differences, these nuances, life stories, to build something that is really, really vibrant and beautiful. Something that looks like a functioning democracy, a beloved community.

Virginia: In terms of the current political moment, what kinds of challenges do you think are arising for us in the post-Obama, post–Hillary Clinton era, when many people seem less willing to name sexism, racism, homophobia, capitalism as what they are?

Barbara: I think we have these moments. It's hard to deny that racism is a force when you have the murder of Trayvon Martin.* You can try to hide from racism in the United States, or pretend, but these contradictions just continue to manifest themselves.

---

*On February 26, 2012, an unarmed teenager, Trayvon Martin, returning from buying snacks at 7–11 was shot and killed by volunteer neighborhood watchman George Zimmerman in Sanford, Florida. Martin was visiting his father, who lived in a gated community. Zimmerman considered him suspicious.

So, for example, we live in a period when the president of the United States affirms equality for people of all sexual orientations, focused upon lesbian and gay marriage, but if you look at the hate crimes statistics, they will show that some of the people who are most endangered of being beaten up are gays, lesbians, and transgendered people.*

There are always things that we can question, interrogate, struggle with, and organize around. As long as there is injustice, we have reason to organize and struggle. Apparently, injustice is not over! We are in a historical period when a lot of things have changed, as a result of the struggles of prior periods. But that doesn't mean it's done.

Virginia: I find, at least with my students, that one of the things that seems unique to this historical moment is a real unwillingness to name difference. The post–Civil Rights, post–identity politics response among white people often is, "If I just don't mention race ever, then nobody can accuse me of being a racist," which actually makes it really difficult to talk about the ongoing realities of racism, or sexism, or homophobia.

"Those of us who have struggled around our identities or have struggled against racism, we actually like to be acknowledged and respected for who we are. We want the whole heritage, the whole struggle, the whole history to be acknowledged. You can't do that if you can't bring it up."

Probably the most compelling example for me is when I was trying to talk to a class about racialization—the process by which an ethnic, geographic, religious, or linguistic group "becomes" a race—and particularly about the category "Arab" in post–9-11 America. So I asked my class, "Who are Arabs?," trying to get at the fact that it is a linguistic group, not a religious or geographic group. And a student literally gasped. When I asked him why, he said, "Oh my god, you said 'Arab.' That's so offensive." There was so much resistance in the room to even using the word.

Barbara: Would it be offensive to call someone Greek or Turkish? Is that offensive? That would be a great question to ask.

Virginia: There's a fear-based response . . .it's about being afraid of being seen to hold racist ideas, which keeps the analysis focused on individual intentions and behaviors and keeps you from recognizing or discussing structural and institutional racism, classism, sexism, or homophobia. Can you offer any insight into how to deal with that political moment?

Barbara: The students you are describing don't have a place to have a public

---

* See note in chapter 6.

dialogue about these differences. They don't have terminology. They also don't have the experience of having engaged in dialogue about these issues and differences that has wonderful, positive results.

Pat Parker, a Black lesbian poet who died in the 1989, wrote this poem about what her white friends need to know, and she basically says, "You need to forget that I'm Black. And you need to *never* forget that I'm Black."* It's possible to balance these two opposite things at the same time. Those of us who have struggled around our identities or have struggled against racism, we actually like to be acknowledged and respected for who we are. We want the whole heritage, the whole struggle, the whole history to be acknowledged. You can't do that if you can't bring it up.

> **"There is virtually no place in United States society where you can have sane and productive dialogues about differences, specifically race."**

Now, that doesn't mean you have to say ridiculous and offensive things. I guess there's still a lot of room for what we did in the 1970s, which was consciousness-raising around race. I love it when someone asks me a question that makes sense around my experience as a person of color. Something that is not insulting, but actually something that shows some insight, curiosity, and respect. I think it's hard because we don't have a lot of role-modeling for it. Look at what happened when President Obama said that if he had a son, he would look like Trayvon Martin. People went *off*. They accused him of being racist, of bringing politics into it. But he was just saying, if he had a son, he would look like Trayvon Martin, and he might be equally endangered.

Virginia: We don't have very many good forums in which to have those conversations.

Barbara: That's correct. There is virtually no place in United States society where you can have sane and productive dialogues about differences, specifically race. So wherever you are along the continuum, instead of beating yourself up about that, think to yourself, "I didn't learn it in school, I didn't hear it at home, I don't get it in social settings, I'm not getting it in church, mosque, synagogue, or temple. I'm just not getting it! Nobody's talking about it!" We need to examine that and try to figure out how to make it different.

---

*From the poem "For the White Person Who Wants to Know How to Be My Friend." The first two lines of the poem are:

   The first thing you do is to forget that I'm black.

   Second, you must never forget that I'm black.

See Parker (1978).

The power structure in this country does *not* want people to talk about race and other oppressions in any realistic way. If people understand how the pieces fit together, people in power will have a lot of problems. In the 1960s, in some ways, that's exactly what happened. The movements did it. Malcolm X was doing it. You couldn't run away from it. Even people who wished to avoid it, who wished to remain ignorant, couldn't escape. You'd turn on the television and you'd see Mike Wallace asking James Baldwin, "James Baldwin, what does the Negro want?" And James Baldwin saying back to him, "What do white people want?" Unforgettable.

"The most progressive parts of the women's movement became sites and places where people could talk about these things, and not only live but find joy in doing so."

Virginia: That's so indicative of the difference. Today's Mike Wallace would never ask that question. That's progress, in some ways, to not ask ignorant questions. But many people have gone right past not asking ignorant questions to not asking any questions at all. Finding space where people can make mistakes, and deal legitimately and honestly with their own lack of awareness, is one important things those forums could accomplish. Let's have a place where we can do that, a place where you can be respectful and responsible but also show your ignorance and recover. And live. I think that's one of the challenges younger folks face today. They don't feel like they can show their ignorance and survive. So they don't risk it.

Barbara: Indeed. The most progressive parts of the women's movement became sites and places where people could talk about these things, and not only live but find joy in doing so.

Alethia Jones: Your writing gives us a glimpse of how to build analysis and theory based on actual work to make real changes in real places. Sometimes that dimension of grassroots organizing work can get lost, but that kind of grounded experience makes a very important difference in finding concrete ways to collaborate with others to make change around key issues.

Barbara: I absolutely believe that. You have to be in touch with what is happening on the ground, day to day, where people are trying to support themselves and take care of their families and loved ones, and all the things that human beings have to do. In addition, if you don't have some kind of organizational capacity, when things occur, you have to scramble to be in a position to address them, whereas if you have the organizational existence, you're much more ready. It's very, very different for a political organization or a policy organization to come together around what's happening now as opposed to an individual saying, "Oh, wow, I don't even know where we would begin."

Some people can't really get through life without deciding to work for justice. They just need it. They look at the situation, they are not pleased with what they see, they know other people who feel similarly [about] whatever the issue is, and they move into action. So there will always be people who decide that they must act, they must communicate, they must take a stand for justice.

And then there are probably a larger segment of people who agree with all of that passionate commitment and the integrity of the people who are acting and with what the activists are asserting, but they don't necessarily feel like they have to be there. They think, "I'll help in other ways, I'll support in other ways." I have great admiration for those who are willing to get their hands dirty, who are willing to roll up their sleeves and get involved.

The Legacy of Combahee's Organizing: Coalitions for Conscious Collective Solutions

Combahee's work was rooted in creative and vocal interventions into systems of oppression in specific places through concerted joint action with friends and allies. Combahee also tried to keep that complexity front and center, rather than shrink issues and identities into simplistic categories. One recent effort, UBUNTU, directly involves this chapter's interviewer, Alexis Pauline Gumbs, and consciously pursues this pathway as it tackles issues of sexual violence in Durham, North Carolina. UBUNTU was founded in 2006 in response to the sexual assault tragedy at Duke University. Dr. Ron Daniels, who currently heads the Institute of the Black World, reconsiders Occupy Wall Street through a Black lens on economic justice. The institute is a longstanding base for Black nationalist activism and strongly influenced the training and perspectives of some of the members of Combahee.

Interview with Alexis Pauline Gumbs

Alexis Pauline Gumbs: How would you describe your work with the Combahee Collective in Boston?

Barbara Smith: I think it was really fated that I ended up there, because I realize that if I had moved to another eastern city, there might not have been the combination of factors and ingredients that made the kind of organizing we did viable. In Boston there's something about the size and the scale of the city that made it more possible for those of us who were like-minded and who cared about these things to find each other. It's a real city. It's smaller than New York, but it's not a backwater . . . except racially. But it had a lot of the components, like an organized Left, that were very important.

There were Black progressive people in Boston; there were people who were artists. The person who was the community activities coordinator for the

Blackstone Community School, she was a dancer who did African dance. So there were all these kinds of lovely intertwinings. There was a filmmaker there named Alonzo Speight, who made a film about police brutality called *The People United* and decided to include the murders of Black women that Combahee organized around in the film.

The fact that there was such a vibrant women's community in the Boston area didn't hurt, either! You had organizations, institutions, and individuals to link with who could help with different kinds of things that you were involved in. There was a women's bookstore, one of the best in the country—New Words. There was a women's restaurant. There was a credit union. There was a women's health center. There was a socialist feminist women's union there, primarily made up of white women, but with politics that actually had a race, class, and gender analysis. So the institutional face of the women's movement was helpful.

The socialist feminists started the Committee to End Sterilization Abuse (CESA), and some people from Combahee were involved in that work. CESA offered the opportunity to meet other feminists of color who were not a part of Combahee but with whom we shared politics. We focused on violence against women in general. There was an annual Take Back the Night march, probably the earliest [such] march in the country. Combahee had impact because we changed the route of the march following the murders of Black women. We actually had feeder marches that started in the people of color communities that eventually got connected [to the main march].

Alexis: The work of Combahee really, really impacted us in Durham when we were organizing in response to the Duke lacrosse rape scandal, and responding to the media and all this bashing of Black women and sex workers and survivors of sexual violence. It was interesting to look at the structure of your organizing when the murders were just continuing to happen. Of course, the pamphlet of *Six [Black] Women: Why Did They Die?* becomes [eleven] and keeps going up. Even on the day of the march, you had to change the signs, right?

Barbara: Indeed, indeed. I'm getting chills.

Alexis: It gives me chills, and I wasn't born at the time! We were faced with this challenge: How do you speak, and how do you raise your voice, and how do you have visibility in these circumstances that are so violent and so clearly trying just to remove us from the whole scene literally and physically and metaphysically, in so many ways?

Barbara: We were just so galvanized around the murders, around making things different for ourselves and people like ourselves.

We were challenging ourselves to work in contexts that were not necessarily comfortable, like Bernice Johnson Reagon talks about in her wonderful article "Coalition Politics: Turning the Century." She says if you're organizing, if it's like a womb, than you're not really doing any organizing. It's not supposed to be comfortable. It's not supposed to be your home. We did challenge ourselves to be out there, but it was painful, so it was great that we had allies. There was a lot of great cross-pollination happening during those years in Boston that made the work vibrant and made us, at times, successful.

Alexis: It does have a huge legacy, being able to look into different women's periodicals that were covering the work that you all were doing at that time, being able to see that trajectory and look at the strategy, an example of what a coalition can do at such an urgent time. The way people even *use* the term "coalition" now [is partly based on the work of Combahee]. When I think about how we can have a balance, a space that is so specifically aligned with everything that we believe, with the choir, with the people that believe what we believe, but then have each other's support to work across . . .

"We were always finding ways and places to try to uplift the organizing to the level where it should be. And some of that work actually took root and then bore fruit."

Barbara: . . .it's wonderful to hear that there was at least one person involved in that organizing around the Duke lacrosse team who was looking at work that had been done previously, to see if there were any insights and strategies to be borrowed.

Alexis: There certainly, certainly were.

Barbara: Another thing that is not well known is how much work the Combahee River Collective did to build an anti-racist women's movement. We worked with Transition House, one of the earliest shelters for battered women in the entire country. Beverly and I wrote the first fundraising letter for Transition House literally at the kitchen table. We had women of color sitting out in the yard of this house, and they had found a place to be away from the violence and the threats. It was really quite amazing.

Renee Franco called to ask if the Combahee River Collective would consider doing an anti-racism training workshop for workers at Transition House, where women of different races were coming together. The staff was primarily white, and many of the women coming to utilize their services were women of color. So we said we would, and we did that more than once. And then other women's groups in the Boston area found out that we were doing this and they would ask us, too. Talk about putting yourself out on a limb!

We did it in a way that consciousness-raising was generally done at that time, which was to speak from your own experience, everyone has a voice, and you don't attack people for their lived experience. You try to listen to what people are bringing, and then figure out what to do with that shared knowledge, information, and feelings, as opposed to attack, attack, attack. So we really did subject ourselves to hearing stuff that most of us really wouldn't have wanted to hear.

Not only did we work to build a more anti-racist women's and feminist movement in Boston, we did that nationwide. We had opportunities to do that kind of work for the National Women's Studies Association's 1981 conference at the University of Connecticut in Storrs and visited the regional women's studies organizations around the country. We were always finding ways and places to try to uplift the organizing to the level where it should be. And some of that work actually took root and then bore fruit. We see the results of what we did in people's consciousness now.

Alexis: UBUNTU was the name of the coalition that we created [to do work around the Duke lacrosse rape scandal]. UBUNTU was about the concept of "I Am Because We Are," about the concept of community. But we were also influenced by the way that poetry was mobilized as a tool to create a space for conversation about [Ntozake Shange's poem] "With No Immediate Cause." We printed it in the pamphlet and we started doing performances of "With No Immediate Cause" in Durham thirty years [after it was written].

Barbara: Isn't that wonderful. There's an anthology of poetry that was published during those years called *The World Split Open*, edited by Louise Bernikow, and that was what it was like for us—the world split open when we saw the play. [Shange's] *For Colored Girls* was just amazing. It was our truth in artistic form.

Alexis: Absolutely. It was really a major lesson to say: These things are all together. Black women telling their stories and raising awareness about violence looks all these different poetic ways. Audre Lorde created *Need* out of these kinds of conversations, you sending her the clippings of what was happening in Boston, your being part of the fund-raising for the battered women's shelter.* Those things stay connected. It is a major model for those of us coming afterwards to say: Poetry belongs right here, it's what allows us to do this work, and it changes the way that we think about what life can mean.

Barbara: Right. Right. Adrienne Rich and Audre did a poetry reading at Sanders Theatre at Harvard to benefit the Coalition for Women's Safety, and that was a really big deal. It shows the kind of reach that we had. Having my feet in different worlds—the literary world, the publishing world, the organizing and activist world, the academic and women's studies world—didn't hurt. We could call upon people from different streams of the very exciting things that were going on. It was the Black women's Renaissance. We could call upon people who were involved in the Renaissance and the revolution to cross-pollinate and to really make a change.

Alexis: In the introduction to *The Truth That Never Hurts*, you talk about the person who holds it down, makes sure that a vision continues. You really

---

* *Need* was the sixth Freedom Organizing pamphlet.

"UBUNTU Statement of Purpose," UBUNTU (2012)

WHO WE ARE: PURPOSE & GOALS

UBUNTU was born in the aftermath of the March 13, 2006 rape of a Durham, NC Black woman by members of the Duke University Lacrosse team.... We are Women, Men, and people who do not fit into the gender binary. We are non-trans and trans. We are People of Color, Multi-racial, and white. We come from throughout the Triangle area and have roots both within and outside of the United States. We are sex workers, students, and community members. We are workers. We are Lesbian, Gay, Bisexual, Two-Spirit, and Questioning. We are Queer and Straight. We are young, old, and in-between. We come from a broad range of economic, geographic, spiritual, and political experiences, backgrounds, and perspectives.

UBUNTU is Women of Color and Survivor-led. This means that we emphasize people most affected by sexual violence as public representatives of the group (i.e., media, mobilizations, public meetings, events, etc.), and in the group's internal structure and processes (membership/composition, roles, and decision-making). This is our way of reclaiming power. The name UBUNTU reflects a commitment to a traditional sub-Saharan African concept of the same name, which roughly translated means "I am because we are."

We have joined together through our rage, our pain, and our hope to generate strategies and actions that prevent, disrupt, transform, and heal sexual violence. We are committed to challenging oppression in all forms because we recognize that none of us is free until we all are. We are committed to envisioning a just and loving world.

We center ourselves in work to end sexual violence. Our survival demands this. However, we know that the daily violence of racism/white supremacy, sexism/transphobia/patriarchy, classism/capitalism, and homophobia/heterosexism are the intersecting sources of sexual violence, the reasons it happens. If we want to end sexual violence, we must end these belief systems and the institutions that support them. We work to transform ourselves and our society along the way to clear a path for healthy, affirming cultures and communities.

were that person for Kitchen Table Press. I appreciate that the work is in print because that's the only way I was able to find it two generations later. But that also entailed major decisions for you to prioritize this legacy, this collective vision, over some things that could have been individually positive or careerist for you. That's one of the things that I admire most, and feel most grateful for. Both that Kitchen Table Press continued to exist, and that it offered a model of leadership and commitment that's not individualistic, that is actually collective.

Barbara: I really believe in that. Even in what I'm doing now, I always feel that it's the collective mind that has the most insight and sharpness. When people ask me individually, What do I think about X? Do you think that your group should. . . ? I say, "I have to ask them. I can't make that decision by myself. It's up to us to figure it out." That's how collective organizing and political work plays itself out. The intelligence of the group speaks. We figure out what to do based upon collective consciousness and will as opposed to individualized "I'm gonna do it this way" dictatorial type stuff. We have far too much of that model.

Alexis: What do you feel has changed since the time that you were organizing in Boston? What do you see in terms of Black women's organizing visions and Black feminists' organizing today? What do you think is different?

Barbara: It's really exciting that there are Black women who say explicitly that they are doing Black feminist organizing, like the Crunk Feminist Collective, or Black women in other countries who see themselves as being engaged in and committed to Black feminist organizing and work. In some ways they're drawing from our work. We've become predecessors in people's political understandings.

"This is not just an intellectual pursuit. . . . If you're not dealing with root causes and material conditions then you're not really making change."

I think what's different is at the time that we were organizing we were still very much affected by the Civil Rights, the Black Power, and the Black nationalist movements. Those ideas, those formations, those organizations were still visible. It's very different to do challenging, radical, groundbreaking organizing in a context where other people aren't doing the same thing. It is energizing when you feel that you're a part of something much bigger than you are. We were actually quite isolated, but there were still glimmers. I can't speak for your generation, but now, because so many years have elapsed, I imagine that you might not feel as connected to something big and world-shaking. We knew that we were about changing the world. It was true in the women's movement; it was true in the lesbian and gay movement.

I'm really glad to hear about the organizing that happened at Duke, because one of the things I hope is that people understand that this is not just an intellectual pursuit. That what we're trying to deal with is material conditions. That's what organizing deals with—material conditions and root causes. *If you're not dealing with root causes and material conditions then you're not really making change.* You've got to deal with what most affects people on a daily basis where they live. You don't necessarily get to decide what that is either. You've got to listen and see what people are about.

I've always been organizing around violence: war, the anti–Vietnam War/peace movement, violence against women, murders, sexual assault, rape, battering, you name it. Now I'm organizing against Black and Brown youth killing each other, shooting each other in our streets. But the roots, some of the roots are similar; some of the causes are similar. One of the things about the work that I'm doing now is that a lot of the people I deal with still are Black women. That's who I hear from. We're not necessarily doing Black feminist organizing but who's calling me up to say that they didn't shovel her street and she has to take her grandchild to school and there's no place for them to stand waiting for the school bus? It all seems on a continuum to me.

Alexis: I would love to share the way I'm seeing organizing in Durham. I say in Durham and not *at Duke* because it was some violence from Duke students that [caught the attention] of the media. But there [was so much more going on]. People who were community organizers, who'd been organizing around economic justice, around racial justice, around educational inequalities, found [the Duke lacrosse rape case] so traumatizing. When something like this happens, people who support violence against women of color, or are violent against women of color, really try to reinforce that we should be silent and that sex workers deserve to be beaten . . .

Barbara: . . .which is backwards and toxic.

Alexis: And just traumatizing. What is miraculous to me was somebody had a potluck meeting in their home to talk about the traumatic nature of the situation and what we can do about it. We decided we wanted to create a coalition. The media is looking at it from this whole standpoint of the courts and who's right and who's wrong, how can you prove this and where's this type of evidence and that type of evidence.

But what people in that room really said was, "We need an actual community." We believe that there would not be gendered violence if all of our needs were met, if we had a way to take care of our children together, if we had access to food, and we had a space to build a shared analysis of the politics of sex workers and why they have rights as workers—also a shared analysis of the legacy of Black feminist organizing against violence against women. So community gardening projects came out of that, educational projects came out of that, material resource sharing came out of that, and direct responses, people opening up their homes when somebody needed a safe place to get away.

Then, someone wrote and asked if there was a multimedia way to share all the great insight we were learning. And so we made print publications and uploaded them to the web so people who are in Rio Grande Valley, Texas, can also use these resources. The issues that we were facing were dramatized by the media in a particular way that was very specific, but the issues that we were talking about are everywhere.

It was amazing to be able to do what you all were saying in that paragraph of the Combahee River Collective Statement—to create a shift in consciousness that drew on our specific local experience of trying to create a community that addresses our needs directly; but, since these issues are unfortunately shared, the strategies and resources we created were also able to be used in different local struggles.

"Occupy Wall Street: Black Voices for Economic Justice Must Be Heard"
Ron Daniels (n.d.)

. . .A disparate band of mostly young protesters from around the country, disgusted with the rapacious behavior of 21st century "Robber Barons," marched on Wall Street and set up a camp called "Occupy Wall Street." As an organizer one never knows what event, what incident or action will be the spark that galvanizes a movement for change. In the face of a Great Recession, precipitated by the greed-driven and reckless behavior of the bandits on Wall Street, there has been growing discontent among the American people, but with rare exception (mass actions by labor and allies in Wisconsin and Ohio) there has been a noticeable absence of mass action, particularly on the Left. . . .

What has now become the Occupy Wall Street movement that is spreading across the nation like wildfire is potentially a game changer, a turning point, a social movement with the potential to impact the political discourse by refocusing on the urgent need to preserve and expand the budding culture of rights fought for by generations of progressives. . . . According to a recent *New York Times* editorial, the top 1% now accounts for nearly 24% of the nation's income, "the highest since 1928." And still Wall Street craves more. . . .

Occupy Wall Street has exploded onto the scene in this moment of grave crisis in the economic and political life of the nation, providing a much needed outlet and target for the pervasive rage rampant among millions ravished by joblessness, mortgage foreclosures, and financial institutions shamelessly eager to rape them with fees calculated to evade the constraints imposed by the newly created Consumer Protection Agency. But, thus far Occupy Wall Street is a self-proclaimed "leaderless," politically non-aligned movement with a multiplicity of messages, grievances, and righteous slogans but no coherent set of goals/demands. And, there are scant numbers of Blacks and other people of color in the ranks of the protesters. The movement is overwhelmingly white. . . .

I'm not certain that anger and outrage without a message and agenda will ultimately transform Wall Street or break the gridlock in Washington that is tantamount to fiddling while countless millions suffer. . . .

There is a special need for Black people to seize upon the momentum created by Occupy Wall Street to identify with and mobilize our forces to add fuel to the fire. The Great Recession precipitated by the unconscionable behavior of Wall Street did not just ruin the lives of white people; it was an equal opportunity destroyer that disproportionately wreaked havoc on Black people and Black communities. Already plagued by a wealth gap that has persisted for generations, the sub-prime mortgage scam that targeted Black consumers wiped out billions of dollars in wealth, liquidating decades of gains by the Black middle class. George Fraser, President/CEO of FraserNet, estimates that it may take a century to recoup the wealth lost by Black America as a consequence of a scam that preyed on victims yearning to realize the "American dream."

As Vernon Jordan, former President of the National Urban League once put it, "when white America gets a cold, Black America gets pneumonia." Nothing is more illustrative of this dictum than the Great Recession. Most political economists concede that the unemployment rate in Black America is at least twice the official rate of 9.1% and perhaps triple when one takes into account the unemployed who have simply given up the search for work. By some estimates 40–50% of Black youth/young people between the ages of 16–30 are jobless! Moreover, the dramatic rise in poverty attributed to the Great Recession has disproportionately impacted Black people. White America is experiencing a Great Recession—Black America is in the throes of a debilitating social and economic Depression borne of decades of benign and blatant neglect, exacerbated by racist and criminal behavior of the barracudas on Wall Street.

Black Voices for Economic Justice have every reason and right to be heard. The fact that white protesters initiated and have led Occupy Wall Street should not be a deterrent to Black engagement. We should view the current conflagration as an opening to raise our specific issues and demands, as we add our voices to the growing amorphous movement to confront and change America's capitalist political economy as symbolized by Wall Street. As a people whose leaders and organizations have often been the conscience of the nation and the vanguard of major social movements, Africans in America should seize every opportunity to expose the hypocrisy and contradictions of an unjust system as we struggle to create a just and humane society. The challenge is to find our own voice to express issues of particular interest to Black people within the context of the broader struggle for reform and transformation.

By organizing Black Voices for Peace and Justice, our late beloved Brother Damu Smith developed a principled and creative avenue to meet this challenge.

Damu recognized that issues of concern to Black people may be ignored or avoided as "divisive" even among white liberals and progressives. He also recognized that Blacks might not be equitably included in the planning and leadership of protests and demonstrations initiated by whites. As opposition to the War in Iraq grew, Damu organized Black Voices for Peace and Justice to ensure that the push to end the war would relate to the urgent need for resources to address the ongoing crises in Black America. Rather than dismiss the anti-war movement as a "white" initiative, Damu created a vehicle for Black people to add their voices to a just struggle while simultaneously insisting that Black issues be addressed. . . .

We should adopt a similar approach as it relates to Occupy Wall Street. As an expression of solidarity and acknowledgment of the harm inflicted on Black people by Wall Street, we should encourage Black people to attend "Occupy" protests in New York and cities across the country. . . .

Since bank foreclosures have disproportionately devastated Black families and communities as a result of the sub-prime mortgage scam and the onslaught of the Great Recession, Black Voices for Economic Justice should demand a Moratorium on Home Foreclosures and a massive federal and bank industry sponsored program to "Bail Out Homeowners." We should demand that the Attorney General investigate and prosecute the criminals whose reckless behavior created the crises—Jail the Criminals on Wall Street. We should demand that the banks most responsible for perpetrating the sub-prime mortgage scam on Black people create Investment Funds to provide grants and low interest loans for business/economic development in Black neighborhoods—Rebuild Black Neighborhoods. We should demand a "Bailout for Students" burdened by loans to pay for the escalating cost of a college education. Black voices should be heard loud and clear demanding a Massive Jobs program to immediately put at least 2 million people to work hired directly by the federal government to perform public sector jobs (something similar to Congresswoman Jan Schakowsky's Emergency Jobs to Restore the American Dream Act)—with an emphasis on targeting neighborhoods/communities with the highest levels of joblessness. . . .

Africans in America should heed the admonition of the Gary Black Political Agenda; our voices must be heard "because it is our people who are most deeply hurt and ravaged by the present systems of society." Black Voices for Economic Justice should gear up to Occupy Wall Street and march on ballot boxes with a vengeance in 2012 to vigorously advance an agenda for reform and fundamental change!

Dr. Ron Daniels is President of the Institute of the Black World 21st Century and Distinguished Lecturer at York College, City University of New York.* Used with permission.

---

*Daniels ran for president of the United States as an independent candidate in 1992. Barbara

Black Feminist Futures

Black feminism's deep roots, many branches, and fruitful seeds ensure that it will be a vibrant and growing part of the future. Traditional organizing techniques and new technology allow women in many places to find each other and knit together a shared conversation that inspires action and change. Barbara considers the joys and difficulties of a well-lived feminist life in conversations with Alexis, Alethia, and Virginia. A "Letter to Patriarchy" from Crunkista offers a feminist critique in characteristic hip hop style. Crunk is a distinct form of hip hop originating in the South from which the Crunk Feminist Collective takes its name.

Interviews with Alexis Pauline Gumbs, Alethia Jones, and Virginia Eubanks

Barbara Smith: Do you think that people who are doing Black feminist and feminist of color organizing are well networked? Or are there lots of things going on where people don't really know who the participants are?

Alexis Pauline Gumbs: We are well networked, but it could be better. Moya Bailey and I cofounded a social networking site called Quirky Black Girls, and she is also a cofounder of the Combahee Survival Project. We asked different organizers to respond to poetic exercises drawn from the Combahee River Collective Statement. When we re-circulated the phrase "It is difficult to even announce in certain spaces that we are Black feminists," the response we got from self-identified Black feminists was amazing. They described why it's important to them that they identify as Black feminists and also the continuing difficulties of claiming that identity in spaces where feminism has been co-opted by mainstream white women who are not feminists. We would say that they are female self-aggrandizers and not feminists. That conversation is really happening and people are using these tools [to connect with each other]. In almost every city in this country I know something that a Black feminist is doing that is inspiring work.

Barbara: That's fantastic. Do you think having a physical conference, an actual gathering could help?

Alexis: I do. We want to have a place where people can see each other and discuss what they are doing, and what did and didn't work out. There is still an issue of access. It's hard for a lot of folks who are doing this work to leave, travel, and stay somewhere. But we had Combahee Survival Revival Week in Durham.

It was like a down-home revival: we created a 'zine together, we had different days around food justice, and we had a ceremony in the river. Kids were there the

---

Smith worked to place him on the ballot in New York State, making it the first presidential campaign she worked on. Sharon Bourke, a key member of the Combahee River Collective, worked closely with the institute in the seventies.

whole time. We ate collectively the whole time. It was mostly people in Durham. There were Black feminists who came from different parts of the country who participated, but it was amazing to have something different than a conference. Something that drew on the resources of a specific place, and then reinvested resources [back] into that place, around that conversation.

Barbara: That's wonderful. Great thinking.

Alexis: We could do more of that. And we can document it. We can Skype people in. Mai'a Williams, a Black feminist who lives in Cairo, Skyped in and participated in the part specifically about mothers of color. There's opportunity for us to see each other even though there's nothing that replaces physically being together.

Barbara: So what do *you* think the major differences in organizing now and then are?

Alexis: You spoke about clarity and about collective action. I guess I shouldn't speak for everybody, but I do think that right now there's so much individualism. Such that even when there're major historical events happening, there's the election of a Black president, which was a collective effort, it is seen as an individual achievement . . .

Barbara: . . .like, I worked on the Obama campaign, aren't I cool—is that the attitude you are talking about?

Alexis: . . .and I have the T-shirt. It's not grounded in changing material conditions and being accountable to a collective struggle. It's invisible. I think that's a danger because our organizing as Black feminists is influenced by that. Sometimes it makes it possible for us to measure our success only in capitalist terms. It makes it possible for us to only measure our success by our individual visibility or by how much money we're able to fund-raise—all of these things that are not markers of our actual impact in community. One of the major reasons that I've looked for the primary documents and tried to make them accessible is because I want people to have different markers or measurement for what their work means. I don't think that real, radical, transformative Black feminist work is ever going to be rewarded by capitalism in capitalist terms.

Barbara: I can definitely attest to that. I'm retirement age. But I'm not retired by any definition. I don't really foresee ever being able to have so much put aside that I don't have to worry. It's haunting. I try not to dwell on it too much. But the thing is that I made the choices that didn't translate into material success or comfort, although I certainly had the tools to go that route.

I have also felt excluded. When I used to talk to a dear friend of mine, Naomi Jaffe, about things I was excluded from or not invited to, she would say, "It's your politics Barbara, it boils down to your politics." That was, in some ways, clarifying and comforting, because being excluded never feels good. She was saying they're not buying radical, Black, socialist, lesbian feminist anything. They're not that comfortable with that so they'd rather have people who have a less challenging critique of the status quo.

Alethia Jones: When you face major turning points and life changes, have certain guiding principles informed your choices?

Barbara: The most important thing is for me to really be excited about and interested in what it is I'm doing. That's why at the age of sixty-four-and-a-half, I'm facing economic challenges yet again. In my twenties and thirties, I never could have imagined taking a job just because of a paycheck. Now, of course, it's coming back to bite me big time. It certainly made for a stimulating and fulfilling work life, making those kinds of decisions. But because my life has been so difficult economically, I am envious of people who don't have to worry about paying their bills.

> "I have always found a tremendous amount of joy in organizing. That's, to me, where the hope is. I love the fact that it is unfettered, unbridled.... I love the in-your-face part of organizing."

A friend of mine said, "Well not everyone has been as fortunate as you are." I said, "*Fortunate?*" I made my own fortune, by having that real connection and desire to be deeply connected to the work that I do. To me, it's really taking very risky chances and standing on principle. I didn't have a silver spoon hanging out of my mouth; I was making choices.

The other guiding principle is fighting for justice, and always having a very keen and clear sense of who was most oppressed, who was most in need, who was facing the biggest injustices and assaults on their freedom.

The other thing that comes to mind is being ethical, being very clear about lines that I do not cross and would not cross even if it might be to my great benefit. Also treating people as I would wish to be treated and trying to treat everyone basically the same way, which is with fairness, and kindness, and compassion.

Alethia: If you could do it over, would you make different choices? Can you, in hindsight, see a way to live in integrity and be economically comfortable?

Barbara: I can't really say. Being who I am and have generally always been, it's hard for me to imagine being satisfied and feeling that I had accomplished the things I wanted to have accomplished if I had gone for the gold. My interest was always towards culture, the arts, activism, things you don't make money from. But it's hard now. It's hard.

Alethia: That's something that seems really unfair. There's a systemic element to it, it does not feel like an individual choice.

Barbara: Twenty years ago, I used to hear about people who I idolized, Black women, who were in poverty, who were old and ill and living in poverty—I always used to think, "Oh my god, that's so horrible. Don't let that be me." I feel like whatever I did, I didn't quite do it right.

"Crunk Letter to Patriarchy," Crunk Feminist Collective (2012)

Dear Patriarchy,

This isn't working. We both know that it hasn't been working for a very long time.

It's not you . . .no actually, it is you. This is an unhealthy, dysfunctional, abusive relationship because of you. You are stifling, controlling, oppressive, and you have never had my best interest at heart. You have tricked me into believing that things are the way they are because they have to be, that they have always been that way, that there are no alternatives and that they will never change. Anytime I questioned you or your ways, you found another way to silence me and coerce me back into submission. I can't do this anymore. I've changed and in spite of your shackles, I've grown. I have realized that this whole restrictive system is your own fabrication and that the only one that is gaining anything from it is you. You selfish dick.

I will not continue to live like this. I will not continue to settle. I know now that there is a better way.

Before you hear about it from one of your boys, you should know that I have met someone. Her name is Feminism. She is the best thing that has ever happened to me. She validates and respects my opinions. She ALWAYS has my best interest at heart. She thinks that I am beautiful and loves me just the way I am. She has helped me find my voice and she makes me happier than I have ever been. We have made each other stronger. Best of all, we encourage and challenge each other to grow. And the sex . . .the sex is so much hotter.

I'm leaving you. You're an asshole. We can never be friends. Don't call me. Ever.

Never yours,

Crunkista*

Crunk Feminist Collective. Used with permission.

---

* From the mission statement:

The Crunk Feminist Collective will create a space of support and camaraderie for hip hop generation feminists of color, queer and straight, in the academy and without, by building a rhetorical community, in which we can discuss our ideas, express our crunk feminist selves, fellowship with one another, debate and challenge one another, and support each other, as we struggle together to articulate our feminist goals, ideas, visions, and dreams in ways that are both personally and professionally beneficial. . . . Crunk(ness) is our mode of resistance that finds its particular expression in the rhetorical, cultural, and intellectual practices of a contemporary generation. . . . Beat-driven and bass-laden, Crunk music blends Hip Hop culture and Southern Black culture in ways that are sometimes seamless, but more often dissonant. But where merely getting crunk signaled that you were out of your mind, a crunk feminist mode of resistance will help you get your mind right, as they say in the South. . . . [W]hat others may call audacious and crazy, we call CRUNK because we are drunk off the heady theory of feminism that proclaims that another world is possible. Crunk feminists don't take no mess from nobody! (crunkfeministcollective.wordpress.com/)

Virginia Eubanks: What should activists and organizers today take from your life as lessons for being more effective in this political moment?

Barbara: If it's making you feel miserable, then it's not the right thing. If you are involved in organizing and you are burnt out, depressed, put upon, just unhappy, then it is not the right thing. I have always found a tremendous amount of joy in organizing. That's, to me, where the hope is. I love the fact that it is unfettered, unbridled. You face roadblocks, but your job is how do we make something out of this that isn't what they expect, and how do we triumph? I just love that part of it. I love the in-your-face part of organizing.

> "I think if we got rid of violence we'd probably go a long way to getting rid of sexism and gender oppression, homophobia, and heterosexism because those all have violence at their roots."

You have to stick with it. You have to listen as well as you talk. Only commit to what you can actually get done, no matter how much less it is than you wish it could be. Everything goes so much better, and people get along so much better, have so much more trust and good feeling about each other, if they're not constantly being disappointed by over-promising and unfulfilled expectations.

Create a context for doing your organizing work that feeds your soul and your spirit. And if it's not doing that, try to figure out why and what you need to do to get to a place where you feel some joy. That's just bottom line. You can't expect instant fixes. Even if it is not the most dynamic and exciting of times, the most exhilarating, you do it on a regular basis for the overall payoff, for the greater good of keeping at it, and to keep that flame of hope burning.

Alexis: If you were to envision the type of future that Black feminism makes possible, what does that future include?

Barbara: The first thing would be an end to violence. I'm so tired of it I don't know what to do. I'm talking about all kinds of violence. I'm talking about warfare, I'm talking about crimes. I'm always haunted by what a violent world we live in. The shootings that happened two days ago in Ohio? It's just like, "When, when, when, when?" I am so haunted by the young man at Rutgers who killed himself because of the incredibly violent act of his roommate.* I am sick and tired of it. The bombing of the people coming into that compound in Afghanistan. Now that I am an elected official, I get reports from the police department directly. So every crime like that that happens, I get it right in my e-mail. We have had stabbings, an

---

*On September 22, 2010 Tyler Clementi committed suicide upon learning that his freshman college roommate secretly recorded and broadcasted Tyler's intimate encounters with a man in their dorm room with a webcam. Dharun Ravi was convicted in 2012 and sentenced to 30 days in jail.

armed robbery. And, of course, I am actively involved in working around the issue of gun violence and street violence primarily among youth of color.

After that would be for everyone to have what they need materially so that they can not just survive, but thrive. We wouldn't have incredible disparities of wealth and of poverty and exploitation and subjugation that characterize not just this country but our global political economy. It's not acceptable to have some people living on a dollar a day or less, not having access to clean water, a decent food supply, housing and health care, and then others who can write checks for seven million dollars and it makes no difference whatsoever in their daily life.

People get so excited when wealthy people contribute or donate. My question always is, was it a sacrifice in any way? Because people who have cajillions of dollars, they can give millions of dollars and it doesn't affect their functioning, their quality of life. To me, real generosity has to do with, "Do I have to sacrifice in some way? Is there something that I'm going to have to give up so that I can help somebody who has less?" Some of our richest people are quite philanthropic. That's much better than for them to be stingy and self-involved. But their generosity, to me, doesn't measure up to the person who makes a decision not to buy a hot cup of coffee so that they can send ten dollars to the Rosenberg Fund for Children. To me that's real generosity.

I think if we got rid of violence we'd probably go a long way to getting rid of sexism and gender oppression, homophobia, and heterosexism because those all have violence at their roots. I certainly want to see racism and white supremacy end. I'm not too optimistic about that. From my vantage point of being almost sixty-four-years-old, it seems like people are very comfortable with white supremacy in this country. That's their default position. Most people don't even acknowledge that white supremacy exists. So how do you get rid of it if they won't even acknowledge that it's operative?

We have to do something in relationship to the planet and how we are marauding around it and getting rid of other species who should be like our sisters and brothers. We're not doing that. And then the water and the air. It's all a part of that system. If you exploit human beings, you think nothing of exploiting animals and natural resources. If you can enslave and entrap and demonize human beings, then you'll have no problem putting as much oil in the water as you possibly can.

To put it in a nutshell, get rid of injustice and have people live in community the way that I believe we were intended to live, and not the way that very toxic and oppressive systems have made us relate to each other and live. Basic pervasive justice. Worldwide. That's what I want to see.

Alexis: Well, thank you. I'm twenty-eight, but your work has such a huge impact on the decisions I've made so far. When I see your name, it's like a refrain in my head like, "It is possible, it is possible, it is possible." Seeing the decisions that you've made and the amazing work that you've done and the impact that it's had is, for me, a testimony that life can be what it should be. It can be a collective commitment; it can be an awareness, a collaborative, creative, inventive process.

Editorial Note

This collection includes articles and interviews spanning forty years. Word usage conventions varied between articles and over time. In our own writing and in the interview transcripts, we made several stylistic choices, some of which depart from conventions in use for some of the previously published documents. The most frequent style differences occur with respect to the following: Black is capitalized when referring to persons (as opposed to a color); African American is not hyphenated; and Third World is capitalized. Today, "people of color" is the term of choice. In the 1970s and early 1980s, many progressive activists used "Third World" to refer to both international and U.S.-based populations of color, based on a political analysis that racial minorities were colonies located within the United States and, like their overseas counterparts, were economically exploited as well as socially and politically oppressed and controlled. We try to refer to the United States instead of saying America, and when American is used, it is modified (Black, North, Latin, and so on). We capitalize Left when referring to a political movement, but women's movement, women's studies, and second wave are not capitalized. Numbers, abbreviations, and times have been standardized, and other style choices generally follow the Baylor University Institute for Oral History's "Style Guide: A Quick Reference for Editing Oral Memoirs" (2007).

Almost every reprinted item in this book has been edited for length, and occasionally for clarity. Some of the original articles can be located online or in published anthologies, but many are hard to find and can only be located in libraries and archives. We use ellipses to indicate where sentences or paragraphs have been removed. See the originals for the full content. Notes in original documents are placed in brackets (e.g., [2]) and appear at the bottom of the page. Notes added by the editors with additional historical detail appear at the bottom of the page preceded by *, †, ‡, §, or ¶.

Eleven previously unpublished interviews are utilized in this volume. Transcribing and editing involves choices as one adapts the informality of the spoken word to the formal standards of the printed word. The verbatim transcripts of the full interviews are on file. They were initially edited for readability and accuracy, which preserves character and meaning while removing false starts, filler words and phrases, et cetera. Interviewers then had an opportunity to review the transcripts to adjust their language and ensure that fact and meaning were correct. For the book, we selected the best and most topical portions of each interview for publication. These sections were subsequently edited extensively to ensure flow by eliminating repetition, fixing grammar and punctuation, eliminating sentence fragments, ensuring consistent verb tenses, and other changes for clarity. Similar topics appear together despite where they occurred in the original interview. When topics overlap between the interviews, often with new insights and directions, we insert material from other interviewers to "extend the conversation." When we do so, we use the full name of the interviewer on first appearance and first names subsequently. This interweaving of interviews meant selecting excerpts and placing them in a new context. Barbara Smith made the most changes, however, clarifying facts and meaning where necessary to appropriately convey her points. To minimize distraction to the reader, ellipses and brackets [ ] are largely not used to capture this extensive editing process. Brackets appear when essential factual information is inserted, and editorial notes are added at the bottom of the page for more detailed additions.

How We Built This Book

Barbara shaped the project from its inception because she knows her life best. Her primary roles were that of interviewee and as a reviewer who gave vital insight on our editorial choices, including historical accuracy and the tone and substance of our claims. Working with Barbara has been gratifying because we love working with individuals and institutions that devote themselves to truth telling in the service of justice.

This book began with a mountain of material—documents, interviews, and articles. University at Albany graduate student Mishel Filisha lovingly collected almost two hundred articles, images, and recordings by, with, or about Barbara Smith by scouring multiple archives, Smith's personal papers, interlibrary loans, and the Internet to assemble and digitize these materials into a database. From this we selected our favorite pieces, which resulted in an eight-hundred-page manuscript. We subsequently selected items that we thought best captured an era, a moment, an argument, a hope or vision. We commissioned almost a dozen new interviews with Barbara between 2010 and 2012, and selected excerpts from the transcripts that enhanced the historical material and extended the discussion to the current historical moment. Although we present only a small fraction of everything we collected, we are still afraid that we "have tried to say too much and at the same time, left too much unsaid" (Smith, 1977).

We have worked on this project in distinct and complementary ways. Nothing is exactly fifty-fifty, but we shared the burdens equally from start to end. We often took turns in carrying the primary burden on a certain portion of the project before handing it off to the other person for review, discussion, and major changes. Virginia took the lead on creating the chapters addressing Barbara's youth, impact on Black women's studies, and the operation of Kitchen Table Press (chapters 2, 4, and 5). Alethia took the lead on creating the chapters on Black feminism, Barbara's work as an Albany elected official, and her legacy (chapters 3, 7, and 8). We shared responsibility for the chapter on multi-issue movement building (chapter 6), with Alethia working on the LGBTQ section and Virginia on the Black Radical Congress section). We both worked on the book and chapter introductions by creating, modifying, and merging different drafts. We produced the final manuscript by working iteratively.

Bibliography

Aguilar, Mila D. *A Comrade Is as Precious as a Rice Seedling*. Latham, NY: Kitchen Table: Women of Color Press, 1987.

Alea, Tomás Gutiérrez, and Juan Carlos Tabío. *Strawberry and Chocolate*. Burbank, CA: Miramax; Distributed by Buena Vista Home Entertainment, 2003.

Baldwin, James. *The Fire Next Time*. New York: Dell Press, 1963.

Bambara, Toni Cade. *The Black Woman: An Anthology*. New York: New American Library, 1970.

Beck, Tito Ben-Ysrael, Mandy Carter, Chandra L. Ford, Kara Keeling, and Barbara Smith. "Will People of Color Pay the Price? A Statement by People of Color in Support of the Ad Hoc Committee for an Open Process." 1999.

Bell, Roseann P., Bettye J. Parker, and Beverly Guy-Sheftall. *Sturdy Black Bridges: Visions of Black Women in Literature*. Garden City, NY: Anchor Press/Doubleday, 1979.

Bernikow, Louise, ed. *The World Split Open: Four Centuries of Women Poets in England and America, 1552–1950*. New York: Vintage Books, 1974.

Black Feminist Working Group (Iresha Picot, Tiamba Wilkerson, Nuala Cabral, Ladi'Sasha Jones, Darasia Selby, and Kim Murray). "What Sistas Want, What Sistas Believe: Black Feminist Twelve Point Plan." 2011. http://blackfeministworkinggroup.wordpress.com/2011/08/30/what-sistas-want-what-sistas-believe-black-feminist-twelve-point-plan/ (accessed April 1, 2013).

Blackside, Inc., and PBS Video. *Eyes on the Prize: Mississippi, Is This America? 1962–1964*. Alexandria, VA: PBS Video, 1987.

Boggs, Grace Lee, and Scott Kurashige. *The Next American Revolution: Sustainable Activism for the Twenty-First Century*. Berkeley: University of California Press, 2011.

Boston Women's Health Collective. *Our Bodies, Ourselves*. New York: Simon and Schuster, 1973.

Bowles, Juliette, ed. *In the Memory and Spirit of Frances, Zora and Lorraine: Essays and Interviews on Black Women and Writing 1979*. Washington, DC: Institute for the Arts and the Humanities, Howard University, 1979.

Boylorn, Robin. "Letter to Barbara Smith." In *I Am Not Meant to Be Alone and without You Who Understand: A Tribute of Letters for Ms. Barbara Smith*, ed. Department of Gender and Race Studies, The University of Alabama, 17–18. Tuscaloosa: The University of Alabama, 2010.

BRC Organizing Committee. "The Struggle Continues: Setting a Black Liberation Agenda for the 21st Century: Call for Participation in the Black Radical Congress," 1998.

———. Black Radical Congress Principles of Unity, 1998.

Brown, Elsa Barkley, Deborah King, and Barbara Ransby. "African American Women in Defense of Ourselves." *New York Times*, November 17, 1991, 47.

Brown, Wilmette. "The Autonomy of Black Lesbian Women." Speech delivered in Toronto, Canada, 1976.

Bryant, Anita, and Bob Green. *At Any Cost*. Grand Rapids, MI: Fleming H. Revell, 1978.

Bulkin, Elly. "An Interview with Adrienne Rich: Part I." *Conditions: One* (April 1977): 62.

Bulkin, Elly, Minnie Bruce Pratt, and Barbara Smith. *Yours in Struggle: Three Feminist Perspectives on Anti-Semitism and Racism*. Brooklyn, NY: Long Haul Press, 1984.

Carter, David. *Stonewall: The Riots That Sparked the Gay Revolution*. New York: St. Martin's Griffin, 2010.

Case Western Reserve University. "Klunder, Bruce W." *The Encyclopedia of Cleveland History*. Cleveland: Case Western Reserve University, 1997.

Clarke, Cheryl. *Narratives: Poems in the Tradition of Black Women*. New York: Kitchen Table: Women of Color Press, 1983.

Cole, Johnnetta B., and Beverly Guy-Sheftall. *Gender Talk: The Struggle for Women's Equality in African American Communities*. New York: Ballantine Books, 2003.

Combahee River Collective. "The Combahee River Collective Statement." In *Capitalist Patriarchy and the Case for Socialist Feminism*, ed. Zillah Eisenstein, 362–372. New York: Monthly Review Press, 1979.

———. *The Combahee River Collective Statement: Black Feminist Organizing in the Seventies and Eighties*. Albany, NY: Kitchen Table: Women of Color Press, 1986.

Conrad, Earl. *Harriet Tubman, Negro Soldier and Abolitionist*. New York: International Publishers, 1942.

Cotten, Trystan T., and Kimberly Springer, eds. *Stories of Oprah: The Oprahfication of American Culture*. Jackson: University Press of Mississippi, 2009.

Crenshaw, Kimberlé Williams. "Mapping the Margins: Intersectionality, Identity

Politics, and Violence against Women of Color." *Stanford Law Review* 43, no. 6 (1991): 1241–99.

———. "Black Women Still in Defense of Ourselves." *The Nation* 293, no. 17 (2011): 14–15.

Cross, Tia, Freada Klein, Barbara Smith, and Beverly Smith. "Face-to-Face, Day-to-Day—Racism CR." In *All the Women Are White, All the Blacks Are Men, but Some of Us Are Brave: Black Women's Studies*, ed. Gloria T. Hull, Patricia Bell-Scott, and Barbara Smith, 52–56. New York: The Feminist Press at City University of New York, 1982.

Crunkista. "Crunk Letter to Patriarchy." 2012. http://www.crunkfeministcollective.com/2012/08/02/throwback-thursday-dear-patriarchy/ (accessed April 1, 2013).

Daniels, Ron D. "Occupy Wall Street: Black Voices for Economic Justice Must Be Heard," circa 2011/2012. http://ibw21.org/vantage-point/occupy-wall-street-black-voices-for-economic-justice-must-be-heard/ (accessed April 1, 2013).

Davis, Angela Y. *Women, Race & Class*. New York: Vintage Books, 1983.

———. *Violence against Women and the Ongoing Challenge to Racism*. New York: Kitchen Table: Women of Color Press, 1985.

Davis-Faulkner, Sheri. "Letter to Barbara Smith." In *I Am Not Meant to Be Alone and without You Who Understand: A Tribute of Letters for Ms. Barbara Smith*, ed. Department of Gender and Race Studies, The University of Alabama, 5. Tuscaloosa: The University of Alabama, 2010.

Democracy Now! "More Highlights from the Black Radical Congress." June 24, 1998. http://www.democracynow.org/1998/6/24/more_highlights_from_the_black_radical (accessed April 1, 2013).

Department of Gender and Race Studies, The University of Alabama, ed. *I Am Not Meant to Be Alone and without You Who Understand: A Tribute of Letters for Ms. Barbara Smith*. Tuscaloosa: The University of Alabama, 2010.

Domini, John "Roots and Racism: An Interview with Ishmael Reed." *Boston Phoenix*, April 5, 1977, 20.

Duberman, Martin. *Stonewall*. New York: Plume, 1994.

Eisenstein, Zillah R., ed. *Capitalist Patriarchy and the Case for Socialist Feminism*. New York: Monthly Review Press, 1978.

Ella's Daughters. "Ella's Daughters Seven Sisters Campaign." n.d. (no longer available online).

Faderman, Lillian. *Odd Girls and Twilight Lovers: A History of Lesbian Life in Twentieth-Century America*. New York: Penguin Books, 1992.

Faulkner, William. *Light in August*. New York: Modern Library, 1950.

Field, Connie, Marilyn Mulford, Michael Chandler, Rhonnie Lynn Washington, Productions Clarity Educational, and Newsreel California. *Freedom on My Mind*. San Francisco: California Newsreel, 1994.

Fraser, Nancy. *Justice Interruptus: Critical Reflections on the "Postsocialist" Condition*. New York: Routledge, 1997.

Fundi Productions. *Fundi: The Story of Ella Baker*. New York: Fundi Productions; First Run (distributor), 1981.

"Glenville Shootout." *The Encyclopedia of Cleveland History*. Cleveland: Case Reserve Historical Society, 1998. http://ech.case.edu/ech-cgi/article.pl?id=GS1 (accessed April 1, 2013).

Giddings, Paula. *When and Where I Enter: The Impact of Black Women on Race and Sex in America*. New York: William Morrow, 1984.

Gluckman, Amy, and Betsy Reed. "Where Has Gay Liberation Gone? An Interview with Barbara Smith." In *Homo Economics: Capitalism, Community, and Lesbian and Gay Life*, ed. Amy Gluckman and Betsy Reed, 195–207. New York: Routledge/Taylor & Francis Group, 1997.

Gómez, Alma, Cherríe Moraga, and Mariana Romo-Carmona. *Cuentos: Stories by Latinas*. New York: Kitchen Table: Women of Color Press, 1983.

Gomez, Jewelle L., and Barbara Smith. "Taking the Home Out of Homophobia: Black Lesbian Health." In *The Black Women's Health Book: Speaking for Ourselves*, ed. E .C. White, 198–213. Seattle, WA: The Seal Press, 1990.

Grant, Jaime M. "Building Community-Based Coalitions from Academe: The Union Institute and the Kitchen Table: Women of Color Press Transition Coalition." *Signs: Journal of Women in Culture and Society* 21, no. 4 (1996): 1024–1033.

Guy-Sheftall, Beverly, ed. *Words of Fire: An Anthology of African-American Feminist Thought*. New York: New Press: Distributed by W.W. Norton, 1995.

Guy-Sheftall, Beverly, and Johnnetta B. Cole, eds. *Who Should Be First? Feminists Speak Out on the 2008 Presidential Campaign*. Albany: State University of New York Press, 2010.

Harris, Duchess. *Black Feminist Politics from Kennedy to Clinton*. New York: Palgrave Macmillan, 2009.

Henderson, Stephen Evangelist. *Understanding the New Black Poetry; Black Speech and Black Music as Poetic References*. New York: Morrow, 1973.

Hill Collins, Patricia. *Black Feminist Thought: Knowledge, Consciousness, and the Politics of Empowerment*. New York: Routledge, 1998a.

——. *Fighting Words: Black Women and the Search for Justice*. Minneapolis: University of Minnesota Press, 1998b.

Howe, Florence. *The Politics of Women's Studies: Testimony from the 30 Founding Mothers*. New York: Feminist Press, 2000.

Hughes, Langston. *The Best of Simple*. New York: Hill and Wang, 1961.

Hull, Gloria T. *Healing Heart: Poems, 1973–1988*. Latham, NY: Kitchen Table: Women of Color Press, 1989.

Hull, Gloria T., Patricia Bell-Scott, and Barbara Smith. *All the Women Are White, All the Blacks Are Men, But Some of Us Are Brave: Black Women's Studies*. Old Westbury, NY: The Feminist Press, 1982.

Hull, Gloria T., and Barbara Smith. "Introduction: The Politics of Black Women's Studies." In *All the Women Are White, All the Blacks Are Men, But Some of Us Are Brave: Black Women's Studies*, ed. Gloria T. Hull, Patricia Bell-Scott, and Barbara Smith, xxxii. Old Westbury, NY: The Feminist Press, 1982.

Hurston, Zora Neale. *Their Eyes Were Watching God*. Greenwich, CT: Fawcett Publications, 1969.

James, Stanlie M., Frances Smith Foster, and Beverly Guy-Sheftall, eds. *Still Brave: The Evolution of Black Women's Studies*. New York, NY: The Feminist Press, 2009.

Johnson, James Weldon, and Arna Wendell Bontemps. *The Autobiography of an Ex-Colored Man*. New York: Hill and Wang, 1960.

Jones, Gayl. *Corregidora*. Boston: Beacon Press, 1986.

Jordan, June, and Albert Williams. *Fannie Lou Hamer*. New York: Crowell, 1972.

Kahn, Karen, and Robin Morgan, eds. *Frontline Feminism 1975–1995: Essays from Sojourner's First 20 Years*. San Francisco: Aunt Lute Books, 1997.

King, Jamilah. "A New LGBT Politics Seeks to Marry Issues, Not Just People." *Colorlines* (June 19, 2012). http://colorlines.com/archives/2012/06/new_lgbt_politics_marries_issues_not_just_people.html (accessed April 1, 2013).

Lerner, Gerda. *Black Women in White America: A Documentary History*. New York: Pantheon Books, 1972.

Lorde, Audre. *Between Ourselves*. Point Reyes: Eidolon Editions, 1976.

———. *Zami, a New Spelling of My Name*. Trumansburg, NY: Crossing Press, 1982.

———. *I Am Your Sister: Black Women Organizing across Sexualities*. New York, NY: Kitchen Table: Women of Color Press, 1985.

———. *Need: A Chorale for Black Woman Voices*. Latham, NY: Kitchen Table: Women of Color Press, 1990.

———. *I Am Your Sister: Collected and Unpublished Writings of Audre Lorde*. Ed. Rudolph P. Byrd, Johnnetta B. Cole, and Beverly Guy-Sheftall. New York: Oxford University Press, 2009.

Lorde, Audre, and Merle Woo. *Apartheid U.S.A. / Freedom Organizing in the Eighties*. New York: Kitchen Table: Women of Color Press, 1986.

Mankiller, Wilma Pearl, Gwendolyn Mink, Marysa Navarro, Barbara Smith, and Gloria Steinem, eds. *The Reader's Companion to U.S. Women's History*. Boston, MA: Houghton Mifflin, 1998.

Miller, James. *Democracy Is in the Streets: From Port Huron to the Siege of Chicago*. Cambridge, MA: Harvard University Press, 1994.

Millett, Kate. *Sexual Politics*. Garden City, NY: Doubleday, 1970.

Modern Language Association Commission on the Status of Women in the Profession. "Black Women and Publishing: Statement of the Modern Language Association Commission on the Status of Women in the Profession." Barbara Smith Papers, Lesbian Herstory Archives, Box 1, Folder 17, 1976.

Moore, Lisa C. *Does Your Mama Know? An Anthology of Black Lesbian Coming Out Stories*. Decatur, GA: RedBone Press, 1997.

——. "Letter to Barbara Smith." In *I Am Not Meant to Be Alone and without You Who Understand: A Tribute of Letters for Ms. Barbara Smith*, ed. Department of Gender and Race Studies, The University of Alabama, 7. Tuscaloosa, AL: The University of Alabama, 2010.

Moraga, Cherríe, and Gloria Anzaldúa. *This Bridge Called My Back: Writings by Radical Women of Color*. New York: Kitchen Table: Women of Color Press, 1983.

Morgen, Sandra. *Into Our Own Hands: The Women's Health Movement in the United States, 1969–1990*. New Brunswick, NJ: Rutgers University Press, 2002.

Morrison, Toni. *Sula*. New York: Vintage Books, 2004.

——. *The Bluest Eye*. New York: Plume Book, 1994.

Mumininas of Committee for Unified Newark. *Mwanamke Mwananchi (The Nationalist Woman)*. Newark, NJ: 1971, 4–5.

Mustufa, Asraa. "North Carolina Confronts the Ugly Past of Its Eugenics Law." *Colorlines* (2011). http://colorlines.com/archives/2011/06/north_carolina_sterilization_victims_to_share_stories.html (accessed April 1, 2013).

National Black Feminist Organization (NBFO). National Black Feminist Organization Statement of Purpose. http://www-personal.umd.umich.edu/~ppennock/doc-BlackFeminist.htm (accessed April 1, 2013).

Naylor, Gloria. *The Women of Brewster Place*. New York: Penguin Books, 1983.

Nelson, Jill. *Straight, No Chaser: How I Became a Grown-up Black Woman*. New York: G.P. Putnam's Sons, 1997.

New York Radicalesbians. "The Woman-Identified Woman." In *Lesbians Speak Out*, ed. Carol Wilson. Oakland, CA: Women's Press Collective, 1974.

O'Brien, John. *Interviews with Black Writers*. New York: Liveright, 1973.

O'Reilly, Kenneth. *Racial Matters: The FBI's Secret File on Black America, 1960–1972*. New York: Free Press, 1991.

Omolade, Barbara. *It's a Family Affair: The Real Lives of Black Single Mothers*. Latham, NY: Kitchen Table: Women of Color Press, 1986.

Parker, Pat. *Movement in Black: The Collected Poetry of Pat Parker*. Ed. Audre Lord and Judy Grahn. Trumansburg, NY: The Crossing Press, 1978.

Perkins, Janet. "The Religious Right: Dividing the African American Community." *Transformation* July/August (1993).

Perry, Tyler. *For Colored Girls*. Santa Monica, CA: Lionsgate, 2011.

Petry, Ann. *The Street*. Boston: Houghton Mifflin, 1991.

Pharr, Suzanne. "Racist Politics and Homophobia." *Transformation* July/August (1993).

Radford, Jill, and Diana E. H. Russell. *Femicide: The Politics of Woman Killing*. New York: Maxwell Macmillan International, 1992.

Ransby, Barbara. *Ella Baker and the Black Freedom Movement: A Radical Democratic Vision*. Chapel Hill: University of North Carolina Press, 2003.

———. *Eslanda: The Large and Unconventional Life of Mrs. Paul Robeson*. New Haven: Yale University Press, 2013.

Reagon, Bernice Johnson. "Coalition Politics: Turning the Century." In *Home Girls: A Black Feminist Anthology*, ed. Barbara Smith, 356–368. New York: Kitchen Table: Women of Color Press, 1983.

Rich, Adrienne. *Of Woman Born: Motherhood as Experience and Institution*. New York: Norton, 1976.

Richardson, Matt. *The Queer Limit of Black Memory: Black Lesbian Literature and Irresolution*. Columbus: Ohio State University Press, 2013.

Roberts, Dorothy E. *Killing the Black Body: Race, Reproduction, and the Meaning of Liberty*. New York: Pantheon Books, 1997.

Roberts, J. R. *Black Lesbians: An Annotated Bibliography*. Tallahassee, FL: Naiad Press, 1981.

Rosenfeld, Seth. *Subversives: The FBI's War on Student Radicals, and Reagan's Rise to Power*. New York: Farrar, Straus and Giroux, 2012.

Sack, Kevin. "Demonstrators Foil Plans for a Ku Klux Klan Rally." *New York Times*. January 21, 1991.

Sanders, Gerald. "What Next for the Black Radical Congress?" *The Organizer* (Summer 1998). http://www.hartford-hwp.com/archives/45a/230.html (accessed March 7, 2014).

Sarachild, Kathie. "Consciousness-Raising: A Radical Weapon." In *Feminist Revolution*, ed. Redstockings, 144–50. New York: Random House, 1978.

Sears, James T. *Rebels, Rubyfruit, and Rhinestones: Queering Space in the Stonewall South*. New Brunswick, NJ: Rutgers University Press, 2001.

Shange, Ntozake. *For Colored Girls Who Have Considered Suicide When the Rainbow Is Enuf: A Choreopoem*. New York: Macmillan, 1977.

———. *Nappy Edges*. New York: St. Martin's Press, 1978.

Shreve, Anita. *Women Together, Women Alone: The Legacy of the Consciousness-Raising Movement*. New York, NY: Ballantine Books, 1990.

Silliman, Jael Miriam, Marlene Gerber Fried, Loretta Ross, and Elena Gutierrez. *Undivided Rights: Women of Color Organize for Reproductive Justice*. Cambridge, MA: South End Press, 2004.

Smith, Barbara. "'Beautiful, Needed, Mysterious': Review of *Sula* by Toni Morrison." *Freedomways* 14, no. 1 (1974): 69–72.

———. "Doing Research on Black American Women, or; All the Women Are White, All the Blacks Are Men, But Some of Us Are Brave." Boston, MA: University of Massachusetts, Boston, 1975.

———. "Toward a Black Feminist Criticism." *Conditions: Two* 11 (1977): 25–44.

———. "Toward a Black Feminist Criticism." In *All the Women Are White, All the Blacks Are Men, But Some of Us Are Brave: Black Women's Studies*, ed. Gloria

T. Hull, Patricia Bell Scott, and Barbara Smith, 157–175.Old Westbury, NY: The Feminist Press, 1982.

———. "Racism and Women's Studies." *Frontiers: A Journal of Women's Studies* 5, no. 1 (1980): 48–49.

———, ed. *Home Girls: A Black Feminist Anthology*. New York: Kitchen Table: Women of Color Press, 1983.

———. "Black Feminism: A Movement of Our Own." In *Frontline Feminism 1975–1995: Essays from Sojourner's First 20 Years*, ed. Karen Kahn and Robin Morgan, 22–27. San Francisco: Aunt Lute Books, 1997. Originally published as "Barbara Smith on Black Feminism," *Sojourner: The Women's Forum* (December 31, 1984).

———. "Our Stories: Women of Color." *The New Statesman* 107, no. 2777 (1984): 23–24.

———. "Soul on Hold." *Village Voice* (July 2, 1985): 22–24.

———. "A Press of Our Own: Kitchen Table: Women of Color Press." In *Communication at the Crossroads: The Gender Gap Connection*, ed. Romana R. Rush and Donna Allen, 202–207. New York: Ablex Publishing, 1989.

———. "Blacks and Gays: Healing the Great Divide." *Gay Community News* (October 1993).

———. *The Truth That Never Hurts: Writings on Race, Gender, and Freedom*. New Brunswick, NJ: Rutgers University Press, 1998.

———. "Establishing Black Feminism." *Souls: A Critical Journal of Black Politics, Culture and Society* 2, no. 4 (2000): 50–54.

———. "Organizing in Albany: Justice for Diallo." *News & Letters* (March 2000). http://www.newsandletters.org/Issues/2000/March/3.2000_diallo.htm (accessed March 8, 2014).

———. "Please Don't Fan Flames of Bigotry." *Albany Times Union* (January 23, 2011): B4.

———. "It's a Diverse World, and That Includes Sexuality." *Daily Gazette* (Schenectady, New York) (January 22, 2011): Letters to the Editor.

———. "Black Feminist Activism: My Next Chapter." Russell Sage College, Troy, New York, 2012.

Smith, Barbara, and Loretta Ross. "Interview by Loretta Ross." Transcript of video recording, May 7–8, 2003. Voices of Feminism Oral History Project. Northampton, MA, Sophia Smith Collection, Smith College, 2003.

Sojourner Editorial Collective. "Packing Boxes and Editing Manuscripts: Women of Color in Feminist Publishing." *Sojourner Women's Forum* 9 (August 1993): 10–11B.

Speight, Alonzo R., Abbey Lincoln, and Newsreel. *The People United*. Boston, MA: Third World, 1985.

Sperazi, Laura, and Barbara Smith. "Breaking the Silence: A Conversation in Black and White." *Equal Times* (March 26, 1978): 8–12.

Springer, Kimberly. *Still Lifting, Still Climbing: Contemporary African American Women's Activism.* New York: New York University Press, 1999.

———. *Living for the Revolution: Black Feminist Organizations, 1968–1980.* Durham, NC: Duke University Press, 2005.

Tough, Paul. *Whatever It Takes: Geoffrey Canada's Quest to Change Harlem and America.* Boston: Houghton Mifflin, 2008.

The Trustees of the John F. Slater Fund for the Education of Freedmen. "Proceedings and Reports." Baltimore: John Murphy & Co., 1882.

UBUNTU. "Who We Are: Purpose & Goals." (2012) http://iambecauseweare. wordpress.com/ (accessed April 1, 2013).

Walker, Alice. *The Third Life of Grange Copeland.* New York: Harcourt, Brace, Jovanovich, 1970.

———. *In Love & Trouble: Stories of Black Women.* New York: Harcourt, Brace, Jovanovich, 1973.

———. "In Search of Our Mother's Gardens." *Ms.* 105 (May 1974): 64–70.

———. *The Color Purple.* New York: Simon and Schuster, 1982.

Wallace, Michele. "A Black Feminist's Search for Sisterhood." *Village Voice*, July 28, 1975, 6–7.

———. *Black Macho and the Myth of the Superwoman.* New York: Dial Press, 1979.

Washington, Harriet A. *Medical Apartheid: The Dark History of Medical Experimentation on Black Americans from Colonial Times to the Present.* New York: Doubleday, 2006.

Washington, Mary Helen. *Black-Eyed Susans: Classic Stories by and About Black Women.* Garden City, NY: Anchor Books, 1975.

———. *Midnight Bird: Stories by Contemporary Black Women Writers.* Garden City, NY: Anchor Books, 1980.

Wilkerson, Isabel. *The Warmth of Other Suns: The Epic Story of America's Great Migration.* New York: Random House, 2010.

Williamson, Terrion L. "'Who Is Killing Us.'" *The Feminist Wire* (2012). http:// thefeministwire.com/2012/01/who-is-killing-us/ (accessed April 1, 2013).

Wilson, Carol, and Collective Women's Press. *Lesbians Speak Out.* Oakland, CA: Women's Press Collective, 1974.

Yamada, Mitsuye. *Desert Run: Poems and Stories.* Latham, NY: Kitchen Table: Women of Color Press, 1988.

Yamada, Mitsuye. *Camp Notes and Other Writing*s. Latham, NY: Kitchen Table: Women of Color Press, 1992.

Yamamoto, Hisaye. *Seventeen Syllables and Other Stories.* Latham, NY: Kitchen Table: Women of Color Press, 1992.

Zinn, Howard. *SNCC: The New Abolitionists.* Boston: Beacon Press, 1964.

Interviews Commissioned for this Volume

(listed alphabetically by interviewer)

Virginia Eubanks. June 12, 2012. Department of Women's Studies. University at Albany, State University of New York, Albany, New York.

———. August 13, 2012. School of Social Welfare. University at Albany, State University of New York, Albany, New York.

Alexis Pauline Gumbs. October 25, 2010. The Women's Building. 373 Central Avenue, Albany, New York.

Beverly Guy-Sheftall. October 29, 2010. Women's Research and Resource Center, Spelman College, Atlanta, Georgia.

Alethia Jones. August 1, 2011. School of Social Welfare. University at Albany, State University of New York, Albany, New York.

———. July 3, 2012. School of Social Welfare. University at Albany, State University of New York, Albany, New York.

Joo-Hyun Kang. January 21, 2011. Joseph S. Murphy Institute for Worker Education and Labor Studies, CUNY School of Professional Studies, 25 West 43rd Street, New York, New York.

Vera "Mike" Michelson. February 10, 2011. Rockefeller College of Public Affairs and Policy. University at Albany, State University of New York, Albany, New York.

Barbara Ransby. January 21, 2011. Joseph S. Murphy Institute for Worker Education and Labor Studies, CUNY School of Professional Studies, 25 West 43rd Street, New York, New York.

Matt Richardson. January 10, 2011. Joseph S. Murphy Institute for Worker Education and Labor Studies, CUNY School of Professional Studies, 25 West 43rd Street, New York, New York.

Kimberly Springer. December 2, 2010. Lesbian Herstory Archives. 484 14th Street, Brooklyn, New York.

Interviewer and
Contributor Biographies

Virginia Eubanks is the author of *Digital Dead End: Fighting for Social Justice in the Information Age* (MIT Press, 2011) and the cofounder of Our Knowledge, Our Power (OKOP), a grassroots economic justice and welfare rights organization, and the Popular Technology Workshops, which help community organizations and social movements link technology tools to their social justice goals. She teaches in the Department of Women's, Gender, and Sexuality Studies at the University at Albany, State University of New York. In past lives, she edited the cyberfeminist 'zine *Brillo* and was active in the community technology center movements in the San Francisco Bay Area and Troy, New York.

Alexis Pauline Gumbs is a queer black feminist troublemaker from Durham, North Carolina. Alexis is the founder of the Eternal Summer of the Black Feminist Mind educational program and the co-creator of the Mobile Homecoming experiential archive, amplifying generations of LGBTQ Black brilliance. She earned her PhD in English, Africana studies, and women's studies from Duke University in 2010 and is widely published in national print and online publications and scholarly journals. Her poetry appears in poetry journals *Kweli*, *Vinyl*, *Turning Wheel*, *Everyday Genius* and in many anthologies. As a twenty-first-century cyber-enabled schoolteacher, Alexis currently runs the Indigo Afterschool program for creative black girl geniuses in sixth grade; Indigo Night School, a ritual space for grown Indigos to hone their new moon intentions; and Brilliance Remastered, an international service reconnecting visionary underrepresented graduate students and emerging community accountable scholars with their profound purpose and the communities they love. Alexis was named one of *UTNE Reader*'s "50 Visionaries Transforming the World" in 2009, a Black Women Rising Nominee and a Reproductive Reality Check Shero in 2010, a recipient of the Too Sexy for 501C-3 trophy in 2011 and one of *The Advocate*'s "Forty under 40" in 2012.

Beverly Guy-Sheftall is the founding director of the Women's Research and Resource Center and Anna Julia Cooper Professor of Women's Studies at Spelman College. She has published many seminal texts within African American and Women's Studies, starting with the first anthology on Black women's literature, *Sturdy Black Bridges: Visions of Black Women in Literature* (Doubleday, 1980), coedited with Roseann P. Bell and Bettye Parker Smith. Other publications include her dissertation, *Daughters of Sorrow: Attitudes Toward Black Women, 1880–1920* (Carlson, 1991); a book coauthored with Johnnetta Betsch Cole, *Gender Talk: The Struggle for Women's Equality in African American Communities* (Random House, 2003); and *I Am Your Sister: Collected and Unpublished Writings of Audre Lorde*, coedited with Rudolph P. Byrd and Johnnetta B. Cole (Oxford University Press, 2011). She published an anthology coedited with Johnnetta B. Cole, *Who Should Be First: Feminists Speak Out on the 2008 Presidential Campaign* (State University of New York Press, 2010). In 1983 she became founding coeditor of *SAGE: A Scholarly Journal of Black Women*, which was devoted exclusively to the experiences of women of African descent. She is the past president of the National Women's Studies Association.

Alethia Jones is director of education and leadership development at 1199 SEIU United Healthcare Workers East, a social justice union headquartered in New York City. Formerly an assistant professor of public policy at the University at Albany, State University of New York, she researched the politics of immigrant inclusion into U.S. institutions, with a focus on social networks and community banks. She is a former fellow at the Center for Reflective Community Practices (now the Community Innovators Lab) at MIT. Her publications include "Identity Politics: Part of a Reinvigorated Class Politics," which appeared in the *New Labor Forum* (Spring 2010) and "Immigration and Institutional Change: The Urban Origins of U.S. Postal Savings Banks" in *The City and American Political Development* (Routledge, 2009). A devoted practitioner of the art of transformative dialogue, she coauthored the "Let's Talk Immigration!" curriculum (with Guillermo Perez) and the Service Employees International Union's (SEIU) "Immigration and SEIU: Why We Care" curriculum (with Maria Robalino).

Joo-Hyun Kang is an activist fighting for racial/gender justice, self-determination, and LGBTST (lesbian, gay, bisexual, two-spirit, and transgender) liberation. Formerly affiliated with Astraea Lesbian Foundation for Justice, the Audre Lorde Project, and Kitchen Table: Women of Color Press, she currently directs Communities United for Police Reform, which is leading a movement to end discriminatory and abusive policing practices in New York, including the NYPD's stop-and-frisk policy. She is a licensed acupuncturist.

Robin D. G. Kelley is the Gary B. Nash Professor of American History at the University of California, Los Angeles. His books include the prize-winning *Thelonious Monk:*

The Life and Times of an American Original (Free Press, 2009); *Africa Speaks, America Answers: Modern Jazz in Revolutionary Times* (Harvard University Press, 2012); *Hammer and Hoe: Alabama Communists during the Great Depression* (University of North Carolina Press, 1990); *Race Rebels: Culture Politics and the Black Working Class* (The Free Press, 1994); *Yo' Mama's DisFunktional! Fighting the Culture Wars in Urban America* (Beacon Press, 1997), which was selected one of the top ten books of 1998 by the *Village Voice*; *Three Strikes: Miners, Musicians, Salesgirls, and the Fighting Spirit of Labor's Last Century*, written collaboratively with Dana Frank and Howard Zinn (Beacon, 2001); and *Freedom Dreams: The Black Radical Imagination* (Beacon Press, 2002). He also edited (with Earl Lewis), *To Make Our World Anew: A History of African Americans* (Oxford University Press, 2000) and is currently completing a general survey of African American history coauthored with Tera Hunter and Earl Lewis to be published by Norton. Kelley's essays have appeared in several anthologies and journals, including *The Nation*, *Monthly Review*, *The Voice Literary Supplement*, *New York Times (Arts and Leisure)*, *New York Times Magazine*, *Rolling Stone*, *Colorlines*, *Code Magazine*, *UTNE Reader*, *Lenox Avenue*, *African Studies Review*, *New Labor Forum*, and *Souls*, to name a few.

Vera "Mike" Michelson is an activist and community organizer based in Albany, New York. Vera is involved in (among other things) SNUG/CeaseFire, an anti-violence community-driven effort to reduce gun violence; ROOTS (Re-Entry Opportunities and Orientation Toward Success), an organization established by ex-offenders and supporters to mentor persons who were formerly incarcerated; the Underground Railroad History Project, which preserves and promotes the history of anti-slavery organizing; Capital District's Working Families Party, which endorses and elects progressive candidates for public office; and has provided leadership on multiple local political campaigns. She was a leader in the Capital District Coalition against Apartheid and Racism from 1981–1994, participating in local and international efforts to defeat apartheid in South Africa and recognized as a leading U.S.-based anti-apartheid organization by the United Nations, the African National Congress, and South West Africa People's Organization (SWAPO). She continues to work on peace and justice issues at home in the United States.

Barbara Ransby, Professor of History and African American Studies, University of Illinois at Chicago, is author of *Ella Baker and the Black Freedom Movement* (University of North Carolina Press, 2005) and *Eslanda: The Large and Unconventional Life of Mrs. Paul Robeson* (Yale University Press, 2012). She is cofounder of the Black feminist network, Ella's Daughters.

Barbara Smith is an author, activist, and independent scholar who has played a groundbreaking role in opening up a national cultural and political dialogue about the intersections of race, class, sexuality, and gender. She has been politically active in many movements for social justice since the 1960s and was among the first to define an African American women's literary tradition and to build Black women's studies and Black feminism in the United States. She has edited three major collections about Black women: *Conditions: Five, The Black Women's Issue* with Lorraine Bethel (1979); *All the Women Are White, All the Blacks Are Men, But Some of Us Are Brave: Black Women's Studies* with Gloria T. Hull and Patricia Bell-Scott (The Feminist Press, 1982); and *Home Girls: A Black Feminist Anthology* (Kitchen Table: Women of Color Press, 1983). She is also the coauthor with Elly Bulkin and Minnie Bruce Pratt of *Yours in Struggle: Three Feminist Perspectives on Anti-Semitism and Racism* (Firebrand Books, 1984). She is the general editor of *The Reader's Companion to U. S. Women's History* with Wilma Mankiller, Gwendolyn Mink, Marysa Navarro, and Gloria Steinem (Mariner Books, 1998). A collection of her essays, *The Truth That Never Hurts: Writings on Race, Gender, and Freedom*, was published by Rutgers University Press in 1998. In 2005 she was nominated for the Nobel Peace Prize, one of one thousand women from all over the globe who were nominated to call attention to women's extreme underrepresentation as recipients of this honor. In 2012 she was chosen for the AOL and PBS multiplatform "Makers: Women Who Make America" initiative that profiles distinguished women in all walks of life who have transformed the nation. She was cofounder and publisher until 1995 of Kitchen Table: Women of Color Press, the one of the first U.S. publishers for women of color. She resides in Albany, New York, and served two terms as a member of the City of Albany's Common Council.

Matt Richardson has been a feminist activist and writer for over twenty years. He has published in journals including *Sexuality Research and Social Policy: Journal of the NSRC* and *The Journal of Women's History*. He was chosen by the coordinators of the Ford Foundation Report on Black Sexuality to coauthor an article with Enoch Page entitled, "On the Fear of Small Numbers: A 21st Century Prolegomenon of the U. S. Black Transgender Experience," which appeared in *Black Sexualities: Probing Powers, Passions, Practices, and Policies* (Rutgers University Press, 2009). He was also the coeditor of the Summer 2011 Transgender Studies and Race special issue of *Feminist Studies* with Leisa Meyer. He is the author of *The Queer Limit of Black Memory: Black Lesbian Literature and Irresolution* (Ohio State University Press, 2013). Matt Richardson was associate publisher at Kitchen Table: Women of Color Press from 1992–1995.

Kimberly Springer has written extensively on Black feminism, race, sexuality, and social movements. She is author of *Living for the Revolution: Black Feminist Organizations, 1968–1980* (2005), editor of *Still Lifting, Still Climbing: African American Women's Contemporary Activism* (1999), and coeditor of *Stories of Oprah: The Oprahfication of American Culture* (2009).

Index

abolitionist movement, 204, 213–14, 255. *See also* slavery

abortion, 56–57, 72, 137, 202. *See also* sterilization abuse

Abu-Jamal, Mumia, 87

ACORN (Association of Community Organizations for Reform Now), 250

adoptions, 126

Advocate (periodical), 180

affirmative action, 33, 89, 105

Afghanistan, 243, 291

Afric-American Female Intelligence Society of Boston, 110

African American Women in Defense of Ourselves (AAWIDO), 42, 83, 87–91, 160, 164

AIDS, 115, 163, 194–96

Alabama, University of, 111, 112, 254

Alarcón, Norma, 139n

Albany, NY, 92, 96, 158, 193, ; on Amadou Diallo trial in, 189–191; on fighting homophobia in, 162–164, 181–182, 195–198; on moving Kitchen Table: Women of Color Press to, 170–171; on politics and political change in 213–251

Albany Common Council, xxiii, 7, 9, 196–97, 214–33, 240–49

Albany Family Educational Alliance, 236

Albany Neighborhoods First, 224

All the Women Are White, All the Blacks Are Men, But Some of Us Are Brave (Hull et al.), xviii–xix, 74, 146, 148, 257; and Black women's studies, 97–100, 110–11, 113, 129, 265; title of, 97, 150–51

Alvarez, Rosie, 139, 158

Alvarez, Sonia, 170

Amazon Quarterly, 148, 170

American Booksellers Association (ABA), 166–69, 171

American Indians, 64, 144n, 153, 239

Amos, Val, 146

anti-Semitism, 61, 170

Anzaldúa, Gloria, 146–47, 150–53, 156–57, 171, 192, 263–64

Asian Americans, 64, 144n, 153, 161

Association of Black Women Historians, 111

Association of Community Organizations for Reform Now (ACORN), 250n

Audre Lorde Project, 174, 190

Aunt Lute Books, 166

awareness, core practice of, 4–5, 136

Ayim, Martha, 166–69

Azalea magazine, 192

Bailey, Moya, 287

Bain, Myrna, 139, 150–51, 158

Baker, Ella, xxiii, 3, 25–26, 55, 174, 253, 258, 260–62